THE MAJOR POLITICAL WRITINGS

OF JEAN-JACQUES ROUSSEAU

DISCOURSE

WHICH TOOK THE PRIZE OF THE ACADEMY OF DIJON IN THE YEAR 1750

ON THIS QUESTION PROPOSED BY THAT ACADEMY:

Whether the restoration of the sciences and the arts has contributed to purifying morals.

BY A CITIZEN OF GENEVA

Here I am the barbarian, understood by nobody.
—Ovid[1]

GENEVA
BARRILLOT & SON

---

1. Ovid *Tristia* 5.10.37, quoted by Rousseau in Latin: *Barbarus hic ego sum quia non intelligor illis*. Rousseau slightly changes the original Latin. The Roman poet Ovid (43 BC–AD 17/18) wrote the *Tristia* ("Sorrows") when in exile in Tomis on the Black Sea where many inhabitants could not understand Latin, therefore making Ovid the "barbarian" among them. Rousseau would later use this same epigraph for his autobiographical work *Rousseau Judge of Jean-Jacques*.

The University of Chicago Press, Chicago 60637
The University of Chicago Press, Ltd., London
© 2012 by The University of Chicago
All rights reserved. Published 2012.
Paperback Edition 2014
Printed in the United States of America

27 26 25 24 23   12

ISBN-13: 978-0-226-92186-0 (cloth)
ISBN-13: 978-0-226-15131-1 (paperback)
ISBN-13: 978-0-226-92188-4 (ebook)
10.7208/chicago/9780226921884.001.0001

Library of Congress Cataloging-in-Publication Data

Rousseau, Jean-Jacques, 1712–1778.
  [Works, Selections. English. 2012]
  The major political writings of Jean-Jacques Rousseau : the two discourses and the social
contract / translated and edited by John T. Scott.
     pages. cm.
  Includes bibliographical references and index.
  ISBN 978-0-226-92186-0 (cloth : alk. paper) — ISBN 0-226-92186-7 (cloth : alk. paper) —
ISBN 978-0-226-92188-4 (e-book) — ISBN 0-226-92188-3 (e-book)
  I. Scott, John T., 1963– II. Rousseau, Jean-Jacques , 1712–1778. Discours sur les sciences
et les arts. English. 2012. III. Rousseau, Jean-Jacques, 1712–1778. Discours sur l'origine et
les fondements de l'inégalité parmi les hommes. English. 2012. IV. Rousseau, Jean-Jacques,
1712–1778. Du contrat social. English. 2012. V. Title.
  B2132.E5 2012
  320—dc23

                                                          2012019388

⊗ This paper meets the requirements of
ANSI/NISO Z39.48-1992 (Permanence of Paper).

To my teachers. For my students.

CONTENTS

CHRONOLOGY

1712   June 28: Jean-Jacques Rousseau born in Geneva.

1728   March 14: Rousseau runs away from Geneva.

1741   December: Approximate time Rousseau arrives in Paris with system of musical notation.

1742   August 22: Rousseau reads his *Project Concerning New Signs for Music* to the Academy of Sciences.

1743   July: Rousseau leaves for Venice to work as Secretary to the French Ambassador to Venice.

1744   August: Rousseau leaves Venice after quarreling with the Ambassador. Returns to Paris.

1749   January–March: Rousseau writes the articles on music for the *Encylcopédie*.

       October: Rousseau visits Denis Diderot, who is imprisoned in Vincennes, and reads the essay topic proposed by the Academy of Dijon on the effect of the restoration of the sciences and the arts on morals.

1750   July: Rousseau awarded the prize by the Academy of Dijon for his essay.

1751   January: Publication of the Discourse on the Sciences and the Arts.

1752   Summer: Successful performance of Rousseau's opera *The Village Soothsayer* at Fontainebleau.

1753   November: Rousseau begins work on the *Discourse on Inequality*.

1754   June 12: Rousseau dates the Dedication to his *Discourse on Inequality* while at Chambéry.

       August 1: Rousseau regains his Genevan citizenship.

1755   April 24: Publication of the *Discourse on Inequality*.

1758   October: Publication of the *Letter to d'Alembert*.

1761   January: Publication of the novel *Julie, or the New Heloise*, which becomes an immediate bestseller.

1762   April: Publication of the *Social Contract*.

May: Publication of *Emile, or On Education*.

June 9: The Parlement of Paris condemns *Emile*. A warrant for Rousseau's arrest is issued. Rousseau flees Paris.

June 19: *Emile* and the *Social Contract* are burned at Geneva. A warrant is issued there for Rousseau's arrest.

August 28: Publication of the pastoral letter by the Archbishop of Paris condemning *Emile*.

1763   March: Publication of *Letter to Beaumont*, defending *Emile* against its condemnation by the Archbishop of Paris.

1764   December: Publication of the *Letters Written from the Mountain* in defense of the *Social Contract*.

1765   September 6: Rousseau's house at Môtiers, the small Swiss village in which he lived in exile for the previous two years, is stoned by the villagers.

September-October: Rousseau lives on St. Peter's Island in the middle of Lake Bienne until he is expelled.

December: Rousseau arrives in Paris to meet the philosopher David Hume, who will accompany him to England.

1766   January: Rousseau arrives in England.

June–October: Rousseau quarrels with Hume, and their mutually accusatory correspondence is published.

1767   May 21: Rousseau leaves England for France, where he lives under a pseudonym.

1770   June: Rousseau returns to Paris on the condition that he not publish anything.

December: Rousseau completes the *Confessions* and gives the first readings of the work. After complaints, he agrees not to give any more readings.

1772   Rousseau finishes *Considerations on the Government of Poland*, which is not published during his lifetime.

1776   Rousseau attempts to deposit the manuscript of his autobiographical and apologetic work *Rousseau, Judge of Jean-Jacques* on the altar of Notre Dame Cathedral.

1776–78   Rousseau works on his autobiographical *Reveries of the Solitary Walker*, which he leaves unfinished at his death.

1778   July 2: Rousseau dies at Ermenonville, outside Paris.

1794   October 11: Rousseau is reburied in the Panthéon in Paris.

INTRODUCTION

THIS VOLUME contains translations of the major political works by Jean-Jacques Rousseau, one of the most important and influential thinkers in the history of political philosophy. The purpose of this introduction is to provide context for the reader of the political writings contained in this volume and some guidance in their interpretation. After giving background on Rousseau's life and then his philosophy in general, I discuss the main ideas of each of the writings in this volume: the *Discourse on the Sciences and the Arts*, the *Discourse on the Origin and the Foundations of Inequality among Men*, and *On the Social Contract*. Before doing so, however, let me suggest three broad ways in which Rousseau's thought is pivotal.

First, Rousseau marks a turning point as the first great critic of early modern philosophy and political thought. Rousseau questions the benefits of modern natural science and the doctrine of progress envisioned by Bacon, Descartes, Locke, Newton, and other early modern thinkers and proselytized by his contemporaries during the Enlightenment. What they called "progress," he argues, was really decline in terms of virtue and happiness. He criticizes political thinkers such as Hobbes and Locke who promoted a political and social system based on self-interest and mutual dependence. Rather than producing the liberty, prosperity, and softening of mores promised by these thinkers, Rousseau claims that the result was a politics of slavery, inequality, and egoism. The result was not the legitimate and healthy political association of citizens envisioned by Rousseau; it was the corrupt society of the "bourgeois"—a term Rousseau was perhaps the first to use in the sense we know today.

Second, although Rousseau was a critic of early modern philosophy and political theory, his own thought is in important respects a radicalized version of early modern thought. Rather than criticizing modern science, politics, and society from the perspective of ancient republicanism or Christian morality, Rousseau accepts many of the principal arguments of Hobbes, Locke, and others in the individualist and empiricist tradition concerning human nature, but he then turns their arguments against them. On the one hand, then, Rousseau joins Hobbes and Locke in challenging the classical philosophical tradition by arguing that humans are not Aristotle's rational and political animals, but are instead self-interested and asocial by nature, and that reason is the servant of the passions rather than the master. On the other hand, however, Rousseau comes to different conclusions than his predecessors by pressing their arguments further than they themselves had done. If humans are not social animals by their nature, he asks, wouldn't they then be essentially solitary beings with very limited passions and therefore exceedingly limited reason? If so, rather than the state of nature being a state of war of all against all, as Hobbes claimed, wouldn't the natural condition of mankind be a state of peaceful animality? If reason is the servant of the passions, then wouldn't the passions and reason develop together as humans come into society, not by any impulse intrinsic to their nature, but by historical accident? If so, wouldn't human nature therefore be shaped to a great extent by historical, environmental, and social forces instead of having a universal and unvarying form, as perhaps all of his predecessors—Aristotle and Hobbes alike—had assumed? If humans have a malleable nature that leads them to develop from innocent animals living in nature to depraved beings living in society, then could their nature perhaps be intentionally molded to transform them from self-interested creatures of the modern commercial society of the sort envisioned by Locke or Montesquieu into communally interested citizens of a truly legitimate democratic state? In short, Rousseau's thought represents a critique of modern philosophy not from the outside but rather from the inside. Rousseau thereby influenced later romantic, historical, socialist, and other schools of thought that, like him, sought to further early modern thinkers' goals of freedom and progress, prosperity and autonomy, while simultaneously criticizing their philosophical positions.

Third, Rousseau is a seminal democratic theorist: the first major thinker to argue that democracy is the only legitimate form of the state. Today we take the argument for democracy for granted. We therefore fail to appreciate how explosive Rousseau's argument was when he presented it. When he published the *Social Contract* in 1762, there were very few governments in the world that even approached being democratic, and none that measured up to the standard of legitimacy he put forward in his work. Indeed, perhaps no state in existence today meets Rousseau's standard, but his argument that democracy is the only legitimate form of the state might be said to have prevailed, if not everywhere then at least in the West, although not necessarily in the version of direct democracy he himself urged. Considered within his own philosophical system, Rousseau's democratic theory can be understood in relation to the two pivotal aspects of his thought as a whole already discussed. First, his argument for democratic self-governance in the *Social Contract* and his other writings is inspired in part by his concerns about the inequality and dependence he saw generated by the modern state and society envisioned by his predecessors. Second, his project for fashioning self-interested individuals into civic-minded citizens is made possible in part because of his conception of the uniquely malleable character of human nature central to his radicalization of modern thought. As with his thought as a whole, both of these facets of his political theory have influenced subsequent political thought. The same concerns about inequality and dependence that inspired Rousseau to offer a vision of democratic self-governance have motivated later political thinkers and reformers, and likewise his project for crafting citizens has inspired hopes for radical political and social reform.

The influence of Rousseau's thought has been immense in philosophy, literature, and political theory, but given that this volume contains his major political works, it is appropriate to conclude these general remarks by noting how the demand for democracy so influentially articulated by Rousseau has spurred political reform and even revolution from his century to our own. Rousseau himself predicted an age of revolutions to come that would overthrow the existing political order in Europe, although he was not optimistic about the likely outcome. Somewhat ironically, then, Rousseau's name has long been associated with the French Revolution. To what extent his works inspired revolutionaries such as Robespierre is a difficult question, and certainly it would be rash to either blame the Citizen of Geneva (or give him credit) for the French Revolution. What can be said with certainty is that the revolutionaries themselves appealed to Rousseau as an authority to justify their actions, either sincerely or cynically and whether or not they understood his thought properly. They forever yoked Rousseau to their Revolution in 1794 when they unearthed his coffin from its resting place on a peaceful island in the middle of a lake on the bucolic estate outside Paris where he died in 1778, proceeded in solemn procession to the city while playing music Rousseau himself had composed, and then interred him in the Panthéon, a church converted to serve as an eternal shrine to the Revolution.

ROUSSEAU'S LIFE

The life and thought of Jean-Jacques Rousseau (1712–78) are intertwined to an unusual degree for a political thinker. In addition to writing autobiographical works that he saw as part of his thought, Rousseau himself suggested that his unusual life enabled him to grasp the variety of human nature and to see through the conventions of his time.

Rousseau was born in Geneva to a mother who died giving him birth and to a watchmaker father who would soon abandon him. His early education was sporadic and largely informal, the result of his early love of reading romantic novels and ancient history, reading that activated his imagination and made him dissatisfied with the more mundane world he actually inhabited. Apprenticed to an engraver, Rousseau first learned the evils of personal dependence. At sixteen he ran away from his native city and began a life of wandering and exile that lasted for the rest of his days. Roaming through the alpine region of what is today eastern France and northern Italy, Rousseau earned his bread as a lackey, a seminarian, an interpreter for a fake churchman soliciting contributions for the Holy Land, a music teacher, and a tutor. For over a decade, he lived with Mme de Warens, a woman some thirteen years his senior whom he affectionately called "Maman" and whose lover he soon became. She encouraged his intellectual and artistic interests. He read widely in literature, history, philosophy, and science, and, with little formal training in music, presented himself as a music teacher. As his relationship with "Maman" cooled and his ambition warmed, Rousseau left for Paris sometime around the end of 1741 with two operas and a new system of musical notation in hand, determined to conquer the intellectual capital of Europe.

After his system of musical notation failed to win the sponsorship of the Academy of Sciences, Rousseau found himself just one among the many ambitious young men who flocked to Paris. He was employed as secretary to the French ambassador to Venice in 1743–44, leaving after he quarreled with his superior. Although his stay in the serene republic was brief, it stirred his first serious thoughts on politics. Returning to Paris, he went to work on an opera but once again failed to gain recognition. He became close friends during this period with Denis Diderot, along with d'Alembert, Condillac, and other intellectuals—called "philosophes"—just beginning to achieve success and notoriety. During this same period, he began his relationship with Thérèse Levasseur, who would be his lifelong mistress and, eventually, his wife. Diderot invited Rousseau to write the articles on musical theory for the *Encyclopédie*, the great Enlightenment project he was undertaking. By the time Rousseau's collaboration in the work was announced in the "Preliminary Discourse" to the *Encyclopédie* of 1751, however, Rousseau had emerged suddenly from obscurity to become the most controversial author in Europe.

Rousseau's metamorphosis began in the fall of 1749. Walking to the chateau of Vincennes to visit Diderot, who was imprisoned there for his subversive writings, Rousseau paused to read the *Mercure de France*, a gazette he had brought along with him. He read there an announcement for a prize-essay competition sponsored by the Academy of Dijon on the question of whether the restoration of the sciences and arts had tended to purify morals. Rousseau was blinded by a sudden inspiration, the so-called "Illumination of Vincennes," in which he later claimed to have seen in a single glimpse his entire philosophical system. "At the moment of that reading I saw another universe and became another man," he later recalled, "and from that instant I was lost."[1]

Rousseau's negative answer to the Academy of Dijon's question, arguing that the advancement of the science and arts tends to corrupt morals, won him the prize. When the *Discourse on the Sciences and the Arts* was published in early 1751, the "Citizen of Geneva" became famous. The work was widely seen as paradoxical, especially since Rousseau himself was a practicing artist and a contributor to a project dedicated to the advancement of the sciences and arts. Rousseau wrote a number of defenses of his *Discourse*, and of himself. His celebrity spread when he finally succeeded in his original profession with the successful performance of his opera, *The Village Soothsayer (Le Devin du village)*, in 1752. His opera remained one of the most performed pieces at the Paris Opéra well into the nineteenth century.

The *Discourse on the Origin and the Foundations of Inequality among Men* (1755), along with the article "Political Economy" for the *Encyclopédie* (1755), cemented Rousseau's reputation as a controversial political theorist. He later claimed that he only fully revealed the core of his thought in the *Discourse on Inequality*: that man is by nature good and is corrupted in society. His inquiry into human nature and the origins of society in the work culminated in an attack on the corruption and inequalities of his contemporary society.

Shortly after publishing the *Discourse on Inequality*, Rousseau applied the lessons of his thought to his own life by leaving Paris for the nearby countryside to undergo a personal reform. He resolved to make himself financially independent through his trade as a musical copyist, an occupation he pursued

---

1. Rousseau, *Confessions, Collected Writings*, 5:294–95.

for much of the remainder of his life. His decision to distance himself from the corrupt moral and intellectual world of Paris began his alienation from Diderot and his other former friends. His final falling out with Diderot was announced in his next important work, the *Letter to d'Alembert* (1758), which was occasioned by d'Alembert's article on "Geneva" for the *Encyclopédie*. In his *Letter*, Rousseau objected to d'Alembert's suggestion that a theater should be established in his native city, where such entertainments were prohibited due to the republic's Calvinist heritage, and he argued that the theater was appropriate only for corrupted peoples. Rousseau would soon make the same argument about romantic novels—paradoxically enough in the preface to his own romantic novel, *Julie, or the New Heloise* (1761). Set in the foothills of the Alps, his novel, Rousseau explained, was meant to give his readers a taste for the countryside and to make them disgusted with the corrupt cities that drew them. Rousseau viewed his turn to literature as part of his philosophical mission, and as a way to reach a popular audience by appealing to their literary taste while at the same time redirecting that taste toward more virtuous ends. *Julie* would prove the most popular novel of the eighteenth century, and Rousseau was known by his contemporaries foremost for it.

Rousseau's reputation today as a political theorist rests largely on his treatise, *On the Social Contract*. Published in April 1762, the *Social Contract* was joined a month later by Rousseau's educational treatise, *Emile, or On Education*, which also contains a précis of the *Social Contract* as well as a lengthy treatment of religion. The publication of these two works quickly changed his life.

In June 1762, *Emile* was condemned by the Parlement of Paris and the Sorbonne for its unorthodox theological views, and an order for the arrest of its author was issued. Rousseau fled Paris on the morning of June 9, passing the men sent to arrest him as he rode out in his carriage. He traveled toward Geneva, only to learn that both the *Social Contract* and *Emile* were condemned and burned in his native city. Rousseau settled in Môtiers, a small village in the mountains in the north of Switzerland, where he lived for the next three years. During this period, he published defenses of his two condemned works, justifying *Emile* in his *Letter to Beaumont* (1763), the Archbishop of Paris who had also issued a proclamation condemning the work, and defending the *Social Contract* against its condemnation by Geneva in the *Letters Written from the Mountain* (1764). His later political works include two "applied" works: the *Constitutional Project for Corsica*, begun in 1764–65 at the request of a Corsican patriot, and the *Considerations on the Government of Poland*, written in 1770–71.

Rousseau's stay in Môtiers became increasingly difficult, and he left the village in September 1765 when the inhabitants stoned his house at the instigation of a local preacher. After a month-long idyll on St. Peter's Island in the middle of Lake Bienne that he later immortalized in his *Reveries of the Solitary Walker*, Rousseau made his way to his next place of exile, England. He traveled to England at the invitation and in the company of David Hume, but the two philosophers quickly quarreled. Rousseau returned to France in 1767, eventually resettling in Paris, where the authorities agreed not to arrest him as long as he did not publish any works.

Rousseau completed his first major autobiographical work, the *Confessions* in 1770. Generally considered the first modern autobiography, in the work Rousseau not only recounts his life but presents it as a uniquely honest and accurate portrait of human nature. In giving readings from the work in small gatherings, Rousseau honored the letter if not the spirit of his agreement with the authorities not to publish. When listeners became uneasy with Rousseau's revelations about himself or offended by his revelations about them, the police ordered him to cease. Rousseau wrote two other autobiographical works, *Rousseau, Judge of Jean-Jacques*, commonly known as the *Dialogues* and completed in 1776, and the *Reveries of the Solitary Walker*, which he left uncompleted at his death.

In May 1778, Rousseau moved outside of Paris to Ermenonville , the estate of one of his admirers. This would be Rousseau's last refuge, as he died of a massive apoplexy on the morning of July 2nd. He was buried on a poplar-covered island in the middle of a lake and rested there until 1794, when the French revolutionaries moved his body in a great procession and interred it in the Panthéon.

ROUSSEAU'S "SYSTEM" OF THE
NATURAL GOODNESS OF MAN

Ever since Rousseau's own time, questions have been raised about the unity or coherence of his writings. Readers of the *Discourse on the Sciences and the Arts*, his first philosophical work, were struck by the paradoxical character of an essay against the progress of the sciences and arts written by a practicing musician and a contributor to the veritable Bible of the Enlightenment, the *Encyclopédie*. Readers of the *Social Contract* have struggled to understand how a treatise arguing that a legitimate state required the total alienation of each individual to the community could be by the same author as the *Discourse on Inequality*, with its praise of natural freedom and ringing criticism of inequality and dependence. Part of the challenge of finding unity in Rousseau's writings stems from the sheer diversity of those writings: political treatises, educational tracts, essays, a novel and other literary works, operas, and autobiographical writings. However, the principal challenge arises from perhaps the most characteristic feature of his writing: paradox.

Rousseau himself readily admits his paradoxes, and from the very beginning of his philosophical career he located himself in the tradition of the most paradoxical of philosophers: Socrates. Like Socrates, he proclaimed that he followed the inscription written on the Temple of Delphi— "Know Thyself"—and admitted that his wisdom consisted in knowing that he did not know. Paradox does not entail contradiction, however, for a paradox only seems to be contradictory; the truth contained within the paradox becomes manifest once the appearance of contradiction is resolved. While acknowledging his paradoxes, Rousseau also insists upon the fundamental unity of his philosophy. He claimed that all of his works were based on the same principle or "system" of thought: the natural goodness of man and his corruption in society.

In a moving letter written over a decade after the event it describes, Rousseau recounts the philosophical vision that changed his life and directed his thought:

I was going to see Diderot, at that time a prisoner in Vincennes; I had in my pocket a *Mercury of France* which I began to leaf through along the way. I fell across the question of the Academy of Dijon which gave rise to my first writing. If anything has ever resembled a sudden inspiration, it is the motion that was caused in me by that reading; suddenly I felt my mind dazzled by a thousand lights; crowds of lively ideas presented themselves at the same time with a strength and a confusion that threw me into an inexpressible perturbation; I feel my head seized by a dizziness similar to drunkenness. . . . Oh Sir, if I had ever been able to write a quarter of what I saw and felt under that tree, how clearly I would have made all the contradictions of the social system seen, with what strength I would have exposed all the abuses of our institutions, with what simplicity I would have demonstrated that man is naturally good and that it is from these institutions alone that men become wicked.[2]

---

2. Rousseau to Malesherbes, January 12, 1762, in *Collected Writings*, 5:575.

Rousseau goes on to explain that the thoughts and feelings that came to him in the "Illumination of Vincennes" were contained in his three "principal" writings, which he claims together formed a single whole: the *Discourse on the Sciences and the Arts*, the *Discourse on Inequality*, and *Emile, or On Education*.[3] To these three writings we can confidently add the *Social Contract* and, indeed, all of Rousseau's writings from the *Discourse on the Sciences and the Arts* onward. As Rousseau claims in defense of *Emile* against the Archbishop of Paris, who condemned the work: "The fundamental principle of all morality about which I have reasoned in all my writings and developed in [*Emile*] with all the clarity of which I was capable, is that man is a naturally good being, loving justice and order; that there is no original perversity in the human heart, and that the first movements of nature are always right."[4] The fact that Rousseau's argument ran directly counter to the Christian doctrine of original sin was lost on neither the Archbishop of Paris nor Rousseau himself.

Rousseau's statements about the coherence of his writings and on the shared foundation in his "system" of the natural goodness of man are retrospective, that is, written from the perspective of an author looking back on his works and defending them. We may be inclined either to trust the author or to suspect his statements of being self-serving, but either way a principal challenge for interpreting Rousseau's writings is to understand how his "system" is presented across his works. He himself later suggested that reading his major writings in backward order—beginning from *Emile* and the *Social Contract*, going back to the *Discourse on Inequality* and other works, and ending with the *Discourse on the Sciences and the Arts*—would more clearly reveal "the development of [my] great principle that nature made man happy and good, but that society depraves him and makes him miserable."[5] His suggestion implies that his "system" of thought only becomes fully evident over time.

Strangely enough, but in keeping with Rousseau's suggestion about the order in which his works might be read, the *Discourse on the Sciences and the Arts*—the very work he claims was the direct result of the "illumination of Vincennes"—is the work in which it is perhaps the most difficult to see the traces of his "system." More will be said about this subject when we turn to the prize essay itself in the next section, but for now it suffices to say that Rousseau's claims to coherence would have to hinge on his remark in the letter quoted above that, like his works as a whole, the argument of the *Discourse*

3. Ibid.
4. Letter to Beaumont, in *Collected Writings*, 9:28.
5. *Rousseau Judge of Jean-Jacques: Dialogues*, in *Collected Writings*, 1:212–13.

concerning the corrupting effects of the advancement of the sciences and arts somehow reveals "the contradictions of the social system" and "all the abuses of our institutions." In this light, his remark in a defense of the first *Discourse* is revealing. Within a broadside against how the taste for philosophy and for the letters and arts leads men away from their duties as men and citizens, a taste that he says dominates the philosophy and politics of his century, he explains:

> What a strange and deadly constitution in which accumulated wealth facilitates the means of accumulating more, and in which it is impossible for those who have nothing to acquire something; in which the good man has no means of escaping from misery; in which the greatest rogues are the most honored, and in which one must necessarily renounce virtue to become an honest man! I know that the declaimers have said all this a hundred times; but they say it while declaiming, and I say it based on reasons; they have perceived the evil, and I have discovered its causes, and above all I have shown a very consoling and useful thing by show-ing that all these vices do not belong so much to man as to man poorly governed.[6]

Rousseau's subsequent works would be devoted to showing both the sources of political corruption and the possibility of legitimate politics.

If man is naturally "good," then in what does this "goodness" consist? Rousseau first announces the principle of the natural goodness of man in the *Discourse on Inequality*. However, even then he does so only in one of his notes to the work (a procedure that should indicate the importance of those notes) and in a manner that does not make his meaning entirely clear. "Men are wicked; sad and continual experience spares the need for proof," Rousseau writes near the beginning of note IX: "Yet man is naturally good—I do be-lieve I have demonstrated it" (127). What is this "demonstration"?

Something of Rousseau's meaning about the natural "goodness" of man can be gleaned from a comparison he draws between "savage man" ("savage" in the sense of "wild" or "untamed," not in the sense of "fierce" or "vicious") and "civilized man" shortly after making this claim:

> Savage man, once he has eaten, is at peace with all of nature and the friend of all his fellow humans. Is it sometimes a question of contending

---

6. *Preface to Narcissus*, in *Collected Writings*, 2:194.

for his meal? He never comes to blows without having first compared the difficulty of prevailing with that of finding his subsistence elsewhere. And as pride is not involved in the fight, it ends with a few blows; the victor eats, the vanquished goes off to try his luck, and all is at peace. But with man in society matters are entirely different. First it is a question of providing for what is necessary, and then for what is superfluous; next come delicacies, and then immense wealth, and then subjects, and then slaves. He does not have a moment of respite. What is most singular about it is that the less natural and pressing the needs, the more the passions increase and, what is worse, the power to satisfy them. As a result, after a long period of prosperity, after having swallowed up a good many treasures and having ruined a good many men, my hero will end up by cutting every throat until he is the sole master of the universe. Such in brief is the moral picture, if not of human life, at least of the secret aspirations of every civilized man's heart. (128–29)

Natural or savage man has very few needs by nature and he has the capacity to fulfill them. Further, he has no passions, such as pride, that fundamentally connect him to other human beings or make him dependent upon them. By contrast, civilized man has a multitude of passions which he is unable to satisfy, and these same passions involve him in relations of mastery and servitude, relations that are corrupting for master and slave alike. Man's natural "goodness," then, seems to consist in an equilibrium between his needs and passions, on the one hand, and his ability to satisfy them, on the other. This equilibrium makes man both "good" for himself and also "good"— or at least not harmful— for others. Rousseau's natural "goodness," then, does not mean that humans are naturally benevolent or altruistic, but rather that their natural passions and faculties tend toward their own preservation and well-being.

This reading helps clarify what Rousseau says in the main text of the *Discourse on Inequality* concerning man's natural goodness. Discussing man in the state of nature, he explains: "It appears at first that men in that state, since they have neither any kind of moral relation among themselves nor known duties, could be neither good nor evil, and had neither vices nor virtues—unless, taking these words in a physical sense, one were to call vices in the individual those qualities that can harm his own self-preservation and virtues those that can contribute to it, in which case it would be necessary to call the most virtuous the one who least resists the simple impulses of nature" (81). In speaking of man's natural "goodness," then, Rousseau takes "virtue" and "goodness" in the "physical sense" he suggests here rather than with regard to any moral qualities, qualities which he will deny humans originally possess. Since natural man is able to satisfy his needs and passions by following "the simple impulses of nature" and since he has no qualities that harm his own self-preservation, natural man is naturally "good" in this sense. As man develops in society and acquires new needs and passions, and especially passions such as pride that make him dependent on his fellow human beings, he becomes "wicked" in the sense that his impulses no longer lead to his happiness and that he has acquired qualities harmful to his own self-preservation and well-being. Man's capacity for such a radical change in his nature is what Rousseau terms "the faculty of perfecting himself" or "perfectibility" (72). It is therefore no accident that the note in which he proclaims that he has "demonstrated" that man is naturally good is attached to the paragraph in the main text in which he explains that humans are characterized not by being free, rational, or social animals, as philosophers had traditionally maintained, but instead by their very "perfectibility"—a quality that ironically tends to make them wicked and miserable.

The *Discourse on Inequality* ends with Rousseau's portrait of his own time as hopelessly beset by misery and inequality, but some of his later works offer his constructive projects for restoring something of our natural goodness and happiness—not by "going back" to nature, which Rousseau himself says is impossible, but by reforming our institutions and even our own nature. Rousseau's later literary and autobiographical works may offer such possible courses of reform, through retreat from the city to the countryside as he depicts in his novel *Julie* or through retreat from society itself into philosophic solitude in his autobiographical writings, but these possibilities are beyond the scope of his political theory and consideration of the writings contained in this volume. However, a statement in his educational treatise, *Emile*, may help clarify Rousseau's theory of the natural goodness of man and the different constructive possibilities for reform he considers. Beginning his work with a statement that alludes to his principle of the natural goodness of man— "Everything is good as it leaves the hands of the Author of things; everything degenerates in the hands of man," including man himself—Rousseau nonetheless goes on to say that we have no choice now that we have left nature but to form or make man: "In the present state of things a man abandoned to himself in the midst of other men from birth would be the most disfigured of all. Prejudices, authority, necessity, example, all the social institutions in which we find ourselves submerged would stifle nature in him and put nothing in its place."[7] What to do, then? "Forced to combat nature or the social institutions," he explains, "one must choose between making a man or a citizen, for one cannot make both at the same time." The routes of "man" and "citizen" are opposed because of how the human being is constituted relative to other human beings. Whereas natural man is "entirely for himself," civil man's very identity consists in being part of the political whole of which he is a member. The citizen "believes himself no longer one but a part of the unity and no longer feels except within the whole." The malleability of human nature makes both routes possible, if nonetheless problematic in various ways, but one has to choose a single route. Otherwise, we risk creating "double men, always appearing to relate everything to others and never relating anything except to themselves alone." In short, we will create the creature of modern society: the "bourgeois."[8] Unlike the being made wicked by living in society, torn between his inclinations and his desires, corrupt and therefore miserable, Rousseau proposes redirecting our natural passions and faculties in such a way that we recreate something like the balance between the desires and ability to satisfy them enjoyed by natural man, who is thereby good and happy. In order to achieve the possibilities of the "man" and the "citizen," very different educations and institutions are required. In the end, however, the different routes offered by Rousseau, including the specifically political path outlined in his *Social Contract*, are all both premised on and patterned on the natural goodness of man.

THE *DISCOURSE ON THE SCIENCES AND THE ARTS*

The prize essay that made him famous, the *Discourse on the Sciences and the Arts* (often referred to as the *First Discourse*), addresses the question posed by the Academy of Dijon concerning whether the restoration of the sciences and arts has tended to purify morals. Rousseau already indicates his reply when he restates the Academy's question at the very outset of the body of the *Discourse*: "Has the restoration of the sciences and the arts contributed to purifying or to corrupting morals?" (9). Although we may today assume that the learned society asking such a question in the center of the Enlightenment would natu-

---

7. *Emile, or On Education*, trans. Allan Bloom (New York: Basic Books, 1979), 37.
8. Ibid., 39–41.

rally expect a response extolling the purifying effects of the sciences and arts, the issue of the relationship between morality and the advancement of the sciences and arts was still hotly contested in Rousseau's time. Indeed, a number of the entrants to the Academy's essay competition joined Rousseau in arguing that the restoration of the sciences and arts had led to moral corruption. Apart from its rhetorical power, what set Rousseau's essay apart was that he does not rely upon traditional religious or civic republican arguments concerning the corrupting effects of secular science and luxurious arts, but instead offers a philosophic or even scientific ("philosophy" and "science" were not fully distinct concepts in the eighteenth century) investigation of the effects of the sciences and arts.

The scientific character of his investigation in the *Discourse* is signaled by Rousseau through a metaphor he uses when he first introduces his thesis in the essay:

> Where there is no effect, there is no cause to seek: but here the effect is certain, the depravity real, and our souls have been corrupted in proportion as our sciences and our arts have advanced toward perfection. Shall it be said that this is a misfortune particular to our age? No, Gentlemen: the evils caused by our vain curiosity are as old as the world. The daily rise and fall of the ocean's waters have not been more regularly subjected to the course of the star that gives us light during the night than has the fate of morals and integrity to the progress of the sciences and arts. Virtue has been seen to flee in proportion as their light dawned on our horizon, and the same phenomenon has been observed in all times and in all places. (14–15)

In this way, then, Rousseau first staked out the paradoxical and complex position he would thereafter occupy: that of a critic of modern thought whose very critique is based upon modern thought itself.

The *Discourse on the Sciences and the Arts* is organized into two parts, as was customary for academic prize essay competitions during that time, but Rousseau signals that the two halves of the work contain arguments of two different types. At the very end of the first part of the work, having presented a number of historical examples that suggest that wherever the sciences and arts have progressed morals have declined, Rousseau writes: "How humiliating these reflections are for humanity! How our pride must be mortified by them! What! Could integrity be the daughter of ignorance? Could science and virtue be incompatible? . . . Let us therefore consider the sciences and the arts in themselves. Let us see what must result from their progress and no longer hesitate to agree on all those points where our reasoning is found to be in accord with historical inductions" (20–21). In other words, Rousseau is admitting here that what he has presented so far in his *Discourse* are "historical inductions" and that the results of such inductions are not conclusive. Rather, the historical examples he has thus far presented must be tested in the light of "reasoning" based on an investigation of "the sciences and arts in themselves." This philosophical investigation is what Rousseau undertakes in the second part of the *Discourse*. Further, it should be noted that Rousseau frames the relationship between science and virtue as a question: "Could science and virtue be incompatible?" Rousseau's investigation in the second part of the work of the sciences and the arts in themselves will reveal that the argument based on historical inductions concerning the incompatibility of science and virtue was incomplete or even misleading and that science and virtue are, in certain cases, compatible.

While Rousseau at first appears in the *Discourse* simply to condemn the effects of the sciences and arts in the name of morality and virtue, religion and patriotism, by the end of the work he praises the benefits of the sciences as advanced by individuals of such intellectual caliber as Bacon, Descartes, and Newton—and, Rousseau hints, himself (34). This praise of the sciences appears at first glance to contradict the main argument of the *Discourse*. But it should be recalled that Rousseau actually began the first part of the work with a praise of enlightenment: "It is a grand and beautiful spectacle to see man emerging, as it were, out of nothingness through his own efforts; dissipating by the light of his reason the shadows in which nature has enveloped him; rising above himself; soaring by his mind to the celestial regions; traversing with the steps of a giant, like the sun, the vast expanse of the universe; and, what is even grander and more difficult, returning into himself in order there to study man and to know his nature, his duties, and his end. All these marvels have been revived in the past few generations" (11). How can the praise of the advancement of the sciences and arts that comes at both the beginning and the end of the work be reconciled with the apparent argument of the work itself that the advancement of the sciences and arts brings about moral corruption?

We can start to understand the apparently contradictory argument of the *Discourse*—or, rather, we can begin to resolve Rousseau's paradoxical presentation of his argument—by considering a statement he makes at the very beginning of the second part of the work, where he turns from uncertain "historical inductions" to philosophical "investigation":

> Indeed, whether one leafs through the annals of the world, whether one supplements uncertain chronicles with philosophic research, human knowledge will not be found to have an origin that corresponds to the idea one would like to have of it. Astronomy was born from superstition; eloquence from ambition, hatred, flattery, lying; geometry from avarice; physics from vain curiosity; all of them, and even moral philosophy, from human pride. The sciences and the arts therefore owe their birth to our vices. (23)

In short, our vices as they develop in society, and above all human pride, are the source of the corrupting effects of the advancement of the sciences and arts. The sciences and arts "in themselves" are not necessarily corrupting: witness the capacity of the likes of Bacon, Descartes, and Newton to pursue the sciences from uncorrupted motives. "If some men must be allowed to give themselves over to the study of the sciences and the arts, it is only those who feel they have the strength to walk alone in their footsteps and go beyond them. It belongs to this small number to raise monuments to the glory of the human mind" (35). When the advancement of the sciences and arts becomes fashionable, however, the motives for pursuing them are corrupt: pride, the desire for inequality and luxury, etc. Such is Rousseau's criticism of the century of Enlightenment. As he writes in the Preface to the *Discourse* when explaining his decision in answering the Academy's question: "I have taken a side; I do not care about pleasing either the witty or the fashionable. In all times there will be men destined to be subjugated by the opinions of their age, their country, their society. . . . One must not write for such readers when one wants to live beyond one's age" (7).

The *Discourse on the Sciences and the Arts* made Rousseau famous, and it also provoked numerous replies and attacks. Rousseau wrote a number of answers to his critics that are helpful for understanding his argument in the *Discourse*.[9] Many of the points raised by his critics are easily dismissed by Rousseau as misstatements of his argument or even caricatures of it. For example, he had

---

9. The writings to which Rousseau responded and Rousseau's own responses can be found in *Collected Writings*, vol. 2.

never argued that we should burn libraries nor had he simply praised ignorance. More interestingly, when asked why he thought virtue and learning were incompatible, he replied that he had done no such thing: he had raised it as a question and given examples of virtuous men who were also learned, above all Socrates, who, like Rousseau himself, praised a certain kind of "ignorance": knowing that you do not know.

When it comes to many of the criticisms leveled against the *Discourse* it is fairly easy upon reexamining his prize essay to agree with its author that his argument had been misunderstood, but Rousseau makes some more audacious claims about his true argument that prove more challenging to reconcile with the contents of the *Discourse* itself. These claims have been at the heart of scholarly disputes about the relationship of the *Discourse on the Sciences and the Arts* to Rousseau's later works and the extent to which his "system" of the natural goodness of man is or is not present in his first essay. Two passages from his replies are particularly important in this regard, and rather than attempting to resolve the issues they raise, I will simply present the passages to serve as a challenge to readers to investigate for themselves whether Rousseau's own interpretation of the *Discourse* squares with their own.

The first of these passages in which Rousseau characterizes his actual argument in the *Discourse* comes from his reply to King Stanisław I Leszczyński of Poland. Stanisław had suggested that rather than arguing that the sciences and arts caused moral corruption, Rousseau should have argued that moral corruption and pernicious luxury have arisen from wealth. Rousseau replies that this was in fact his argument:

> I had not said either that luxury was born from the sciences, but that they were born together and that one scarcely went without the other. This is how I would arrange this genealogy. The first source of evil is inequality. From inequality came wealth, for those words poor and rich are relative, and everywhere that men are equal, there are neither rich nor poor. From wealth are born luxury and idleness. From luxury come the fine arts and from idleness the sciences.[10]

In other words, Rousseau claims that his actual argument was not that the advancement of the sciences and the arts causes moral corruption, but that moral

---

10. *Observations by Jean-Jacques Rousseau of Geneva on the Reply Made to his Discourse*, in *Collected Writings*, 2:48.

corruption born of inequality causes the advancement of the sciences and the arts, which, in turn, result in further moral corruption since they nourish pride and the other corrupt motives for which they are pursued in the first place. If this was Rousseau's actual argument in the *Discourse*, then why did he not present it more clearly? Rousseau addresses this question in another reply to a critic:

> Having so many interests to contest, so many prejudices to conquer, and so many harsh things to state, in the very interest of my readers, I believed I ought to be careful of their pusillanimity in some way and let them perceive only gradually what I had to say to them. . . . Some precautions were thus at first necessary for me, and it is in order to be able to make everything understood that I did not wish to say everything. It was only gradually and always for a few readers that I developed my ideas. It is not myself that I treated carefully, but the truth, so as to get it across more surely and make it useful. I have often taken great pains to try to put into a sentence, a line, a word tossed off as if by chance the result of a long sequence of reflections. Often, most of my readers must have found my discourses badly connected and almost entirely rambling, for lack of perceiving the trunk of which I showed them only the branches. But that was enough for those who know how to understand, and I have never wanted to speak to the others.[11]

Again, it is for readers to examine Rousseau's *Discourses* in order to see whether they accept the author's interpretation of his own work. Whatever the result of such an investigation, it is clear that the *Discourse on the Sciences and the Arts* is a complex work that demands careful reading and interpretation.

THE *DISCOURSE ON INEQUALITY*

The Academy of Dijon provided Rousseau with the opportunity to write his next major work when it proposed a question for its 1754 prize competition asking about the origin of inequality among men and whether it was authorized by natural law. Once again, Rousseau provides a glimpse of his answer by restating the Academy's question, this time in the title to the work: *Discourse on the Origin and the Foundations of Inequality among Men* (often referred to as

---

11. *Preface to a Second Letter to Bordes*, in *Collected Writings*, 2:185.

the *Second Discourse*). Gone was the Academy's inquiry about whether existing inequalities were authorized by natural law: "a question perhaps good for slaves to debate within earshot of their masters," Rousseau remarks at the outset of the body of the discourse, "but not befitting rational and free men who seek the truth" (61). Instead, Rousseau will inquire about the "foundations" of inequality, a formulation that leaves open the question of the legitimacy of existing inequalities. Rousseau fully reveals his hand at the very end of the *Discourse* with a ringing condemnation of the political, social, and economic conditions of modern states:

> It follows from this account that inequality, being almost nonexistent in the state of nature, derives its force and growth from the development of our faculties and from the progress of the human mind, and eventually becomes stable and legitimate by the establishment of property and laws. It further follows that moral inequality, authorized by positive right alone, is contrary to natural right whenever it is not exactly proportioned to physical inequality—a distinction which sufficiently determines what ought to be thought in this regard of the sort of inequality that prevails among all civilized peoples, because it is manifestly contrary to the law of nature, however it may be defined, that a child command an old man, that an imbecile lead a wise man, and that a handful of people be glutted with superfluities while the starving multitude lacks necessities. (117)

As Rousseau would later explain in the *Confessions* concerning the *Discourse on Inequality*: "I began to put my principles in open view a little more than I had done until then."[12] If we accept his claims about the true, if veiled, argument of the *Discourse on the Sciences and the Arts*, then the *Discourse on Inequality* provides the missing premise to his earlier prize essay by revealing the sources of the corruption, inequality, and other vices besetting modern society.

Having been asked a question about human inequality, Rousseau transforms his inquiry into an examination of human nature. One of the principal arguments he makes in the *Discourse* is that all of his predecessors had made the fundamental mistake of assuming that human nature is the same in all times and places. "The philosophers who have examined the foundations of society have all felt the necessity of going back to the state of nature, but

---

12. *Confessions*, in *Collected Writings*, 5:326.

none of them has reached it. . . . In short, all of them, speaking continually of need, greed, oppression, desires, and pride, have carried into the state of nature ideas they have taken from society: they spoke of savage man and they were depicting civil man" (62). In this statement Rousseau aligns himself with Hobbes, Locke, and other thinkers in the tradition of political theory that approaches the examination of the foundations of society with the concepts of the state of nature, the natural rights of the individual, and the social contract while simultaneously declaring how he departs from them. His kinship to these thinkers is evident from the manifest falseness of his initial statement: not *all* philosophers have thought it necessary to "go back" to the state of nature. Indeed, Plato, Aristotle, Augustine, Machiavelli, and many other thinkers did not do so. Rousseau thereby signals that Hobbes, Locke, and others in the state of nature tradition had adopted the *proper* mode of inquiry into political and moral questions. However, he also argues that they did not go far enough with it. They did not go far enough because they falsely assumed that human nature was everywhere the same: they spoke of "savage man" and they were depicting "civil man."

As often with Rousseau, his critique is based on a fundamental agreement with his predecessors. Like Hobbes, Locke, and others in the individualist and empiricist tradition, and against Aristotle and other more classical thinkers, Rousseau agrees that reason is subordinate to the passions, and especially to self-love. But he then questions the extent of our natural passions and therefore the extent of our natural reason. "Savage man" does not have the "need, greed, oppression, desires, and pride" that we see in "civil man." As Rousseau restates this argument at the end of the work when enunciating the principal lessons an "attentive reader" should draw from it, there is an "immense distance" between the "natural state" and the "civil state" because of the change in human nature. "In a word, he will explain how the soul and human passions, altering imperceptibly, so to speak change their nature; why our needs and our pleasures change objects in the long run; why, with original man gradually vanishing, society no longer offers to the eyes of the wise man anything but an assemblage of artificial men and fabricated passions that are the work of all these new relations and have no true foundation in nature" (116).

According to Rousseau, human passions and faculties are dynamic rather than stationary. The dynamics of human psychology he outlines in the work informs both his argument that humans naturally have very limited passions and reason and his account of how the passions and reason develop once humans enter into society. In a particularly important passage he explains:

Whatever the moralists may say about it, human understanding owes much to the passions which, as is generally acknowledged, owe much to it as well. It is by their activity that our reason is perfected. We seek to know only because we desire to have pleasure, and it is not possible to conceive why someone who had neither desires nor fears would go to the trouble of reasoning. The passions, in turn, derive their origin from our needs and their progress from our knowledge. For one can desire or fear things only through the ideas one can have of them or by the simple impulsion of nature; and savage man, deprived of every kind of enlightenment, experiences only the passions of this latter type. His desires do not exceed his physical needs. (73).

With so few needs, savage man has very limited passions and therefore very limited reason. As he comes to have new needs or experiences new passions, and especially needs and passions connected to his fellow human beings, however, his reasoning develops in order to satisfy them. In turn, as his reasoning develops he develops new needs. For example, foresight enables him to anticipate needs he will have to satisfy in the future and he now has a new need for which he has to provide. Human nature is therefore shaped by various forces and especially by social relations.

For Rousseau, human nature is malleable to an extent that no other thinker had previously realized. Humans are "historical" beings. Rousseau terms this capacity for change in our passions and faculties the "faculty of perfecting himself" or "perfectibility": "a faculty which, with the aid of circumstances, successively develops all the others and resides among us as much in the species as in the individual, whereas an animal is at the end of a few months what it will be all its life and its species will be at the end of a thousand years what it was the first year of that thousand" (72). Rousseau maintains that the defining characteristic of human beings is perfectibility, and not reason or speech, as Aristotle and Hobbes both thought, or being the "political animal," as Aristotle argued. Indeed, natural man for Rousseau does not possess reason or speech and is radically asocial.

Despite the seemingly positive connotations of "perfectibility," a term Rousseau coined or was at least among the first to use, the consequences of "this distinctive and almost unlimited faculty" (72) are almost entirely negative in Rousseau's initial characterization of it. Rather than arguing that perfectibility is the capacity for the improvement of the individual and the species, he claims that our capacity for change generally leads to our corruption and misery. "It would be sad for us to be forced to agree that this distinctive and almost unlimited faculty is the source of all man's misfortunes, that it is this faculty which, by dint of time, draws him out of that original condition in which he would pass tranquil and innocent days, that it is this faculty which, over the centuries, by causing his enlightenment and his errors, his vices and his virtues, to bloom, makes him in the long run the tyrant of himself and of nature" (72–73). Despite his generally pessimistic account of perfectibility, however, Rousseau never denies that the highest capacities of humans, both intellectual and moral, also depend upon our capacity for development. Rather, his argument is that the advances that make possible the intellectual and moral development of a few individuals tend to come at the expense of the corruption and misery of the majority.

From the beginning of the *Discourse on Inequality*, Rousseau recognizes that his theory of the malleable and historical character of human nature poses almost insuperable obstacles to his examination:

> And how will man ever manage to see himself as nature formed him, through all the changes that the sequence of time and of things must have produced in his original constitution, and to disentangle what he retains of his own stock from what circumstances and his progress have added to or changed in his primitive state? Like the statue of Glaucus, which time, sea, and storms had so disfigured that it resembled less a god than a ferocious beast, the human soul, altered in the bosom of society by a thousand continually renewed causes, by the acquisition of a mass of knowledge and error, by changes that took place in the constitution of bodies, and by the continual impact of the passions, has, so to speak, changed in appearance to the point of being almost unrecognizable. (51)

His task in the work, then, is to persuade his reader that the primitive natural man he depicts in the beginning of the work could become the being we now have before our eyes.

Rousseau's presentation in the *Discourse on Inequality* takes the form of a hypothetical history of human nature, beginning from our original or natural condition and tracing our development up to the present day. In the first part of the *Discourse*, Rousseau describes "natural man" in the "pure state of nature" as an essentially solitary and stupid creature, initially little different than the other beasts. His presentation of the state of nature is directed largely at

Hobbes' account of the state of nature as a war of all against all. Far from being a state of war, the state of nature is generally peaceful (although the attentive reader will note that it is far from idyllic). Once again, however, Rousseau accepts Hobbes' basic premises concerning the natural egoism of humans and the instrumental role of reason in relation to the passions. According to Rousseau, Hobbes has illegitimately assumed that humans naturally have the needs and passions that would require permanent contact with their fellow humans. Humans can satisfy their primary desire for self-preservation without developing the psychological traits—pride, fear of death, etc.—and their social manifestations—competition, war, etc.—that Hobbes attributes to them.

Particularly important for Rousseau's understanding of human nature are the "two principles preceding reason" that he states in the Preface to the work (54) he found after "meditating on the first and simplest operations of the human soul": self-love and pity. Within the discourse itself, Rousseau expounds on these two principles in direct response to Hobbes: "There is, besides, another principle that Hobbes did not notice and which—having been given to man in order to soften, under certain circumstances, the ferocity of his pride [*amour-propre*], or the desire to preserve himself before the birth of this pride [*amour-propre*] . . . tempers the ardor he has for his own well-being by an innate repugnance to see his fellow human being suffer. . . . I speak of pity" (82–83). While pity may restrain the activity of natural man's self-love and thereby make the state of nature less violent than in Hobbes' account, Rousseau's employment of the passion in this context seems dangerous for his argument, for pity would seem to require imagination he wants to deny to natural man and implies a connection to other human beings, even a social inclination, that Rousseau claims does not exist in the state of nature. The role of pity in his account in the *Discourse on Inequality* and his other works has been the subject of extensive scholarly debate. No less important than pity, however, is the distinction Rousseau makes in the passage quoted above between natural self-love ("the desire to preserve himself") and a unnatural or developed form of self-love, "pride" (*amour-propre*). He expands on this distinction in a note (XV) attached to this passage:

Pride [*amour-propre*] and self-love [*amour de soi-même*]—two passions very different in their nature and their effects—must not be confused. Self-love [*amour de soi-même*] is a natural feeling that inclines every animal to look after its own self-preservation and that, directed in man by reason and modified by pity, produces humanity and virtue. Pride [*amour-propre*] is only a relative feeling, fabricated and born in society, that inclines every individual to attach more importance to himself than to anyone else, that inspires in men all the harm they do to one another, and that is the true source of honor. (147)

As will be explained in editorial notes to these passages, Rousseau uses two different French terms to label the two forms of self-love: *amour de soi* (or *amour de soi-même*) for the natural form of self-love by which all beings, including human beings, seek their self-preservation and well-being, and *amour-propre* for the developed form of self-love that includes being concerned with how one looks in the eyes of others and, indeed, understanding our very selves in terms of how we believe we are seen by others. Rousseau often uses the term *amour-propre* in the negative sense of "pride" or "vanity," but the term can also have a positive sense, like in the notion of taking "pride" in one's work. In any case, his main point is clear: natural man is limited to the natural form of self-love because, as an essentially limited, solitary, and asocial being, he lacks the means, the motive, and the opportunity to conceive of how he looks to others. In sum, Rousseau argues that humans naturally do not possess any passions or other attributes that essentially or necessarily connect them to their fellow human beings, much less make them dependent upon them.

Finally, and centrally for Rousseau's thought, he argues in the first part of the *Discourse on Inequality* that humans are naturally "good" (see the section above, "Rousseau's 'System' of the Natural Goodness of Man"). Rousseau does not mean by this that humans are naturally moral, virtuous, or beneficent, since he argues that humans originally are not social, rational, or moral creatures. Rather, humans are naturally "good" in that their natural passions and faculties tend toward their self-preservation and well-being as individuals and as a species. In this sense, then, Rousseau can claim that humans as Hobbes described them are "evil" in that their natural passions and faculties lead to their misery and even destruction. Rousseau clarifies this argument in *Emile*: "But when Hobbes called the wicked man a robust child, he said something absolutely contradictory. All wickedness comes from weakness. The child is wicked only because he is weak. Make him strong; he will be good."[13] As discussed above, the natural "goodness" of man consists in an equilibrium between his needs and passions and his ability to satisfy them, an equilibrium that makes him good for himself and also not dependent on others, for it is de-

---

13. *Emile*, 67.

pendence above all that makes men evil. For Rousseau it is the social relations that are not natural to man that "make a being evil while making him sociable, and eventually to bring man and the world from so distant a beginning to the point where we now see them" (90).

In the second part of the *Discourse on Inequality*, Rousseau traces the development of humans out of the original state of nature into society, and then sketches the development of society up to the present time. According to Rousseau, although humans possess the potential for development, or perfectibility, that potential need never have developed. Human development, therefore, must be due to external and extrinsic causes, such as climate or natural disasters or overpopulation, which brought humans into permanent contact with one another and thereby created the conditions for their development. Rousseau imagines how the family and then larger societies might have been established, and suggests how reason, language, and other faculties could have developed under those changed conditions. Most importantly, he portrays how our fundamental passions alter, changing the natural self-love (*amour de soi*) simply concerned with self-preservation into other-regarding pride (*amour-propre*), and how, more generally, our hearts and minds are transformed due to these new relations. Up to this point in our development, these changes constitute a corruption of our nature to some extent, but they also make us recognizably "human." Contrary to the common misinterpretation that sees him as romanticizing the original condition of "noble savages" (a term he never uses), Rousseau explicitly argues that the stage of largely developed humans living in small "savage societies" is the best condition for humankind: "this period of the development of human faculties, occupying a golden mean between the indolence of the primitive state and the petulant activity of our pride [*amour-propre*], must have been the happiest and most durable epoch. The more one reflects on it, the more one finds that this state was the least subject to revolutions, the best for man . . . and that he must have left it only by some fatal accident which for the sake of the common utility ought never to have happened" (97).

This happy stage of human development comes to an end, perhaps inevitably, with the invention of property. Property makes humans dependent upon one another—economically, socially, and psychologically—and corrupts rich and poor, master and slave alike:

> To be and to appear to be became two entirely different things, and from this distinction came ostentatious display, deceitful cunning, and all the

vices that follow in their wake. From another point of view, having previously been free and independent, here is man, subjected, so to speak, by a multitude of new needs to all of nature and especially to his fellow humans, whose slave he in a sense becomes even in becoming their master. Rich, he needs their services; poor, he needs their help, and being in a middling condition does not enable him to do without them. He therefore constantly has to seek to interest them in his fate and to make them find their own advantage, in reality or appearance, in working for his. (100)

Property makes it possible for unnatural inequalities such as birth and wealth to have a permanent effect on the fates of individuals. Disputes over property lead to a war of all against all, and political society therefore becomes necessary. However, in Rousseau's account, the very establishment of political society, and then government, ultimately leads to the condition of radical inequalities and corruption that he argues characterizes his own time. Although he describes the initial pseudo-contract that created political society as a fraudulent ploy by the rich to secure their property against the poor (102−3), unlike Marx and other thinkers who would follow him, he sees the establishment of property and of political society as an inevitable development.

But what, then, is the lesson of the *Discourse on Inequality*? Voltaire effectively posed this question in his typically sarcastic manner in a letter he wrote to Rousseau after reading the work: "I have received, Sir, your new book against the human race. . . . One acquires the desire to walk on all fours when one reads your work. Nevertheless, since I lost this habit more than sixty years ago, I unfortunately feel that it is impossible for me to take it up again."[14] In response to Voltaire, Rousseau himself explains: "you have characterized as a book against the human race a writing wherein I pleaded the cause of the human race against itself."[15] What does Rousseau mean? His answer is that he has shown in the *Discourse on Inequality* that man is naturally good, and that the evil we experience in ourselves and amongst ourselves is not from our nature, or from original sin, but is a historical accident. Yet Voltaire's question still stands: what, then, should we do after reading the *Discourse on Inequality*? Rousseau in fact anticipates this question in the *Discourse* itself when he writes at the end of note IX: "What, then? Must we destroy societies, annihilate thine

---

14. Letter from Voltaire to Rousseau, August 30, 1755, in *Collected Writings*, 3:102.
15. Letter from Rousseau to Voltaire, August 18, 1756, in *Collected Writings*, 3:108.

and mine, and return to live in the forests with bears? A conclusion in the manner of my adversaries which I much rather prefer to anticipate than to leave them the shame of drawing it." Nonetheless, in the difficult passage that follows this preemptive strike against the shameless Voltaire, Rousseau is still unclear about the lesson:

> As for men like me, whose passions have forever destroyed their original simplicity, who can no longer feed on grass and acorns nor do without laws and leaders . . . they will scrupulously obey the laws and the men who are their authors and ministers; they will honor above all the good and wise princes who know how to prevent, cure, or palliate that throng of abuses and evils that are always ready to crush us; they will animate the zeal of these worthy leaders by showing them, without fear and without flattery, the greatness of their task and the rigor of their duty. But, for all this, they will scorn no less a constitution that can be maintained only with the assistance of so many respectable people—which is desired more often than obtained—and from which, in spite of all their efforts, more real calamities than apparent advantages always arise. (133)

In short, Rousseau appears to be suggesting that the reader of the *Discourse on Inequality* will at least know the source of the evil, dependence, and inequality he now experiences in society. But is there any constructive lesson to take from the work? Is there a path open to us to improve our condition?

THE *SOCIAL CONTRACT*

"Man is born free, and everywhere he is in chains," Rousseau proclaims near the beginning of his major political treatise, *On the Social Contract; Or Principles of Political Right* (I.1; 163). If he revealed the foundations of society and our chains in the *Discourse on Inequality*, the task he sets for himself in the *Social Contract* is to legitimate the "chains" that bind us to one another and to achieve a new kind of political and moral freedom through democratic self-legislation.

The nature and extent of his project can be seen from his statement, just before the ringing statement about our freedom and chains, about his intention in the work: "I want to inquire whether there can be some legitimate and reliable rule of administration in the civil order, taking men as they are and laws as they can be. In this inquiry I will always try to join what right permits with what interest prescribes, so that justice and utility are not always found at odds" (Proemium; 163). Rousseau will attempt to reconcile "right" and "interest," "justice" and "utility." His goals are therefore at once theoretical—to establish the principles of political right, of legitimacy—and practical—to show us how a properly formed political union would be in our interest and useful to us. By speaking of "interest" and "utility," Rousseau takes "men as they are": naturally self-interested. Somehow this natural self-love must be and can be reconciled with obedience to the laws, or "laws as they can be," truly legitimate laws. As Rousseau later explained in a letter to Mirabeau: "Here, according to my ideas, is the great problem of politics, which I compare to that of squaring the circle in geometry, and of longitudes in astronomy: *To find a form of government that might place the laws above man.*"[16] Rousseau elaborates this claim in *Emile*:

> There are two sorts of dependence: dependence on things, which is from nature; dependence on men, which is from society. Dependence on things, since it has no morality, is in no way detrimental to freedom and engenders no vices. Dependence on men, since it is without order, engenders all the vice, and by it, master and slave are mutually corrupted. If there is any means of remedying this ill in society, it is to substitute law for man and to arm the general wills with a real strength superior to the action of every particular will. If the laws of nations could, like those of nature, have an inflexibility that no human force could ever conquer, dependence on men would then become dependence on things again.[17]

Human societies as Rousseau portrays them in the *Discourse on Inequality* are riddled with dependence on men, a dependence that corrupts us and makes us unfree. Rousseau's project in the *Social Contract*, therefore, is to find a form of association where we are insofar as possible dependent only on the laws of our own free choosing.

Like his predecessors in the social contract tradition, Rousseau argues that individuals are naturally free and that legitimate authority must therefore originate not in natural relationships or through force, but in a formal convention or agreement among these individuals. Unlike his predecessors, however, Rousseau insists that we must somehow remain as free as we were before

---

16. Rousseau to Mirabeau, July 26, 1767, in *Rousseau's Social Contract and Other Later Political Writings*, ed. and trans. Victor Gourevitch (Cambridge: Cambridge University Press, 1997), 269.

17. *Emile*, 85.

entering the political association for this contract to be legitimate. Rousseau frames the problem in this way: "'How to find a form of association that defends and protects the person and goods of each associate with all the common force, and by means of which each, uniting with all, nonetheless obeys only himself and remains as free as before?' Such is the fundamental problem to which the social contract provides the solution" (I.6; 172). For Rousseau, we cannot alienate our freedom by consenting to allow others to rule over us, even as elected representatives. His solution to this problem is paradoxical: the total alienation of all those joining the political association to the association itself through the social contract:

> The clauses of this contract are so completely determined by the nature of the act that the slightest modification would render them null and void. As a result, although they may never have been formally enunciated, they are everywhere the same, everywhere tacitly acknowledged and recognized; they are such until that point when, the social compact having been violated, each person recovers his first rights and regains his natural freedom while losing the conventional freedom for which he renounced it.
>
> These clauses, properly understood, all come down to a single one, namely the total alienation of each associate with all his rights to the whole community. For, in the first place, since each gives himself entirely, the condition is equal for all, and since the condition is equal for all, no one has an interest in making it burdensome for the others. (I.6; 172–73)

The social contract of all the associates creates a political whole where the people as a single body legislates for itself. For Rousseau, the "sovereign" does not rule over "subjects," as does Hobbes' sovereign or Locke's legislative, but rather the people as a whole makes laws for itself in its role as "sovereign" and all obey those same laws in their role as "subjects." The only legitimate form of political authority is democratic self-legislation, and the members of this republic achieve the civil and moral freedom of true "citizens."

The "general will" is the term Rousseau uses to describe the will of the sovereign people in its legislative capacity, and this term has caused considerable confusion and controversy. Striking statements by Rousseau such as "whoever refuses to obey the general will be constrained to do so by the whole body, which means nothing else but that he will be forced to be free" (I.7; 175) and "the general will is always right" (II.3, 182) have only made debates more heated. The "general will" is sometimes conceived by interpreters as a mystical popular will, perhaps accessible only to those who rule in the name of the people, as claimed by the French Revolutionaries inspired by Rousseau. Rousseau's actual conception of the general will, however, can be understood by beginning from its voluntarist foundation, that is, as having its basis in the will of the naturally self-interested human being. The "will" of the individual is the desire for self-preservation and well-being natural to all humans. The problem that arises as humans develop is that this desire is frustrated, making the political association necessary. The "general will," then, is fundamentally the same desire of the individual when he considers himself as part of the entire political association, as a "citizen." The general will is always "right" in principle, then, because the citizens by definition desire what is in their interest, but it does not follow that they are always properly informed about that interest. Likewise, the person who refuses to obey the general will must be "forced to be free" both because he wants the benefits of the political association without bearing the costs and because he cannot otherwise achieve civil and moral freedom. Moreover, insufficiently appreciated is what Rousseau writes immediately after his shocking statement about forcing someone to be free: "For such is the condition that, by giving each citizen to the fatherland, guarantees him against all personal dependence—a condition that makes for the ingenuity and the functioning of the political machine and that alone makes legitimate civil engagements which would otherwise be absurd, tyrannical, and liable to the most enormous abuses" (I.7; 175). The freedom realized in the properly organized political association saves us from the corrupting effects of the personal dependence we experience once we come into society. Rousseau nonetheless recognizes that there is a persistent tension between the "particular will" an individual has when considered as an individual and the "general will" he has when considered as a citizen (see I.7; 175). This tension is a fundamental problem of politics for Rousseau.

The difficulty of getting naturally self-interested individuals to see themselves as citizens, a problem that stems from his theory of human nature, leads Rousseau to discuss the need for the "lawgiver" (II.7). The lawgiver is a kind of founder that makes a people into a people, and Rousseau refers to such traditional examples as Moses and Lycurgus, but reconceives their role in terms of his own theory of human nature and its fundamental malleability:

> He who dares to undertake to establish a people's institutions must feel
> that he is capable of changing, so to speak, human nature; of transform-

ing each individual, who by himself is a complete and solitary whole, into a part of a greater whole from which that individual receives as it were his life and his being; of weakening man's constitution in order to reinforce it; of substituting a partial and moral existence for the physical and independent existence we have all received from nature. In a word, it is necessary for him to take away man's own forces in order to give him forces which are foreign to him and of which he cannot make use without the help of others. The more these natural forces are dead and annihilated, the more powerful and lasting are the ones he has acquired, and the more solid and complete is the institution as well. As a result, when each citizen is nothing, can do nothing, except with all the others, and when the force acquired by the whole is equal or superior to the sum of the natural forces of all the individuals, the legislation can be said to be at the highest point of perfection it might attain. (II.7; 191)

Rousseau's lawgiver has an extraordinary role in the state. The lawgiver cannot accomplish his task of refashioning human nature through legislation, since laws can only legitimately come from the people itself. Rather, the lawgiver creates a shared culture through common customs, mores, and opinions: "a part of the laws unknown to our politicians, but upon which the success of all the others depends, a part to which the great lawgiver attends in secret while he appears to restrict himself to particular regulations which are merely the sides of the arch of which morals—slower to arise—ultimately form the unshakeable keystone" (II.12; 202–3). In addition, Rousseau speaks approvingly of the lawgiver's resort to religion to give divine sanction to the community and its laws (II.7; 193), and he devotes the longest chapter in the *Social Contract* (IV.8) to a discussion of civil religion.

   While Rousseau insists that the only legitimate form of sovereignty is democratic *self-legislation*, he does not argue that democratic *government* is the best or the only form of government and, in fact, he argues that democracy as a form of government is both unattainable for human beings and also ultimately incompatible with democratic sovereignty. In order to understand this claim, we must keep in mind the precise terminology Rousseau uses when it comes to "government." Rousseau discusses "government" and its various forms (democracy, aristocracy, and monarchy) in Book III of the *Social Contract*. He begins the first chapter of Book III, the chapter on government in general, with a warning: "I warn the reader that this chapter should be read with due care, and that I do not know the art of being clear for those who are not willing to be attentive" (III.1; 205). For Rousseau, the "government" is the power that executes the laws made by the people in its capacity as sovereign, and the executive power is therefore strictly subordinate to the legislative power in his theory, not a co-equal branch or a version of mixed sovereignty or mixed government, which he rejects. The main reason the executive power must be separate from the legislative power, according to Rousseau, is that the laws enacted by the people must be general in form and application to be legitimate whereas the execution of the laws is necessarily particular in form, that is, applied to particular individuals. Mixing the legislative and executive powers therefore has the danger of adulterating the generality of the laws and thereby rendering them unjust or abusive. Hence Rousseau's argument that democratic government (as opposed to democratic sovereignty) is ultimately unworkable and also his argument that the aristocratic form of government is the best, understanding by "aristocratic" a natural aristocracy based on merit. However, Rousseau's separation of the executive and legislative powers carries with it a fatal flaw. Given the naturally self-interested nature of humans, he admits that the members of the government and the government as a body will ultimately pursue their own interests as individuals or as a body at the expense of the common interest of the state as a whole (III.1; 209). The tendency for the government to usurp sovereign power is perhaps the reason why Rousseau warns his reader at the outset of his discussion of government to pay particular attention.

Due in large part to the tendency of the government to degenerate, Rousseau does not believe that legitimate political institutions and a shared culture can permanently solve the problem of politics. Given the inclination for the natural self-interest of individuals to reassert itself against their identity as citizens, as well as the related tendency for the government to usurp the power of the sovereign people, Rousseau argues that the natural path for all political associations is ultimately decline and death. His prescriptions are meant to make the chains that bind us in society as legitimate, beneficial, and enduring as possible. The fundamental question for interpreting Rousseau's thought, given his core argument that humans are naturally good but are corrupted in society, then, is to ask to what extent even a properly ordered society can prevent our corruption. To what extent are "men as they are" and "laws as they can be" reconcilable even in the best ordered society? The author of the *Social Contract* seems simultaneously to raise our hopes for the possibilities of politics and to warn us about its ultimately insoluble and even tragic character.

SELECT BIBLIOGRAPHY

·⊏══════⊐·

ROUSSEAU'S LIFE and thought have attracted an unusually large amount of scholarly attention. Given the breadth of his corpus of writings, this scholarship includes contributions from a wide variety of disciplines, including literature, political theory, and philosophy. It also includes work in numerous languages, including English and, of course, French. The following bibliography is therefore necessarily selective. These suggested readings are limited to work available to the English-language reader and focus on studies of the political writings contained in this volume.

ROUSSEAU'S LIFE

The standard biography in English is Maurice Cranston's three-volume work:

Jean-Jacques: The Early Life and Work of Jean-Jacques Rousseau, 1712–1754. Chicago: University of Chicago Press, 1991.

The Noble Savage: Jean-Jacques Rousseau, 1754–1762. Chicago: University of Chicago Press, 1999.

The Solitary Self: Jean-Jacques Rousseau in Exile and Adversity. Chicago: University of Chicago Press, 1999.

ROUSSEAU'S WRITINGS

The standard editions of Rousseau's corpus in French and English translation are:

Oeuvres complètes. 5 vols. Paris: Gallimard, Bibliothèque de la Pléiade, 1959–95.

The Collected Writings of Rousseau. 13 vols. Edited by Roger D. Masters and

Christopher Kelly. Hanover, N.H.: Dartmouth College / University Press of
New England, 1990–2010.

Rousseau's complete correspondence, which is cited in the present volume on a
number of occasions, is also useful:

Correspondence complète. 51 vols. Edited by Ralph A. Leigh. Geneva, Banbury,
and Oxford: Voltaire Foundation, 1965–95.

ROUSSEAU'S THOUGHT IN GENERAL

Among studies of Rousseau's thought as a whole or of his political thought in
general, the following are perhaps the most influential and valuable.

Cassirer, Ernst. *The Question of Jean-Jacques Rousseau.* 2d ed. Edited and translated by Peter Gay. New Haven: Yale University Press, 1989. (Originally
published in German in 1932.)

Cooper, Laurence D. *Rousseau, Nature, and the Good Life.* University Park:
Penn State University Press, 1999.

de Jouvenel, Bertrand. "Essay on Rousseau's Politics." In *Jean-Jacques Rousseau:
Critical Assessments of Leading Political Philosophers,* ed. John T. Scott, 4 vols.,
1:79–140. London: Routledge, 2006. (Originally published in French in 1947.)

De Man, Paul. *Allegories of Reading: Figural Language in Rousseau, Nietzsche,
Rilke, and Proust.* New Haven: Yale University Press, 1982.

Gauthier, David. *Rousseau: The Sentiment of Existence.* Cambridge: Cambridge
University Press, 2006.

Kelly, Christopher. *Rousseau as Author: Consecrating One's Life to the Truth.* Chicago: University of Chicago Press, 2003.

Masters, Roger D. *The Political Philosophy of Rousseau.* Princeton: Princeton
University Press, 1968.

Arthur M. Melzer. *The Natural Goodness of Man: On the System of Rousseau's
Thought.* Chicago: University of Chicago Press, 1990.

Neuhouser, Frederick. *Rousseau's Theodicy of Self-Love: Evil, Rationality, and
the Drive for Recognition.* Oxford: Oxford University Press, 2008.

O'Hagan, Timothy. *Rousseau.* London: Routledge, 1999.

Shklar, Judith N. *Men and Citizens: A Study of Rousseau's Social Theory.* Cambridge: Cambridge University Press, 1969.

Starobinski, Jean. *Jean-Jacques Rousseau: Transparency and Obstruction.* Translated by Arthur Goldhammer. Chicago: University of Chicago Press, 1988.
(Originally published in French in 1958.)

Starobinski, Jean. "The Antidote in the Poison: The Thought of Jean-Jacques Rousseau." In Starobinski, *Blessings in Disguise, or, The Morality of Evil*. Translated by Arthur Goldhammer. Cambridge, Mass.: Harvard University Press, 1993. (Originally published in French in 1989.)

Strauss, Leo. "The Crisis of Modern Natural Right: Rousseau." In *Natural Right and History*, 252–94. Chicago: University of Chicago Press, 1953.

Strong, Tracy B. *Jean-Jacques Rousseau: The Politics of the Ordinary*. Thousand Oaks, Calif.: Sage, 1994.

Wokler, Robert. *Rousseau: A Very Short Introduction*. Oxford: Oxford University Press, 2001.

DISCOURSE ON THE SCIENCES AND THE ARTS

The prize essay that made Rousseau famous has not received nearly as much attention as it should.

Campbell, Sally H., and John T. Scott. "The Politic Argument of Rousseau's *Discourse on the Sciences and the Arts*." *American Journal of Political Science* 49 (October 2005): 818–28.

Gourevitch, Victor. "Rousseau on the Arts and Sciences." *Journal of Philosophy* 69 (1972): 737–54.

Mason, John Hope. "Reading Rousseau's *First Discourse*." *Studies in Voltaire and the Eighteenth Century* 249 (1986): 251–66.

Keohane, Nannerl O. "'The Masterpiece of Policy in Our Century': Rousseau on the Morality of the Enlightenment." *Political Theory* 6 (1978): 457–84.

Strauss, Leo. "On the Intention of Rousseau." *Social Research* 14 (1947): 455–87.

Wokler, Robert. "The *Discours sur les sciences et les arts* and its Offspring: Rousseau in Reply to His Critics." In *Reappraisals of Rousseau: Studies in Honour of R. A. Leigh*, ed. S. Harvey, M. Hobson, D. Kelley, and S.S.B. Taylor, 250–78. Manchester: Manchester University Press, 1980.

DISCOURSE ON THE ORIGINS AND THE FOUNDATIONS OF INEQUALITY AMONG MEN

Among the many studies of Rousseau's *Discourse on Inequality*, the following are particularly valuable.

Cooper, Laurence D. "Between Eros and Will to Power: Rousseau and 'The Desire to Extend Our Being.'" *American Political Science Review* 98 (2004): 105–19.

De Man, Paul. "Theory of Metaphor in Rousseau's *Second Discourse*." *Studies in Romanticism* 12 (1973): 475–98.

Dent, N.J.H. "Rousseau on *Amour-Propre*." *Proceedings of the Aristotelian Society* 72 (1998): 57–74.

Gourevitch, Victor. "Rousseau on Providence." *Review of Metaphysics* 53 (2000): 565–611.

Grace, Eve. "The Restlessness of 'Being': Rousseau's Protean Sentiment of Existence." *History of European Ideas* (2001): 133–51.

Kelly, Christopher, and Roger D. Masters. "Human Nature, Liberty and Progress: Rousseau's Dialogue with the Critics of the *Discours sur l'inégalité*." In *Rousseau and Liberty*, ed. Robert Wokler, 53–69. Manchester: Manchester University Press, 1995.

O'Hagan, Timothy. "Rousseau on *Amour-Propre*." *Proceedings of the Aristotelian Society* 72 (1999): 91–107.

Okin, Susan Moller. "Rousseau's Natural Woman." *Journal of Politics* 41 (1979): 393–416.

Scott, John T. "The Theodicy of the *Second Discourse*: The 'Pure State of Nature' and Rousseau's Political Thought." *American Political Science Review* 86 (1992): 696–711.

Scott, John T. "Rousseau and the Melodious Language of Freedom." *Journal of Politics* 59 (1997): 803–29.

Velkley, Richard. *Being After Rousseau: Philosophy and Culture in Question*, chap. 1. Chicago: University of Chicago Press, 2002.

ON THE SOCIAL CONTRACT

Rousseau's political treatise has received considerable attention from a wide variety of scholarly perspectives.

Affeldt, Stephen. "The Force of Freedom: Rousseau on Forcing to Be Free." *Political Theory* 27 (1999): 299–333.

Althusser, Louis. "Rousseau: The Social Contract." In *Politics and History: Montesquieu, Rousseau, Marx*, 113–60. London: Verso, 1982.

Bertram, Christopher. *Rousseau and "The Social Contract."* London: Routledge, 2003.

Carter, Richard. "Rousseau's Newtonian Body Politic." *Philosophy and Social Criticism* 7 (1980): 144–67.

Cohen, Joshua. "Reflections on Rousseau: Autonomy and Democracy," *Philosophy and Public Affairs* 15 (1986): 275–97.

Fralin, Richard. "The Evolution of Rousseau's View of Representative Government." *Political Theory* 6 (1978): 517–36.

Gildin, Hilail. *Rousseau's "Social Contract": The Design of the Argument.* Chicago: University of Chicago Press, 1983.

Kateb, George. "Aspects of Rousseau's Political Thought." *Political Science Quarterly* 76 (1961): 519–43.

Kelly, Christopher. "'To Persuade without Convincing': The Language of Rousseau's Legislator." *American Journal of Political Science* 31 (1987): 321–35.

Neuhouser, Frederick. "Freedom, Dependence, and the General Will." *Philosophical Review* 102 (1993): 363–95.

Plamenatz, John. "'Ce qui ne signifie autre chose sinon qu'on le forcera d'être libre.'" In *Hobbes and Rousseau: A Collection of Critical Essays*, ed. M. Cranston and R. S. Peters, 318–32. Garden City, N.Y.: Doubleday, 1972.

Riley, Patrick. "The General Will Before Rousseau." *Political Theory* 6 (1978): 485–516.

Scott, John T. "Rousseau's Anti-Agenda-Setting Agenda and Contemporary Democratic Theory." *American Political Science Review* 99 (February 2005): 137–44.

ACKNOWLEDGMENTS

THIS TRANSLATION would not have been possible without the encouragement, advice, and assistance of a number of people.

Several people encouraged me to undertake this project and generously offered their good counsel along the way. In addition to Susan Collins, Stuart Warner, and Robert Zaretsky, who all helped me with the initial proposal for the project, I would particularly like to thank several people who played important roles. First, John Tryneski, my editor at University of Chicago Press, for his enthusiasm for the project and his sound advice. Second, Christopher Kelly and Roger Masters for their generosity and encouragement from the outset. I want to thank Roger Masters in particular, for it was as his student that I first encountered Rousseau through his own translations and editions of the Citizen of Geneva. Third, and most of all, my wife, Adrienne, without whose love and support I could not have done this project or any other.

Translating inevitably raises questions regarding nuances of meaning, historical usage, and other issues, and I have profited from the advice of a number of individuals in this regard, including Henry Clark, Ryan Patrick Hanley, Christine Henderson, Ourida Mostefai, and especially Michael O'Dea. All of these individuals also read part or all of my translations and offered useful suggestions. R. Lee McNish compiled the index, and also provided invaluable editorial assistance for the volume as a whole.

Finally, I gladly acknowledge the assistance of two of my students who worked as research assistants on this project. Michelle Schwarze and John Warner sat with me for hours a day, days a week, and week after week reading the manuscript of the translation aloud, checking it against the French, consulting other translations, and offering their own suggestions about how to solve the innumerable and often insoluble issues of translation we faced on every page, page after page. Their own scholarly abilities, hard work, and continual good humor can be only partly repaid with my gratitude.

NOTE ON THE
TRANSLATION AND EDITION

TRANSLATING IS LIKE doing a crossword puzzle which, perhaps unbeknownst to the poor puzzle-doer, does not have a solution. There is rarely simply a correct answer to any issue encountered when translating, and almost every decision involves simultaneous gains and losses. Translating Rousseau poses particular difficulties because he is such a great stylist. The power of his writing draws on an unusually wide variety of rhetorical devices, syntactic variation, rhythmic prose, and changing tone that are ultimately impossible to capture in translation. My goal, then, has been to produce an accurate and readable translation in contemporary English that seeks to convey, first, his meaning and, second, to the extent possible, the power of his prose.

Writing to the publisher of his *Letter to d'Alembert* in 1758 to complain about the corrections the publisher had made to his prose, Rousseau wrote: "harmony appears to me of such great importance in matters of style that I put it immediately after clarity, even before correct grammar."[18] In doing this translation, I have attempted to follow Rousseau's own statement about his priorities as a writer.

First, I have tried to make Rousseau's meaning clear. Questions about meaning always pose questions of interpretation: what does the author *mean*—intend to convey to the reader— in a given sentence, even by a given word choice? This issue is especially nettlesome considering that words or sentence constructions can sometimes have multiple meanings or shades of meaning, a multiplicity of meanings perhaps intended by the author. These complications suggest that a translation should be as literal as possible in keeping with clear

---

18. Rousseau to Marc-Michel Rey, July 8, 1758, *Correspondence complète*, 5:111. See also Rousseau to Du Peyrou, April 12, 1765.

English. By "literal" I do not mean a one-for-one correspondence of word to word. Such literalness is impossible in translating from one language to another, including from French to English, or would at least produce unreadable results. More importantly, over-literalness would not produce accurate results in the most important sense: with regard to the author's intended meaning. The meaning can be captured and conveyed in a translation only by mirroring the original in a way that mirrors as closely as possible the meaning in another language. This goal is, of course, one that can only be approached and not achieved. In order to minimize the contrary problem of allowing the translator too much interpretative license, however, I have attempted to keep the vocabulary and other relevant aspects of the translation as consistent as possible throughout so that the reader can follow Rousseau's own usage through any given work and across works with confidence. So as not to unduly interrupt the experience of reading Rousseau in English, I have also tried to keep to a minimum editorial notes that explain difficult or important translation issues.

Second, I have tried to capture something of the harmony of Rousseau's prose in order to convey some idea of the effect on the reader of reading him in the original. Such a task is a Sisyphean one. Part of the musical effect of Rousseau's prose—its melody, harmony, and rhythm—is produced by his syntactic variety and his punctuation, which are often unusual even by the standards of eighteenth-century French. Attempting to mimic this syntax and punctuation, however, would produce unreadable or ungrammatical English, especially since eighteenth-century French punctuation and syntax is simply not the same as twenty-first century English, or twenty-first century French for that matter. Rather than trying to retain the original punctuation, therefore, I have intentionally broken up Rousseau's sentences or punctuated them differently when I judged that doing so would achieve a gain in clarity of meaning or capture what I take to be Rousseau's intended rhetorical effect, tone, etc. Such choices are inevitably matters of interpretation. Likewise, I have decided not to retain the original capitalization. This decision is based on several considerations, including the fact that doing so consistently and accurately is ultimately impossible since English and French do not have the same syntax and therefore the same rules for capitalization, and also because the French capitalization is not consistent with contemporary English usage. Rousseau's famous opening salvo in the *Social Contract*—"L'homme est né libre, et partout il est dans les fers"—illustrates this problem. If translated "Man is born free, and everywhere he is in chains," then it appears that "Man" (*homme*) is capitalized, whereas it is not in the original, while translating it overly literally as "The man is born free . . ." would correctly capture the original capitalization of "The" (*L'*), but would not be English. Readers interested in examining Rousseau's prose more closely ultimately have a single route open to them: read him in the original French.

Finally, although Rousseau exercises his authority as an author to sometimes deviate from proper grammar, I have not dared to follow in his footsteps him in this regard, at least not intentionally.

This translation is based on the 1782 edition of Rousseau's works. I have also consulted the current standard French edition of the *Oeuvres complètes* (see Select Bibliography) and the original editions of these works and, in the case of the *Discourse on Inequality*, the edition by Heinrich Meier (5th ed.; Paderborn: Ferdinand Schöningh, 2001), which contains some important corrections and information. Where there are differences across editions published during Rousseau's lifetime or by his literary executors, I have followed the 1782 edition, which includes corrections and occasional additions based on Rousseau's own manuscript copies. I have not noted these changes, so the reader should consult the French critical edition in this regard.

There are numerous previous English translations of the writings contained in this volume. While I hope that my own translations are an improvement upon those of my predecessors, if they are indeed an improvement it is due in part to the skillful work of those who came before me. Particularly valuable have been the translations and editions of Judith Bush and Roger Masters, now included in the *Collected Writings of Rousseau* (vols. 2, 3, and 4; see Select Bibliography), and those of Victor Gourevitch, *The Discourses and Other Early Political Writings* and *The Social Contract and Other Later Political Writings* (both published by Cambridge University Press). Readers who would like to encounter Rousseau in somewhat different translations, and especially those who would like to read more of his political and other writings, would do well to consult these fine translations.

Finally, I have made the editorial notes short and informative and have placed them as footnotes to the main text so that the reader can consult them easily. In order to keep these notes short, I do not include bibliographic information for the sources Rousseau cites. For ancient sources, I simply provide the standard references for these works (e.g., Stephanus numbers for Plato's works). For modern sources, where appropriate I include a page reference to a contemporary edition of the work (e.g., Frame's translation of Montaigne's *Essays*), and list these editions at the end of the volume in a Bibliography of Rousseau's Sources.

DISCOURSE ON
THE SCIENCES AND THE ARTS

Satyr, you do not know it.
See the note, p. 23

DISCOURSE

WHICH TOOK THE PRIZE OF THE ACADEMY OF DIJON IN THE YEAR 1750

ON THIS QUESTION PROPOSED BY THAT ACADEMY:

Whether the restoration of the sciences and the arts has contributed to purifying morals.

BY A CITIZEN OF GENEVA

Here I am the barbarian, understood by nobody.
—Ovid[1]

GENEVA
BARRILLOT & SON

---

1. Ovid *Tristia* 5.9.37, quoted by Rousseau in Latin: *Barbarus hic ego sum quia non intelligor illis.* Rousseau slightly changes the original Latin. The Roman poet Ovid (43 BC–AD 17/18) wrote the *Tristia* ("Sorrows") when in exile in Tomis on the Black Sea where many inhabitants could not understand Latin, therefore making Ovid the "barbarian" among them. Rousseau would later use this same epigraph for his autobiographical work *Rousseau Judge of Jean-Jacques.*

NOTICE

WHAT IS FAME? This is the unfortunate work to which I owe mine. Certainly this piece, which won me a prize and made a name for me, is at best mediocre and I dare add that it is one of the slightest in this entire collection. What an abyss of miseries would the author have avoided if only this first work had been received as it deserved to be! But as it happened, a favorable reception that was initially unjustified gradually brought upon me a harsh penalty that is even more unjustified.[2]

---

2. The Notice was written by Rousseau in 1763 for a collected edition of his works, hence his remark in the Notice that the *Discourse* is "one of the slightest in this entire collection." In speaking of the "harsh penalty" he has suffered for his fame as a writer, Rousseau refers foremost to the condemnation of his *Emile* and *Social Contract* in 1762, a year before this collected edition appeared. See the editor's introduction.

PREFACE

HERE IS ONE of the greatest and noblest questions ever debated. This discourse is not concerned with those metaphysical subtleties that have spread to all fields of literature and from which the announcements of academies are not always exempt. Rather, it is concerned with one of those truths that pertain to the happiness of the human race.

I foresee that I will not easily be forgiven for the side I have dared to take. Clashing head on with everything that nowadays attracts men's admiration, I can expect only universal blame, and it is not for having been honored with the approbation of a few wise men that I should count on that of the public. As such, I have taken a side; I do not care about pleasing either the witty or the fashionable. In all times there will be men destined to be subjugated by the opinions of their age, their country, their society. Someone who today plays the freethinker and the philosopher would, for the same reason, have been a fanatic at the time of the League.[3] One must not write for such readers when one wants to live beyond one's age.

Another word and I am done. Little expecting the honor I received, after submitting it I reworked and expanded this discourse to the point of turning it, as it were, into a different work. I now consider myself obligated to restore it to the state in which it was awarded the prize. I have merely thrown in some notes and let stand two passages which are easily recognized and which the Academy would perhaps not have approved of.[4] I thought that equity, respect, and gratitude required this notice of me.

---

3. The League, or Holy League, was a Catholic faction that attempted to suppress Protestantism during the French wars of religion of the latter part of the sixteenth century.

4. Contrary to Rousseau's suggestion, these passages are not easily recognized and their identity has been a matter of dispute among scholars.

DISCOURSE

We are deceived by the appearance of rectitude.[5]

HAS THE RESTORATION of the sciences and the arts contributed to purifying or to corrupting morals?[6] This is what is to be examined. Which side should I take in this question? That, Gentlemen, which suits a decent man who knows nothing and who does not think any the less of himself for it.

It will be difficult, I feel, to adapt what I have to say to the tribunal before which I appear. How do I dare blame the sciences before one of Europe's most learned societies, praise ignorance in a famous academy, and reconcile contempt for study with respect for the truly learned? I have seen these contradictions, and they have not rebuffed me. It is not science I abuse, I told myself; it is virtue I defend before virtuous men. Integrity is even more dear to good men than erudition is to scholars. What, then, have I to fear? The enlightenment[7] of the assembly listening to me? I admit it, but this fear regards the composition of the discourse and not the sentiment of the speaker. Equitable sovereigns have never hesitated to condemn themselves in doubtful disputes, and the most advantageous position in a just cause is to have to defend oneself against an upright and enlightened opponent who is judge in his own case.

---

5. Horace *On the Art of Poetry (Ars poetica)* 5.25, quoted by Rousseau in Latin: *Decipimur specie recti.*

6. "Morals" translates *moeurs*, which might also be translated "mores" and has a broad sense of morals, manners, and even customs. The broad sense of the term should be kept in mind.

7. "Enlightenment" translates *lumières*, here and throughout. The term refers to the "illumination" or "light" of the mind. Although Rousseau's contemporaries referred to their era as the "century of enlightenment" (*siècle des lumières*), the term "Enlightenment" as used to refer to the intellectual movement of the eighteenth century did not come into English usage until about a century after the publication of the *Discourse on the Sciences and the Arts.*

To this motive which encourages me is joined another which decides me: it is that, after having upheld the side of truth according to my natural lights, there is, regardless of the outcome, a prize I cannot fail to receive. I will find it in the depths of my heart.

FIRST PART

·⊂▭▭▭▭▭▭▭⊃·

IT IS A GRAND and beautiful spectacle to see man emerging, as it were, out of nothingness through his own efforts; dissipating by the light of his reason the shadows in which nature has enveloped him; rising above himself; soaring by his mind to the celestial regions; traversing with the steps of a giant, like the sun, the vast expanse of the universe; and, what is even grander and more difficult, returning into himself in order there to study man and to know his nature, his duties, and his end. All these marvels have been revived in the past few generations.

Europe had fallen back into the barbarism of the first ages. Just a few centuries ago the peoples of that part of the world today so enlightened lived in a condition worse than ignorance. I know not what scientific jargon, even more despicable than ignorance, had usurped the name of knowledge and posed an almost invincible obstacle to its return.[8] A revolution was needed to bring men back to common sense. It eventually came from the quarter from which it was least expected. It was the stupid Muslim, it was the eternal scourge of letters who brought about their rebirth among us. The fall of Constantine's throne carried into Italy the debris of ancient Greece.[9] France in turn was enriched by those precious spoils. Soon the sciences followed letters, the art of writing joined the art of thinking, a sequence which appears strange and is perhaps only too natural, and people began to feel the principal advantage of

---

8. Rousseau alludes to the technical vocabulary of Scholastic philosophy that predominated in medieval theology and philosophy.

9. Rousseau refers to the fall of Constantinople in 1453 to the invading Ottoman Turks. Constantinople was founded by the Emperor Constantine as the eastern capital of the Roman Empire and became the capital of the Byzantine Empire. The refugees from Constantinople carried with them many Greek literary and philosophical works that served as an inspiration for the revival of learning in Italy and elsewhere during the Renaissance.

communing[10] with the Muses, that of making men more sociable by inspiring in them the desire to please one another with works worthy of their mutual approbation.

The mind has its needs, as does the body. The latter make up the foundations of society, the former make it pleasant. While government and laws provide for the security and well-being of assembled men, the sciences, the letters, and the arts—less despotic and perhaps more powerful—spread garlands of flowers over the iron chains with which men are burdened, stifle in them the feeling of that original freedom for which they seemed to have been born, make them love their slavery and fashion them into what are called civilized peoples. Need raised thrones; the sciences and the arts have strengthened them. Earthly powers: love talents and protect those who cultivate them.* Civilized peoples: cultivate them; happy slaves: you owe to them that delicate and refined taste on which you like to pride yourselves; that softness of character and urbanity of morals that make relations[11] among you so affable and so easy; in a word, the appearance of all the virtues without having any of them.

This is the sort of civility, the more amiable as it affects to display itself less, that formerly distinguished Athens and Rome in the much lauded days of their magnificence and their splendor. It is through it, no doubt, that our age and our nation will surpass all times and all peoples. A philosophic tone without pedantry, natural and yet engaging manners, as far removed from Teutonic rusticity as from Italian pantomime: these are the fruits of the taste acquired through good education and perfected by moving in polite society.[13]

---

* Princes always view with pleasure the taste for the agreeable arts and for superfluities that do not result in the exportation of money spread among their subjects. For aside from thereby nurturing in them that pettiness of soul so appropriate to servitude, they well know that all the needs which the people gives itself are so many chains with which they burden themselves. Alexander, wanting to keep the Ichthyophagi dependent on him, compelled them to give up fish and to feed themselves on foods common to other peoples,[12] and the savages of America who go around totally naked and who live only on the yield of their hunting have never been subdued. Indeed, what yoke could be imposed on men who need nothing?

---

10. "Communing" translates *commerce*, which has the general sense of interactions or dealings among individuals or groups, which is the sense here, or sometimes the specific sense of commercial relations. Given the importance of the term for eighteenth-century thought about the origins and effects of "commerce" in both senses of the term, *commerce* has either been translated as "commerce" or a note will identify an alternative translation such as "relations" or "interactions."

11. Or: commerce (*commerce*).

12. Alexander the Great encountered a group of people called the Ichthyophagi (Fish-Eaters) in what is today Pakistan who ate primarily fish.

13. Or: "through social commerce" (*commerce*).

How sweet it would be to live among us if outward appearances were always the image of the dispositions of the heart, if propriety were virtue, if our maxims served us as rules, if genuine philosophy were inseparable from the title of philosophy! But so many qualities are all too rarely found together, and virtue hardly proceeds with such pomp. Richness of attire may announce an opulent man, and his elegance a man of taste. The healthy and robust man is recognized by other signs: it is beneath the rustic clothes of a farmer and not beneath the gilt of a courtier that strength and vigor of body will be found. Finery is no less foreign to virtue, which is strength and vigor of soul. The good man is an athlete who enjoys competing in the nude. He spurns all those vile ornaments which would hinder the use of his strength, and most of which have been invented solely to hide some deformity.

Before art had fashioned our manners and taught our passions to speak a borrowed language, our morals were rustic but natural, and differences in conduct announced those of character at first glance. Human nature, at bottom, was not better. But men found their security in the ease of seeing through one another, and that advantage, of which we no longer sense the value, spared them many vices.

Today, when more subtle study and a more refined taste have reduced the art of pleasing to a set of principles, a vile and deceitful uniformity reigns in our morals, and all minds seem to have been cast from the same mold. Incessantly civility requires, propriety demands; incessantly it is customs that are followed, never one's own genius. One no longer dares to appear to be what one is; and under this perpetual constraint, the men who make up that herd called society, placed in the same circumstances, will all do the same things unless more powerful motives deter them from doing so. One will therefore never really be able to know those with whom one is dealing. To know one's friend, one will therefore have to wait for momentous occasions—that is, to wait until it is too late, because it is these very occasions for which it would have been essential to know him.

What a procession of vices must accompany this uncertainty! No more sincere friendships, no more real esteem, no more well-founded confidence. Suspicions, offenses, fears, coolness, reserve, hatred, betrayal continually conceal themselves behind that uniform and deceitful veil of civility, behind that much lauded urbanity we owe to the enlightenment of our age. The name of the master of the universe will no longer be profaned by swearing, but it will be insulted by blasphemies without our scrupulous ears being offended by them. People will not boast of their own merit, but they will belittle that of others. They will not coarsely insult their enemy, but they will artfully malign him. National hatreds will die out, but they will do so along with love of fatherland.[14] Scorned ignorance will be replaced by a dangerous Pyrrhonism.[15] There will be some forbidden excesses, some dishonored vices, but others will be dignified with the name of virtues; one will either have to have them or to affect them. Let those who so wish boast of the sobriety of the wise men of the age; as for me, I see in it merely a refinement of intemperance as unworthy of my praise as their artful simplicity.*

Such is the purity our morals have acquired. This is how we have become affable men. It is for the letters, the sciences, and the arts to claim their share in such a salutary bit of work. I will only add one thought: that if an inhabitant of some far-off land sought to form an idea of European morals based on the state of the sciences among us, on the perfection of our arts, on the propriety of our theater, on the civility of our manners, on the affability of our discourse, on our perpetual professions of goodwill, and on that tumultuous competition of men of all ages and of all social conditions who seem anxious to oblige one another from the dawn of morn to the setting of the sun; that this stranger, I say, would guess our morals to be precisely the opposite of what they are.

Where there is no effect, there is no cause to seek: but here the effect is certain, the depravity real, and our souls have been corrupted in proportion as our sciences and our arts have advanced toward perfection. Shall it be said that this is a misfortune particular to our age? No, Gentlemen: the evils caused by

---

* *I like*, states Montaigne, *to argue and discuss, but only with a few men and for my own sake. For to serve as a spectacle for the great and to vie with others by parading one's wit and chatter is, I find, a most unbecoming occupation for a man of honor.* This is the occupation of all our wits, save one.[16]

---

14. "Fatherland" translates *patrie*. *Patrie* might also be translated "country" in the sense of the phrase "love of country," hence "patriotism." However, aside from the fact that "country" also translates *pays*, which does not have the strong political sense of *patrie*, Rousseau argues that modern peoples can have a "country" (*pays*) without having a true "fatherland" (*patrie*). Although the term "fatherland" in contemporary English often has a pejorative sense stemming from the nationalist movements and wars of the twentieth century, *patrie* will be translated as "fatherland" throughout.

15. Pyrrhonism was an ancient philosophical doctrine, named after Pyrrho of Elis, that taught suspension of judgment in the face of uncertainty about truth. In Rousseau's time the doctrine that was taken to be a form of radical skepticism.

16. Michel de Montaigne, *Essays* (1580–92), "Of the Art of Discussion," 3.8, p. 704. The exception that Rousseau makes for one of his contemporaries who does not talk merely to display his wit is generally agreed to refer to Denis Diderot, his closest friend at the time he wrote this *Discourse*.

our vain curiosity are as old as the world. The daily rise and fall of the ocean's waters have not been more regularly subjected to the course of the star that gives us light during the night than has the fate of morals and integrity to the progress of the sciences and the arts. Virtue has been seen to flee in proportion as their light dawned on our horizon, and the same phenomenon has been observed in all times and in all places.

Behold Egypt, that first school of the universe, that climate so very fertile beneath a brazen sky, that famous land from which Sesostris long ago set out to conquer the world. It becomes the mother of philosophy and the fine arts, and, soon thereafter, the conquest of Cambyses, then that of the Greeks, of the Romans, of the Arabs, and finally of the Turks.[17]

Behold Greece, formerly peopled by heroes who twice vanquished Asia, once in front of Troy and once at their very hearths. Nascent letters had not yet carried corruption into the hearts of its inhabitants, but the progress of the arts, the dissolution of morals, and the yoke of the Macedonian closely followed upon one another, and Greece — ever learned, ever voluptuous, and ever enslaved — no longer experienced anything but a change of masters in the course of its revolutions. All Demosthenes' eloquence could never revive a body that luxury and the arts had enervated.[18]

It is in the time of the likes of Ennius and of Terence that Rome, founded by a shepherd and made illustrious by farmers, begins to degenerate. But after the likes of Ovid, of Catullus, of Martial, and that crowd of obscene authors whose names alone alarm modesty, Rome, formerly the temple of virtue, becomes the theater of crime, the disgrace of nations, and the plaything of barbarians. This capital of the world ultimately succumbs to the yoke it had imposed on so many peoples, and the day of its fall was the eve of the day on which the title of arbiter of good taste was given to was given to one of its citizens.[19]

---

17. Sesostris could refer to a number of legendary Egyptian rulers. The Persian king Cambyses conquered Egypt in 525 BC. In turn, Alexander the Great conquered it in 332 BC, the Romans under Augustus in 30 BC, the Arabs under Caliph Omar I in 639–42, and the Ottoman Turks in 1517.

18. The Athenian orator Demosthenes (384–322 BC) spoke in opposition to the Macedonian expansion into the Greek city-states.

19. Ennius (c. 239–c. 169 BC), who is considered the father of Roman poetry, and Terence (c. 195/185–159 BC), the great dramatist, both lived during the period of the Roman Republic. The poet Ovid (43 BC–AD 17/18), who was well known for his erotic poems, lived during the early Roman Empire. Catullus (84–54 BC), an erotic poet, lived during the time of the collapse of the Roman Republic. Martial (40–c.104) wrote satirical poems and lived during a tumultuous period of the early Roman Empire. The citizen named "arbiter of good taste" was Petronius (c. 27–66), the satirical writer who was a courtier to Nero and who was renowned for his debauchery.

What shall I say about that metropolis of the Eastern Empire which, by its location, seemed destined to be the metropolis of the entire world, of that refuge of the sciences and arts banned from the rest of Europe, perhaps more out of wisdom than barbarism? All that is most shameful in debauchery and corruption; the blackest of betrayals, assassinations, and poisonings; a contest among all of the most atrocious crimes: this is what makes up the fabric of the history of Constantinople, this is the pure source from which we have received the enlightenment in which our time takes such great pride.

But why seek in remote times proofs of a truth for which we have enduring evidence before our eyes? In Asia there is an immense land where literary honors lead to the state's highest offices. If the sciences purified morals, if they taught men to shed their blood for the fatherland, if they animated courage, the peoples of China should be wise, free, and invincible. But if there is not a single vice that does not dominate them, not a single crime that is not familiar to them, if neither the enlightenment of government officials, nor the alleged wisdom of the laws, nor the large number of inhabitants of that vast empire have been able to protect it from the yoke of the ignorant and coarse Tartar, of what use have all these learned men been to them? What benefit have they derived from the honors bestowed on them? Is it to be populated by slaves and wicked men?

Let us contrast these scenes with that of the morals of the small number of peoples that, protected from that contagion of vain knowledge, have created their own happiness as well as an example for other nations by their virtues. Such were the first Persians, a singular nation in which virtue was learned as science is learned among us, which subjugated Asia with so much ease, and which alone has had the glory of having the history of its institutions mistaken for a philosophic novel.[20] Such were the Scythians, of whom such magnificent praise has come down to us. Such were the Germans, whose simplicity, innocence, and virtues a pen — weary of depicting the crimes and foul deeds of an educated, opulent, and voluptuous people — took solace in portraying.[21] Such was Rome itself in the times of its poverty and its ignorance. Such, finally, has that rustic nation — so lauded for its courage, which adversity has not

---

20. The "philosophic novel" in question is the *Education of Cyrus*, written by Xenophon (c. 430–354 BC), who was an associate of Socrates.

21. The author of the "pen" in question is Tacitus (56–117), whose *Histories* and *Annals* chronicle the history of the early Roman Empire and who was the also the author of the *Germania*, which described the rustic Germanic tribes.

been able to fell, and for its fidelity, which bad examples have not been able to corrupt—proven itself to be to this very day.[22]*

It is not owing to stupidity that they have preferred other forms of exercise to those of the mind. They were not unaware that in other lands idle men spent their lives arguing over the sovereign good, over vice and virtue, and that prideful reasoners, bestowing the greatest praise on themselves, lumped together other peoples under the contemptuous name of barbarians. But they considered their morals and learned to disdain their doctrine.†

Could I forget that it was in the very bosom of Greece that a city was seen to arise which was as famous for its happy ignorance as for the wisdom of its laws, that republic of demigods rather than of men, so superior to humanity did their virtues seem? O Sparta! Eternal source of shame for a vain doctrine! While the vices carried by the fine arts were introduced together into Athens, while a tyrant was there assembling the works of the prince of poets with such care,[25] you drove away from your walls the arts and the artists, the sciences and the learned.

The outcome marked the difference. Athens became the abode of politeness and good taste, the country of orators and philosophers. The elegance of the buildings there corresponded to that of the language. Marble and canvas, brought to life by the hands of the most skillful masters, were there seen all over. It is from Athens that those astonishing works that will serve as models in every corrupted age have come. The picture of Lacedaemon is less brilliant. *There*, said other peoples, *men are born virtuous and the very air of the country*

---

* I dare not speak of those happy nations which do not even know the name of the vices we have so much trouble suppressing, of those savages of America whose simple and natural ordering Montaigne does not hesitate to prefer, not only to the laws of Plato, but even to everything that philosophy could ever imagine as most perfect for governing peoples. He cites numerous striking examples for those who know how to appreciate them. "But just think!" he says, "they don't wear breeches!"[23]

† Really, will someone tell me what opinion the Athenians themselves must have had of eloquence when they kept it away with such care from that upright tribunal whose judgments the gods themselves did not appeal?[24] What did the Romans think of medicine when they banished it from their republic? And when what little humanity they retained led the Spaniards to forbid their lawyers from entering America, what idea must they have had of jurisprudence? Might it not be said that they believed that by this single act they atoned for all the evils they had done to those unfortunate Indians?

---

22. Rousseau appears to refer to the Swiss.

23. See Montaigne, *Essays* (1580–92), "Of Cannibals," 1.31, p. 159.

24. Rousseau refers to the Areopagus, the highest judicial court in ancient Athens.

25. The Athenian tyrant Peisistratos (d. c. 527 BC) commissioned what became the standard edition of Homer's poetry.

seems to inspire virtue. Of its inhabitants the only thing that remains for us is the memory of their heroic actions. Are such monuments worth less to us than the curious marbles Athens has left us?

Some wise men, it is true, resisted the general torrent and protected themselves against vice while in the abode of the Muses. But listen to the verdict that the foremost and most unfortunate among them passed on the learned men and artists of his time.

"I examined," he says, "the poets, and I regard them as people whose talent impresses both themselves and others, who present themselves as wise men, who are taken to be such, and who are nothing of the sort.

"From the poets," continues Socrates, "I went on to the artists. No one is more ignorant about the arts than I am; no one was more convinced that the artists possessed some very fine secrets. Yet I perceived that their condition is no better than that of the poets and that both of them have the same bias. Because the most skillful among them excel in their specialty, they regard themselves as the wisest of men. This presumption altogether tarnished their knowledge in my eyes. As a result, putting myself in the place of the oracle and asking myself which I would prefer to be, what I am or what they are, knowing what they have learned or knowing that I know nothing, I answered myself and the god: I want to remain what I am.

"We do not know—neither the sophists, nor the poets, nor the orators, nor the artists, nor I—what is the true, the good, and the beautiful. But there is this difference between us: that although these people know nothing, they all believe that they know something, whereas I, if I know nothing, am at least not in doubt about it. As a result, this entire superiority of wisdom that is accorded to me by the oracle amounts simply to being fully convinced that I am ignorant of what I do not know."[26]

Here, then, is the wisest of men in the judgment of the gods and the wisest of the Athenians according to the view of all Greece, Socrates, speaking in praise of ignorance! Is it credible that, if he were brought back to life among us, our learned and our artists would cause him to change his opinion? No, Gentlemen, that just man would continue to scorn our vain sciences, he would

---

26. Rousseau here paraphrases Plato *Apology of Socrates* 21b–22e. Plato has Socrates recount there how Socrates, having learned that the Oracle of Dephi declared that no one is wiser than he, went to those reputed wisest among his fellow-citizens—the politicians, then the poets, and finally the manual artisans or craftsmen—and concluded from his inquiries that his wisdom consisted in knowing that he did not know anything. Among other alterations or admissions in his paraphrase, Rousseau most significantly omits any discussion of politicians and replaces manual artisans or craftsmen with artists.

not help to enlarge that mass of books with which we are inundated from every direction, and he would leave behind—as he did before—as the sole precept to his disciples and to our posterity merely the example and the memory of his virtue. Now that is a fine way to teach men!

What Socrates had begun in Athens, Cato the Elder continued in Rome by loosing his fury upon those artificial and subtle Greeks who were seducing the virtue and softening the courage of his fellow-citizens.[27] But the sciences, the arts, and dialectic still prevailed. Rome was filled with philosophers and orators. Military discipline was neglected, agriculture spurned, sects were embraced, and the fatherland forgotten. The sacred names of freedom, disinterestedness, obedience to the laws were replaced by the names of Epicurus, Zeno, Arcesilaus.[28] *Ever since learned men began to appear among us,* said their own philosophers, *good men have been eclipsed.*[29] Until then the Romans had been content to practice virtue; all was lost when they began to study it.

O Fabricius! What would your great soul have thought if—to your own misfortune, called back to life—you had seen the pompous appearance of that Rome saved by your might and made more illustrious by your respectable name than by all its conquests? "Gods!" you would have said, "what has become of those thatched huts and those rustic hearths where moderation and virtue once dwelled? What fatal splendor has replaced Roman simplicity? What is this strange language? What are these effeminate morals? What is the meaning of these statues, these paintings, these buildings? Mad men, what have you done? You, the masters of nations, have you made yourselves the slaves of the frivolous men you vanquished? Is it rhetoricians who govern you? Was it to enrich architects, painters, sculptors, and historians that you shed your blood in Greece and Asia? Are the spoils of Carthage booty for a flute player? Romans, hasten to tear down these amphitheaters, break these marble statues, burn these paintings, drive away these slaves who have subjugated you and whose fatal arts are corrupting you. Let other hands win renown through vain talents; the sole talent worthy of Rome is that of conquering the world and making virtue reign in it. When Cineas took our Senate for an assembly of kings, he was dazzled neither by vain pomp nor by an overly refined elegance.

27. Marcus Porcius Cato or Cato the Elder (234–149 BC) was a Roman statesman famous for his adherence to old-fashioned Roman virtues and his opposition to the introduction into the city of the Greek philosophical sects.

28. Epicurus (341–270 BC) was the founder of the Epicurean sect, Zeno of Citium (c. 334–c. 262 BC) was the founder of the Stoic sect, and Arcesilaus (c. 316–c. 240 BC) was the founder of a form of skepticism associated with the later Platonic Academy.

29. Rousseau here paraphrases Seneca *Letters* 95.13.

He did not hear in it that frivolous elegance, the object of study and the delight of trifling men. What, then, did Cineas see that was so majestic? O citizens! He saw a spectacle that neither your wealth nor all your arts will ever produce, the noblest spectacle that has ever appeared beneath heaven: the assembly of two hundred thousand virtuous men, worthy of commanding Rome and of governing the earth."[30]

But let us leap over the interval of space and time and see what has happened in our lands and before our eyes. Or, rather, let us set aside the repugnant canvases that would offend our delicacy and spare ourselves the difficulty of repeating the same things under different names. It is not in vain that I evoked the shade of Fabricius, and what did I make that great man say that I could not have put in the mouth of Louis XII or of Henri IV?[31] Among us, it is true, Socrates would not have drunk the hemlock; but he would have drunk a still more bitter cup: insulting raillery and scorn a hundred times worse than death.

This is how luxury, licentiousness, and slavery have in all ages been the punishment for the prideful efforts we have made to leave that happy ignorance in which eternal wisdom had placed us. The thick veil with which it has covered all its operations seemed to warn us clearly enough that it did not destine us for vain studies. But is there even one of its lessons from which we have been able to profit or which we have neglected with impunity? Peoples: know once and for all, then, that nature wanted to keep you from science just as a mother tears a dangerous weapon from the hands of her child, that all the secrets it hid from you are so many evils from which it protects you, and that the difficulty you find in educating yourselves is not the least of its blessings. Men are perverse; they would be even worse if they had had the misfortune to be born learned.

How humiliating these reflections are for humanity! How our pride must be mortified by them! What! Could integrity be the daughter of ignorance? Could science and virtue be incompatible? What consequences might be drawn from these prejudices? But in order to reconcile these apparent contradictions, it is only necessary to examine closely the emptiness and meaninglessness of those

---

30. Gaius Fabricius Luscinus was a Roman statesman and general who was elected consul in 282 and 278 BC. He was known for his austere morals and for his negotiation of peace terms with the Greek king Pyrrhus, who was so impressed with Fabricius' immunity to bribery that he released his Roman prisoners without any ransom. Cineas was sent by Pyrrhus to Rome to negotiate for peace.

31. Louis XII was king of France from 1498 to 1515 and Henri IV from 1589 to 1610. The interval between the reigns of these two kings was a period of intense religious conflict in France between Catholics and Protestants.

prideful titles which dazzle us and which we give so gratuitously to human knowledge. Let us therefore consider the sciences and the arts in themselves. Let us see what must result from their progress and no longer hesitate to agree on all those points where our reasoning is found to be in accord with historical inductions.

SECOND PART

·◦〓〓〓〓〓◦·

IT WAS AN ANCIENT tradition passed down from Egypt to Greece that a god who was hostile to men's tranquility was the inventor of the sciences.* What, then, must the Egyptians themselves, among whom they were born, have thought of them? It was that they saw up close the sources that had produced them. Indeed, whether one leafs through the annals of the world, whether one supplements uncertain chronicles with philosophic research, human knowledge will not be found to have an origin that corresponds to the idea one would like to have of it. Astronomy was born from superstition; eloquence from ambition, hatred, flattery, lying; geometry from avarice; physics from vain curiosity; all of them, and even moral philosophy, from human pride. The sciences and the arts therefore owe their birth to our vices. We would be in less doubt regarding their advantages if they owed it to our virtues.

The defectiveness of their origin is only too clearly brought back to mind for us in their objects. What would we do with the arts without the luxury that nourishes them? Without men's injustices what purpose would jurisprudence

---

* The allegory of the fable of Prometheus is easily grasped, and it does not appear that the Greeks, who nailed him to the Caucasus, scarcely thought more favorably of him than the Egyptians did of their god Thoth.[32] "The satyr," an ancient fable goes, "wanted to kiss and embrace the fire the first time he saw it, but Prometheus cried out to him: Satyr, you will mourn the beard on your chin, for it burns when it is touched."[33] This is the subject of the frontispiece.

---

32. See Plato *Phaedrus* 274c–275b, where Socrates tells a story about the god Thoth (or Theuth) displaying his arts to the Egyptian pharaoh, who questions the good or harm that may come from them. See also Plato *Protagoras* 320c–322d.

33. Rousseau closely paraphrases Plutarch, "How to Profit by One's Enemies," 2. The continuation of the passage is instructive for understanding the complexity of Rousseau's argument in the *Discourse on the Sciences and the Arts*: "Yet this very fire is a most beneficial thing to mankind: it bestows upon us the blessings both of light and heat, and it serves those who know how to use it for the most excellent instruments of the arts."

serve? What would history become if there were neither tyrants, nor wars, nor conspirators? Who, in a word, would want to spend his life in sterile contemplation if each person, consulting only the duties of man and the needs of nature, had time only for the fatherland, the unfortunate, and his friends? Are we then destined to die fastened to the edge of the well into which the truth has withdrawn?[34] This reflection alone should rebuff from the very outset every man who would seriously attempt to educate himself through the study of philosophy.

How many dangers! How many false paths in the investigation of the sciences! How many errors, a thousand times more dangerous than the truth is useful, must be braved in order to reach it! The disadvantage is evident, for falsehood admits of an infinite number of combinations, but the truth has but one mode of being. Furthermore, who really seeks it sincerely? Even with the best of intentions, by what signs is one certain to recognize it? Amid this host of differing sentiments, what will be our criterion for judging it correctly?* And what is most difficult, if by good fortune we eventually find it, who among us will know how to make good use of it?

If our sciences are vain in the object they propose for themselves, they are still more dangerous through the effects they produce. Born in idleness, they nourish it in their turn, and the irreparable loss of time is the first injury they necessarily do to society. In politics, as in morals, it is a great evil not to do good, and every useless citizen can be regarded as a pernicious man. Answer me, then, illustrious philosophers—you, thanks to whom we know in what proportions bodies attract one another in a vacuum; what in the orbits of the planets are the ratios of the areas covered in equal times; what curves have conjugate points, inflexion points, and cusps; how man sees everything in God; how the soul and the body are, like two clocks, in harmony without

---

* The less one knows, the more one believes one knows. Did the Peripatetics doubt anything? Did not Descartes construct the universe with cubes and vortices?[35] And even today is there in Europe a physicist, however shabby, who does not rashly explain that profound mystery of electricity, which will perhaps forever remain the despair of true philosophers?

---

34. Truth withdrawing into a well or pit or abyss is an image commonly attributed to the ancient atomist philosopher Democritus (see Democritus, Fragment 17). Rousseau could have taken the image from a number of sources, including Montaigne, *Essays* (1580–92), "Of the Art of Discussion," 3.8, p. 708.

35. The Peripatetics were the sect of philosophy associated with the Lyceum, originally founded by Aristotle. René Descartes (1596–1650), the philosopher, natural scientist, and mathematician, proposed a theory of planetary orbits and other celestial phenomena based on a series of interlocking vortices, or large bands of material particles moving in a circular manner.

communicating; what planets might be inhabited; what insects reproduce in an extraordinary manner?[36] Answer me, I say, you from whom we have received so much sublime knowledge: even if you had never taught us any of these things, would we be any less populous, less well-governed, less formidable, less flourishing or more perverse? Reexamine, then, the importance of your productions, and if the labors of the most enlightened of our learned and our best citizens procure us so little utility, tell us what we must think of that crowd of obscure writers and idle men of letters who devour the state's substance at a pure loss.

What am I saying, idle? And would to God they were indeed! Morals would be healthier and society more peaceful. But those vain and futile declaimers go about everywhere, armed with their deadly paradoxes, undermining the foundations of faith and annihilating virtue. They laugh disdainfully at those old-fashioned words "fatherland" and "religion" and consecrate their talents and their philosophy to destroying and degrading all that is sacred among men. Not that at bottom they hate either virtue or our dogmas: it is public opinion to which they are hostile, and in order to bring them back to the feet of the altars, it would be enough to banish them among the atheists. O rage for distinction! What will you not do?

The misuse of time is a great evil. Other evils still worse accompany the letters and the arts. One of them is luxury, born like them from men's idleness and vanity. Luxury rarely proceeds without the sciences and the arts, and never do they proceed without it. I know that our philosophy, ever fertile in singular maxims, claims—against the experience of every age—that luxury makes for the splendor of states. But, having forgotten the need for sumptuary laws, will it dare deny as well that good morals are essential to the continuance of empires and that luxury is diametrically opposed to good morals? Let luxury be a certain sign of wealth, let it even serve, if you like, to increase it. What must be concluded from this paradox so worthy of being born in our time, and what will virtue become when it is necessary to enrich oneself

---

36. The discoveries of the "illustrious philosophers" are as follows: the first three (the proportions by which bodies attract one another in a vacuum, the ratios of the areas covered in equal times by the planets, and the conjugate points, inflexion points, and cusps of various curves) were discovered or developed by Isaac Newton (1643–1727), although the ratios of planetary motion were first formulated by Johannes Kepler (1571–1630); the doctrine that man sees everything in God was put forth by Nicholas Malebranche (1638–1715); the notion of the harmony between the soul and body as illustrated by two synchronous clocks was advanced by Gottfried Wilhelm Leibniz (1646–1716); speculation that other planets might be inhabited refers to Bernard Le Bovier de Fontenelle (1657–1757) and his work *Conversations on the Plurality of Worlds* (1686); finally, probably the best known investigations into the reproduction of insects were done by the naturalist René Antoine Ferchault de Réaumur (1683–1757).

at any cost? The ancient politicians spoke constantly of morals and virtue; ours speak only of commerce and money.[37] One will tell you that a man in a given land is worth the sum for which he would be sold in Algiers. Another, working through this calculation, will discover countries in which a man is not worth anything, and others in which he is worth less than nothing.[38] They evaluate men like herds of cattle. According to them, a man is worth to the state only what he consumes in it. Thus, a Sybarite might well be worth thirty Lacedaemonians. Let one guess, then, which of these two republics, Sparta or Sybaris, was subjugated by a handful of peasants and which made Asia tremble.[39]

The monarchy of Cyrus was conquered with twenty thousand men by a prince poorer than the least of Persia's satraps, and the Scythians, the most miserable of all peoples, resisted the most powerful monarchs in the universe. Two famous republics contested the empire of the world: one was very rich, the other had nothing, and it was the latter that destroyed the former. The Roman Empire, in its turn, after having gobbled up all the riches in the universe, was the prey of peoples who did not even know what wealth was. The Franks conquered the Gauls, the Saxons England, without any other treasure than their bravery and their poverty. A band of poor mountaineers the sum of whose greed was limited to some sheepskins, after breaking Austrian pride crushed the opulent and formidable House of Burgundy that made the potentates of Europe tremble. Finally, all the power and all the wisdom of the heir of Charles V, supported by all the treasures of the Indies, came to be shattered by a handful of herring-fishers.[40] Let our politicians deign to suspend their

37. Compare Montesquieu, *Spirit of the Laws* (1748), 3.2, pp. 22–23: "The political men of Greece who lived under popular government recognized no other force to sustain it than virtue. Those of today speak to us only of manufacturing, commerce, finance, wealth, and even luxury."

38. See Montesquieu, *Spirit of the Laws*, 23.17, p. 439: "Sir William Petty has assumed in his calculations that a man in England is worth what he would be sold for in Algiers. This can be good only for England: there are countries in which a man is worth nothing; there are some in which he is worth less than nothing."

39. Sybaris was an ancient city in what is today southern Italy whose wealth was legendary that was conquered by Croton, another city in the same region, in 510 BC. Contrary to Rousseau's exaggerated claim, Croton was also a wealthy city and not "a handful of peasants." Sparta (or Lacedaemon) was the Greek city that, along with Athens, led Greek resistance to the Persian Empire during the 5th century BC.

40. In this paragraph, Rousseau refers to the following historical events, often with a degree of exaggeration: the conquest of Persia ("the monarchy of Cyrus") by Alexander the Great in 334–330 BC; the failure of the Persians to conquer the Scythians during the sixth century BC; the wars between Rome and Carthage ("two famous republics") known as the Punic Wars in 264–241 BC, 218–201 BC, and 149–146 BC; the invasions of Rome by the Goths, Huns, and Vandals and the ultimate fall of the Roman Empire in 476; the conquest of the Gauls by the Franks and the Saxon invasions of Britain, both during the fifth century AD; the successful resistance by the Swiss ("a band of poor mountaineers") against the Austrian Habsburg Empire during the fourteenth century and then their victory over Charles the Bold, Duke of Burgundy in 1476; the successful

calculations in order to reflect on these examples, and let them learn for once that with money one has everything, save morals and citizens.

What, then, precisely is at issue in this question of luxury? To know what is more important for empires: to be brilliant and transitory or virtuous and lasting. I say brilliant, but with what luster? The taste for splendor is hardly ever combined in the same souls with the taste for the honorable. No, it is not possible for minds degraded by a host of trivial concerns to ever rise to anything great, and even if they had the strength to do so they would lack the courage.

Every artist wants to be applauded. The praise of his contemporaries is the most precious portion of his reward. What will he do to obtain it, then, if he has the misfortune to be born among a people and in a time when the learned, having become fashionable, have put frivolous youth into a position where they set the tone; when men have sacrificed their taste to the tyrants of their freedom;* when, since one of the sexes has dared to approve only what is proportioned to the pusillanimity of the other, masterpieces of dramatic poetry are dropped from repertoires and wonders of harmony are rejected? What will he do, Gentlemen? He will lower his genius to the level of his age and he will prefer to compose ordinary works that are admired during his lifetime rather than marvels that would be admired only long after his death. Tell us, famous Arouet, how much you have sacrificed manly and strong beauties to our false delicacy, and how much the spirit of gallantry, so fertile in petty things, has cost you great ones?[41]

This is how the dissolution of morals, a necessary consequence of luxury, leads in turn to the corruption of taste. If, by chance, someone among those men of extraordinary talent is found who has firmness of soul and who refuses

---

* I am quite far from thinking that this ascendency of women is in itself an evil. It is a gift nature has given them for the happiness of the human race. Better directed, it could produce as much good as it now does evil. It is not sufficiently appreciated what advantages would arise for society if a better education were given to that half of the human race which governs the other. Men will always be what is pleasing to women. If you want to become great and virtuous, therefore, teach women what greatness of soul and virtue are. The reflections this subject furnishes, and which Plato long ago made, greatly deserve to be more fully developed by a pen worthy of writing after the model of such a master and of defending so great a cause.[42]

---

revolt of the Netherlands against King Philip II of Spain ("the heir of Charles V," that is, the Habsburg Holy Roman Emperor Charles V, who was also king of Spain) from 1566 to 1579.

41. "Famous Arouet" is the poet, dramatist, and historian Voltaire (1694–1778), whose given name was François-Marie Arouet. By using Voltaire's given name rather than his pen name, Rousseau emphasizes Voltaire's desire for fame.

42. See Plato *Republic* 5 (451b–457b), where Socrates proposes that the men and women of the best city are equal and should therefore have the same education and roles in the city.

to yield to the genius of his age and to debase himself with childish works, woe unto him! He will die in poverty and oblivion. If only this were a prognostication I am making and not an experience I report! Carle, Pierre: the moment has come when that brush destined to increase the majesty of our temples with sublime and sacred images will fall from your hands or it will be prostituted to decorate the panels of a carriage with lascivious paintings.[43] And you, rival of the likes of Praxiteles and of Phidias; you, whose chisel the ancients would have utilized to make gods capable of excusing their idolatry in our eyes: inimitable Pigalle, your hand will bring itself to sculpting the belly of a grotesque figurine or it must remain idle.[44]

One cannot reflect on morals without taking delight in recalling the image of the simplicity of the earliest times. It is a lovely shore, fashioned by the hand of nature alone, toward which one continually turns one's eyes and from which one reluctantly feels oneself moving away. When innocent and virtuous men enjoyed having the gods as witnesses of their actions, they lived together in the same huts. But soon, becoming wicked, they grew weary of these inconvenient spectators and relegated them to magnificent temples. They eventually chased them out in order to take up residence there themselves, or at least the temples of the gods were no longer distinguished from the houses of the citizens. This was the height of depravity, and the vices were never carried further than when they could be seen, so to speak, set up on marble columns and engraved on Corinthian capitals at the entry of the palaces of the great.

While the conveniences of life multiply, while the arts are perfected and luxury spreads, true courage is enervated, the military virtues vanish, and this too is the work of the sciences and of all those arts practiced in the shade of the study. When the Goths ravaged Greece, all the libraries were saved from being burned only by that opinion, spread by one of them, that they should let their enemies keep belongings so well suited to deterring them from military training and to amusing them with idle and sedentary occupations. Charles VIII found himself master of Tuscany and the Kingdom of Naples almost without having drawn his sword, and his entire court attributed this unexpected ease to the fact that the princes and nobility of Italy amused themselves by becom-

---

43. Carle or Charles-André Van Loo (1705−65) and Jean-Baptiste-Marie Pierre (1714−89) were well-known painters of the period.

44. Jean-Baptiste Pigalle (1714−85) was one of the most popular sculptors of the time. Praxiteles (4th century BC) was the most famous sculptor of ancient Greece, and Phidias (5th century BC) was the most famous sculptor, artist, and architect of ancient Athens and was commissioned by Pericles to make several statues for the Parthenon.

ing ingenious and learned more than they worked at becoming vigorous and warlike. Indeed, states the sensible man who relates these two anecdotes, all examples teach us that in such military regulations, and in all those similar to them, the study of the sciences is much more likely to soften and emasculate men's courage than to strengthen and animate it.[45]

The Romans confessed that military virtue was extinguished among them in proportion as they began to become connoisseurs of paintings, engravings, jeweled vases, and to cultivate the fine arts. And, as if that famous land were destined ever to serve as an example to other peoples, the rise of the Medici and the restoration of letters brought about anew, and perhaps forever, the downfall of that warlike reputation Italy seemed to have recovered a few centuries ago.

The ancient republics of Greece, with that wisdom which shined forth in most of their institutions, forbade their citizens all those sedate and sedentary occupations which, by weighing down and corrupting the body, soon enervate the vigor of the soul. How, indeed, do you think men whom the slightest need crushes and the slightest difficulty rebuffs would envision hunger, thirst, fatigue, danger, and death? With what courage will soldiers endure excessive labors to which they have not become accustomed? With what spirit will they make forced marches under officers who do not even have the strength to travel on horseback? Let no one raise as an objection against me the renowned valor of all those modern warriors who are so scientifically trained. I hear their bravery on a single day of battle highly lauded, but I am not told how they endure excessive labor, how they resist the harshness of the seasons and the inclemency of the weather. All it takes is a bit of sunshine or snow, the lack of a few superfluities, to dissolve and destroy the best of our armies in a few days. Intrepid warriors: endure for once the truth that is so rare for you to hear: you are brave, I know; you would have triumphed with Hannibal at Cannae and at Trasimene, with you Caesar would have crossed the Rubicon and enslaved his country; but it is not with you that the one traversed the Alps and the other vanquished your ancestors.[46]

---

45. King Charles VIII of France invaded Italy in 1494 in order to claim the throne of the Kingdom of Naples and Sicily, and he marched through Tuscany and other areas of Italy while meeting little resistance. The "sensible man" who relates these stories is Montaigne. See Montaigne, *Essays* (1580–92), "Of Pedantry," 1.26, p. 106.

46. The Carthaginian general Hannibal successfully crossed the Alps with his army in 218 BC in order to attack Rome, and among the battles he fought were at Cannae (216 BC) and Lake Trasimene (217 BC). The Roman general Julius Caesar crossed the river Rubicon with his army in 49 BC, defying the Senate and igniting the civil war that ultimately led to the downfall of the Roman Republic.

Success in combat does not always lead to success in war, and for generals there is an art superior to that of winning battles. Someone may run intrepidly into the line of fire and yet be a very bad officer; even in a soldier, a little more strength and vigor would perhaps be more necessary than so much bravery, which does not protect him from death. And what does it matter to the state whether its troops perish by fever and cold or by the enemy's sword?

If the cultivation of the sciences is harmful to warlike qualities, it is even more so to moral qualities. From our earliest years a foolish education adorns our minds and corrupts our judgment. I see everywhere immense establishments in which youth are raised at great expense in order to teach them everything, except their duties. Your children will not know their own language, but they will speak others which are nowhere in use. They will know how to compose verses they have difficulty understanding. Without knowing how to disentangle error from the truth, they will possess the art of making it unrecognizable to others through specious arguments. But as for the words magnanimity, equity, moderation, humanity, courage—they will not know what they are. The sweet name of fatherland will never strike their ear, and if they hear God spoken of, it will be less to fear him than to be scared of him.* I would as soon, said a wise man, have had my pupil spend his time on a tennis court: at least his body would be more fit.[47] I know that children must be kept busy and that idleness is for them the danger to be most feared. What, then, must they learn? This is certainly a fine question! Let them learn what they ought to do as men,† and not what they ought to forget.

---

* *Philosophical Thoughts.*[48]

† Such was the education of the Spartans, according to the greatest of their kings.[49] It is, states Montaigne,[50] a thing worthy of great consideration that there is so little discussion of doctrine, even in the very home of the Muses, in those excellent, and in truth monstrously perfect, orders of Lycurgus even though they were so concerned with the raising of children, as if this were their principal task—as if those noble youth, spurning every other yoke, had to be furnished only with teachers of valor, prudence, and justice instead of our teachers of science.

Let us now see how the same author speaks of the ancient Persians. Plato, he states, recounts that the eldest son in their royal line was raised in the following way. After his birth, he was given not to the women but to the eunuchs who had the greatest authority with the king due to their virtue. They took charge of making his body handsome and healthy, and after he was seven they taught him to ride and hunt. When he reached fourteen, they placed him in the hands of four men: the wisest, the most just, the most moderate, the most valiant in the

---

47. The "wise man" is Montaigne. See Montaigne, *Essays* (1580–92), "Of Pedantry," 3.8, p. 101.

48. Denis Diderot, *Philosophical Thoughts* (1746), section 8: "There are people of whom it must not be said that they fear God, but rather that they are scared of him."

49. The "greatest of kings" of Sparta refers to Agesilaus (444–360 BC). For the saying attributed to him quoted by Rousseau in the main text, see Plutarch *Sayings of the Spartans* 67.

50. This long note draws heavily on Montaigne, *Essays* (1580–92), "Of Pedantry," 3.8, pp. 104–5, although with significant changes by Rousseau.

Our gardens are adorned with statues and our galleries with paintings. What would you think these masterpieces of art, exhibited for public admiration, represent? The defenders of the fatherland? Or those still greater men who have enriched it by their virtues? No. They are the images of all the aberrations of heart and head, painstakingly drawn from ancient mythology and early on presented to the curiosity of our children, doubtless so that they have before their eyes models of evil actions before even knowing how to read.

From where do all these abuses arise, if not from the fatal inequality introduced among men by the distinction of talents and by the degradation of virtues? This is the most obvious effect of all our studies and the most dangerous of all their consequences. It is no longer asked of a man whether he has integrity but whether he has talents, or of a book whether it is useful but whether it is well written. Rewards are bestowed on the witty and virtue remains without honors. There are a thousand prizes for fine discourses, none for fine actions. Will someone tell me, however, whether the glory attached to the best of the discourses that will be crowned by this academy is comparable to the merit of having founded the prize?

The wise man does not run after fortune, but he is not insensitive to glory. And when he sees it so poorly distributed, his virtue, which a little emulation would have animated and made advantageous to society, falls in lassitude and is extinguished in misery and oblivion. This is what the preference for agreeable talents over useful talents must in the long run everywhere produce, and what experience has confirmed only too well since the revival of the sciences and the

---

nation. The first taught him religion, the second always to be truthful, the third to conquer his appetites, the fourth to fear nothing.[51] All, I will add, to make him good, none to make him learned.

Astyages, in Xenophon, asks Cyrus to recite his latest lesson. It is this, says he: in our school a large boy, having a small tunic, gave it to one of his smaller classmates and took away from him his tunic, which was larger. Our preceptor, having made me judge of this dispute, I judged that things should remain as they were and that both seemed to be better suited in this respect. Whereupon he reprimanded me for having done wrong: for I had limited myself to considering suitability, when it was necessary to have first provided for justice, which demands that no one be compelled with regard to what belongs to him. And he says that he was punished for it, just like we are punished in our villages for having forgotten the first aorist of τύπτω. My schoolmaster would have to give a fine harangue, *in genere demonstrativo*, before he could persuade me that his school is as good as that one.[52]

---

51. For Montaigne's source, see Plato *Alcibiades I* 121d–122a.

52. For Montaigne's source, see Xenophon *Education of Cyrus* 1.3.16–17. Astyages, the king of the Median Empire, was the grandfather of the future Persian emperor Cyrus the Great, who would later dethrone him in 550 BC. The Greek verb τύπτω means "to strike or hit," so the joke is that the schoolmaster strikes the student for not knowing how to conjugate the verb, thus providing a lesson *in genere demonstrativo*, or of the kind through demonstration.

arts. We have physicists, geometers, chemists, astronomers, poets, musicians, painters. We no longer have citizens, or, if we still have some, dispersed in our abandoned countryside, they perish there impoverished and scorned. Such is the condition to which those who provide us with bread and who give our children milk are reduced, such is the regard they get from us.

I admit, however, that the evil is not as great as it might have become. Eternal foresight, by placing salutary herbs next to certain noxious plants, and the remedy for the wounds inflicted by various harmful animals within their bodies, has taught sovereigns, who are its ministers, to imitate its wisdom. It is after its example that that great monarch whose glory will acquire only new luster from one age to another drew from the very bosom of the sciences and the arts, sources of a thousand disorders, those famous societies responsible simultaneously for the dangerous trust of human knowledge and for the sacred trust of morals through the attention they have given to maintaining among themselves every purity and to requiring it of all the members they admit.[53]

These wise institutions, strengthened by his august successor[54] and imitated by all the kings of Europe, will at least serve as a check on men of letters, all of whom, aspiring to the honor of being admitted to the academies, will keep watch over themselves and will strive to make themselves worthy of being admitted through useful works and irreproachable morals. Those among these societies that choose subjects fit for reviving love of virtue in citizens' hearts for the prizes with which they honor literary merit will show that this love reigns among them and will give peoples that pleasure, so rare and so sweet, of seeing learned societies dedicated to disseminating not only agreeable enlightenment, but also salutary teachings throughout the human race.

Let no one therefore raise as an objection against me what I regard as merely a new proof. So many precautionary measures show only too well the necessity of taking them, and one does not seek remedies for evils that do not exist. Why should it be the case that, despite this, these very remedies are just as inadequate as ordinary remedies? So many establishments created for the benefit of the learned are only all the more capable of impressing people with regard to the object of the sciences and of steering minds toward their cultivation. It seems, from the precautions that are taken, that there are too many farmers and that a shortage of philosophers is feared. I do not wish to risk a comparison between agriculture and philosophy here; it would not be

---

53. Rousseau refers to King Louis XIV of France (1638–1715), who established a number of academies.
54. The "august successor" of Louis XIV as king of France was Louis XV (1710–74).

tolerated. I will simply ask: what is philosophy? What do the writings of the best known philosophers contain? What are the teachings of those friends of wisdom? To listen to them, wouldn't one take them for a troop of charlatans crying out, each from his spot on the public square: "Come to me, it is I who alone does not deceive"? One claims that there is no body and that everything is an idea. Another that there is no substance but matter nor any other God than the world. This one proposes that there are neither virtues nor vices, and that moral good and evil are chimeras. That one, that men are wolves and can devour one another with a clear conscience.[55] O great philosophers! Why do you not save these profitable teachings for your friends and your children? You would soon reap the reward, and we would no longer fear finding any of your sectarians among our own.

These, then, are the wondrous men on whom the esteem of their contemporaries has been bestowed during their lifetimes and for whom immortality is reserved after their demise! These are the wise maxims we have received from them and which we will transmit to our descendants from one age to another. Did paganism, given over to all the aberrations of human reason, leave to posterity anything that could be compared to the shameful memorials that printing has prepared for it under the reign of the Gospel? The impious writings of the likes of Leucippus and of Diagoras perished along with them.[56] The art of immortalizing the extravagances of the human mind had not yet been invented. But, thanks to typography* and to the use we make of it, the dangerous reveries of the likes of Hobbes and of Spinoza will last forever.[57] Go, famed writings of which the ignorance and rusticity of our forefathers would not have been capable: escort to our descendants those even more dangerous

---

* Considering the frightful disorders that printing has already caused in Europe, judging the future by the progress that the evil makes from one day to the next, one can easily foresee that sovereigns will not delay in devoting as much care to banish this terrible art from their states as they took to establish it. Sultan Ahmed,

---

55. In the previous four sentences Rousseau appears to refer, respectively, to the philosophical doctrines of George Berkeley (1685–1753), who denied the existence of material substances or bodies and argued that these objects are only ideas in the mind; Baruch Spinoza (1632–77), who equated God and nature or the world, although he did not directly claim that all substances were material; Bernard Mandeville (1670–1733), who famously argued that private vices produce public benefits (or "private vice makes public virtue"), but did not claim that there are no vices or virtues; and Thomas Hobbes (1588–1679), who wrote that "man is a wolf to man" (see *De Cive*, Epistle Dedicatory, p. 3).

56. Leucippus (5th century BC) was a philosopher of atomism. Diagoras (5th century BC) was a sophist regarded as an atheist.

57. The philosophers Thomas Hobbes (1588–1679) and Baruch Spinoza (1632–77) were widely regarded in Rousseau's time as atheists.

works that reek of the corruption of our own age's morals and together transmit to the ages to come a faithful history of the progress and advantages of our sciences and our arts. If they read you, you will not leave any doubt regarding the question we are debating today, and unless they are more foolish than we are, they will throw up their hands to heaven and will say with a bitter heart: "Almighty God, thou who holds all spirits in thy hands, deliver us from the enlightenment and fatal arts of our fathers and give us back ignorance, innocence, and poverty, the sole goods that might create our happiness and which are precious in thy sight."

But if the progress of the sciences and the arts has added nothing to our genuine felicity, if it has corrupted our morals, and if the corruption of morals has tainted purity of taste, what shall we think of that throng of rudimentary authors who have removed from the temple of the Muses the difficulties that guarded access to it and that nature placed there as a test of the strength of those who might be tempted to know? What shall we think of those compilers of works who have indiscreetly broken down the door of the sciences and let into their sanctuary a populace unworthy of approaching them, whereas one would hope that all those who could not advance very far in the career of letters would have been rebuffed from the outset and would have been directed into arts useful to society. Someone who for his entire life will be a bad versifier, a subaltern geometer, would perhaps become a great cloth maker. Those whom nature destined to make its disciples needed no teachers. The likes of Verulam, of Descartes, and of Newton[61]—those preceptors of the human race—had none themselves, and what guides would have led them to

---

giving into the importuning of some supposed men of taste, consented to establish a printing press at Constantinople.[58] But hardly had the press begun operating than it had to be destroyed and the equipment thrown into a well. They say that Caliph Omar, when consulted regarding what should be done with the library at Alexandria, responded in the following terms. If the books in that library contain things contrary to the Koran, they are wicked and must be burned. If they contain nothing but the doctrine of the Koran, burn them anyway: they are superfluous. Our learned men have cited this reasoning as the height of absurdity.[59] Yet, imagine Gregory the Great in place of Omar and the Gospel in place of the Koran: the library would still have been burned, and this would perhaps be the finest moment in that illustrious Pontiff's life.[60]

---

58. The Ottoman sultan Ahmed III (1673–1736) patronized the arts and authorized the first printing press used to print works in Arabic and Turkish.

59. Caliph Omar reputedly ordered the destruction of the famous library of Alexandria after the city was captured by the invading Muslims in 642.

60. Pope Gregory the Great (c. 540–604) allegedly had all the pagan books in the Palatine library destroyed.

61. Francis Bacon (1561–1626), created Baron Verulam in 1618, René Descartes (1596–1650), and Isaac Newton (1643–1727) were all important philosophers and natural scientists.

the point their vast genius carried them? Ordinary teachers could only have narrowed their understanding by confining it within the narrow capacity of their own. It is by the first obstacles that they learned to exert themselves and that they trained themselves to traverse the immense space they covered. If some men must be allowed to give themselves over to the study of the sciences and the arts, it is only those who feel they have the strength to walk alone in their footsteps and go beyond them. It belongs to this small number to raise monuments to the glory of the human mind. But if one wants nothing to be above their genius, nothing must be beyond their hopes. This is the sole encouragement they need. The soul imperceptibly proportions itself to the objects that occupy it, and it is great occasions that make great men. The prince of eloquence was consul of Rome, and perhaps the greatest of philosophers chancellor of England.[62] Is it to be believed that if the former had only held a chair in some university or the latter had obtained only a modest pension from an academy, is it to be believed, I say, that their works would not have reflected their status? Let kings therefore not consider it beneath them to admit into their counsels those men most capable of advising them well. Let them renounce that old prejudice, invented by the pride of the great, that the art of leading peoples is more difficult than that of enlightening them, as if it were easier to get men to do good willingly than to constrain them to do so. Let the learned of the first rank find honorable asylum in their courts. Let them there obtain the sole recompense worthy of them: that of contributing by their reputation to the happiness of the peoples to whom they will have taught wisdom. It is only then that it will be seen what virtue, science, and authority can do when animated by a noble emulation and working in concert for the felicity of the human race. But as long as power is by itself on the one side, enlightenment and wisdom by themselves on the other, the learned will rarely think of great things, princes will even more rarely do noble things, and people will continue to be abject, corrupt, and unhappy.

As for us, common men, to whom heaven has not imparted such great talents and has not destined for so much glory, let us remain in our obscurity. Let us not run after a reputation which would elude us and which, in the present state of things, would never give back what it would have cost us, even if we possessed all the qualifications for obtaining it. What good is it to seek our happiness in the opinion of others if we cannot find it in ourselves? Let us

---

62. Rousseau refers to Marcus Tullius Cicero (106–43 BC), who was elected Consul in 63 BC, and Francis Bacon, who served as lord chancellor of England.

leave to others the task of instructing peoples in their duties and let us limit ourselves to fulfilling our own well: we do not need to know anything more.

O virtue! Sublime science of simple souls, are then so many efforts and preparations needed to know you? Are not your principles engraved in all hearts, and is it not enough to learn your laws to return into oneself and to listen to the voice of one's conscience in the silence of the passions? This is genuine philosophy, let us know how to be satisfied with it; and without envying the glory of those famous men who are immortalized in the republic of letters, let us try to establish that glorious distinction between them and us long ago noted between two great peoples: that the one knew how to speak well, and the other to act well.[63]

THE END

---

63. That is, the Athenians and Spartans.

DISCOURSE

ON THE ORIGIN AND THE
FOUNDATIONS OF INEQUALITY
AMONG MEN

He goes back to his equals.
See note XVI, p. 147

DISCOURSE

ON THE ORIGIN AND THE
FOUNDATIONS OF INEQUALITY
AMONG MEN

BY JEAN-JACQUES ROUSSEAU
CITIZEN OF GENEVA

What is natural has to be considered not in beings that are corrupted,
but in those that truly act in accordance with their nature.
—Aristotle, *Politics*, Book I[1]

AMSTERDAM
CHEZ MARC MICHEL REY, MDCCLV

---

1. Aristotle *Politics* 1.5 (1254a), quoted by Rousseau in Latin: *Non in depravatis, sed in his quae bene secundum naturam se habent, considerandum est quid sit naturale.* The context of the passage is Aristotle's discussion of natural slavery, where he examines whether there is a natural inequality between those who are slaves by nature and those who are not and whether this inequality would justify natural slaves being ruled. The quotation Rousseau chooses is part of Aristotle's more general argument that humans and other beings should be investigated in terms of their "end" (*telos*), or most complete or realized form.

TO THE REPUBLIC OF GENEVA

MAGNIFICENT, MOST HONORED, AND SOVEREIGN LORDS

Convinced that it is fitting only for the virtuous citizen to pay to his father-land[2] such tribute as it may acknowledge, for thirty years I have worked to de-serve to offer you public homage. And as this happy occasion makes up in part for what my efforts have been unable to accomplish, I believed that I might be allowed to be guided here by the zeal that animates me rather than by the right that ought to authorize me.[3] Having had the good fortune to be born among you, how could I meditate on the equality nature has placed among men and on the inequality they have instituted without thinking of the profound wis-dom with which both, happily combined in this state, work together in the manner most closely approximating natural law and most favorable to society for the maintenance of public order and the happiness of private individuals? While seeking the best maxims that good sense might dictate concerning the constitution of a government, I was so struck to see them all in operation in

2. "Fatherland" translates *patrie*. *Patrie* might also be translated "country" in the sense of the phrase "love of country," hence "patriotism." However, aside from the fact that "country" also translates *pays*, which does not have the strong political sense of *patrie*, Rousseau argues that modern peoples can have a "country" (*pays*) without having a true "fatherland" (*patrie*). Although the term "fatherland" in contemporary English often has a pejorative sense stemming from the nationalist movements and wars of the twentieth century, *patrie* will be translated as "fatherland" throughout.

3. Even though Rousseau calls himself a "Citizen of Geneva" on the title page, when he wrote this Dedica-tion he had not regained his citizenship and therefore did not formally have the right to use this title. Rousseau lost his citizenship when he left the city at sixteen years of age and converted to Catholicism. The Dedication is dated June 12, 1754 from Chambéry, a city in the far eastern part of present-day France and then in the King-dom of Savoy. When he wrote this Dedication, Rousseau was returning to his native city, where he formally returned to the Protestant faith and regained his citizenship on August 1, 1754. See the editor's introduction.

yours that, even had I not been born within your walls, I would have believed myself unable to refrain from offering this picture of human society to that people which, of all others, appears to me to possess its greatest advantages and to have best prevented its abuses.[4]

If I had had to choose my birthplace, I would have chosen a society of a size limited by the extent of human faculties—that is, by the possibility of being well governed—and where, each person being up to his task, no one was compelled to entrust others with the functions with which he was charged; a state where, all individuals knowing one another, neither the obscure maneuvers of vice nor the modesty of virtue could be hidden from the public's notice and judgment, and where that sweet habit of seeing and knowing one another made love of the fatherland a love of the citizens rather than love of the soil.

I would have wished to be born in a country where the sovereign and the people could have only one and the same interest, so that all the movements of the machine always tended only to the common happiness. Since this would not be possible unless the people and the sovereign were one and the same person, it follows that I would have wished to be born under a democratic government, wisely tempered.

I would have wished to live and die free, that is, so subject to the laws that neither I nor anyone else could shake off their honorable yoke—that salutary and gentle yoke which the proudest heads bear all the more docilely as they are made to bear no other.

I would therefore have wished that no one inside the state could declare himself to be above the law and that no one outside it could impose any law the state was obliged to recognize. For regardless of what the constitution of a government may be, if there is a single man[5] who is not subject to the law,

---

4. Rousseau's highly flattering portrait of Geneva in the Dedication contains thinly veiled criticism of the failure of the city to live up to its relatively democratic constitution. Most importantly, many of the sovereign powers or functions of the representative assembly elected by the citizen body, known as the Conseil Général, had been effectively usurped by the twenty-five magistrates appointed for life, known as the Petit Conseil. As a former government official wrote Rousseau: "You have followed the movements of your heart in the Dedicatory Epistle, and I fear it will be found that you flatter us too much; you represent us as we ought to be, and not as we are" (Jean-Louis Du Pan to Rousseau, in Rousseau, *Correspondance complète*, 3:136). Rousseau offers an extensive critical examination of the actual condition of Geneva's politics in his *Letters Written from the Mountain* (1764), which is a defense of the *Social Contract* against its condemnation by Geneva.

5. "Man" translates *homme*, which can mean either "man" (that is, male human being) or "human being" (applying to both sexes). While it is tempting to translate *homme* as "human being" (or perhaps "person" in this context), it is arguable that Rousseau's usage of the word is often not gender-neutral and so the word will be consistently translated as "man" (or "men" in the plural) throughout.

all the others are necessarily at his discretion (I [p. 119]).[6] And if there is a national leader[7] and another foreign leader, regardless of the division of authority they may make, it is impossible for both of them to be well obeyed and for the state to be well governed.

I would not have wished to live in a newly instituted republic, however good its laws might be, for fear that—the government, perhaps being constituted otherwise than necessary for that point in time, with the government not being suited to the new citizens or the citizens to the new government—the state would be susceptible to being shaken and destroyed almost from its birth. For freedom is like those hearty and succulent foods or those full-bodied wines which are fit for nourishing and fortifying robust temperaments which are accustomed to them, but which overwhelm, ruin, and intoxicate those weak and delicate temperaments which are not up to them. Once peoples are accustomed to masters, they are no longer capable of doing without them. If they try to shake off the yoke, they move all the further away from freedom since, mistaking freedom for an unbridled license that is opposed to it, their revolutions almost always deliver them up to seducers who only make their chains heavier. The Roman people itself—that model for all free peoples—was not capable of governing itself upon being released from the oppression of the Tarquins.[8] Debased by the slavery and the ignominious labors the Tarquins had imposed on it, it was at first merely a stupid mob that needed to be handled and governed with the greatest wisdom, so that, being accustomed little by little to breathe the salutary air of freedom, those souls, enervated or rather made brutish under tyranny, acquired by degrees that severity of morals[9] and that pride of courage which eventually made of them the most respectable of all peoples. I would therefore have sought for my fatherland a happy and tranquil republic whose antiquity was, as it were, lost in the darkness of time, which had suffered only those attacks fit for demonstrating and strengthening

---

6. Rousseau's notes to the *Discourse on Inequality* are reproduced after the body of the work, starting on p. 119 below. See Rousseau's "Notice on the Notes," p. 57 below.

7. "Leader" translates *chef*, which might also be translated "chief." The French term *chef* has a number of applications and can be used with regard to the "chief" or "head" of a political or business organization (hence the head of a restaurant kitchen is a "chef") and also the head of a family. Although the English term "leader" has a somewhat more democratic connotation than the French term *chef*, especially in Rousseau's time, the term has been translated as "leader" when used with regard to politics.

8. The Tarquins were a series of semi-legendary kings in early Rome. The overthrow of the last Tarquin and the establishment of the Roman Republic were traditionally held to have occurred in 509 BC.

9. "Morals" translates *moeurs*, which might also be translated "mores" and has a broad sense of morals, manners, and even customs. The broad sense of the term should be kept in mind throughout.

courage and love of the fatherland in its inhabitants, and where the citizens, long accustomed to a wise independence, were not only free, but worthy of being so.

I would have wished to choose for myself a fatherland deflected from the fierce love of conquests by a fortunate powerlessness and protected by a still more fortunate situation from the fear of itself becoming the conquest of another state; a free city located amidst a number of peoples none of whom had an interest in invading it and each of whom had an interest in preventing the others from themselves invading it; a republic, in a word, which did not tempt the ambition of its neighbors and which could reasonably count on their help in case of need. It follows that, in such a fortunate situation, it would have had nothing to fear except from itself, and that if its citizens were trained in the use of arms, it would have been rather so as to maintain among themselves that warlike ardor and that pride of courage which befits freedom so well and which nourishes a taste for it, rather than from the necessity of providing for their own defense.

I would have sought a country where the right of legislation was common to all citizens, for who can know better than they the conditions under which it suits them to live together in the same society? But I would not have approved of plebiscites like those of the Romans, where the state's leaders and those most interested in its preservation were excluded from deliberations on which their safety often depended, and where, by an absurd inconsistency, the magistrates were deprived of the rights enjoyed by ordinary citizens.

On the contrary, I would have desired that, in order to check the self-interested and ill-conceived projects and the dangerous innovations that eventually ruined the Athenians, everyone did not have the power to propose new laws according to his fancy; that this right belonged to the magistrates alone; that they even exercised it with such circumspection that the people, for its part, was so hesitant to give its consent to these laws and that their promulgation could only be done with such solemnity that, before the constitution was shaken, they had the time to be convinced that it is above all the great antiquity of the laws which makes them sacred and venerable, that the people soon scorns those laws which it sees change daily, and that by becoming accustomed to neglect ancient practices on the pretext of doing better, great evils are often introduced to correct lesser ones.

I would above all have fled, as necessarily ill-governed, a republic where the people, believing it could do without its magistrates or allowing them merely a precarious authority, imprudently retained the administration of civil affairs and the execution of its own laws. Such must have been the crude constitution of the earliest governments immediately upon emerging from the state of nature, and such was also one of the vices that ruined the republic of Athens.

Rather, I would have chosen a republic where individuals, content with sanctioning the laws and deciding the most important public affairs as a body and upon the report of their leaders, established respected tribunals, carefully distinguishing their various jurisdictions, annually elected the most capable and most upright of their fellow citizens to administer justice and govern the state, and where the virtue of the magistrates thus bearing witness to the wisdom of the people, each would do credit to the other. As a result, if ever some fatal misunderstanding happened to disturb public concord, even those times of blindness and errors would be marked by expressions of moderation, reciprocal esteem, and a common respect for the laws—harbingers and guarantees of a sincere and perpetual reconciliation.[10]

Such are, MAGNIFICENT, MOST HONORED, AND SOVEREIGN LORDS, the advantages I would have sought in the fatherland I would have chosen for myself. And if to these providence had also added a charming location, a temperate climate, a fertile soil, and the most delightful vistas beneath heaven, to complete my happiness I would have desired only to enjoy all these goods in the bosom of that happy fatherland, living peacefully in sweet society with my fellow citizens, practicing toward them—and following their own example—humanity, friendship, and all the virtues, and leaving behind me the honorable memory of a good man and an honorable and virtuous patriot.

If, less happy or too late wise, I had seen myself reduced to ending a crippled and languishing career in other climes, uselessly regretting the peace and quiet of which my imprudent youth had deprived me, I would have at least nurtured in my soul those same sentiments I was unable to put to use in my country, and filled with a tender and disinterested affection for my distant fellow citizens, I would have addressed to them from the bottom of my heart something like the following discourse.

My dear fellow citizens, or rather my brothers, since the ties of blood as well as the laws unite almost all of us, it gives me pleasure to be unable to think of you without thinking at the same time of all the good things you enjoy and of which none of you perhaps senses the value better than I, who has lost them.

10. The history of Geneva in the eighteenth century was marked by considerable political conflict, and the "fatal misunderstandings" to which Rousseau refers were far from reconciled when he wrote this. Most importantly, a serious conflict between the citizen body and its magistrates that occurred in 1737–38 required the intervention and mediation of France, Zurich, and Bern.

The more I reflect on your political and civil situation, the less I can imagine that the nature of human things could admit of a better one. In all other governments, when it is a question of ensuring the greatest good of the state, everything is always limited to fanciful projects and at the very most to mere possibilities. As for you, your happiness is established, you need only enjoy it, and to become perfectly happy you need nothing more than to know how to be content with being so. Your sovereignty, acquired and recovered at sword's point, and preserved through two centuries by dint of valor and wisdom, is at last fully and universally acknowledged. Honorable treaties determine your boundaries, ensure your rights, and strengthen your tranquility. Your constitution is excellent, dictated by the most sublime reason and guaranteed by friendly and respectable powers. Your state is tranquil, you have neither wars nor conquerors to fear. You have no masters other than those wise laws you have made, administered by upright magistrates of your choosing. You are neither so rich as to be enervated by softness and to lose the taste for true happiness and solid virtue amidst vain delights, nor so poor as to need outside help beyond what your industry procures for you. And this precious freedom, which is maintained by large nations only through exorbitant taxes, costs you almost nothing to preserve.

May a republic so wisely and so happily constituted last forever, both for its citizens' happiness and as an example to all peoples! This is the sole wish that remains for you to make, and the sole concern that remains for you to attend to. Henceforth it is up to you alone, not to create your happiness—your ancestors have spared you the trouble—but to make it lasting through the wisdom of using it well. It is on your perpetual union, on your obedience to the laws, on your respect for their ministers that your preservation depends. If there remains among you the least germ of bitterness or distrust, hasten to destroy it as a fatal leaven from which your miseries and the ruin of the state would sooner or later result. I implore you all to look into the depths of your heart and consult the secret voice of your conscience. Does anyone among you know of a more upright, more enlightened, more respectable body in the universe than that of your magistracy? Do not all of its members offer you an example of moderation, simplicity of morals, respect for the laws, and the most sincere reconciliation? Then grant without reservation to such wise leaders that salutary confidence which reason owes to virtue. Consider that they are of your choosing, that they justify that choice, and that the honors owed to those you have established in the dignity of office necessarily redound to yourselves. None of you is so unenlightened as to be unaware that there can be neither security nor freedom for anyone where the rigor of the laws and the authority of their defenders cease. What is it a question for you to do, then, except to do wholeheartedly and with just confidence what you would in any event be obliged to do out of true interest, duty, and reason? May a guilty and fatal indifference to the maintenance of the constitution never cause you to neglect in time of need the wise advice of the most enlightened and most zealous among you. Rather, may equity, moderation, the most respectful firmness continue to regulate all your undertakings and display in you to the whole universe the example of a proud and modest people, as jealous of its glory as of its freedom. Beware above all—and this will be my final piece of advice—of ever heeding those sinister interpretations and venomous discourses whose secret motives are often more dangerous than the objectives at which they aim. An entire household awakens and takes warning at the first cries of a good and loyal guardian that never barks except at the approach of thieves, but people hate the importunity of those noisy animals that repeatedly disturb public tranquility and whose continual and misplaced warnings are not even heeded at the moment of need.

And you, MAGNIFICENT AND MOST HONORED LORDS, you worthy and respectable magistrates of a free people: allow me to offer my homage and my respects to you in particular.[11] If there is anywhere in the world a rank likely to render those who occupy it illustrious, it is without doubt that which is bestowed by talents and virtue, that of which you have shown yourselves worthy and to which your fellow citizens have raised you. Their own merit adds yet new luster to yours, and I find you, having been chosen to govern men by men themselves capable of governing others, as superior to other magistrates as a free people—and especially the one you have the honor of leading—is, by its enlightenment and its reason, superior to the populace of other states.

May I be allowed to cite an example of which there ought to remain better traces and which will always be present in my heart. I never recall without the sweetest emotion the memory of the virtuous citizen to whom I owe my being, and who throughout my childhood instilled in me the respect that was

---

11. Note that while Rousseau addresses his fellow citizens as a whole as "MAGNIFICENT, MOST HONORED, AND SOVEREIGN LORDS," he pointedly omits the term "SOVEREIGN" when he turns to address Geneva's magistrates in particular. As noted above, Rousseau's Dedication contains a thinly veiled critique of the effective usurpation of sovereign power by the magistrates.

owed to you.[12] I see him still, living by the work of his hands and nurturing his soul with the most sublime truths. I see Tacitus, Plutarch, and Grotius[13] before him, mingled with the tools of his trade. I see at his side a beloved son, receiving with too little profit the tender instruction of the best of fathers. But if the aberrations of a foolish youth caused me forget such wise lessons for a time, I have the happiness to feel at last that no matter what inclination one may have toward vice, it is difficult for an education in which the heart is involved to remain forever lost.

Such are, MAGNIFICENT AND MOST HONORED LORDS, the citizens and even the non-citizen residents born in the state you govern;[14] such are those educated and sensible men, called "workers" and "the people," about whom they have such base and such false ideas in other nations. My father, I gladly admit it, was not distinguished among his fellow citizens. He was only what they all are, and such as he was, there is no country where his company would not have been sought after, cultivated, and even profitably so, by the most respectable people. It is not up to me—and, thank heaven, it is not necessary—to speak to you of the regard men of that stamp can expect from you: your equals by education as well as by the rights of nature and of birth, your inferiors by their will, by the preference they owe your merit, which they have recognized, and for which you in your turn owe them a kind of gratitude. I learn with lively satisfaction how much in dealing with them you temper the gravity suitable for ministers of the laws with gentleness and condescension, how much you grant to them in esteem and attentiveness what they owe you in obedience and respect—conduct full of justice and wisdom, suitable for making the unhappy events which must be forgotten in order that they never be seen again grow all the more distant, conduct all the more judicious as this equitable and generous people makes a pleasure of its duty, as it naturally loves

---

12. Rousseau's portrayal of his father is highly idealized. Isaac Rousseau was a watchmaker who left his newly married wife for over six years while he worked in Constantinople, returning at her request only a year before Jean-Jacques was born. Isaac was charged several times with poaching and engaged in a duel in the streets of Geneva in 1722, after which he fled the city to avoid prosecution, effectively abandoning the ten-year-old Jean-Jacques. Rousseau rarely saw or had contact with his father afterward. Isaac Rousseau died in 1747.

13. Tacitus (56–117), Roman historian of the early Roman Empire. Plutarch (c. 46–120), Greek historian, biographer, and moralist whose *Parallel Lives* of eminent Greeks and Romans is his best known work. Hugo Grotius (1583–1645), natural law theorist best known for his *Rights of War and Peace*.

14. The citizens (*citoyens*) and burghers (*bourgeois*) of Geneva, which together elected the Grand Conseil, made up only a portion of those residing in Geneva, which included resident aliens or "non-citizen residents" (*habitants*).

to honor you, and as the most ardent in upholding their rights are those most inclined to respect yours.

It should not be surprising that the leaders of a civil society love its glory and happiness, but it is altogether astonishing that those who regard themselves as the magistrates, or rather as the masters, of a more holy and more sublime fatherland exhibit any love for the terrestrial fatherland that sustains them. How sweet it is for me to be able to make such a rare exception in our favor, and to rank among our best citizens those zealous trustees of the sacred dogmas authorized by the laws, those venerable pastors of souls, whose lively and sweet eloquence carries the maxims of the gospel all the better into hearts as they are always themselves the first to practice them! Everyone knows with what success the great art of preaching is cultivated in Geneva. But, too accustomed to see things spoken of in one manner and done in another, few people know the extent to which the spirit of Christianity, sanctity of morals, severity toward oneself and gentleness toward others, reign in the body of our ministers. Perhaps it belongs to the city of Geneva alone to offer the edifying example of such a perfect union among a society of theologians and men of letters. It is in large part on their acknowledged wisdom and moderation, it is on their zeal for the prosperity of the state, that I base hope for its eternal tranquility. And I note, with a pleasure mixed with astonishment and respect, how much they abhor the frightful maxims of those barbarous holy men of whom history furnishes more than one example, and who, in order to uphold the pretended rights of God—that is, their own interests—were all the less sparing of human blood as they flattered themselves that their own would always be respected.

Could I forget that precious half of the republic which creates the other's happiness, and whose gentleness and wisdom maintain its peace and good morals? Amiable and virtuous citizen-women, the fate of your sex will always be to govern our own. How fortunate when your chaste power, exercised solely in conjugal union, makes itself felt only for the state's glory and the public happiness! This is how women commanded in Sparta, and this is how you deserve to command in Geneva. What barbarous man could resist the voice of honor and of reason in the mouth of a tender wife, and who would not despise vain luxury on seeing your simple and modest attire which, by the luster it derives from you, seems to be the most favorable to beauty? It is up to you to always maintain the love of laws in the state and concord among the citizens by your amiable and innocent dominion and by your engaging ways; to reunite divided families by happy marriages; and above all to correct, by the persuasive sweetness of your lessons and by the modest graciousness of your conversation, the faults our young people acquire in other countries, from which, instead of the many useful things from which they could profit, they bring back, along with a puerile tone and ridiculous air acquired among debauched women, only admiration for I know not what supposedly grand things—the frivolous compensations for servitude that will never be worth as much as august freedom. Therefore be always what you are, chaste guardians of morals and gentle bonds of peace, and continue to assert, at every opportunity, the rights of the heart and of nature to the benefit of duty and of virtue.

I flatter myself that events will not prove me wrong in basing hope for the common happiness of the citizens and the glory of the republic on such guarantors. I admit that, for all these advantages, it will not shine with that brilliance by which most eyes are dazzled and the puerile and fatal taste which is the most mortal enemy of happiness and freedom. Let dissolute youth look elsewhere for easy pleasures and lasting remorse. Let supposed men of taste elsewhere admire the grandeur of palaces, the beauty of carriages, superb furnishings, the pomp of spectacles, and all the refinements of softness and luxury. In Geneva only men will be found; yet such a spectacle also has its value, and those who seek it out will be worth just as much as the admirers of the rest.

May you all, MAGNIFICENT, MOST HONORED, AND SOVEREIGN LORDS, deign to receive with the same kindness the respectful testimonies of the interest I take in your common prosperity. If I were unfortunate enough to be guilty of some indiscreet outpouring of emotion in this lively outpouring of my heart, I beg you to pardon it as the tender affection of a true patriot and as the ardent and legitimate zeal of a man who envisions no greater happiness for himself than that of seeing you all happy.

I am with the most profound respect
MAGNIFICENT, MOST HONORED, AND SOVEREIGN LORDS,
Your most humble and most obedient servant and fellow citizen.

JEAN-JACQUES ROUSSEAU
At Chambéry, June 12, 1754

PREFACE

THE MOST USEFUL and the least advanced of all human knowledge appears to me to be that of man (II [p. 119]), and I dare say that the inscription on the Temple of Delphi[15] alone contained a more important and more difficult precept than all the hefty books of the moralists. As such I consider the subject of this discourse to be one of the most interesting questions philosophy might propose, and unfortunately for us one of the thorniest philosophers might resolve. For how will the source of inequality among men be known unless one begins by knowing men themselves? And how will man ever manage to see himself as nature formed him, through all the changes that the sequence of time and of things must have produced in his original constitution, and to disentangle what he retains of his own stock from what circumstances and his progress have added to or changed in his primitive state? Like the statue of Glaucus,[16] which time, sea, and storms had so disfigured that it resembled less a god than a ferocious beast, the human soul, altered[17] in the bosom of society by a thousand continually renewed causes, by the acquisition of a mass of knowledge and error, by changes that took place in the constitution of bodies, and by the continual impact of the passions, has, so to speak, changed in appearance to the point of being almost unrecognizable. And, instead of a being always acting according to certain and invariable principles, instead of that

---

15. "Know thyself."

16. Glaucus was in mythology a fisherman who became a sea god. See Plato *Republic* 10 (611b-d), where Socrates uses the image to represent the original simple and divine nature of the human soul that is concealed by the conflicting passions.

17. "Altered" translates *altérée* from the verb *altérer*. Although the word in its various grammatical forms as a verb, noun, or adjective can mean simply "alter" or "change," it generally has a negative connotation of distortion, degeneration, corruption, or adulteration. This negative connotation should be kept in mind throughout.

celestial and majestic simplicity its author imprinted upon it, one no longer finds anything but the deformed contrast of passion which believes it reasons and of understanding caught in delirium.

What is crueler still is that, since all the progress of the human species continually moves it further from its primitive state, the more we accumulate new knowledge, the more we deprive ourselves of the means of acquiring the most important knowledge of all, and it is, in a sense, by dint of studying man that we have rendered ourselves incapable of knowing him.

It is easy to see that it is in these successive changes in the human constitution that one must seek the first origin of the differences that distinguish men, who, as is generally acknowledged, are naturally as equal among themselves as were the animals of each species before various physical causes introduced into some of them the different varieties we notice in them. Indeed, it is not conceivable that these first changes, by whatever means they occurred, altered all the individuals of the species all at the same time and in the same way. Rather, while some of them having been perfected or deteriorated and having acquired various good or bad qualities that were not inherent to their nature, the others remained in their original state for a longer time. And such was among men the first source of inequality, which is easier to demonstrate to be so in general than it is to assign its true causes with precision.

Let my readers not imagine, then, that I dare flatter myself with having seen what appears to me so difficult to see. I have begun some lines of reasoning, I have hazarded some conjectures, less in the hope of resolving the question than with the intention of clarifying it and reducing it to its genuine state. Others will easily be able to go farther along the same path, without it being easy for anyone to reach the end. For it is no light undertaking to disentangle what is original from what is artificial in the present nature of man, and to know correctly a state which no longer exists, which perhaps never did exist, which probably never will exist, and about which it is nevertheless necessary to have correct notions in order to judge our present state properly. Even more philosophy than might be supposed would be necessary for whoever will undertake to determine precisely which precautions to take in order to make solid observations on this subject. And a good solution to the following problem would not appear to me unworthy of the Aristotles and Plinys of our age: *What experiments would be necessary in order to gain knowledge of natural man; and what are the means for doing these experiments in the midst of society?* Far from undertaking to resolve this problem, I believe I have sufficiently meditated on the subject to dare answer in advance that the greatest philosophers will not be too good to direct these experiments nor the most powerful sovereigns to carry them out—mutual assistance scarcely reasonable to expect especially given the perseverance or, rather, the continuing enlightenment and good will needed from both parties in order to achieve success.

This research, so difficult to carry out, and to which so little thought has been given until now, is, however, the sole means left to us for removing a multitude of difficulties that conceal from us the knowledge of the real foundations of human society. It is this ignorance of man's nature that throws so much uncertainty and obscurity on the true definition of natural right. For the idea of right, says M. Burlamaqui, and still more that of natural right, are manifestly ideas relative to man's nature. It is therefore from this very nature of man, he continues, from his constitution and from his state, that the principles of this science must be deduced.[18]

It is not without surprise and without scandal that one notes how little agreement concerning this important matter prevails among the various authors who have dealt with it. Among the most serious writers one can hardly find two of them who are of the same view on this point. Without speaking of the ancient philosophers, who seem to have set out to contradict each other as best they could concerning the most fundamental principles, the Roman jurists indiscriminately subject man and all the other animals to the same natural law, because they consider this word "law" to express what nature imposes on itself rather than what it prescribes, or, rather, due to the particular sense in which these jurists understood the word "law," which in this case they seemed to have taken merely as the expression of the general relations established by nature among all animate beings for their common preservation.[19] The moderns, recognizing the term "law" as applying only to a rule prescribed to a moral being—that is, a being that is intelligent, free, and considered in its relations with other beings—consequently restrict the province of natural law to the sole animal endowed with reason, namely man.[20] But while each defines this law after his own fashion, all of them base it on such metaphysical principles

18. Jean-Jacques Burlamaqui, *The Principles of Natural and Politic Law* (1747), 1.1.1, p. 32. Rousseau's paraphrase of Burlamaqui is nearly a direct quotation.

19. See, e.g., Justinian *Institutes* 1.2.1: "The law of nature is what nature teaches all animals; this law is not peculiar to the human race alone, but belongs to all living creatures."

20. By the "moderns," Rousseau appears primarily to mean modern jurists such as Hugo Grotius, Samuel von Pufendorf, and Jean-Jacques Burlamaqui, who restricted the province of natural law and natural right to rational and moral beings. See, e.g., Grotius, *The Rights of War and Peace* (1625), 1.1.10, vol. 1:150–51: "Natural right is the rule and dictate of right reason, showing the moral deformity or moral necessity there is in any act, according to its suitableness or unsuitableness to a rational and sociable nature."

that even among us there are very few people capable of comprehending these principles, far from being able to discover them by themselves. As a result, all the definitions of these learned men, otherwise in perpetual contradiction with one another, agree only on this: that it is impossible to understand the law of nature and consequently to obey it without being a very great reasoner and a profound metaphysician. Which means precisely that to establish society men must have utilized enlightenment that develops only with much difficulty and for very few people in the midst of society itself.

Knowing nature so little and agreeing so poorly on the meaning of the term *law*, it would be quite difficult to agree on a good definition of natural law. As such, all those found in books, aside from not being uniform, have the further defect of being drawn from several kinds of knowledge men do not naturally have and from advantages the idea of which they are able to conceive only after having left the state of nature. One begins by searching for the rules on which it would be appropriate for men to agree among themselves for the sake of common utility; and then one applies the term "natural law" to the collection of these rules, without any further proof than the good they consider would result from their universal application. This is surely a most convenient way of putting together definitions and of explaining the nature of things by nearly arbitrary preferences.

But as long as we do not know natural man, it will be vain for us to try to determine the law he has received, or that which best suits his constitution. All that we can see very clearly on the subject of this law is that not only must the person's will it obligates be able to submit to it knowingly for it to be law, but also it must speak directly through the voice of nature for it to be natural.

Setting aside, therefore, all scientific books that teach us only to see men as they have made themselves, and meditating on the first and simplest operations of the human soul, I believe I perceive in it two principles preceding reason, one of which interests us ardently in our well-being and our self-preservation, and the other of which inspires in us a natural repugnance to see any sensitive being, and principally our fellow humans,[21] perish or suffer. It is from the concurrence[22] and combination that our mind is capable of making of these two

---

21. "Fellow humans" translates *semblables*. Although the term generally refers to one's fellow humans, it has the root sense of "like" or "similar" and so can also have the more extended sense of beings which are recognized as being similar to oneself. The term could also therefore potentially apply to non-humans insofar as they are viewed by humans as similar to themselves.

22. "Concurrence" translates *concours*, which has the literal meaning of "racing together," and therefore has the sense of either competition or cooperation.

principles, without it being necessary to introduce that of sociability,[23] that all the rules of natural right appear to me to flow—rules which reason is later compelled to reestablish on other foundations when, through its successive developments, it has succeeded in stifling nature.

In this way, one is not obliged to make a philosopher of man before making a man of him. His duties toward others are not dictated to him solely by the belated lessons of wisdom; and as long as he does not resist the inner impulse of commiseration, he will never do harm to another man or even another sensitive being, except in the legitimate case when, his self-preservation being involved, he is obliged to give preference to himself. By this means, the ancient disputes over the participation of the animals in natural law are also brought to an end. For it is clear that, being devoid of enlightenment and freedom, they cannot recognize this law; but since they share something of our nature through the sensibility with which they are endowed, it must be concluded that they should also participate in natural right and that man is subject to some sort of duties toward them. It seems, indeed, that if I am obligated to not do any harm to my fellow human being, it is less because he is a rational being than because he is a sensitive being, a quality that, since it is common to beast and man, should at least give the beast the right not to be needlessly mistreated by man.

This same study of original man, of his true needs, and of the fundamental principles of his duties is also the only proper means that may be used to dispel those crowds of difficulties which present themselves regarding the origin of moral inequality, the true foundations of the body politic, the reciprocal rights of its members, and a thousand other similar questions, as important as they are poorly elucidated.

When considering human society with a calm and disinterested eye, it seems at first to exhibit only the violence of powerful men and the oppression of the weak. The mind revolts against the harshness of the former; one is led to deplore the blindness of the latter; and as nothing is less stable among men than those external relationships which chance produces more often than wisdom, and which are called weakness or might, wealth or poverty, human establishments appear at first glance to be founded on piles of quicksand. It is only by examining them closely, it is only after having swept away the dust and

---

23. Rousseau alludes in particular to the natural law theorist Samuel von Pufendorf, who considered "sociability" as an essential characteristic of human beings and as the fundamental law of natural right. See Pufendorf, *The Whole Duty of Man According to the Law of Man* (1673), 1.3.7–8, pp. 55–56, and *De jure naturae et gentium* (1672), 2.3.15.

sand which surround the edifice, that one perceives the unshakeable base upon which it is built and that one learns to respect its foundations. Now, without the serious study of man, of his natural faculties, and of their successive developments, one will never succeed in making these distinctions and in separating what, in the present constitution of things, the divine will has done from what human art has claimed to do. The political and moral research occasioned by the important Satires question I am examining is therefore useful in every way, and the hypothetical history of governments is an instructive lesson for men in every respect. By considering what we would have become, left to ourselves, we ought to learn to bless him whose beneficent hand, by correcting our institutions and giving them an unshakeable basis, has prevented the disorders which must otherwise have resulted and has caused our happiness to arise from the very means that seemed bound to render our misery complete.

> *Learn what the god has ordained for you,*
> *And what is your place in human affairs.*[24]

---

24. Persius *Satires* 3.71–73, quoted by Rousseau in Latin: *quem te deus esse / Jussit et humana qua parte locatus es in re / Disce.*

NOTICE ON THE NOTES [25]

I HAVE ADDED SOME notes to this work in accordance with my lazy custom of working in fits and starts. These notes sometimes stray far enough from the subject that they are not good to read with the text. I have therefore relegated them to the end of this discourse, in which I have tried my best to follow the straightest path. Those who have the courage to start over again will be able to amuse themselves the second time with beating the bushes, and to try to peruse the notes. There will be little harm in others' not reading them at all.

---

25. The numbering of the notes in this edition (I, II, III, etc.) follows the Pléiade edition, which itself follows the posthumous 1782 edition of Rousseau's works in this regard. However, as Heinrich Meier notes in his edition of the *Discourse on Inequality* (see Bibliography), the editions of the work published in Rousseau's lifetime used a combination of numbers (1, 2, 3, etc.) and letters (a, b, c, etc.) for the notes. Rousseau's reason for numbering the notes in this manner is unclear, although it is possible that he added the notes indicated by letters while the work was already in press, in which case it would have been expensive to renumber all the notes. The original sequence was as follows: I = (*), II = (*2.), III = (*3.), IV = (*a), V = 4, VI = 5, VII = (*d), VIII = 6, IX = 7, X = 8, XI = 9, XII = 10, XIII = (*b), XIV = 11, XV = 12, XVI = 13, XVII = (*c), XVIII = 14, XIX = 15.

QUESTION PROPOSED BY THE ACADEMY OF DIJON

What is the origin of inequality among men,
and whether it is authorized by natural law.[26]

---

26. The prize competition for 1754 was announced by the Academy of Dijon in the November 1753 edition of the *Mercure de France*. The precise wording of the question was: "What is the source of inequality among men, and whether it is authorized by natural law."

DISCOURSE

ON THE ORIGIN, AND THE

FOUNDATIONS OF INEQUALITY

AMONG MEN

IT IS OF MAN that I am to speak, and the question I am examining tells me that I am going to speak to men, for such questions are not proposed by those who are afraid to honor the truth. I will therefore confidently defend the cause of humanity before the wise men who invite me to do so, and I will not be dissatisfied with myself if I prove myself worthy of my subject and my judges.

I conceive of two sorts of inequality in the human species: one which I call natural or physical because it is established by nature, and which consists in the difference in age, health, strength of the body, qualities of the mind, or of the soul; the other, which may be called moral or political inequality because it depends upon a sort of convention and is established, or at least authorized, by the consent of men. The latter consists in the different privileges that some enjoy at the expense of others, such as being more wealthy, more honored, more powerful than they are, or even in making themselves obeyed by them.

It is not possible to ask what the source of natural inequality is, because the answer would be expressed in the mere definition of the word. Still less can one inquire whether there might not be some essential connection between the two inequalities. For that would be asking, in other terms, whether those who command are necessarily better than those who obey, and whether strength of body or of mind, wisdom or virtue, are always found in the same individuals in proportion to their power or riches—a question perhaps good for slaves to debate within earshot of their masters, but not befitting rational and free men who seek the truth.

What, then, precisely is at issue in this discourse? To indicate in the progression of things the moment when, right replacing violence, nature was subjected to law; to explain by what chain of marvelous circumstances the strong could have resolved to serve the weak, and the people to purchase fanciful tranquility at the expense of real felicity.

The philosophers who have examined the foundations of society have all felt the necessity of going back to the state of nature, but none of them has reached it. Some have not hesitated to attribute to man in that state the notion of the just and the unjust, without bothering to show that he had to have that notion, or even that it was useful to him. Others have spoken of the natural right everyone has to keep what belongs to him, without explaining what they meant by "belong." Others, granting authority to the stronger over the weaker from the very outset, have had government arising right away, without considering the time that must have elapsed before the words "authority" and "government" could have existed among men. In short, all of them, speaking continually of need, greed, oppression, desires, and pride, have carried into the state of nature ideas they have taken from society: they spoke of savage man and they were depicting civil man.[27] It did not even enter the minds of most of our philosophers to doubt that the state of nature existed, whereas it is evident from reading the Sacred Books that the first man, having received enlightenment and precepts directly from God, was not himself in that state, and that, granting the books of Moses the faith that any Christian philosopher owes them, it must be denied that men were ever found in the pure state of nature,[28] even before the Flood, unless they fell back into it by some extraordinary event—a paradox highly difficult to defend and altogether impossible to prove.

Let us therefore begin by setting aside all the facts, for they have no bearing on the question. The research that may be undertaken regarding this subject must not be taken for historical truth, but only for hypothetical and conditional reasoning, more appropriate for clarifying the nature of things than for showing their genuine origin, and similar to the reasoning our physicists employ all the time with regard to the formation of the world.[29] Religion orders us to

27. "Savage man" is "savage" in the sense of "wild" or "untamed," not in the sense of "fierce" or "vicious." The contrast Rousseau develops is therefore between uncivilized man and civilized man.

28. The "pure state of nature" was a term originally used by medieval or early modern natural law thinkers such as Thomas Aquinas and Francisco Suarez to refer to the natural state of mankind without divine dispensation or prior to it, with the "state of nature" itself referring to the state of mankind prior to the Fall. See, e.g., Aquinas, *Summa Theologica* (written 1265–74), I-II, q. 109, art. 8; Francisco Suarez, *De legibus ac Deo legislatore* (1612), 1.3.11–12 and 2.8.8–9.

29. See Descartes, *Discourse on Method* (1637), part 5, beginning. After first referring to the condemnation of Galileo by the Catholic Church for his examination of the Copernican system, and remarking that he suppressed his own book on the formation of the world due to the controversy, Descartes explains that his examination of the formation and laws of the physical universe will be strictly hypothetical.

believe that since God himself took men out of the state of nature immediately after the creation, they are unequal because he intended them to be so. But it does not forbid us from forming conjectures, drawn solely from the nature of man and of the beings surrounding him, about what the human race might have become if it had been left to its own devices. This is what is asked of me, and what I propose to examine in this discourse. As my subject concerns man in general, I will try to adopt a language that suits all nations—or, rather, forgetting times and places, considering only the men to whom I speak, I will imagine myself in the Lyceum of Athens, rehearsing the lessons of my masters, with the likes of Plato and of Xenocrates as my judges, and the human race as my audience.[30]

O man, whatever land you may be from, whatever your opinions may be, listen: here is your history such as I have found it reads, not in the books of your fellow men, who are liars, but in nature, which never lies. Everything that comes from nature will be true; there will be nothing false in it except what I may have unintentionally mixed in it of my own. The times of which I am going to speak are very far off. How much you have changed from what you were! It is, so to speak, the life of your species that I am going to describe to you according to the qualities you received, which your education and your habits may have been able to corrupt, but have not been able to destroy. There is, I feel, an age at which the individual man would want to halt. You will seek the age at which you would wish your species had halted. Dissatisfied with your present state for reasons that herald even greater dissatisfactions for your unhappy posterity, perhaps you would want to be able to go backward. And this sentiment must serve as the praise of your earliest ancestors, the criticism of your contemporaries, and the terror of those who will have the misfortune to live after you.

---

30. The Lyceum of Athens was the school founded by Aristotle in 335 or 334 BC. Xenocrates (c. 395–314 BC), the philosopher and mathematician, was a student of Plato who later headed Plato's school, the Academy.

FIRST PART

HOWEVER IMPORTANT it may be, in order to judge the natural state of man correctly, to consider him from his origin and to examine him, so to speak, in the first embryo of the species, I will not follow his physical organization through its successive developments. I will not stop to investigate in the animal system what he could have been at the beginning so as eventually to become what he is. I will not examine whether, as Aristotle thinks, his elongated nails were not at first hooked claws,[31] whether he was not hairy like a bear, and whether, his walking on all fours (III [p. 120]), his gaze directed toward the earth and limited to a horizon of a few paces, did not indicate the character as well as the limitations of his ideas.[32] On that subject I could form only vague and almost imaginary conjectures. Comparative anatomy has as yet made too little progress, the observations of naturalists are as yet too uncertain, to be able to establish the basis for solid reasoning upon such foundations. Thus, without having recourse to the supernatural knowledge we have on this point, and without regard to the changes that must have occurred in the structure of man, internal as much as external, as he gradually applied his limbs to new uses and as he consumed new foods, I will suppose him formed from all time as I see him today: walking on two feet, using his hands as we do ours, directing his gaze toward the whole of nature, and surveying with his eyes the vast expanse of heaven.

---

31. Although Aristotle does speak of the analogy between the nails of human beings and the claws of animals, he does not claim that nails evolved from claws (see *Parts of Animals* 687a-b). Aristotle's discussion in this context is his claim that human beings are not disadvantageously physically constituted compared to other animals since they are adaptable, for example being able to use their hands for many purposes.

32. Aristotle suggests that human beings' upright posture is a sign of our rational and divine nature. See *Parts of Animals* 686a.

Stripping this being, so constituted, of all the supernatural gifts he could have received and of all the artificial faculties he could have acquired only by prolonged progress—considering him, in a word, such as he must have come from the hands of nature—I see an animal less strong than some, less agile than others, but, all things considered, the most advantageously physically organized of all. I see him satisfying his hunger beneath an oak, quenching his thirst at the first stream, finding his bed at the foot of the same tree that had furnished his meal, and with that his needs satisfied.

The earth, left to its natural fertility (IV [p. 122] and covered by immense forests which no axe has ever mutilated, at every step offers storehouses and shelter to the animals of every species. Men, dispersed among them, observe and imitate their industry, and so raise themselves up to the level of the instinct of beasts, with the advantage that each species has only its own instinct, and man—perhaps having none that belongs to him—appropriates them all to himself, feeds himself equally well on most of the various foods (V [p. 123]) which the other animals divide among themselves, and consequently finds his subsistence more easily than any of them can.

Accustomed from childhood to the inclemency of the weather and the rigor of the seasons, habituated to fatigue, and forced—naked and without arms—to defend their lives and their prey against other ferocious beasts or to escape them by running, men develop a robust and almost unalterable temperament. Children, bringing into the world the excellent constitution of their parents and strengthening it by the same training which produced it, thereby acquire all the vigor of which the human species is capable. Nature makes use of them precisely as the law of Sparta did with the children of its citizens: it renders strong and robust those who are well constituted and causes all the others to perish, differing in this regard from our societies, where the state, by rendering them burdensome to their parents, kills them indiscriminately before their birth.

Savage man's body being the only implement with which he is familiar, he puts it to various uses of which ours are incapable for lack of practice, and it is our industry that deprives us of the strength and agility that necessity obliges him to acquire. If he had had an axe, would his wrist break such strong branches? If he had had a sling, would he throw a stone so hard? If he had had a ladder, would he climb a tree so nimbly? If he had had a horse, would he run so fast? Give civilized man time to gather all his machines around him, and there can be no doubt that he will easily overcome savage man. But if you want to see an even more unequal fight, put them face to face, naked and disarmed, and you will soon recognize the advantage of constantly having all one's strength at one's disposal, of always being ready for any eventuality, and of always carrying oneself, so to speak, wholly with oneself (VI [p. 124]).

Hobbes claims that man is naturally intrepid and seeks only to attack and fight.[33] An illustrious philosopher thinks, and Cumberland and Pufendorf also affirm, that, on the contrary, nothing is as timid as man in the state of nature, and that he is always trembling and ready to flee at the slightest noise that strikes him, at the slightest movement that he perceives.[34] This may be so for objects with which he is not familiar, and I do not doubt that he is frightened by every new sight that presents itself to him whenever he cannot discern the physical good and evil that must be expected from it or compare his strength with the danger he runs—rare circumstances in the state of nature, where everything proceeds in such a uniform manner and where the face of the earth is not subject to those sudden and continual changes caused in it by the passions and inconstancy of united peoples. But savage man, living dispersed among the animals and early finding himself in the position of having to measure himself against them, soon makes the comparison, and, sensing that he surpasses them in skill more than they surpass him in strength, he learns to fear them no more. Pit a bear or a wolf against a savage who is robust, agile, courageous, as they all are, armed with stones and a good stick, and you will see that the danger will at the very least be reciprocal and that, after several such experiences, ferocious beasts, which do not like to attack each other, will not willingly attack man, who they will have found to be just as ferocious as themselves. With regard to those animals that actually have more strength than man has skill, he is in the same position with respect to them as other weaker species, which nonetheless continue to subsist, with this advantage for man: that, no less prepared than they are to run and finding almost certain refuge in trees, he always has the option of accepting or refusing the encounter and the choice of fleeing or fighting. Let us add that it does not appear that any animal naturally makes war upon man, except in the case of self-defense or extreme hunger, or

---

33. See Hobbes, *On the Citizen* (1642), 1.4: "All men in the state of nature have a desire, and will to hurt . . ." (p. 26). See also Hobbes, *Leviathan* (1651), chap. 13.

34. The "illustrious philosopher" is Charles-Louis de Secondat, baron de Montesquieu (1689–1755), who argues in the *Spirit of the Laws* (1748) that man in the state of nature "would at first feel only his weakness; his timidity would be extreme; and as for evidence, if it is needed on this point, savages have been found in the forests; everything makes them tremble, everything makes them flee" (1.2, p. 6). Richard Cumberland argues in *A Treatise of the Laws of Nature* (1672), against Hobbes, that human passions would not necessarily lead to the war of all against all described by Hobbes (1.32, p. 350]). For Pufendorf's account of man's fearfulness in the natural state, see *De jure naturae et gentium* (1672), 2.1.8 and 2.2.2; see also 2.3.16.

displays those violent antipathies toward him that seem to announce that one species is destined by nature to serve as food for the other.

These are undoubtedly the reasons why Negroes and savages are so little concerned about the ferocious beasts they encounter in the woods. The Caribs of Venezuela, among others, live in this regard in the most profound security and without the slightest inconvenience. Although they go nearly naked, says François Corréal, this does not keep them from boldly exposing themselves in the woods armed only with bow and arrow, but no one has ever heard that any of them has been devoured by beasts.[35]

Other more formidable enemies, against which man does not have the same means of defending himself, are natural infirmities: childhood, old age, and illnesses of all types—sad signs of our weakness, of which the first two are common to all animals and the last of which belongs principally to man living in society. I even observe on the subject of childhood that the mother, since she carries her child with her everywhere, can feed it more easily than the females of a number of animals, which are forced to come and go repeatedly with great fatigue, this way to seek their food and that way to suckle or feed their young. It is true that if the mother happens to perish, the child greatly risks perishing with her; but this danger is common to a hundred other species, whose young are for a long time unable to go seek their nourishment themselves. And if childhood lasts longer among us, since we live longer as well, everything is also more or less equal in this respect (VII [p. 126]), although there are other rules regarding the duration of infancy and the number of young (VIII [p. 126]) which do not pertain to my subject. Among old people, who act and perspire little, the need for food diminishes along with the ability to provide for it. And as savage life keeps gout and rheumatism away from them, and as old age is, of all ills, that which human assistance can least alleviate, they eventually expire without anyone perceiving that they cease to exist and almost without perceiving it themselves.

With regard to illnesses, I will not repeat the empty and false declamations against medicine made by most healthy people, but I will ask whether there is any solid observation from which it might be concluded that the average lifespan of man is shorter in countries where this art is most neglected than in those where it is cultivated with the greatest care. And how could that be, unless we give ourselves more ills than medicine can furnish us remedies! The extreme inequality in our way of life—excess of idleness among some, excess

---

35. Rousseau cites François Corréal, *Voyages de François Corréal aux Indes Occidentales* (rev. ed. 1722), 1.8.

of labor among others; the ease with which our appetites and our sensuality are aroused and satisfied; the overly refined foods of the rich, which feed them with rich sauces and overwhelm them with indigestion; the bad food of the poor, which they are even short of most of the time and the lack of which leads them to greedily stuff their stomachs when they get the chance; late nights, excesses of every kind, immoderate outpourings of all the passions, bouts of fatigue, and exhaustion of the mind; innumerable sorrows and pains which are experienced in every social station and which perpetually gnaw away at men's souls: these are the fatal proofs that most of our ills are our own work, and that we would have avoided almost all of them by preserving the simple, uniform, and solitary way of life which was prescribed to us by nature. If nature intended us to be healthy, I almost dare affirm that the state of reflection is a state contrary to nature, and that the man who meditates is a depraved animal. When one considers the good constitution of savages, at least of those whom we have not ruined with our strong liquors, when one learns that they experience almost no illnesses except wounds and old age, one is strongly inclined to believe that the history of human illnesses could easily be written by following that of civil societies. Such at least is the view of Plato, who judges, based on certain remedies used or approved by Podalirius and Machaon at the siege of Troy, that various illness these very remedies should have brought on were not yet then experienced by men.[36] And Celsus reports that dieting, so necessary nowadays, was invented only by Hippocrates.[37]

With so few sources of ills, man in the state of nature therefore scarcely has need of remedies, and still less of doctors. The human species is in this respect no worse off than all the others, and it is easy to learn from hunters whether they come across many sick animals in their treks. They do find some that have received considerable wounds which healed quite well, that have had bones and even limbs broken and set again by no other surgeon than time, with no other regimen than their ordinary life, and that are no less perfectly cured for not having been tormented by incisions, poisoned by drugs, or worn out by fasts. Finally, however useful well-administered medicine may be among us, it is still certain that if a sick savage left to his own devices has nothing to hope for except from nature, in return he has nothing to fear except from his illness, which often makes his situation preferable to ours.

---

36. See Plato *Republic* 405d–408c. Compare Homer *Iliad* 11.639–40. Podalirius and Machaon were the sons of the legendary healer Asclepius.

37. See A. Cornelius Celsus *De Medicina* Preface. Hippocrates was the great medical doctor who flourished in the fourth century BC after whom the "Hippocratic Oath" is named.

Let us therefore beware of confusing savage man with the men we have before our eyes. Nature treats all the animals left to its care with a partiality that seems to show how jealous it is of this right. The horse, the cat, the bull, even the ass are mostly taller, all of them have a more robust constitution, more vigor, more strength in the forests than in our houses. They lose half of these advantages in becoming domesticated, and it might be said that all our care to treat and feed these animals well only ends up causing them to degenerate. It is the same with man himself: in becoming sociable and a slave, he becomes weak, timid, groveling, and his soft and effeminate way of life completes the enervation of both his strength and his courage. Let us add that in savage and domesticated conditions the difference between one man and another must be yet greater than that between one beast and another; for since both animal and man have been treated equally by nature, all the comforts man provides for himself above and beyond those he provides for the animals he tames are so many particular causes that make him degenerate more perceptibly.

Nakedness, lack of dwelling, and deprivation of all those useless things we believe so necessary are not, therefore, such a great misfortune for these first men, nor above all are they such a great obstacle to their self-preservation. If they do not have hairy skin, they have no need of it in warm countries, and in cold countries they soon learn to appropriate the skins of the beasts they have overcome. If they have only two feet for running, they have two arms to provide for their defense and for their needs. Their children perhaps walk late and with difficulty, but mothers carry them with ease—an advantage lacking in other species in which the mother, being pursued, finds herself forced to abandon her young or to adjust her pace to theirs.* Finally, unless one supposes those singular and fortuitous combinations of circumstances of which I will speak hereafter, and which might very well never have occurred, it is in any case clear that the first who made himself clothes or a dwelling thereby gave himself things that were hardly necessary, since he had done without

---

* There may be some exceptions to this. For example, that of the animal from the province of Nicaragua which resembles a fox, has feet like a man's hands, and, according to Corréal, has a pouch under its belly into which the mother puts her young when she is obliged to flee. This is doubtless the same animal that is called a Tlaquatzin in Mexico, and to the female of which Laët attributes a similar pouch for the same use.[38]

---

38. For Corréal, see n. 35 to p. 68. Jan Laët's account of the West Indies first appeared in 1625. The animal to which Laët refers is the opossum.

them until then and since it is hard to see why he could not endure as a grown man a mode of life he had endured from his childhood.

Alone, idle, and always near danger, savage man must like to sleep and be a light sleeper like the animals, which, since they think little, so to speak sleep the entire time they are not thinking. His own preservation being almost his only care, his best trained faculties must be those whose principal object is attack and defense, either to overcome his prey or to guard against being another animal's prey. By contrast, the organs perfected only by softness and sensuality must remain in a state of coarseness that precludes any kind of delicacy in him; and since his senses are not alike in this respect, he will have extremely crude touch and taste and highly acute sight, hearing, and smell. Such is the animal state in general, and, according to travelers' reports, such also is that of most savage peoples. Thus it is not surprising that the Hottentots of the Cape of Good Hope catch sight of vessels on the high seas with their naked eyes from as far away as do the Dutch with spyglasses, nor that the savages of America track the Spaniards by smell just as well as the best dogs could have done, nor that all these barbarous nations endure their nakedness without difficulty, whet their appetite with hot peppers, and drink European liquors like water.

I have up to this point considered only physical man. Let us try to look at him now from the metaphysical and moral side.

I see in every animal only an ingenious machine to which nature has given senses to revitalize itself and protect itself, up to a certain point, from everything that tends to destroy or disturb it. I perceive precisely the same things in the human machine, with this difference: that nature alone does everything in the operations of the beast whereas man contributes to his own operations in his capacity as a free agent. The former chooses or rejects by instinct and the latter by an act of freedom, which makes it so that the beast cannot deviate from the rule that is prescribed to it, even when it would be advantageous for it to do so, and that man deviates from it often to his own detriment. So a pigeon would die of hunger near a basin filled with the best meats and a cat atop heaps of fruits or grain even though each could nourish itself very well on the food it disdains if it made up its mind to try some. So dissolute men yield to excesses which cause them fever and death, because the mind depraves the senses, and because the will still speaks when nature is silent.

Every animal has ideas since it has senses, it even combines its ideas up to a certain point, and man differs in this regard from beast only by degree. Some philosophers have even suggested that there is more difference between one given man and another given man than between a given man and a given beast.[39] It is therefore not so much understanding that constitutes the specific difference of man among the animals as it is his capacity as a free agent. Nature commands every animal, and the beast obeys. Man feels the same impetus, but he recognizes that he is free to acquiesce or resist, and it is above all in the consciousness of this freedom that the spirituality of his soul is shown. For physics in a way explains the mechanism of the senses and the formation of ideas, but in the power of willing, or rather of choosing, and in the feeling[40] of this power are found only purely spiritual acts, about which nothing is explained by the laws of mechanics.

But, even if the difficulties surrounding all these questions should leave some room for dispute concerning this difference between man and animal, there is another very specific quality that distinguishes them and about which there can be no argument: that is, the faculty of perfecting himself[41]—a faculty which, with the aid of circumstances, successively develops all the others and resides among us as much in the species as in the individual, whereas an animal is at the end of a few months what it will be all its life and its species will be at the end of a thousand years what it was the first year of that thousand. Why is man alone liable to becoming imbecile? Is it not that he thereby returns to his primitive state and that—while the beast, which has acquired nothing and which also has nothing to lose, always retains his instinct—man, losing again by old age or by other accidents everything that his *perfectibility* has made him acquire thereby falls back lower than the beast itself? It would be sad for us to be forced to agree that this distinctive and almost unlimited faculty is the source of all man's misfortunes, that it is this faculty which, by dint of time, draws him out of that original condition in which he would pass tranquil and innocent days, that it is this faculty which, over the centuries, by causing his enlightenment and his errors, his vices and his virtues, to bloom,

---

39. See Montaigne, *Essays* (1580–92), "Of the Inequality among Us," 1.42, p. 189: "Plutarch says somewhere that he does not find so much difference between one animal and another as he does between one man and another. . . . I would willingly outdo Plutarch and say that there is more distance between a given man to a given man than from a given man to a given animal." Montaigne refers to Plutarch's dialogue "That Beasts Use Reason."

40. "Feeling" translates *sentiment*, which might also be translated "sentiment." As in English, the French term *sentiment* can refer either to a feeling or to an opinion. The term will be translated as "feeling" when it is clear that this is his primary meaning.

41. "The faculty of perfecting himself" translates *la faculté de se perfectionner*. This phrase might also be translated "the faculty of self-perfection" or, more passively, "the faculty of being perfected." Just below, Rousseau will use the term "perfectibility," a term he coined or at least was the first to use in print, to name this uniquely human capacity for change on the level of the individual and species.

makes him in the long run the tyrant of himself and of nature (IX [p. 127]). It would be horrible to be obliged to praise as a beneficent being the person who first suggested to the inhabitants of the banks of the Orinoco the use of those boards he binds to his children's temples, and which assure them at least a portion of their imbecility and of their original happiness.

Savage man, left by nature to instinct alone, or rather compensated for that instinct he perhaps lacks by faculties capable of substituting for it at first and then of raising him far above nature, will therefore begin with purely animal functions (X [p. 134]). To perceive and to feel will be his first state, which he will have in common with all the animals. To will and to not will, to desire and to fear, will be the first and almost the only operations of his soul until new circumstances cause new developments in it.

Whatever the moralists may say about it, human understanding owes much to the passions which, as is generally acknowledged, owe much to it as well. It is by their activity that our reason is perfected. We seek to know only because we desire to have pleasure, and it is not possible to conceive why someone who had neither desires nor fears would go to the trouble of reasoning. The passions, in turn, derive their origin from our needs and their progress from our knowledge. For one can desire or fear things only through the ideas one can have of them or by the simple impulsion of nature; and savage man, deprived of every kind of enlightenment, experiences only the passions of this latter type. His desires do not exceed his physical needs (XI [p. 141]). The only goods he knows in the universe are food, a female, and rest; the only evils he fears are pain and hunger. I say pain and not death, for an animal will never know what it is to die, and the knowledge of death and its terrors is one of the first acquisitions man has made in moving away from the animal condition.

It would be easy for me, if it were necessary, to support this view by facts and to show that in all the nations of the world the progress of the mind has been precisely proportioned to the needs that peoples received from nature or to those to which circumstances subjected them, and consequently to the passions, which prompted them to provide for these needs. I would show the arts being born in Egypt and spreading with the flooding of the Nile. I would follow their progress among the Greeks, where they were seen to sprout, grow, and rise up to the heavens amidst the sands and rocks of Attica without being able to take root on the fertile banks of the Eurotas.[42] I would note that in

---

42. Rousseau makes the traditional contrast between Athens, located in Attica and known for its cultivation of the arts, and Sparta, the city on the banks of the river Eurotas and known for its neglect of the arts. Compare *Discourse on the Sciences and the Arts*, p. 36 above.

general the peoples of the north are more industrious than those of the south because they can less afford not to be so, as if nature wanted to equalize things in this way by giving to minds the fertility it denies the soil.

But without resorting to the uncertain evidence of history, who does not see that everything seems to remove from savage man the temptation and the means of ceasing to be savage? His imagination portrays nothing to him; his heart asks nothing of him. His modest needs are so easily found at hand, and he is so far from the degree of knowledge necessary for desiring to acquire greater knowledge, that he can have neither foresight nor curiosity. The spectacle of nature becomes indifferent for him by dint of becoming familiar to him. There is always the same order, there are always the same revolutions. He does not have the mind to wonder at the greatest marvels, and it is not in him that one must seek the philosophy man needs in order to know how to observe once what he has seen every day. His soul, which nothing agitates, gives itself over to the sole feeling of its present existence, without any idea of the future, however near it may be, and his projects, as limited as his views, hardly extend to the end of the day. Such is, even today, the degree of the foresight of the Carib: in the morning he sells his bed of cotton and in the evening he comes weeping to buy it back for not having foreseen that he would need it for the coming night.

The more one meditates on this subject, the more the distance from pure sensations to the simplest knowledge increases in our eyes; and it is impossible to conceive how a man, by his strength alone, without the aid of communication, and without the spur of necessity, could have bridged so great an interval. How many centuries perhaps elapsed before men were at the point of seeing a fire other than that of heaven? How many different chance events were needed to learn the most common uses of this element? How many times must they have let it go out before they acquired the art of reproducing it? And how many times did each of these secrets perhaps die along with the one who discovered it? What shall we say of agriculture, an art which requires so much labor and foresight, which depends on other arts, which quite obviously is practicable only in a society that has at least begun, and which serves us less to bring forth from the earth those foods it would readily yield without this art than to force it to yield those we prefer as being most to our taste? But let us suppose men had multiplied so much that the products of nature no longer sufficed to feed them—a supposition which, incidentally, would indicate a great advantage for the human species in that way of life. Let us suppose that, without forges and without workshops, the tools for farming had fallen from heaven into the savages' hands, that these men had conquered the mortal hatred they all have for sustained work, that they had learned to foresee their needs so far in advance, that they had guessed how the earth must be cultivated, grain sowed, and trees planted, that they had discovered the art of grinding wheat and fermenting grapes—all things that would have had to be taught to them by the gods, as it is impossible to conceive how they could have learned them by themselves. What man, after all this, would be foolish enough to torment himself by cultivating a field that will be plundered by the first comer, whether man or beast, for whom the crop was agreeable? And how could anybody resolve to spend his life doing hard work when the more he needs its reward, the more certain he is of not reaping it? In a word, how could this situation lead men to cultivate the earth as long as it is not divided among them—that is, as long as the state of nature is not entirely destroyed?

Even if we were to suppose a savage man to be as skillful in the art of thinking as our philosophers make him out to be, even if we were to make him, following their example, a philosopher himself—discovering the most sublime truths on his own, making for himself, by extremely abstract chains of reasoning, maxims of justice and reason drawn from the love of order in general or from the known will of his creator; in a word, even if we were to suppose him to have as much intelligence and enlightenment in his mind as he would have to have—and to the degree that dullness and stupidity is in fact found in him—what use would the species derive from all this metaphysics, which could not be communicated and which would perish with the individual who had invented it? What progress could the human race make, scattered in the woods among the animals? And to what point could men perfect themselves and enlighten one another who, having neither fixed domicile nor any need for one another, would encounter one another perhaps hardly twice in their lives, without recognizing one another and without speaking to one another?

Consider how many ideas we owe to the use of speech; how much grammar trains and facilitates the operations of the mind; and think of the inconceivable difficulties and the infinite time the first invention of languages must have cost. Add these reflections to those that preceded, and it will be possible to judge how many thousands of centuries would have been necessary in order to successively develop in the human mind the operations of which it was capable.

Let me be allowed to consider for a moment the predicaments faced in the study of the origin of languages. I could content myself with citing or repeating here the investigations the abbé de Condillac has carried out concerning this matter, which all fully confirm my view and which, perhaps, gave me my first idea regarding it.[43] But since the way this philosopher resolves the difficulties he himself raises concerning the origin of instituted signs shows that he assumed what I question—namely, some sort of society already established among the inventors of language—I believe that, in referring to his reflections, I ought to add my own to them in order to exhibit these same difficulties in the light that suits my subject. The first difficulty that arises is to imagine how languages could have become necessary, for since men have neither relations among themselves nor any need of them, neither the necessity of this invention nor its possibility is conceivable unless it were indispensable. I might well say, as many others do, that languages arose in the domestic relations[44] among fathers, mothers, and children. But, aside from the fact that this would not resolve the objections, it would be committing the error of those who, in reasoning about the state of nature carry into it ideas taken from society, always see the family gathered in one and the same dwelling and its members maintaining among themselves a union as intimate and permanent as among us, where so many common interests unite them. Instead, in this primitive state, having no houses, nor huts, nor property of any kind, each took up his lodging at random and often for a single night. Males and females united fortuitously according to encounter, opportunity, and desire, without speech being an especially necessary interpreter of the things they had to say to one another; they parted just as readily (XII [p. 141]). The mother nursed her children at first for her own need; then, habit having endeared them to her, she nursed them afterward for their need. As soon as they had the strength to seek their food, they did not delay in leaving the mother herself. And as they had almost no other way to find one another than not to lose sight of one another, they were soon at the point of not even recognizing each other. Note also that since the child has all his needs to explain and consequently more things to say to the mother than the mother does to the child, it is he who must bear the greatest burden with regard to its invention, and that the language he uses must be in large part his own work. This multiplies languages as many times

---

43. Etienne Bonnot de Condillac, *Essay on the Origin of Human Knowledge* (1746), part 2, Preamble. After acknowledging the biblical account of Adam and Eve, who were able to reflect and communicate with one another, Condillac states that in his own hypothetical investigation of the origin of language he will suppose a society of two children of different sexes who survived the Flood.

44. "Relations" translates *commerce*, which has the general sense of interactions or dealings among individuals or groups, which is the sense here, or the specific sense of commercial relations. Given the importance of the term for eighteenth-century thought about the origins and effects of "commerce" in both senses of the term, *commerce* has either been translated as "commerce" or a note will identify an alternative translation such as "relations," "interactions," etc.

as there are individuals to speak them, to which their wandering and vagabond life further contributes since it does not allow any idiom enough time to gain any consistency. For to say that the mother teaches the child the words it will have to use to ask her for this thing or that is to show quite clearly how already formed languages are taught, but this does not tell us how they are formed.

Let us suppose this first difficulty overcome. Let us momentarily leap over the immense distance there must have been between the pure state of nature and the need for languages, and, supposing them to be necessary (XIII [p. 145]), let us try to find out how they could begin to be established. New difficulty, even worse than the preceding one: for if men needed speech in order to learn to think, they had an even greater need of knowing how to think in order to discover the art of speech. And even if it were understood how the sounds of the voice came to be taken for the conventional interpreters of our ideas, it would remain to see what possibly could have been the specific interpreters of this convention for ideas that, having no perceptible object, could be indicated neither by gesture nor by voice. As a result, it is scarcely possible to form tenable conjectures concerning the birth of this art for communicating one's thoughts and establishing exchanges[45] between minds—a sublime art which is already so far from its origin, but which the philosopher views as still being so incredibly far from its perfection that no man is bold enough to contend that it would ever be reached, even were the revolutions that time necessarily brings about suspended on its behalf, were prejudices to quit the academies or fall silent before them, and were they able to attend to this thorny question for centuries on end without interruption.

Man's first language—the most universal, most energetic, and only language he needed before it was necessary to persuade assembled men—is the cry of nature. As this cry was wrested from him only by a sort of instinct on urgent occasions to implore help in cases of great danger or relief in cases of violent pain, it was not of much use in the ordinary course of life, where more moderate feelings prevail. When men's ideas began to extend and multiply, and when closer communication was established among them, they sought more numerous signs and a more extensive language. They multiplied inflexions of the voice and added to it gestures, which by their nature are more expressive and whose meaning depends less on a prior determination. They therefore expressed visible and moving objects by gestures and audible ones by imitative sounds. But as gesture indicates hardly anything but objects which are

---

45. Or: commerce (*commerce*).

present, or easily described, and visible actions, as it is not universally practicable since darkness or the interposition of a body render it useless, and as it requires rather than stimulates attention, men finally thought of substituting vocal articulations, which, while they do not have the same relation to specific ideas, are better suited to represent them all inasmuch as they are instituted signs—a substitution which could not be made except by common consent and in a such a manner as is rather difficult to put into practice for men whose crude organs as yet had little training, and which is even more difficult to conceive in itself, because this unanimous agreement must have had a motive and because speech appears to have been highly necessary in order to establish the use of speech.

It must be considered that the first words of which men made use had a much more extensive signification in their minds than do those used in already formed languages, and that, since they were ignorant of the division of discourse into its constituent parts, they at first gave each word the meaning of an entire proposition. When they began to distinguish subject from attribute and verb from noun, which was no small effort of genius, substantives were at first so many proper nouns, the present infinitive the only verb tense, and as for adjectives, the very notion of them must have developed only with great difficulty, because every adjective is an abstract word and because abstractions are difficult and not especially natural mental operations.

Each object at first received a particular name, without regard to genera and species, which these first institutors were incapable of distinguishing; and all individual things were presented to their minds in isolation, just as they are in the tableau of nature. If one oak was called "A," another was called "B," for the first idea derived from two things is that they are not the same, and much time is often needed to observe what they have in common. In this way, the more limited the knowledge, the more extensive the dictionary became. The obstacle posed by all this nomenclature could not easily be removed, for in order to arrange beings under common and generic denominations, they needed to know their properties and differences, they needed observations and definitions, that is, much more natural history and metaphysics than the men of that time could have had.

Besides, general ideas can enter the mind only with the aid of words, and the understanding grasps them only by means of propositions. This is one of the reasons why animals can neither form such ideas nor acquire the perfectibility which depends on them. When a monkey goes without hesitating from one nut to another, are we to think that he has the general idea of this sort of fruit and that he compares its archetype to these two individuals? Doubtless not; rather, the sight of one of these nuts recalls to his memory the sensations he received from the other, and his eyes, being modified in a certain way, announce to his taste the modification it is about to receive. Every general idea is purely intellectual; if imagination becomes the least bit involved, the idea immediately becomes particular. Try to draw for yourself the image of a tree in general: you will never succeed in doing so. In spite of yourself, it will have to be seen as small or large, bare or leafy, light or dark; and if it were up to you to see in it only what is found in every tree, this image would no longer resemble a tree. Purely abstract beings are seen in the same way, or they are conceived of only through discourse. The definition of the triangle alone gives you the genuine idea of it: as soon as you represent one for yourself in your mind, it is a given triangle and not another, and you cannot help making its lines perceptible or its plane colored. It is therefore necessary to state propositions, it is therefore necessary to speak in order to have general ideas; for as soon as the imagination stops, the mind no longer advances except with the aid of discourse. If, then, the first inventors could give names only to the ideas they already had, it follows that the first substantives could never have been anything but proper nouns.

But when, by what means I cannot conceive, our new grammarians began to extend their ideas and to generalize their words, the inventors' ignorance must have subjected this method to narrow bounds. And just as they at first overly multiplied the names of individual things for not knowing genera and species, they subsequently made too few species and genera for not having considered beings in terms of all their differences. To extend the divisions far enough would have required more experience and enlightenment than they could have had and more research and work than they were willing to apply to it. So if even today new species are daily discovered that had eluded all our observations until now, let one consider how many must have remained hidden from men who judged things only at first glance! As for primary classes and the most general notions, it is superfluous to add that they too must have eluded them. How, for example, would they have imagined or understood the words "matter," "mind," "substance," "mode," "figure," "movement," since our philosophers, who have used them for such a long time, themselves have considerable difficulty understanding these words and since, as the ideas attached to these words are purely metaphysical, they found no model for them in nature?

I stop after these first steps, and I beg my judges to suspend their reading here in order to consider, with regard to the invention of nouns for physical things alone—that is, concerning the easiest part of language to discover—how far it still has to go in order to express all of men's thoughts, in order to assume a consistent form, be capable of being spoken in public, and have an influence on society. I beg them to reflect upon how much time and knowledge were needed to discover numbers (XIV [p. 146]), abstract nouns, aorists and all the tenses of verbs, particles, syntax, to link propositions, reasonings, and to formulate the entire logic of discourse. As for myself, frightened by the multiplying difficulties and convinced of the almost demonstrated impossibility that languages could have arisen and been established by purely human means, I leave it to anyone who should wish to undertake it the examination of this difficult problem: Which was more necessary, an already formed society for the institution of languages or already invented languages for the establishment of society?

Whatever the case may be regarding these origins, it is at least clear from how little care nature has taken to bring men together through mutual needs and to facilitate their use of speech, how little it has prepared their sociability and how little it has contributed for its part to all they have done to establish social bonds. Indeed, it is impossible to imagine why in that primitive state a man would need another man any more than a monkey or a wolf would need its fellow creature,[46] nor, assuming this need, what motive could induce the other to provide for it; nor even, if he did, how they could agree with one another on the terms. I know that we are repeatedly told that nothing would have been so miserable as man in that state;[47] and if it is true, as I believe I have proved, that he could have had the desire and the opportunity to leave it only after many centuries, this would be a charge to level against nature and not against him whom nature had so constituted. But, if I understand this term *miserable* correctly, it is a word that is either meaningless, or that signifies solely a painful privation and suffering of the body or soul. Now, I would very much like someone to explain to me what kind of misery there can be for a free being whose heart is at peace and whose body is healthy. I ask which—civil or natural life—is more liable to become intolerable to those who enjoy it? We nearly always see around us only people who complain about their existence, and some even deprive themselves of it insofar as they are able to do so, and the combination of divine and human laws hardly suffices to stop this disor-

---

46. "Fellow creature" translates *semblable*. See n. 21 to p. 54.

47. See Pufendorf, *The Whole Duty of Man According to the Law of Man* (1673), 2.5.2, pp. 187–88; *De jure naturae et gentium* (1672), 2.2.8. See also Hobbes, *Leviathan* (1651), chap. 13.

der. I ask whether anyone has ever heard it said that a savage who is free even so much as considered complaining about his life and killing himself? Let it therefore be judged with less pride on which side genuine misery lies. Nothing, on the contrary, would have been so miserable as savage man dazzled by enlightenment, tormented by passions, and reasoning about a state different from his own. It was by a very wise providence that the faculties he had in potential were to develop only with the opportunities to exercise them, so that they were neither superfluous and burdensome to him beforehand nor belated and useless when needed. He had, in instinct alone, everything necessary for him to live in the state of nature; he has in cultivated reason only what is necessary for him to live in society.

It appears at first that men in that state, since they have neither any kind of moral relation among themselves nor known duties, could be neither good nor evil, and had neither vices nor virtues—unless, taking these words in a physical sense, one were to call vices in the individual those qualities that can harm his own self-preservation and virtues those that can contribute to it, in which case it would be necessary to call the most virtuous the one who least resists the simple impulses of nature. But without deviating from the usual meaning, it is appropriate to suspend the judgment we might pass on such a situation and to be wary of our prejudices until after having examined, scale in hand, whether there are more virtues than vices among civilized men, or whether their virtues are more advantageous than their vices are fatal, or whether the progress of their knowledge is a sufficient compensation for the harm they do one another in proportion as they learn of the good they ought to do, or whether, all things considered, they would not be in a happier situation for having neither harm to fear nor good to hope from anyone than they are for having subjected themselves to universal dependence and having obligated themselves to receive everything from those who do not obligate themselves to give them anything.

Above all, let us not conclude with Hobbes that since man has no idea of goodness he is naturally evil, that he is vicious because he does not know virtue, that he always refuses his fellow humans services he does not believe he owes them, or that, by virtue of the right he reasonably claims to the things he needs, he foolishly imagines himself to be the sole owner of the entire universe.[48] Hobbes saw very clearly the defect of all modern definitions of natural

48. Hobbes argues that man naturally has "a right to everything, even to one another's body" (*Leviathan* [1651], chap. 14, p. 80). See also Hobbes, *On the Citizen* (1642), 1.10. Contrary to Rousseau's statement, however, Hobbes denies that man is "naturally evil." See Hobbes, *Leviathan*, chap. 13, p. 77; *On the Citizen*, Preface

right, but the conclusions he draws from his own definition show that he takes it in a sense which is no less false. Reasoning on the basis of the principles he establishes, this author ought to say that, since the state of nature is the state in which the care of our self-preservation is the least prejudicial to that of others, this state was consequently the most conducive to peace and the best suited to the human race. He says precisely the opposite since he has improperly included in savage man's care for his self-preservation the need to satisfy a large number of passions which are the product of society and which have made laws necessary. The evil man, he says, is a robust child.[49] It remains to be seen whether savage man is a robust child. Even if we were to grant this to him, what would he conclude from it? That if, since even if this man is robust he would be as dependent on others as if he were weak, there is no extreme to which he would not go, that he would beat his mother when she was too slow to give him her breast, that he would strangle one of his younger brothers when he was inconvenienced by him, that he would bite another's leg when it bumped or bothered him. But to be robust and to be dependent are two contradictory assumptions in the state of nature. Man is weak when he is dependent and he is emancipated before he is robust. Hobbes did not see that the same cause that prevents savages from using their reason, as our jurists claim they do, prevents them at the same time from abusing their faculties, as he himself claims. As a result, it could be said that savages are not evil precisely because they do not know what it is to be good; for it is neither the development of enlightenment nor the restraint of law, but rather the calm of the passions and the ignorance of vice, which prevent them from doing evil. *So much more does the ignorance of vice profit these men than does the understanding of virtue profit those.*[50] There is, besides, another principle that Hobbes did not notice and which—having been given to man in order to soften, under certain circumstances, the ferocity of his pride,[51] or the desire to preserve himself before the

---

to the Readers, p. 11. Rousseau's point is that Hobbes' argument that man's unrestrained natural passions are contrary to his self-preservation and well-being makes man "evil" from the perspective of Rousseau's own understanding, outlined in the previous paragraph, of natural goodness and especially of "goodness" taken in its "physical sense."

49. See Hobbes, *On the Citizen* (1642), Preface to the Readers, p. 11: "Thus an evil man is rather like a sturdy boy, or a man of childish mind. . . . "

50. Justin *Histories* 2.2.15, quoted by Rousseau in Latin: *Tanto plus in illis proficit vitiorum ignoratio, quam in his congnitio virtutis.* "These men" who are ignorant of vice refers to the Scythians, whereas "those" with an understanding of virtue refers to the Greeks.

51. "Pride" here and later in this sentence translates *amour-propre.* As will become clear later in this paragraph, and especially in note XV, Rousseau distinguishes between two kinds of self-love: the natural form of *amour de soi,* translated "self-love" or "love of oneself," and the developed form of *amour-propre.* Like the

birth of this pride (XV [p. 147])—tempers the ardor he has for his own well-being by an innate repugnance to see his fellow human being suffer. I do not believe I need fear any contradiction in granting to man the sole natural virtue that the most extravagant detractor of human virtues was forced to acknowledge.[52] I speak of pity, a disposition suitable to beings as weak and as subject to so many ills as we are, a virtue all the more universal and all the more useful to man as it precedes the use of all reflection in him, and so natural that the beasts themselves sometimes show perceptible signs of it. Without speaking of the tenderness of mothers for their young and of the perils they brave to protect them, we daily observe the repugnance horses have for trampling a living body underfoot. An animal does not pass by a dead animal of its own species without uneasiness. Some of them even give them a kind of burial. And the sad lowing of the cattle entering a slaughterhouse proclaims the impression they receive from the horrible sight that strikes them. It is a pleasure to see the author of *The Fable of the Bees* forced to acknowledge man as a compassionate and sensitive being, abandoning, in the example he gives of it, his cold and subtle style to offer us the pathetic image of an imprisoned man who outside sees a ferocious beast tearing a child from his mother's breast, breaking his weak limbs with its murderous fangs, and tearing the throbbing entrails of this child with its claws. What dreadful agitation must be felt by this witness of an event in which he takes no personal interest? What anguish must he suffer at this sight for not being able to lend any help either to the fainting mother or to the dying child?[53]

Such is the pure movement of nature prior to all reflection. Such is the force of natural pity, which the most depraved morals still have difficulty destroying, since we daily see in our theaters people, being moved and weeping for the miseries of an unfortunate person, who, if they were in the tyrant's place, would further increase their enemy's torments—like bloodthirsty Sulla, so sensitive to ills which he had not caused, or like Alexander of Pherae, who dared not attend the performance of a single tragedy for fear that he be seen

---

English term "pride," *amour-propre* often has the pejorative sense of a corrupted form of self-love as in vanity, a negative sense that Rousseau often emphasizes in his discussions of *amour-propre*, but it also has a potentially positive sense as in "taking pride in one's work," a sense in which Rousseau also uses the term. Given the importance for Rousseau of this distinction between the two forms of self-love, and also given that the French word *orgueil* has also been translated as "pride," a note will indicate when "pride" translates *amour-propre*.

52. As will become clear later in this paragraph, the "extravagant detractor of human virtues" is Bernard Mandeville, who famously argues in *The Fable of the Bees* (1714) that "private vices make public virtue."

53. See Bernard Mandeville, "An Essay on Charity and Charity-Schools" (1723), in *Fable of the Bees*, 1:255–56.

groaning with Andromache and Priam, whereas he listened without emotion to the cries of so many citizens whose throats were daily slit at his orders.[54]

> When nature gave mankind tears,
> She proclaims she gave them tender hearts.[55]

Mandeville has clearly sensed that, for all their morality, men would never have been anything but monsters if nature had not given them pity to support reason; but he did not see that from this single attribute flow all the social virtues he wants to deny to men. Indeed, what are generosity, clemency, humanity except pity applied to the weak, the guilty, or the human species in general? Benevolence and even friendship are, properly understood, products of a constant pity focused on a particular object: For is desiring that someone not suffer anything other than desiring that he be happy? Even if it were true that commiseration were only a feeling that puts us in the place of the one who suffers—an obscure and lively feeling in savage man, developed but weak in civil man—what difference would this make to the truth of what I say, except to give it more strength? Indeed, commiseration will be all the more energetic to the extent that the onlooking animal identifies more intimately with the suffering animal. Now, it is obvious that this identification must have been infinitely closer in the state of nature than in the state of reasoning. It is reason that engenders pride,[56] and it is reflection that fortifies it. It is reason that turns man back upon himself. It is reason that separates him from everything that bothers and afflicts him. It is philosophy that isolates him; it is by means of it that he secretly says at the sight of a suffering man: perish if you will, I am safe. No longer do anything but dangers to the entire society disturb the tranquil slumber of the philosopher and tear him from his bed. His fellow human being can have his throat slit with impunity beneath his window; he has only to put his hands over his ears and argue with himself a bit to keep nature, which rebels within him, from making him identify with the person being assassinated. Savage man does not have this admirable talent, and, for want of wisdom and reason, he is always seen heedlessly yielding to the first feeling of humanity.

---

54. Lucius Cornelius Sulla (c. 138–78 BC) was a Roman general and politician who became dictator after his victory in the civil wars. See Plutarch, *Lives*, "Sulla." Alexander of Pherae (reigned 369–358 BC) was tyrant of Pherae in Thessaly. See Plutarch, *Lives*, "Pelopidas" 29. See also Montaigne, *Essays* (1580–92), "Cowardice, Mother of Cruelty," 2.27, pp. 523–24.

55. Juvenal *Satires* 15.131–33, quoted by Rousseau in Latin: *Molissima corda / Humano generi dare se Natura fatetur, / Quae lacrymas dedit.*

56. "Pride" here translates *amour-propre*.

In riots, in street fights, the populace assembles, the prudent man moves away. It is the rabble, it is the marketwomen, who separate the combatants and keep decent people from slitting one another's throats.

It is therefore quite certain that pity is a natural feeling which, by moderating the activity of love of oneself in each individual, contributes to the mutual preservation of the entire species. It is it that carries us without reflection to the aid of those we see suffering. It is it that, in the state of nature, takes the place of laws, morals, and virtue, with the advantage that no one is tempted to disobey its gentle voice. It is it that will deter every robust savage from robbing a weak child or an infirm old man of his hard-won subsistence, if he himself hopes to be able to find his own elsewhere. It is it that, in place of that sublime maxim of reasoned justice, *Do unto others as you would have them do unto you*, inspires in all men this other maxim of natural goodness, much less perfect but perhaps more useful than the preceding one, *Do what is good for you with the least possible harm to others*. In a word, it is in this natural feeling, rather than in subtle arguments, that we must seek the cause of the repugnance every man would experience in doing evil, even independently of the maxims of education. While it may belong to Socrates and minds of his stamp to acquire virtue through reason, the human race would have ceased to exist long ago if its preservation had depended only on the reasoning of those who make it up.

With such inactive passions and such a salutary restraint, men—fierce rather than wicked and more attentive to protecting themselves from the harm they might suffer than tempted to do harm to others—were not prone to very dangerous disputes. As they did not have any kind of relations[57] with one another, they consequently knew neither vanity, nor consideration, nor esteem, nor contempt. As they had neither the slightest notion of thine and mine nor any genuine idea of justice, as they regarded any violence they might suffer as a harm easily redressed and not as an insult they had to punish, and as they did not even dream of vengeance, unless perhaps mechanically and on the spot like a dog that bites the stone thrown at it, their quarrels would seldom have led to bloodshed unless they had had a more sensitive subject than food. But I see a more dangerous subject that remains for me to discuss.

Among the passions that agitate man's heart, there is an ardent, impetuous one that makes one sex necessary for the other, a terrible passion which braves every danger, overcomes every obstacle, and which, in its fury, seems likely to

57. Or: commerce (*commerce*).

destroy the human race it is meant to preserve. What will become of men tormented by this unbridled and brutal rage, without modesty, without restraint, and daily quarrelling over their loves at the price of their blood?

It must first be agreed that the more violent the passions, the more laws are needed to contain them. But aside from the fact that the disorders and crimes they cause daily among us show clearly enough the insufficiency of laws in this regard, it would also be good to examine whether these disorders do not arise along with the laws themselves. For then, even were they capable of repressing these disorders, the very least that should be demanded of them is to stop an evil that would not exist without them.

Let us begin by distinguishing the moral from the physical in the feeling of love. The physical is that general desire that leads one sex to unite with the other. The moral is that which gives this desire its specific character and focuses it exclusively on a single object, or which at least gives it a greater degree of energy for this preferred object. Now, it is easy to see that the moral aspect of love is an artificial feeling born of social custom and extolled with much skill and care by women in order to establish their empire and to make dominant the sex that ought to obey. Since this feeling is based on certain notions of merit or beauty which a savage is not in a condition to have and on comparisons he is not capable of making, it must be almost nothing for him. For as his mind could not have formed abstract ideas of regularity and proportion, so his heart is not susceptible to the feelings of admiration and love which, even without their being noticed, arise from the application of these ideas. He heeds solely the temperament he has received from nature and not a distaste[58] he could not have acquired, and every woman is good for him.

Limited to the physical aspect of love alone, and fortunate enough to be ignorant of those preferences which enflame the feeling and increase the difficulties related to it, men must feel the ardors of the disposition less frequently and less vividly, and consequently have fewer and less cruel quarrels among themselves. Imagination, which wreaks such havoc among us, does not speak to savage hearts. Each peaceably awaits the impulse of nature, gives himself

---

58. In his corrections to his own copy of the *Discourse on Inequality* incorporated into the 1782 edition of his works, Rousseau here substituted "distaste" (*dégoût*) for "taste" (*goût*), which originally had the sentence say that natural man does not heed "a taste he could not have acquired." Rousseau's substitution, although it makes the sentence more awkward, is also more in keeping with this point that every woman is to natural man's taste ("every woman is good for him") and that only acquired "distaste" for women with certain attributes would prevent him from mating with them.

over to it without choosing with more pleasure than frenzy, and, the need satisfied, all desire is extinguished.

It is therefore indisputable that love itself, like all the other passions, has acquired only in society that impetuous ardor which so often makes it fatal to men, and it is all the more ridiculous to portray savages as continually slitting one another's throats so as to satisfy their brutality since this opinion is directly contrary to experience, and since the Caribs—which of all existing peoples has thus far moved away the least from the state of nature—are precisely the most peaceful in their loves and the least subject to jealousy, even though they live in a scorching climate, which always seems to impart a greater activity to these passions.

With regard to inferences that could be drawn, among various animal species, from the fights between males which bloody our farmyards in every season or which make our forests resound with their cries in springtime as they contend for a female, it is necessary to begin by excluding all species in which nature has manifestly established different relations concerning the relative strength of the sexes than among us. Thus cockfights do not provide an inference for the human species. In species where the proportion is more even, these fights can have as their cause only the scarcity of females in relation to the number of males or the exclusive intervals during which the female constantly refuses the male's advance, which amounts to the first cause, for if each female tolerates the male during only two months of the year, in this respect it is as though the number of females were fewer by five-sixths. Now, neither of these two cases is applicable to the human species, in which the number of females generally surpasses that of males and in which it has never been observed, even among savages, that females have periods of heat and exclusion like those of other species. Moreover, among some of these animals, since the entire species enters into a state of heat at the same time, there comes one terrible moment of common ardor, tumult, disorder, and fighting—a moment which does not take place among the human species, for whom love is never periodic. It therefore cannot be concluded from the fights of certain animals for the possession of females that the same thing would happen to man in the state of nature. And even if this conclusion could be drawn, as these dissensions do not destroy the other species, it has to be thought that they would not be any more fatal to ours, and it is very obvious that they would cause still less havoc in the state of nature than they do in society, especially in countries where, morals still counting for something, the jealousy of lovers and vengeance of husbands daily cause duels, murders, and worse yet, where the duty of eternal fidelity serves only to create adulterers, and where even the laws of continence and honor necessarily spread debauchery and multiply abortions.

Let us conclude that—wandering in the forests, without industry, without speech, without domicile, without war, and without contact, without any need of his fellow humans, likewise without any desire to harm them, perhaps without ever even recognizing anyone individually—savage man, subject to few passions and self-sufficient, had only the feelings and the enlightenment suited to that state, that he felt only his true needs, looked at only what he believed it was in his interest to see, and that his intelligence made no more progress than his vanity. If by chance he made some discovery, he was all the less able to communicate it as he did not recognize even his children. Art perished with the inventor. There was neither education nor progress; the generations multiplied uselessly. And since everyone always started at the same point, the centuries passed by in all the crudeness of the first ages; the species was already old, and man remained ever a child.

If I have elaborated at such length on the assumption of this primitive condition, it is because, having ancient errors and inveterate prejudices to destroy, I believed I had to dig down to the root and show in the portrayal of the genuine state of nature how far inequality—even natural inequality—is from having as much reality and influence in that state as our writers claim.

Indeed, it is easy to see that among the differences that distinguish men, some pass for being natural that are exclusively the work of habit and the various ways of life men adopt in society. Thus a robust or delicate temperament, and the strength or weakness which depend on it, often come more from a severe or effeminate upbringing than from the original constitution of bodies. The same is true for strength of the mind, and not only does education create the difference between cultivated minds and those which are not, but it increases the difference found among the former in proportion to their cultivation; for when a giant and a dwarf walk on the same road, every step they take will give the giant an added advantage. Now, if one compares the prodigious diversity of educations and ways of life that prevail in the different social orders of the civil state with the simplicity and uniformity of animal and savage life, in which all feed on the same foods, live in the same manner, and do exactly the same things, it will be understood how much less the difference from man to man must be in the state of nature than in that of society, and how much natural inequality in the human species must increase through instituted inequality.

But even if nature showed as much partiality in the distribution of its gifts as is claimed, what advantage would the most favored derive from them at the expense of others in a state of things which allowed for almost no kind of relationship among them? Where there is no love, of what use will beauty be? What use is wit for people who do not speak and cunning for those who have no dealings with one another? I hear it always repeatedly said that the stronger will oppress the weak, but let someone explain to me what is meant by this word "oppression." Some will dominate by violence, and the others will groan, subject to all their whims. This is precisely what I observe among us, but I do not see how this could be said of savage men, to whom it would even be very difficult to explain what servitude and domination are. A man may well seize the fruits another has picked, the game he has killed, the cave he used as shelter, but how will he ever succeed in making himself obeyed and what chains of dependence can there be among men who possess nothing? If someone chases me from one tree, I leave it to go to another. If someone harasses me in one place, who will prevent me from going elsewhere? Is there a man whose strength is superior enough to mine and who is, in addition, depraved enough, lazy enough, and fierce enough to force me to provide for his subsistence while he remains idle? He has to resolve not to lose sight of me for a single instant, to keep me very carefully tied up while he sleeps for fear that I may escape or kill him—that is, that he is obliged to willingly incur a great deal more trouble than he wishes to avoid and than he gives to me. After all that, does his vigilance relax for a moment? Does an unexpected noise make him turn his head? I take twenty steps into forest, my chains are broken, and he never sees me again in his life.

Without needlessly drawing out these details, everyone must see that, since the bonds of servitude are formed only by the mutual dependence of men and by the reciprocal needs that unite them, it is impossible to enslave a man without first having put him in the position of being unable to do without another—a situation which, since it does not exist in the state of nature, leaves everyone in it free from the yoke and renders vain the law of the stronger.

After having proved that inequality is barely perceptible in the state of nature and that its influence there is almost nonexistent, it remains for me to show its origin and its progress in the successive developments of the human mind. After having shown that *perfectibility*, the social virtues, and the other faculties natural man had received in potentiality could never develop by themselves, that to do so they needed the fortuitous concurrence of several foreign causes which might never have arisen and without which he would have eternally remained in his primitive constitution, it remains for me consider and to bring together the different chance events that were able to perfect human reason while causing the species to deteriorate, to make a being evil while making him sociable, and eventually to bring man and the world from so distant a beginning to the point where we now see them.

I admit that since the events I have to describe could have happened in several ways, I can choose among them only on the basis of conjectures. But aside from the fact that these conjectures become reasons when they are the most probable that could be drawn from the nature of things and are the only means available to discover the truth, the conclusions I want to deduce from mine will not thereby be conjectural, because, on the principles I have just established, no other system can be conceived that would provide me with the same results and from which I could draw the same conclusions.

This will excuse me from expanding my reflections about how the lapse of time compensates for the slight probability of events; about the surprising power of very trivial causes when they act without interruption; about the impossibility of eliminating certain hypotheses, on the one hand, without being in a position to give them the degree of the certainty of facts, on the other; about how, when two facts taken as real are to be connected by a series of intermediate facts which are unknown or regarded as such, it is up to history, when available, to provide the facts that connect them, and it is up to philosophy, when they are lacking, to ascertain similar facts that might connect them; finally, about how, with reference to events, similarity reduces the facts to a much smaller number of different classes than is imagined. It is enough for me to offer these objects to the consideration of my judges. It is enough for me to have made it so that vulgar readers do not need to consider them.

SECOND PART

THE FIRST PERSON WHO, having enclosed a plot of ground, thought of saying *this is mine* and found people simple enough to believe him was the true founder of civil society. What crimes, wars, murders, what miseries and horrors, would the human race have been spared by someone who, pulling up the stakes or filling in the ditch, had cried out to his fellow humans: "Beware of listening to this imposter. You are lost if you forget that the fruits are everyone's and the earth is no one's!" But in all likelihood things had already reached a point where they could no longer remain as they were. For this idea of property, depending upon many prior ideas which could have arisen only successively, was not formed all at once in the human mind. A great deal of progress had to be made, a great deal of industry and enlightenment had to be acquired, transmitted, and increased from one age to the next before reaching this end point of the state of nature. Let us therefore start further back and try to bring together from a single viewpoint this slow succession of events and of knowledge in their most natural order.

Man's first feeling was that of his existence, his first care that of his preservation. The productions of the earth provided him with all the necessary support, instinct led him to make use of it. While hunger and other appetites caused him to experience by turns various ways of existing, one of these appetites invited him to perpetuate his species, and this blind inclination, devoid of any feeling of the heart, produced only a purely animal act. The need satisfied, the two sexes no longer recognized each other, and even the child no longer meant anything to the mother as soon as he could do without her.

Such was the condition of nascent man. Such was the life of an animal limited at first to pure sensations and scarcely profiting from the gifts nature offered to him, far from dreaming of wresting anything from it. But difficulties soon presented themselves; it was necessary to learn to overcome them. The height of trees, which prevented him from reaching their fruits, the competition of animals that sought to eat these fruits, the ferocity of those that wanted to take his life—everything obliged him to apply himself to bodily exercises. He had to make himself agile, swift at running, strong in combat. Natural weapons—tree branches and stones—were soon at hand. He learned to surmount nature's obstacles, to fight other animals when necessary, even to contend with men for his subsistence or to make up for what had to be yielded to the stronger.

In proportion as the human race spread, difficulties multiplied together with men. Differences of soil, climate, season may have forced them to vary their way of life. Barren years, long and hard winters, scorching summers which consume everything, required renewed industry from them. Along the sea and rivers they invented line and hook, and they became fishermen and icthyophagous. In forests they made for themselves bows and arrows, and they became hunters and warriors. In cold countries they covered themselves with the skins of beasts they had killed. Lightning, a volcano, or some happy accident acquainted them with fire, a new resource against the rigor of winter. They learned to preserve this element, then to reproduce it, and eventually to use it to prepare meats they had previously devoured raw.

This repeated utilization of various beings in relation to himself and of some beings in relation to others must naturally have engendered perceptions of certain relations in man's mind. Those relations that we express by the words "large," "small," "strong," "weak," "fast," "slow," "fearful," "bold," and other similar ideas, compared when necessary, and almost without thinking about it, eventually produced in him reflection of a sort, or rather a mechanical prudence that indicated to him the precautions most necessary for his safety.

The new enlightenment that resulted from this development increased his superiority over the other animals by making him aware of it. He practiced setting traps for them, he tricked them in a thousand ways, and although some of them surpassed him in strength in combat or speed in running, in time he became the master of those that might serve him and the scourge of those that might harm him. This is how the first glance he directed upon himself produced in him the first movement of pride. This is how, as yet scarcely knowing how to distinguish ranks and looking upon himself as in the first rank as a species, he prepared himself from afar to claim the first rank as an individual.

Although his fellow humans were not for him what they are for us, and although he had scarcely more interactions[59] with them than with the other animals, they were not overlooked in his observations. The conformities that time may have enabled him to perceive among them, his female, and himself led him to judge those he did not perceive, and seeing that they all behaved as he would have done under similar circumstances, he concluded that their way of thinking and feeling was entirely in conformity with his own. And this important truth, firmly established in his mind, made him follow, by a premonition as sure as dialectic and more prompt, the best rules of the conduct that suited him to observe toward them for his advantage and security.

Taught by experience that love of well-being is the sole impulse for human actions, he was able to discern the rare occasions when common interest should make him count on the assistance of his fellow humans, and those even rarer ones when competition should make him distrust them. In the first case, he united with them in a herd or at most in some sort of free association that obligated no one and lasted only as long as the passing need that had formed it. In the second case, each sought to obtain his advantage, either by naked force, if he believed he could, or by cleverness and cunning, if he felt he was the weaker.

This is how men might have imperceptibly acquired some crude idea of mutual engagements and the advantage of fulfilling them, but only insofar as present and perceptible interest might require. For foresight meant nothing to them, and far from being concerned with a distant future, they did not even think of the next day. If it was a matter of catching a stag, each clearly sensed that he ought faithfully to keep to his post; but if a hare happened to pass within range of one of them, there can be no doubt that he pursued it without any scruple and that, having obtained his prey, he cared very little about having caused his companions to miss theirs.

It is easy to understand that such interactions[60] did not require a language much more refined than that of crows and monkeys, which group together in more or less the same way. Some inarticulate cries, numerous gestures, and a few imitative sounds must have for a long time made up the universal language, and by adding to this in each region a few articulated and conventional sounds—the institution of which is, as I have already said, not so easy to explain—they had particular languages, but crude, imperfect ones and more or less like those various savage nations have. I cover multitudes of centuries

---

59. Or: commerce (*commerce*).
60. Or: commerce (*commerce*).

in a flash, forced by the time that passes, the abundance of things I have to say, and the almost imperceptible progress at the outset. For the more slowly events succeeded one another, the more quickly can they be described.

These first advances eventually put man within reach of making more rapid ones. The more the mind was enlightened, the more industry was perfected. Soon ceasing to fall asleep underneath the first tree or to withdraw into caves, they found hatchets of a sort, of hard and sharp stones, which they used to chop wood, dig the earth, and make huts from branches which it later occurred to them to strengthen with clay and mud. This was the epoch of a first revolution that brought about the establishment and differentiation of families and that introduced a sort of property, from which perhaps many disputes and fights already arose. However, as the stronger were likely the first to make themselves lodgings since they felt they were capable of defending them, it is to be presumed that the weak found it simpler and safer to imitate them than to try to dislodge them. And as for those who already had huts, seldom must anyone have sought to appropriate his neighbor's, less because it did not belong to him than because it was useless to him and because he could not get hold of it without exposing himself to a very lively fight with the family that occupied it.

The first developments of the heart were the effect of a new situation that brought together husbands and wives, fathers and children, in a common dwelling. The habit of living together gave rise to the sweetest feelings known to men: conjugal love and paternal love. Each family became a little society all the better united as reciprocal attachment and freedom were its only bonds. And it was then that the first difference was established in the way of life of the two sexes, which until then had had only one. Women became more sedentary and became accustomed to looking after the hut and the children, while the men went to seek their common subsistence. The two sexes also began to lose something of their ferocity and their vigor through their somewhat softer life. But if any one of them separately became less fit to fight savage beasts, in turn it was easier to assemble in order to resist in common.

In this new state, with a simple and solitary life, very limited needs, and the implements they had invented to provide for them, men enjoyed a great deal of leisure which they used to procure several sorts of conveniences unknown to their fathers. And this was the first yoke they imposed on themselves without thinking about it and the first source of the evils they prepared for their descendants. For, aside from the fact that they thereby continued to soften both body and mind, since these conveniences lost almost all of their charm through habit, and since they had at the same time degenerated into true needs, being deprived of them became much more cruel than their possession was sweet, and they were unhappy to lose them without being happy to possess them.

Here one catches a slightly better glimpse of how the use of speech is established or is imperceptibly perfected in the bosom of each family, and it can be further conjectured how various particular causes might enlarge the language and accelerate its progress by making it more necessary. Great floods or earthquakes surrounded inhabited districts with water or precipices. Revolutions of the globe detached and broke up portions of the continent into islands. It seems conceivable that a common idiom must have formed sooner among men brought together in this way, and forced to live together, than among those who wandered freely in the forests on the mainland. Thus it is quite possible that islanders, after their first attempts at navigation, brought the use of speech to us, and it is at least quite likely that society and languages came into being on islands and were perfected there before they were known on the continent.

Everything begins to change appearance. Men, who until this point wandered in the woods, having now adopted a more fixed settlement, slowly come together, unite in different bands, and eventually form in each region a particular nation unified in terms of morals and character—not by rules and laws, but by the same type of life and of foods and by the common influence of the climate. A permanent proximity cannot fail eventually to give rise to some sort of connection between different families. With young people of different sexes inhabiting neighboring huts, the intermittent interactions[61] demanded by nature soon lead to another kind, no less sweet and more permanent through visiting one another. They grow accustomed to consider different objects and to make comparisons. They imperceptibly acquire ideas of merit and beauty that produce sentiments of preference. By dint of seeing one another, they can no longer do without seeing one another again. A tender and gentle feeling insinuates itself into the soul and becomes an impetuous fury at the least opposition. Jealousy awakens along with love; discord triumphs, and the gentlest of the passions receives sacrifices of human blood.

In proportion as ideas and feelings succeed one another, as mind and heart are trained, the human race continues to be tamed, contacts spread and bonds draw tighter. They grew accustomed to assemble in front of their huts or around a large tree. Song and dance, true children of love and leisure, became

---

61. Or: commerce (*commerce*).

the amusement or rather the occupation of idle men and women gathered together. Each began to look at the others and to want to be looked at himself, and public esteem had a value. The one who sang or danced the best, the most beautiful, the strongest, the most clever, or the most eloquent became the most highly considered—and this, then, was the first step toward inequality and at the same time toward vice. From these first preferences arose vanity and contempt, on the one hand, and shame and envy, on the other. And the fermentation caused by these new leavens eventually produced compounds fatal to happiness and innocence.

As soon as men had begun to make assessments of one another and the idea of esteem was formed in their minds, each claimed a right to it, and it was no longer possible for anyone to deprive anyone of it with impunity. From this came the first duties of civility, even among savages, and from this any intentional wrong became an affront because, along with the harm that resulted from the injury, the offended person saw in it contempt for his person often more unbearable than the harm itself. This is how, with everyone punishing the contempt shown him in a manner proportioned to the importance he accorded himself, vengeance became terrible and men became bloodthirsty and cruel. This was precisely the stage reached by most of the savage peoples known to us. And it is for want of sufficiently distinguishing among ideas, and noticing how far distant these peoples already were from the first state of nature, that some have hastened to conclude that man is naturally cruel and that he needs civilizing to make him gentle, whereas nothing is as gentle as man in his primitive state, when—placed by nature at equal distances from the stupidity of brutes and the fatal enlightenment of civil man, and limited by instinct and by reason alike to protecting himself from the harm that threatens him—he is restrained by natural pity from doing harm to anyone, as nothing provokes him into doing so himself, even after he himself has been harmed. For, according to the maxim of the wise Locke, *where there is no property, there can be no injury.*[62]

But it must be noted that budding society and the relations already established among men required from them qualities different than those they derived from their primitive constitution; that, since morality began to be introduced into human actions, and since before there were laws each was the sole judge and avenger of the offenses he had received, the goodness suitable to

---

62. Locke, *An Essay Concerning Human Understanding* (1690), 4.3.18. Rousseau uses "injury" where Locke (and also his translator into French) had written "injustice."

the pure state of nature was no longer that which suited nascent society; that punishments had to become more severe in proportion as the occasions for offense became more frequent, and that it was up to the terror of revenge to take the place of the restraint of laws. Thus, although men had become less hardy and although natural pity had already undergone some alteration, this period of the development of human faculties, occupying a golden mean between the indolence of the primitive state and the petulant activity of our pride,[63] must have been the happiest and most durable epoch. The more one reflects on it, the more one finds that this state was the least subject to revolutions, the best for man (XVI [p. 147]), and that he must have left it only by some fatal accident which for the sake of the common utility ought never to have happened. The example of savages, almost all of whom are found at this point, seems to confirm that the human race was made to remain in it forever, that this state is the veritable youth of the world, and that all subsequent progress has been in appearance so many steps toward the perfection of the individual, and in fact toward the decrepitude of the species.

As long as men were content with their rustic huts, as long as they limited themselves to sewing their clothing of skins with thorns and fish bones, adorning themselves with feathers and shells, painting their bodies with various colors, perfecting or embellishing their bows and arrows, carving a few fishermen's canoes or making a few crude musical instruments with sharp stones—in a word, as long as they applied themselves only to tasks a single person could do and only to arts that did not require the cooperation of several hands, they lived free, healthy, good, and happy insofar as they could be by their nature, and continued to enjoy the sweet pleasures of independent interactions[64] with one another. But from the moment that one man needed the help of another, as soon as they perceived it was useful for a single person to have provisions for two, equality disappeared, property was introduced, labor became necessary, and vast forests were changed into smiling fields which had to be watered by the sweat of men and in which slavery and misery were soon seen to sprout and grow together with the harvest.

Metallurgy and agriculture were the two arts whose invention produced this great revolution. For the poet it is gold and silver, but for the philosopher it is iron and grain that have civilized men and ruined the human race. Accordingly, both of them were unknown to the savages of America, who for

---

63. "Pride" here translates *amour-propre.*
64. Or: commerce (*commerce*).

this reason have always remained savage. Other peoples even seem to have remained barbarous as long as they had practiced one of these arts without the other. And perhaps one of the chief reasons why Europe has been civilized, if not earlier then at least more continuously and more so than other parts of the world, is that it is at the same time the most abundant in iron and the most fertile in wheat.

It is very difficult to conjecture how men came to be acquainted with and to use iron, for it is not credible that all by themselves they imagined extracting ore from the mine and making the necessary preparations to smelt it before knowing what would result from doing so. From another point of view, this discovery can be even less attributed to some accidental fire, since mines are formed only in arid places bare of trees and plants, so that it might be said that nature had taken precautions to conceal this deadly secret from us. There remains, then, only the extraordinary circumstance of some volcano which, vomiting its metallic materials in melted form, will have given observers the idea of imitating this operation of nature. Even so, they must be assumed to have had a great deal of courage and foresight to undertake such a difficult labor and to envisage so far in advance the advantages they could derive from it—something that is hardly even suited to minds already more trained than theirs must have been.

As for agriculture, its principle was known long before its practice was established, and it hardly seems possible that men continually occupied with drawing their subsistence from trees and plants would not soon enough have an idea of the means nature uses for the generation of plants. But their industry probably turned in that direction only rather late, either because the trees, which along with hunting and fishing furnished their food, did not require their care, or for want of knowing how to use wheat, or for want of implements with which to cultivate it, or for want of foresight concerning future need, or, finally, for want of means to prevent others from appropriating the fruit of their labor. Once they had become more industrious, it can be conjectured that, using sharp rocks and sharpened sticks, they began by cultivating some vegetables or roots around their huts, long before knowing how to prepare wheat and before having the necessary implements for large-scale cultivation, without taking account of the fact that in order to devote themselves to this occupation and to sow the land, they had to resolve to lose something initially in order to gain a great deal later—a precaution rather far from the turn of mind of savage man, who, as I have said, has great difficulty thinking in the morning of his needs for the evening.

The invention of the other arts was therefore necessary to force the human race to apply itself to the art of agriculture. As soon as some men were needed to smelt and forge iron, other men were needed to feed them. The more the number of workers increased, the fewer hands there were to provide the common subsistence without there being fewer mouths to consume it, and as some needed foodstuffs to exchange for their iron, others eventually found the secret of using iron to increase foodstuffs. From this arose plowing and agriculture on the one hand, and the art of working metals and of multiplying their uses on the other.

From the cultivation of the land its division necessarily followed, and from property, once it was recognized, the first rules of justice. For in order to render unto each his own, each person has to be able to have something. Moreover, as men began to look to the future and as they all saw they had some goods to lose, there was not a single one of them who did not have to fear reprisals against himself for the wrongs he might do to others. This origin is all the more natural as it is impossible to conceive the idea of nascent property arising from anything except manual labor, for it is not clear what a man can add, other than his labor, in order to appropriate things he has not made. It is labor alone that, giving to the cultivator a right to the product of the land he has worked, consequently gives him a right to the soil, at least until the harvest, and thus from one year to the next, which, since it constitutes a continuous possession, is easily transformed into property. When the ancients, says Grotius, gave Ceres the epithet of legislatrix and gave the name Thesmophoria to a festival celebrated in her honor, they thereby made it clear that the division of land produced a new sort of right—that is, the right of property, different from the one that follows from natural law.[65]

Things in this state might have remained equal if talents had been equal, and if, for example, the use of iron and the consumption of foodstuffs had always been exactly balanced. But the proportion, which nothing maintained, was soon upset. The stronger did more work, the more clever turned his work to better advantage, the more ingenious found ways to reduce his labor; the farmer needed more iron or the blacksmith more wheat; and, even though they worked equally, one person earned a great deal while another had difficulty staying alive. This is how natural inequality imperceptibly unfolds together with contrived inequality and how differences among men, developed

---

65. Grotius, *Rights of War and Peace* (1625), 2.2.2, vol. 2:427. The Thesmophoria was an ancient Greek festival held in honor of the goddess Demeter (or Ceres in Latin) and her daughter Persephone.

by their different circumstances, make themselves more perceptible, more permanent in their effects, and begin to have a proportionate influence on the fate of individuals.

Things having reached this point, it is easy to imagine the rest. I will not pause to describe the successive development of the other arts, the progress of languages, the testing and application of talents, the inequality of fortunes, the use or abuse of wealth, or all the details that follow from them and that everyone can easily supply. I will limit myself simply to casting a glance at the human race placed in this new order of things.

Here, then, are all our faculties developed, memory and imagination in play, pride[66] involved, reason activated, and the mind having almost reached the extent of the perfection of which it is susceptible. Here are all the natural qualities set in action, the rank and fate of each man based not only on the quantity of goods and the power to help or to harm, but on the mind, beauty, strength, or skill, on merit or talents. And since these qualities are the only ones that could attract consideration, it was soon necessary to have them or to affect them. For one's advantage, it was necessary to appear to be different from what one in fact was. To be and to appear to be became two entirely different things, and from this distinction came ostentatious display, deceitful cunning, and all the vices that follow in their wake. From another point of view, having previously been free and independent, here is man, subjected, so to speak, by a multitude of new needs to all of nature and especially to his fellow humans, whose slave he in a sense becomes even in becoming their master. Rich, he needs their services; poor, he needs their help, and being in a middling condition does not enable him to do without them. He therefore constantly has to seek to interest them in his fate and to make them find their own advantage, in reality or appearance, in working for his. This makes him deceitful, treacherous, and artful with some, imperious and harsh with others, and makes it necessary for him to mislead all those he needs when he cannot get them to fear him and when he does not find it in his interest to make himself useful to them. Finally, consuming ambition, the ardor to raise one's relative fortune, less out of genuine need than in order to place oneself above others, inspires in all men a dark inclination to harm one another, a secret jealousy all the more dangerous as it often assumes the mask of benevolence in order to strike its blows more surely. In a word, competition and rivalry on

---

66. "Pride" here translates *amour-propre*.

the one side, opposition of interests on the other, and always the hidden desire to profit at the expense of others. All these evils are the first effect of property and follow inevitably in the wake of nascent inequality.

Before representative signs of wealth were invented, it could hardly consist of anything except land and livestock, the only real goods men can possess. Now, once inheritances had accumulated in number and extent to the point of covering all the land and them all bordering one another, none of them could be enlarged any longer except at the expense of the others, and those who were left out, whom weakness or indolence had prevented from acquiring an inheritance, having in their turn become poor without having lost anything—because as everything changed around them, they alone did not change—were obliged to receive or steal their subsistence from the hands of the rich, and from this—in accordance with the different characters of the rich and the poor—domination and servitude, or violence and plunder, began to arise. The rich, for their part, had scarcely experienced the pleasure of dominating than they soon disdained all other pleasures, and using their old slaves to subdue new ones, they thought only of subjugating and enslaving their neighbors—like those ravenous wolves which having once tasted human flesh refuse all other food and no longer want to devour anything but men.

This is how, with the most powerful or the most miserable having made of their strength or their needs a sort of right to another's goods—equivalent, according to them, to the right of property—the breakdown of equality was followed by the most frightful disorder. This is how the usurpations of the rich, the brigandage of the poor, the unbridled passions of all, stifling natural pity and the as yet weak voice of justice, made men greedy, ambitious, and evil. A perpetual conflict arose between the right of the stronger and the right of the first occupant which ended only in fights and murders (XVII [p. 149]). Nascent society gave way to the most horrible state of war. The human race, debased and dispirited, no longer able to retrace its steps, or renounce the unhappy acquisitions it had made, and working only toward its shame by the abuse of the faculties that do it honor, brought itself to the brink of its ruin.

Shocked by the novelty of the evil, both rich and wretched,
He flees his wealth, and hates what he once prayed for.[67]

---

67. Ovid *Metamorphoses* 11.127–28, quoted by Rousseau in Latin: *Attonitus novitate mali, divesque miserque, / Effugere optat opes, et quae modo voverat, odit.* The passage describes Midas after having been granted his wish that everything he touches be turned into gold.

It is not possible that men would not have eventually reflected on such a miserable situation and on the calamities with which they were overwhelmed. The rich above all must have soon sensed how disadvantageous to them was a perpetual war in which they alone paid all the costs and in which the risk to life was common to all, while the risk to goods was theirs alone. Besides, regardless of what gloss they might put on their usurpations, they were sufficiently aware that they were established merely on a precarious and abusive right and that, having been acquired only by force, force could take it away from them without their having any reason to complain about it. Even those who industry alone had enriched could scarcely base their property on better titles. They could well say: "It is I who built this wall; I earned this plot by my labor." "Who gave you its dimensions?" it might be responded to them, "And by virtue of what do you lay claim to be paid at our expense for work we have not imposed on you? Don't you know that a great many of your brethren perish or suffer from need of what you have in excess, and that you had to have express and unanimous consent of the human race to appropriate for yourself anything from the common subsistence above and beyond your own?" Devoid of valid reasons to justify himself and sufficient force to defend himself; easily crushing an individual, but himself crushed by gangs of bandits; alone against all, not being able due to mutual jealousy to unite with his equals against enemies united by the common hope of plunder, the rich man, pressed by necessity, finally conceived the most carefully considered project that ever entered the human mind. It was to use the very strength of those who attacked him in his favor, to make his defenders out of his adversaries, to instill different maxims in them, and to give them different institutions that were as favorable to him as natural right was adverse to him.

With this in mind, after having shown his neighbors the horror of a situation that made them all take up arms against one another, that made their possessions as burdensome as their needs, and in which no one found safety in either poverty or wealth, he easily invented specious reasons to lead them to his goal. "Let us unite," he tells them, "to protect the weak from oppression, restrain the ambitious, and secure for each the possession of what belongs to him. Let us institute rules of justice and peace to which all are obliged to conform, which make no exception for anyone, and which compensate, as it were, for the whims of fortune by subjecting the powerful and the weak alike to mutual duties. In a word, instead of turning our forces against ourselves, let us gather them together into a supreme power that governs us according to wise laws, that protects and defends all the members of the association, repulses common enemies, and maintains everlasting concord among us."

Much less than the equivalent of this discourse was needed to sway crude, easily seduced men, who, moreover, had too many disputes to straighten out amongst themselves to be able to do without arbiters, and too much greed and ambition to be able to do without masters for long. All ran toward their chains, believing they were securing their freedom, for while they had enough reason to sense the advantages of a political establishment, they did not have enough experience to foresee its dangers. Those most capable of anticipating the abuses were precisely those who counted on profiting from them, and even the wise saw that they had to resolve to sacrifice one part of their freedom for the preservation of the other, just as a wounded man has his arm cut off to save the rest of his body.

Such was, or must have been, the origin of society and of laws, which gave new fetters to the weak man and new forces to the rich man (XVIII [p. 150]), irreversibly destroyed natural freedom, forever established the law of property and of inequality, made an irrevocable right out of a clever usurpation, and henceforth subjected the entire human race to labor, servitude, and misery for the profit of a few ambitious people. It is easy to see how the establishment of a single society makes the establishment of all the others indispensible, and how, in order to face united forces, it was necessary to unite in turn. Societies, multiplying or expanding rapidly, soon covered the entire face of the earth, and it was no longer possible to find a single corner in the universe where one could free oneself from the yoke and withdraw one's head from beneath the often poorly guided sword each man saw perpetually suspended over it. Civil right having thus become the common rule of citizens, the law of nature no longer held except between different societies, where, under the name of right of nations, it was tempered by a few tacit conventions to make relations[68] possible and to take the place of natural commiseration, which, losing nearly all of the strength between one society and another that it had between one man and another, no longer resides in any but a few great cosmopolitan souls who surmount the imaginary barriers that separate peoples and who, following the example of the sovereign being that created them, embrace the entire human race in their benevolence.

Political bodies, thus remaining in the state of nature among themselves, felt the effect of the inconveniences that had forced individuals to leave it, and this

---

68. Or: commerce (*commerce*).

state became still more deadly among these great bodies than it had previously been among the individuals of which they were composed. From this arose the national wars, battles, murders, reprisals which make nature tremble and shock reason, and all those horrible prejudices which rank the honor of shedding human blood among the virtues. The most decent men learned to count among their duties that of slitting the throats of their fellow human beings. Men were eventually seen massacring one another by the thousands without knowing why; and more murders were committed in a single day of fighting and more horrors in the taking of a single city than had been committed in the state of nature during whole centuries over the entire face of the earth. Such are the first effects one glimpses of the division of the human race into different societies. Let us return to their institution.

I know that some have attributed other origins to political societies, such as the conquests of the more powerful or the union of the weak, and the choice between these causes does not make any difference for what I want to establish. However, the one I have just presented appears to me to be the most natural for the following reasons. (1) That, in the first case, since the right of the conqueror is not a right, it could not have served as the basis of any other right, for the conqueror and the conquered peoples always remain in a state of war with one another, unless the nation, given back its complete freedom, voluntarily chooses the victor as its leader. Until then, whatever the terms of capitulation were, as they were based only on violence and as they are consequently null and void by that very fact, based on this hypothesis there can be neither genuine society, nor body politic, nor any other law than that of the stronger. (2) That, in the second case, these words *strong* and *weak* are equivocal, since, during the interval between the establishment of the right of property or of the first occupant and that of political governments, the meaning of these terms is better expressed by *poor* and *rich* since, in fact, before the laws a man did not have any other means of subjecting his equals than by attacking their goods or by giving them a portion of his own. (3) That, since the poor have nothing to lose except their freedom, it would have been a very foolish act for them to give away voluntarily the sole good remaining to them without getting anything in exchange. That, on the contrary, since the rich were, so to speak, sensitive in every part of their goods, it was much easier to harm them; they consequently had more precautions to take to protect themselves from harm. And that, finally, it is reasonable to believe that a thing was invented by those for whom it is useful rather than by those it does harm.

Nascent government did not have a constant and regular form. The lack of philosophy and experience allowed only present inconveniences to be perceived, and they thought of remedying others only as they came to light. Despite all the labors of the wisest lawgivers, the political state remained ever imperfect because it was almost the work of chance and because, having begun badly, time revealed the defects and suggested some remedies but could never repair the vices of the constitution. They continually patched it whereas it would have been necessary to begin by sweeping the area clean and throwing away all the old materials, as Lycurgus did in Sparta, in order then to raise a good edifice. Society at first consisted only of a few general conventions which all individuals pledged to observe and of which the community was made the guarantor toward each of them. Experience must have shown how weak such a constitution was, and how easy it was for lawbreakers to avoid conviction or punishment for misdeeds of which the public alone was to be both witness and judge. The law must have been evaded in a thousand ways, inconveniences and disorders must have continually multiplied before it finally occurred to them to entrust private individuals with the dangerous trust of public authority and to commit to magistrates the task of making sure that the people's deliberations were observed. For to say that the leaders were chosen before the confederation was established, and that the ministers of the laws existed before the laws themselves, is a supposition that does not permit of serious debate.

It would be no more reasonable to believe that peoples first threw themselves unconditionally and irrevocably into the arms of an absolute master and that the first means of providing for the common security imagined by proud and untamed men was to rush headlong into slavery. Indeed, why did they give themselves superiors if not to defend themselves against oppression and to protect their goods, their freedoms, and their lives, which are, so to speak, the constituent elements of their being? Now, since the worst thing that can happen in the relations between one man and another is for one of them to find himself at the other's discretion, would it not have been contrary to good sense to begin by surrendering into the hands of a leader the only things they needed his help to preserve? What equivalent could he have offered them for the concession of so fine a right? And, if he had dared to require it under pretext of defending them, would he not straightaway have received the answer of the fable: What more will the enemy do to us? It is therefore incontestable, and it is the fundamental maxim of all political right, that peoples have given themselves leaders to defend their freedom and not to enslave them. *If we have a prince*, said Pliny to Trajan, *it is so that he may preserve us from having a master.*[69]

Our politicians[70] offer the same sophisms about love of freedom as our philosophers do about the state of nature. On the basis of the things they see, they make judgments about very different things that they have not seen, and they attribute a natural inclination to servitude to men due to the patience with which those they have before their eyes bear theirs, without considering that it is the same for freedom as for innocence and virtue, whose value is felt only as long as one enjoys them oneself and the taste for which is lost as soon as they have been lost. I know the delights of your country, said Brasidas to a satrap who compared the life of Sparta to that of Persepolis, but you cannot know the pleasures of mine.[71]

As an untamed steed bristles his mane, stomps the ground with its hoof, and struggles impetuously at the very approach of the bit, whereas a trained horse patiently endures whip and spur, so barbarous man does not bend his head for the yoke civilized man wears without a murmur, and he prefers the most turbulent freedom to a tranquil subjection. Man's natural dispositions for or against servitude therefore have to be judged not by the degradation of enslaved peoples but by the prodigious deeds performed by all free peoples to protect themselves from oppression. I know that the former do nothing but incessantly boast of the tranquility they enjoy in their chains, and that *they call the most miserable servitude peace.*[72] But when I see the latter sacrifice pleasures, tranquility, wealth, power, and life itself for the preservation of this sole good, so disdained by those who have lost it; when I see animals born free and abhorring captivity break their heads against the bars of their prison; when I see large numbers of completely naked savages despise European voluptuousness and brave hunger, fire, the sword, and death to preserve nothing but their independence, I feel that it does not befit slaves to reason about freedom.

With regard to paternal authority, from which some have derived absolute

---

69. Pliny the Younger (61–c. 112), was a leading politician under the Emperor Trajan. See his *Panegyricus* 55.7.

70. "Politicians" translates *politiques*, which can refer to either political actors of various kinds, including political leaders or political thinkers.

71. Rousseau paraphrases Herodotus (*Histories* 7.134–35), who relates the answer of the Spartan emissaries Sperthias and Bulis—not the Spartan general Brasidas—to the Persian satrap Hydarnes after being asked why they refused to become subjects of the Persian king.

72. Tacitus *Histories* 4.17, quoted by Rousseau in Latin: *miserrimam servitutem pacem appelant*. The passage comes in Tacitus' description of Gaius Julius Civilis' attempt in AD 69 to incite his fellow Gauls to revolt against Roman rule. Rousseau's follows Algernon Sidney's version as cited in his *Discourses Concerning Government* (published 1698), 2.15, p. 160.

government and society as a whole, without having recourse to the proofs of Locke and Sidney to the contrary,[73] it suffices to note that nothing in the world is farther from the ferocious spirit of despotism than the gentleness of this authority, which looks more to the advantage of the one who obeys than to the utility of the one who commands; that by the law of nature the father is master of the child only as long as his help is necessary to him, that beyond this point they become equals, and then the son, being perfectly independent of the father, owes him only respect and not obedience, for gratitude is indeed a duty that must be fulfilled, but not a right that can be required. Instead of saying that civil society derives from paternal power, on the contrary it must be said that this power draws its principal force from civil society. An individual was recognized as the father of many only when they stayed assembled around him. The father's goods, of which he is truly the master, are the bonds which keep his children dependent on him, and he can choose to give them no more of a share of his estate than is proportionate to how well they deserved it from him by continual deference to his wishes. Now, far from subjects having any similar favor to expect from their despot, as they and everything they possess belong exclusively to him—or at least so he claims—they are reduced to receiving as a favor what he leaves them of their own goods. He dispenses justice when he despoils them; he dispenses grace when he lets them live.

Continuing in this way to examine the facts in light of right, one would find no more solidity than truth in the argument for the voluntary establishment of tyranny, and it would be difficult to show the validity of a contract that obligated only one of the parties, in which one side was granted everything and the other nothing, and that would work only to the disadvantage of the person who engaged himself. This odious system is quite far from being, even today, that of wise and good monarchs, and especially of the kings of France, as can be seen in various places in their edicts and particularly in the following passage from a famous writing, published in 1667 in the name and by the orders of Louis XIV. *Let it therefore not be said that the sovereign is not subject to the laws of his state, since the contrary proposition is a truth of the right of nations, which flattery has sometimes attacked, but which good princes have always defended as a tutelary divinity of their states. How much more legitimate it is to say with the wise*

73. See Locke, *First Treatise of Government*, in general, and also *Second Treatise of Government* (1690), chap. 6; and Sidney, *Discourses Concerning Government* (1698), 1.7–8, pp. 27–30. Both Locke and Sidney opposed Sir Robert Filmer's patriarchal theory of the origin and transmission of political power through paternal authority as contained in his *Patriarcha* (composed in the 1630s or 1640s and published in 1680). See also Rousseau, *Social Contract*, I.2.

Plato for the perfect felicity of a kingdom is that a prince be obeyed by his subjects, that the prince obey the laws, and that the law be right[74] *and always directed to the public good.*[75] I will not pause to investigate whether, since freedom is the most noble of man's faculties, it is not debasing one's nature, lowering oneself to the level of the beasts enslaved by instinct, even offending the author of one's being, to renounce unconditionally the most precious of all his gifts, to subject oneself to committing all the crimes he forbids us, in order to try to please a ferocious or mad master, and whether this sublime workman must be more irritated at seeing his finest work destroyed than at seeing it dishonored. I will disregard, if one wishes, the authority of Barbeyrac, who explicitly declares, following Locke, that no one may sell his freedom to the point of subjecting himself to an arbitrary power which treats him according to its fancy. *For*, he adds, *that would be to sell one's own life, of which one is not the master.*[76] I will only ask: by what right those who have not been afraid to debase themselves to this point could subject their posterity to the same ignominy, and to renounce on its behalf goods which do not depend on their liberality, and without which life itself is burdensome to all those who are worthy of it?

Pufendorf states that just as one transfers one's goods to another by conventions and contracts, so too can one divest oneself of one's freedom in favor of someone else.[77] This, it seems to me, is a very bad argument. For, first, the good I alienate becomes something altogether foreign to me, and its abuse is indifferent to me; but it is important to me that my freedom not be abused, and I cannot risk becoming the instrument of crime without making myself guilty of the evil I will be forced to do. Moreover, since the right of property is only by convention and human institution, every man can dispose of what he possesses as he pleases; but it is not the same for the essential gifts of nature, such as life and freedom, which each man is allowed to enjoy and of which it is at least doubtful that he has the right to divest himself. By depriving himself of the one, he debases his being; by depriving himself of the other, he destroys it

---

74. "Right" translates *droit*. The sense of *droit* in this usage is that the law is "upright" or "sound."

75. This passage comes from the 1667 *Treatise on the Very Christian Queen to Various States of the Spanish Monarchy* (*Traité des droits de la reine très chrétienne sur divers états de la monarchie d'Espagne*), which was an attempt to justify Louis XIV's claim to the Spanish Netherlands and other lands, a claim that served as the basis for the 1667–68 War of Devolution. Given the context, Rousseau's claim about "wise and good monarchs" rejecting the "odious system" of voluntary tyranny is meant ironically.

76. Jean Barbeyrac makes this statement in his notes to the 1712 edition of his translation and edition of Pufendorf, *De jure naturae et gentium* (1672), 7.8.6 n. 2. For Locke's statement, see *Second Treatise of Government* (1690), 4.23.

77. Pufendorf, *De jure naturae et gentium* (1672), 7.8.1 and 6.5.

insofar as he possibly can. And as no temporal good can compensate for either, to renounce it at any price whatsoever would be simultaneously to offend nature and reason. But even if one were able to alienate one's freedom like one's goods, the case would be very different with regard to children, who enjoy the father's goods only by transmission of his right, whereas since freedom is a gift they have by nature in their capacity as men, their parents had no right to divest them of it. As a result, just as violence had to be done to nature to establish slavery, so nature had to be changed to perpetuate this right. And the jurists who have gravely pronounced that the child of a slave would be born a slave have in other terms decided that a man would not be born a man.

It therefore appears certain to me not only that governments did not begin through arbitrary power—which is only their corruption and extreme limit, and which in the end brings them back to the sole law of the stronger for which they were initially the remedy—but also that, even were they to have begun in this way, since this power is by its nature illegitimate, it could not have served as the foundation for the rights of society or consequently for instituted inequality.

Without entering at present into the research that still remains to be done regarding the nature of the fundamental pact of all government, I limit myself, following common opinion, to considering the establishment of the body politic as a genuine contract between the people and the leaders it chooses for itself—a contract by which the two parties obligate themselves to observe the laws stipulated in it and which form the bonds of their union.[78] Since the people have, with regard to social relations, united all their wills into a single one, all the articles about which this will is explicit become so many fundamental laws which obligate all the members of the state without exception, and one of these laws regulates the selection and power of the magistrates charged with attending to the execution of the others. This power extends to everything that can maintain the constitution without going so far as to change it. To it are joined honors which make the laws and their ministers respectable and, for the ministers personally, prerogatives which compensate them for the difficult labors good administration demands. The magistrate, for his part, obligates

---

78. Note that Rousseau states here that he is following the "common opinion" concerning the establishment of the body politic either through a primary contract between the people and the government or through a "double contract" where first the body politic is established by a contract among individuals and then the government is established by a contract between the people and the government. Locke's political theory would be a prominent example of the latter variety. Rousseau explicitly rejects this theory in the *Social Contract* (III.16–17).

himself to use the power confided to him solely in accordance with the intention of those granting it, to maintain for each person the peaceful enjoyment of what belongs to him, and to prefer on every occasion the public utility to his own interest.

Before experience had shown, or knowledge of the human heart had enabled men to foresee, the inevitable abuses of such a constitution, it must have appeared all the better as those charged with attending to its preservation themselves had the greatest interest in its being preserved. For since the magistracy and its rights are established only on the fundamental laws, as soon as these laws are destroyed the magistrates would cease to be legitimate, the people would no longer be bound to obey them, and as it was not the magistrate but rather the law which constituted the essence of the state, each would by right return to his natural freedom.

With even the slightest careful reflection, this would be confirmed by additional reasons and it would be evident from the nature of the contract that it could not be irrevocable. For if there were no superior power which could be the guarantor of the fidelity of the contracting parties, or force them to fulfill their reciprocal engagements, the parties would remain sole judges in their own cause, and each of them would always have the right to renounce the contract as soon as it found that the other broke its conditions, or as soon as the conditions ceased to suit it. This is the principle on which it seems that the right to abdicate can be founded. Now, considering, as we are doing, only what is of human institution, if the magistrate who has all the power in his hands and who appropriates all the advantages of the contract for himself nonetheless had the right to renounce his authority, there is all the more reason that the people, which pays for all the leaders' failings, should have the right to renounce its dependence. But the frightful dissensions, the infinite disorders which this dangerous power would necessarily entail, show more than anything else how much human governments needed a basis more solid than reason alone, and how necessary it was for public tranquility that the divine will intervene in order to give the sovereign authority a sacred and inviolable character which deprives subjects of the fatal right to do as they like with it. Even if religion had done only this good for men, this would be enough to oblige them all to cherish and adopt it, even with its abuses, because it spares even more blood than fanaticism causes to be shed. But let us follow the thread of our hypothesis.

The different forms of government derive their origin from the greater or lesser differences found among individuals at the time of institution. Was one man preeminent in power, virtue, wealth, or prestige? He alone was elected magistrate, and the state became monarchical. If several who were more or less equal to one another surpassed all the others, they were jointly elected, and there was an aristocracy. Those whose fortune or talents were less disproportionate, and who were the least distant from the state of nature, retained the supreme administration in common, and they formed a democracy. Time verified which of these forms was the most advantageous to men. Some remained solely subject to laws, others soon obeyed masters. Citizens wanted to retain their freedom, subjects thought only of depriving their neighbors of theirs, since it was unbearable to them that others should enjoy a good they themselves no longer enjoyed. In a word, on the one side were wealth and conquests, on the other happiness and virtue.

In these various governments all magistracies were initially elective, and when wealth did not prevail, preference was accorded to merit, which confers a natural ascendency, and to age, which confers experience in doing business and composure in deliberations. The elders of the Hebrews, the Gerontes of Sparta, the Senate of Rome, and the very etymology of our word *Seigneur* shows how respected old age formerly was. The more elections fell to men advanced in age, the more frequent they became and the more their difficulties made themselves felt. Intrigues were introduced, factions formed, parties grew bitter, civil wars broke out, and eventually the blood of citizens was sacrificed to the supposed happiness of the state, and they were on the verge of falling back into the anarchy of former times. The ambition of the most preeminent made the most of these circumstances to perpetuate their offices within their families. The people—already accustomed to dependence, tranquility, and the conveniences of life, and already incapable of breaking its chains—consented to allow its servitude in order to assure its tranquility. And this is how leaders, having become hereditary, grew accustomed to regard their magistracy as a family possession, to regard themselves as the owners of the state of which they were at first merely the officers, to call their fellow citizens their slaves, to count them like cattle among the number of things that belonged to them, and to call themselves the equals of the gods and the kings of kings.

If we follow the progress of inequality in these different revolutions, we will find that the first revolution culminates in the establishment of the law and the right of property, the second in the institution of the magistracy, and that the third and last was the changing of legitimate power into arbitrary power. As a result, the status of rich and poor was authorized by the first epoch, that of powerful and weak by the second, and by the third that of master and slave, which is the utmost degree of inequality and the one in which all the others eventually culminate, until new revolutions either dissolve the government entirely or bring it closer to a legitimate founding.

To understand the necessity of this progress, one must consider less the motives for the establishment of the body politic than the form it takes in its implementation and the inconveniences which follow from it. For the vices that make social institutions necessary are the same ones that make their abuse inevitable. And as—with the sole exception of Sparta, where the law looked primarily to the education of children and where Lycurgus established morals that almost enabled him to dispense with adding laws—laws, in general less strong than the passions, restrain men without changing them, it would be easy to prove that any government which, without being corrupted or altered, always worked exactly according to the end for which it had been instituted would have been instituted unnecessarily, and that a country where no one eluded the laws and abused the magistracy would need neither magistrates nor laws.

Political distinctions necessarily bring about civil distinctions. Growing inequality between the people and its leaders soon makes itself felt among private individuals and is modified among them in a thousand ways according to passions, talents, and circumstances. The magistrate could not usurp power illegitimately without creating some minions to whom he is forced to cede some share of it. Furthermore, citizens let themselves be oppressed only insofar as, being carried away by blind ambition, and looking more beneath than above themselves, domination becomes more precious to them than independence, and they consent to bear chains so that they in their turn can give them to others. It is very difficult to reduce to obedience someone who does not seek to command, and the cleverest politician would never succeed in subjecting men who wished only to be free. But inequality spreads without difficulty among ambitious and cowardly souls, always ready to run the risks of fortune and almost indifferent to whether they dominate or serve, depending on whether fortune becomes favorable or adverse to them. This is how the time must have come when the eyes of the people were so bedazzled that their overseers had only to say to the least significant of men, "Be great, you and your lineage," and he immediately appeared great to everyone as well as in his own eyes, and his descendents were exalted still further in proportion to their distance from him. The more remote and uncertain the cause, the more the effect increased; the more idlers that could be counted in a family, the more illustrious it became.

If this were the place to go into details, I would easily explain how, even without the government becoming involved, inequality of prestige and authority becomes inevitable among private individuals (XIX [p. 150]) as soon as, being united in the same society, they are forced to make comparisons among themselves and to take account of the differences they discover in the continual use they have to make of one another. These differences are of several types, but since wealth, nobility or rank, power, and personal merit are generally the principal distinctions by which one is measured in society, I would prove that the agreement or conflict among these various forces is the surest indication of a well or badly constituted state. I would show that of these four sorts of inequality, since personal qualities are the origin of all the others, wealth is the last to which they are ultimately reduced because, since it is the most immediately useful to well-being and the easiest to transmit, it can readily be used to buy all the rest—an observation which can be utilized to judge fairly accurately the degree to which each people has moved away from its primitive institution and concerning the distance it has traveled toward the extreme limit of corruption. I would note how much this universal desire for reputation, honors, and preferences, which consumes us all, exercises and compares talents and strengths, how much it excites and multiplies the passions, and—by making all men competitors, rivals, or, rather, enemies—how many reverses, successes, and catastrophes of every type it daily causes by making so many contenders run in the same lists. I would show that it is this ardor to be talked about, this frenzy to distinguish ourselves that almost always keeps us outside ourselves, to which we owe what is best and worst among men, our virtues and our vices, our sciences and our errors, our conquerors and our philosophers—that is, a multitude of bad things as against a small number of good ones. Finally, I would prove that if one sees a handful of powerful and rich men at the height of glory and fortune while the crowd grovels in obscurity and misery, it is because the former value the things they enjoy only to the extent that the latter are deprived of them, and that, without any change in their status, they would cease to be happy if the people ceased to be miserable.

But these details alone would comprise the material for a substantial work in which the advantages and inconveniences of every government relative to the rights of the state of nature would be weighed and in which would be disclosed all the various guises inequality has assumed to this day, and might assume in future ages, according to the nature of these governments and to the revolutions that time will necessarily bring about in them. One would see the multitude oppressed from within as a consequence of the very precautions it had taken against what threatened it from without. One would see oppression continually grow without the oppressed ever being able to know what its limit might be or what legitimate means they might have left to halt it. One would see the rights of citizens and national freedoms die out little by little, and the protestations of the weak treated as seditious murmurs. One would see politics restrict the honor of defending the common cause to a mercenary portion of the people. As a result of this, one would see arise the necessity of taxes, the discouraged farmer abandon his field even during peacetime and put aside the plow to buckle on the sword. One would see emerge the fatal and bizarre rules of the point of honor. One would see the defenders of the fatherland sooner or later become its enemies, holding their dagger constantly suspended over their fellow citizens, and a future time would come when they would be heard to say to their country's oppressor:

> *If you command me to plunge my sword in my brother's breast or my parent's throat*
> *Or in the belly of my pregnant wife,*
> *I will do it all, even if my right hand be unwilling.*[79]

From the extreme inequality of conditions and fortunes, from the diversity of passions and talents, from useless arts, from pernicious arts, from frivolous sciences would come throngs of prejudices equally contrary to reason, happiness, and virtue. One would see leaders foment everything that can weaken assembled men by disuniting them, everything that can give society an air of apparent concord while sowing in it a seed of real division, everything that can inspire mistrust and mutual hatred in the different orders of society by setting their rights and their interests in opposition, and consequently strengthen the power that holds them all in check.

It is from the midst of this disorder and these revolutions that despotism, gradually raising its hideous head and devouring everything it perceived to be good and wholesome in every part of the state, would ultimately succeed in

---

79. Lucan (39–65) *Pharsalia* 1.376–78, quoted by Rousseau in Latin: *Pectore si fratris gladium juguloque parentis / Condere me jubeas, gravidaeque in viscera partu / Conjugis, invitâ peragam tamen omnia dextrâ.* The passage comes from the speech by Laelius, Julius Caesar's chief centurion, in which he urges the wavering troops to follow Caesar's call to cross the Rubicon and thus begin the civil wars that resulted in the fall of the Roman Republic. Rousseau substitutes *gravidaeque* (pregnant) for the original *plenaeque* (full or plump), following Algernon Sidney's citation of the verse in his *Discourses Concerning Government* (1698), 2.19, p. 186.

trampling underfoot the laws and the people and in establishing itself on the ruins of the republic. The times preceding this final change would be times of disturbances and calamities, but in the end everything would be swallowed up by the monster, and peoples would no longer have leaders or laws but only tyrants. From that moment on it is also no longer a question of morals and virtue, for wherever despotism reigns—*where there is no hope from honesty*[80]—it tolerates no other master. As soon as he speaks, there is neither uprightness nor duty to consult, and the blindest obedience is the sole virtue left to slaves.

Here is the final limit of inequality and the farthest point that closes the circle and touches the point from which we set out. It is here that all private individuals become equals again because they are nothing and that, since subjects no longer have any law except the will of the master or the master any rule but his passions, the notions of good and the principles of justice vanish once again. It is here that everything is brought back to the sole law of the stronger, and consequently to a new state of nature, different from the one with which we began, in that the first was the state of nature in its purity and this last is the fruit of an excess of corruption. There is, besides, so little difference between these states, and the contract of government is so utterly dissolved by despotism, that the despot is master only as long as he is the stronger, and that as soon as he can be expelled, he cannot complain about the violence. The uprising that ends with a sultan being strangled or dethroned is as lawful an act as those by which, the day before, he disposed of his subjects' lives and goods. Force alone maintained him, force alone overthrows him. Everything thus occurs according to the natural order, and whatever the outcome of these brief and frequent revolutions may be, no one can complain about another's injustice, but only about his own imprudence or his misfortune.

In thereby discovering and following the forgotten and lost routes that must have led man from the natural state to the civil state, in reestablishing, along with the intermediate positions I have just indicated, those which the pressure of time has caused me to omit or which imagination has not suggested to me, every attentive reader will not fail to be struck by the immense distance that separates these two states. It is in this slow succession of things that he will see the solution to an infinite number of problems of morality and politics which philosophers are unable to resolve. He will sense that, since the human race of one age is not the human race of another age, the reason why Diogenes did not

---

80. Derived from Tacitus *Annals* 5.3, and quoted by Rousseau in Latin: *cui ex honesto nulla est spes.* Once again, Rousseau appears to take the phrase from Sidney, *Discourses Concerning Government* (1698), 2.19, p. 191.

find a man is that he was looking among his contemporaries for the man of a time that no longer was.[81] Cato, he will say, perished with Rome and freedom because he was out of place in his age, and the greatest of men only astonished the world he would have governed five hundred years earlier.[82] In a word, he will explain how the soul and human passions, altering imperceptibly, so to speak change their nature; why our needs and our pleasures change objects in the long run; why, with original man gradually vanishing, society no longer offers to the eyes of the wise man anything but an assemblage of artificial men and fabricated passions that are the work of all these new relations and have no true foundation in nature. Observation fully confirms what reflection teaches us on this subject: savage man and civilized man differ so much in the bottom of their hearts and inclinations that what constitutes the supreme happiness of the one would reduce the other to despair. The former breathes only repose and freedom, wants only to live and to remain idle, and not even the ataraxia of the Stoic comes close to his profound indifference to any other object.[83] By contrast, the citizen, forever active, sweats, bustles about, constantly frets to seek ever more laborious tasks: he works to death, he even runs toward it in order to be in a position to live, or he renounces life in order to acquire immortality. He courts the great he hates and the rich he despises; he spares nothing to obtain the honor of serving them; he boasts proudly of his baseness and of their protection and, proud of his slavery, he speaks with contempt of those who do not have the honor of sharing it. What a spectacle the difficult and envied labors of a European minister must be for a Carib! How many cruel deaths would this indolent savage not prefer to the horror of such a life, which is often not even sweetened by the pleasure of doing good? But in order to see the purpose of so many efforts, these words *power* and *reputation* would have to have a meaning in his mind; he would have to learn there are men of a sort who count the esteem of the rest of the universe for something, who know how to be happy and satisfied with themselves based on the testimony of others rather than on their own. Such, indeed, is the genuine cause of all these differences: the savage lives within himself; sociable man, always outside himself, knows how to live only in the opinion of others, and it is from their

---

81. Diogenes (4th century BC) was the Cynic philosopher who famously carried a lantern about in the daylight looking for an honest man.

82. Marcus Porcius Cato (95–46 BC), known as Cato the Younger, was a statesman from the late Roman Republic who opposed Julius Caesar and then committed suicide rather than facing defeat by Caesar. Rousseau often points in his writings to Cato as his example of the exemplary citizen.

83. "Ataraxia" is a Greek term meaning a condition of indifference or tranquility of the soul. The term is associated with several ancient philosophical sects, especially the Stoics.

judgment alone that he, so to speak, derives the feeling of his own existence. It is not part of my subject to show how such a disposition gives rise to so much indifference toward good and evil along with such fine discourses on morality; how everything being reduced to appearances, everything becomes fabricated and staged—honor, friendship, virtue, and often even the vices themselves, which men ultimately discover the secret of boasting about; how, in a word, always asking others what we are and never daring to ask it of ourselves, in the midst of so much philosophy, humanity, politeness, and sublime maxims, we have only a deceitful and frivolous exterior, honor without virtue, reason without wisdom, and pleasure without happiness. It is enough for me to have proved that this is not man's original state, and that it is the spirit of society alone and the inequality it engenders that so changes and alters all our natural inclinations.

I have tried to exhibit the origin and the progress of inequality, the establishment and abuse of political societies, insofar as these things can be deduced from the nature of man by the light of reason alone and independently of those sacred dogmas that give the sanction of divine right to sovereign authority. It follows from this account that inequality, being almost nonexistent in the state of nature, derives its force and growth from the development of our faculties and from the progress of the human mind, and eventually becomes stable and legitimate by the establishment of property and laws. It further follows that moral inequality, authorized by positive right alone, is contrary to natural right whenever it is not exactly proportioned to physical inequality—a distinction which sufficiently determines what ought to be thought in this regard of the sort of inequality that prevails among all civilized peoples, because it is manifestly contrary to the law of nature, however it may be defined, that a child command an old man, that an imbecile lead a wise man, and that a handful of people be glutted with superfluities while the starving multitude lacks necessities.

NOTES

DEDICATION

Note I (p. 43). Herodotus relates that after the murder of the false Smerdis, when the seven liberators of Persia assembled to deliberate about the form of government they would give the state, Otanes was strongly in favor of a republic—an opinion all the more extraordinary in the mouth of a satrap since, aside from the claim he might have to the empire, the great fear more than death any sort of government that forces them to respect men. Otanes, as might be expected, was not heeded, and seeing that they were going to proceed to the election of a monarch, he, who wanted neither to obey nor command, voluntarily gave up his right to the crown to the other competitors, asking as his only compensation that he and his posterity be free and independent, which was granted him. Even had Herodotus not informed us of the restriction that was placed on this privilege, it would necessarily have to be assumed. Otherwise Otanes, not recognizing any sort of law and being accountable to no one, would have been all-powerful in the state and more powerful than the king himself. But there was hardly any likelihood that a man capable in a situation like this of being satisfied with such a privilege was capable of abusing it. Indeed, this right was never seen to have caused the slightest trouble in the kingdom, either by wise Otanes or by any of his descendants.[84]

PREFACE

Note II (p. 51). From my very first step I confidently rely on one of those authorities that are worthy of respect for philosophers because they come

---

84. See Herodotus *Histories* 3.83. The restriction placed on this privilege was that Otanes and his descendants would not transgress the laws of Persia.

from a solid and sublime reasoning, which they alone know how to discover and appreciate.

"Whatever interest we may have in knowing ourselves, I wonder whether we do not know better everything that is not ourselves. Provided by nature with organs intended solely for our self-preservation, we use them only to receive foreign impressions, we seek only to expand outward, and to exist outside ourselves. Too busy multiplying the functions of our senses and increasing the exterior range of our being, rarely do we make use of that interior sense which reduces us to our true dimensions and separates from us everything that is not part of us. However, it is this sense that we must make use of if we wish to know ourselves; it is the only sense by which we can judge ourselves. But how is this sense to be made active and given its full range? How can we rid our soul, in which it resides, of all our mind's illusions? We have lost the habit of using it, it has remained without exercise in the midst of the tumult of our bodily sensations, it has been dried up by the fire of our passions; the heart, the mind, the senses—everything works against it." *Hist. nat.*, vol. 4, p. 151, *de la nat. de l'homme.*[85]

DISCOURSE

Note III (p. 65). The changes that a long practice of walking on two feet may have produced in man's physical structure, the relationships that can still be observed between his arms and the forelegs of quadrupeds, and the inference drawn from their way of walking, could have given rise to some doubts about which way of walking must have been most natural to us. All children begin by walking on all fours and need our example and our lessons to learn to stand upright. There are even savage nations, such as the Hottentots, which, greatly neglecting their children, let them walk on their hands for such a long time that they later experience great difficulty in getting them to straighten up. The children of the Caribs of the Antilles do the same thing. There are various examples of quadruped men, and among others I might cite that of the child who was found in 1344 near Hesse, where he had been raised by wolves, and who afterward said at the court of Prince Henry that, if it had been up to him, he would have preferred to have returned to them rather than to live among

---

85. Georges-Louis Le Clerc, comte de Buffon, *Histoire naturelle générale et particulière*, quoting from the opening passage of the third volume of Buffon's work, *Histoire naturelle de l'homme* (1749). Rousseau cites the 1752 ed. in 12°, p. 151. Buffon was one of the greatest naturalists of Rousseau's time, and his voluminous work covered subjects from geology through biology, including human nature. His theories of the formation and transformation of the earth and his treatment of human beings as animals were censured by the ecclesiastical authorities.

men. He was so thoroughly accustomed to walking like those animals that wood splints had to be tied to him which forced him to hold himself upright and keep his balance on two feet. The same was true for the child found in 1694 in the forests of Lithuania and who lived among bears. He gave, states M. de Condillac, no sign of reason, walked on his hands and feet, had no language, and made sounds that bore no resemblance to those of a man.[86] The little savage from Hanover who was brought to the English court some years ago had all the trouble in the world in making himself walk on two feet, and in 1719 two other savages were found in the Pyrenees who roamed through the mountains in the manner of quadrupeds. As for the objection that might be made that we thus deprive ourselves of the use of our hands, from which we derive so many advantages, aside from the fact that the example of monkeys shows that the hand can very well be used in both ways, this would prove only that man can assign to his limbs a more convenient purpose than nature's, and not that nature has destined man to walk otherwise than it teaches him.

But there are, it seems to me, much better reasons to give for holding that man is a biped. First, even if it were shown that he could originally have been structured otherwise than we see him and yet eventually become what he is now, this would not be enough to conclude that it did happen in this way. For after having shown the possibility of these changes, it would still be necessary, before accepting them, to demonstrate at least their likelihood. Moreover, if man's arms appear to have been able to serve him as legs when needed, this is the only observation that lends support to this system as against a great number of others that are contrary to it. The principal ones are: that the manner in which man's head is attached to his body, instead of directing his sight horizontally—as do all the other animals, and as he himself does when walking upright—would have kept his eyes directly fastened on the ground when walking on all fours, a situation not at all favorable to the preservation of the individual; that the tail he lacks and for which he has no use when walking on two feet is useful to quadrupeds and that none of them is deprived of it; that the woman's breast, very well positioned for a biped that holds her child in her arms, is so poorly positioned for a quadruped that none of them has it placed in this manner; that the hindquarters being inordinately high in relation to the forelegs—which makes it so that we drag ourselves around on our knees when walking on all fours—the whole would have made for an animal that was poorly proportioned and walked awkwardly; that if he had set his foot

---

86. See Condillac, *Essay on the Origin of Human Knowledge* (1746), 1.4.2.23, p. 88.

down flat like his hand, he would have had one fewer articulation in his hind leg than other animals do, namely that which joins the canon bone to the tibia; and that, setting down only the tip of his foot, as he would undoubtedly have been constrained to do, the tarsus—without speaking of the many bones that compose it—appears too large to take the place of the canon bone and its articulations with the metatarsus and the tibia too close together to give the human leg in this position the same flexibility as those of quadrupeds. The example of children, since it is taken from an age in which their natural strength is still not developed nor their limbs firm, proves nothing at all, and I might as well say that dogs are not destined to walk because they only crawl several weeks after their birth. Particular facts also have little force against the universal practice of all men, even of nations which, since they have no communication with others, could not have imitated them in anything. A child abandoned in a forest before he could walk and raised by some beast, will have followed his nurse's example when practicing walking as she does; habit could give him dexterity he did not have from nature; and just as people without arms succeed by dint of practice in doing with their feet everything we do with our hands, so he will ultimately succeed in using his hands as feet.

Note IV (p. 66). Should there be found among my readers so poor a natural scientist as to raise difficulties for me concerning the assumption of this natural fertility of the earth, I am going to respond to him with the following passage.

"As plants draw much more substance from air and water for their nourishment than they draw from the earth, it happens that when they decay they return more to the earth than they had drawn from it. Furthermore, a forest regulates water from rain by preventing evaporation. Thus in woods which have been preserved for a long time without being touched, the layer of the earth that supports vegetation would increase considerably. But since animals give less to the earth than they take from it and since men consume enormous quantities of wood and plants for fire and other uses, it follows that the layer of topsoil in an inhabited country should always diminish and eventually become like the terrain of Arabia Petraea and like that of so many other countries in the Orient—which, in fact, is the most anciently inhabited region—where only salt and sand are now found. For the fixed salt of plants and animals remains, while all the other parts are volatilized." M. de Buffon, *Hist. Nat.*[87]

---

87. Buffon, *Histoire naturelle générale et particulère*, vol. 1 (1749, 2d ed. in 4°), "Proofs of the Theory of the Earth," article 7, pp. 242–43.

To this might be added factual proof from the quantity of trees and plants of every species that fill almost all the uninhabited islands which have been discovered in recent centuries, and from what history teaches about the immense forests that had to be felled all over the earth as it was populated or civilized. I will also make the three following remarks on this subject. First, that if there is a sort of vegetation that might compensate for the loss of vegetable matter which is due to animals, according to M. Buffon's reasoning, it is above all woods, the tops and leaves of which collect and absorb more water and moisture than do other plants. Second, that the destruction of the soil, that is, the loss of the substance suited to vegetation, must accelerate in proportion as the earth is more cultivated and as its most industrious inhabitants consume its products of all kinds in greater abundance. My third and most important remark is that the fruits of trees provide animals with more food than can other vegetation—an experiment I myself have made by comparing the products of two plots of land equal in size and quality, the one covered with chestnut trees and the other sown with wheat.[88]

Note V (p. 66). Among the quadrupeds, the two most universal distinguishing characteristics of meat-eating species are drawn, first, from the shape of the teeth and, second, from the structure of the intestines. The animals that live only on vegetation all have blunt teeth, such as the horse, ox, sheep, hare. But meat-eating ones have pointed ones, such as the cat, dog, wolf, fox. And as for the intestines, frugivores have some, such as the colon, which are not found in meat-eating animals. It therefore seems that man, since he has teeth and intestines like those of the frugivorous animals, should naturally be placed in that class, and not only do anatomical observations confirm this opinion, but the records of antiquity are also very favorable to it. "Dicaearchus," states St. Jerome, "relates in his books on Greek antiquities that during the reign of Saturn, when the earth was still fertile on its own, no man ate flesh, but that all lived on fruits and vegetables that grew naturally" (Bk. 2, *Adv. Jovinian*).[89] This opinion can be further supported by the accounts of several modern travelers. François Corréal, among others, attests that most of the inhabitants of the Lucayas whom the Spanish transported to the

88. Compare Locke, *Second Treatise of Government* (1690), 5.37, p. 294: "For the provisions serving to the support of human life, produced by one acre of inclosed and cultivated land, are (to speak much within compass) ten times more, than those, which are yielded by an acre of land, of an equal richness, lying waste in common. . . . I have here rated the improved land very low in making its product but as ten to one, when it is much nearer an hundred to one."

89. St. Jerome (c. 347–420) *Against Jovinian* 2.13. In citing this passage, Rousseau omits the equation of the reign of Saturn with the Golden Age. Dicaearchus (c. 350–285 BC) was a student of Aristotle.

islands of Cuba, Santo Domingo, and elsewhere died from having eaten flesh.[90] From this it can be seen that I forego many advantages I could exploit. For since prey is almost the sole subject of fighting among carnivorous animals, and since frugivores live in continual peace with one another, if the human species was of this latter genus, it is clear that it would have had a much easier time subsisting in the state of nature and much less need and fewer occasions for leaving it.

Note VI (p. 67). All knowledge that requires reflection, all knowledge that is acquired only by the linking of ideas and is perfected only successively, seems to be altogether beyond the reach of savage man for want of communication with his fellow humans, that is, for want of the instrument used for that communication and of the needs that make it necessary. His knowledge and his efforts are limited to jumping, running, fighting, throwing a stone, climbing a tree. But if he knows only these things, in turn he knows them much better than do we, who do not have the same need of them as he does. And as they depend solely on the use of the body and are not susceptible of any communication or improvement from one individual to another, the first man could have been just as skilled at them as his most remote descendents.

The reports of travelers are full of examples of the strength and vigor of men in barbarous and savage nations. They have almost as much praise for their skill and nimbleness. And as eyes alone are needed to observe these things, nothing prevents us from lending credence to what eyewitnesses attest about them, I draw some examples at random from the first books that come to hand.

"The Hottentots," states Kolben, "comprehend fishing better than the Europeans of the Cape. They are equally skilled with net, hook, and spear, in coves as well as rivers. They are no less skillful at catching fish by hand. They are incomparably skillful at swimming. Their manner of swimming has something surprising about it and which is altogether peculiar to them. They swim with their body upright and their hands stretched out of the water, so that that they appear to be walking on land. In the roughest of seas, when the waves form so many mountains, they as it were dance atop the crest of the waves, rising and falling like a piece of cork."

"The Hottentots," the same author further states, "are surprisingly skilled at hunting, and the nimbleness of their running is beyond imagination." He is

---

90. François Corréal, *Voyages de François Corréal aux Indes Occidentales* (1722), 1.2. The Islas Lucayas are the Bahamas.

amazed that they do not more often put their agility to bad use, which however sometimes happens, as can be judged from the example he gives of it.
"A Dutch sailor disembarking at the Cape," he states, "engaged a Hottentot
to follow him to town with a roll of tobacco weighing about twenty pounds.
When they were both at some distance from the crew, the Hottentot asked
the sailor whether he knew how to run. Run?! answers the Dutchman; yes,
very well. Let's see, replied the African, and running off with the tobacco, he
disappeared almost immediately. The sailor, dumbfounded by such marvelous
speed, gave no thought to pursuing him and never again saw either his tobacco
or his porter.

"They have such quick sight and such a sure hand that the Europeans do
not even come close to them. At a hundred paces they will hit a target the
size of a half-penny with the throw of a stone, and what is more astonishing
is that instead of fixing their eyes on the target as we do, they make continual
movements and contortions. It seems that their stone is carried by an invisible
hand."[91]

Father du Tertre says more or less the same things about the savages of the
Antilles that have just been read concerning the Hottentots of the Cape of
Good Hope. He praises above all their accuracy in killing with their arrows
birds in flight and swimming fish, which they then retrieve by diving.[92] The
savages of North America are no less famous for their strength and skill, and
here is an example that will enable us to judge those of the Indians of South
America.

In the year 1746, an Indian from Buenos Aires, having been sentenced to
the galleys at Cadiz, proposed to the governor to buy back his freedom by
risking his life at a public festival. He promised that he would single-handedly
set upon the most ferocious bull, armed only with a rope, that he would bring
it to the ground, that he would seize it with his rope by whatever part they
should indicate, that he would saddle it, bridle it, mount it, and, thus mounted,
fight two more bulls of the fiercest sort to be let out from the torillo, and that
he would put them all to death, one after another, at the instant he was commanded to do so and without anyone's help. This was granted to him. The
Indian kept his word and succeeded in doing everything he had promised. For
the way in which he did it and for all the detail of the fight, one can consult

---

91. Peter Kolben, *Description du Cap de Bonne-Espérance* (1719), 1.13.7–8. Rousseau quotes loosely from a
French translation of the work.

92. Jean-Baptiste du Tertre, *Histoire générale des Isles de Saint Christophe* (1654), 5.1.4.

the first volume in 12° of M. Gautier's *Observations sur l'histoire naturelle*, page 262, from which this fact is taken.[93]

Note VII (p. 68). "The lifespan of horses," states M. de Buffon, "is, as in all other animal species, proportioned to the length of time of their growth. Man, who takes fourteen years to grow up, can live six or seven times that long, that is, ninety or one hundred years. The horse, whose growth is completed in four years, can live six or seven times that long, that is, twenty-five or thirty years. The examples that might be contrary to this rule are so rare that they should not even be regarded as an exception from which conclusions might be drawn. And as draught horses complete their growth in less time than riding horses, they also do not live as long and are old from the age of fifteen."[94]

Note VIII (p. 68). I believe I see another still more general difference between carnivorous animals and frugivores than the one I remarked upon in note V, because it applies as well to birds. This difference consists in the number of young, which never exceeds two to a litter in species that live only on vegetation and which ordinarily exceeds that number in meat-eating species. It is easy to recognize nature's design in this regard by the number of teats, which is only two in every female of the first species—like the horse, cow, goat, deer, sheep, etc.— and which is always six or eight in the other females—like the dog, cat, wolf, tiger, etc. The chicken, goose, and duck, which are all meat-eating birds—as are the eagle, sparrow hawk, and screech owl—also lay and hatch a great number of eggs, which never happens with the pigeon, dove, or birds that eat absolutely nothing but grain, which hardly ever lay and hatch more than two eggs at a time. The reason that may account for this difference is that the animals that live only on grasses and plants, since they spend almost all day grazing and are forced to spend a great deal of time feeding themselves, could not manage to nurse many young, whereas meat-eating ones, since they take their meal practically in a single instant, can more easily and more frequently return to their young and to their hunting, and make up for the consumption of such a large quantity of milk. All this calls for many particular observations and reflections, but this is not to the place for doing so, and it is enough for me to have shown the most general system of nature in this

---

93. Jacques Gautier d'Agoty, *Observations sur l'histoire naturelle* (1752–55).
94. Buffon, *Histoire naturelle générale et particulère*, "Natural History of the Horse" (1753, 2d ed. in 4°), 4:226–27.

part, a system which provides a new reason for removing man from the class of carnivorous animals and for placing him among the frugivorous species.

Note IX (p. 73). A famous author, calculating the goods and evils of human life and comparing the two sums, has found that the latter greatly surpassed the former and that all things considered life was a rather poor present for man.[95] I am not at all surprised by his conclusion; he drew all his arguments from the constitution of civil man. If he had gone back to natural man, it can be concluded that he would have found very different results, that he would have perceived that man has hardly any other evils than those he has given himself, and that nature would have been justified. It is not without difficulty that we have succeeded in making ourselves so miserable. When, on the one hand, one considers men's tremendous labors, so many sciences fathomed, so many arts invented; so many forces employed; chasms filled, mountains leveled, rocks split, rivers made navigable, lands cleared, lakes dug, swamps drained, enormous buildings raised upon the earth, the sea covered with ships and sailors; and when, on the other hand, one inquires with a little thought into the true advantages that have resulted from all this for the happiness of the human species, one cannot help but be struck by the astonishing disproportion that prevails between these things, and deplore man's blindness, which, to feed his foolish pride and I know not what vain admiration for himself, makes him rush ardently after all the miseries to which he is susceptible and which beneficent nature had taken care to keep from him.

Men are wicked; sad and continual experience spares the need for proof. Yet man is naturally good—I do believe I have demonstrated it.[96] What is it, then, that can have depraved him to this extent if not the changes that have taken place in his constitution, the progress he has made, and the knowledge he has acquired? Let human society be admired as much as one likes; it will remain no less true that it necessarily leads men to hate one another in proportion as their interests conflict, to render one another apparent services and in fact to do one another every imaginable harm. What is to be thought of relations[97] in which each private individual's reason dictates to him maxims

---

95. The "famous author" is probably the philosopher and mathematician Pierre Moreau de Maupertuis, who makes such an argument in his *Essai de philosophie morale* (1749), chap. 2.

96. This is Rousseau's first statement of the principle of the natural goodness of man and his corruption in society that he later claimed was the fundamental principle of his entire philosophical system. See editor's introduction, above pp. xix–xxv.

97. Or: commerce (*commerce*).

directly contrary to those that public reason preaches to the body of society, and in which each profits from the others' misfortune? There is perhaps not a single well-to-do man whose death is not secretly hoped for by greedy heirs and often his own children; not a single ship at sea whose shipwreck would not be good news to some merchant; not a single commercial firm which a dishonest debtor would not like to see burn with all the papers it contains; not a single people that would not rejoice at its neighbors' disasters. This is how we find our advantage in detriment to our fellow humans, and how one person's loss almost always makes for another's prosperity. But what is more dangerous still is that public calamities are awaited and hoped for by a large number of private individuals. Some wish for illnesses, others death, others war, others famine. I have seen horrible men weep with sadness at the prospect of a fertile year, and the great and deadly fire of London, which cost the life and goods of so many unfortunates, perhaps made the fortune of more than ten thousand people. I know that Montaigne blames the Athenian Demades for having had a worker punished who, by selling coffins at a very high price, profited greatly from the citizens' deaths.[98] But since the reason Montaigne advances is that everyone would have to be punished, it is clear that his reasoning confirms my own. Let us therefore see through our frivolous displays of good will to what goes on in the depths of our hearts, and let us reflect on what must be the state of things where all men are forced to flatter and destroy one another and where they are born enemies by duty and knaves by interest. If I am answered that society is so constituted that every man gains by serving the rest, I will reply that this would all be very well if he did not gain still more by harming them. There is no profit so legitimate that is not exceeded by the profit that can be made illegitimately, and the wrong done to one's neighbor is always more lucrative than services are. It is therefore just a question of finding the means to be assured of impunity, and it is to this end that the powerful apply all their strength and the weak all their cunning.

Savage man, once he has eaten, is at peace with all of nature and the friend of all his fellow humans. Is it sometimes a question of contending for his meal? He never comes to blows without having first compared the difficulty of prevailing with that of finding his subsistence elsewhere. And as pride is not involved in the fight, it ends with a few blows; the victor eats, the vanquished goes off to try his luck, and all is at peace. But with man in society matters are

---

98. Montaigne, *Essays* (1580–92), "The Profit of One Man is the Damage of Another," 1.22, p. 77. Demades was a notoriously unscrupulous and greedy Athenian orator who was put to death in about 318 BC.

entirely different. First it is a question of providing for what is necessary, and then for what is superfluous; next come delicacies, and then immense wealth, and then subjects, and then slaves. He does not have a moment of respite. What is most singular about it is that the less natural and pressing the needs, the more the passions increase and, what is worse, the power to satisfy them. As a result, after a long period of prosperity, after having swallowed up a good many treasures and having ruined a good many men, my hero will end up by cutting every throat until he is the sole master of the universe. Such in brief is the moral picture, if not of human life, at least of the secret aspirations of every civilized man's heart.

Compare without prejudices the condition of civil man with that of savage man, and inquire, if you can, how many new doors—aside from his wickedness, his needs, and his miseries— the first condition has opened to suffering and death. If you consider the mental anguish that consumes us, the violent passions that exhaust and grieve us, the excessive labors with which the poor are overburdened, the even more dangerous softness to which the rich abandon themselves, and which cause the former to die of their needs and the latter of their excesses. If you consider the monstrous combinations of foods, their pernicious seasonings, spoiled foodstuffs, adulterated drugs, the knavery of those who sell them, the errors of those who administer them, the poisoned vessels in which they are prepared. If you attend to the epidemic diseases bred by the bad air where large numbers of men are gathered together, to those illnesses brought about by the delicacy of our way of life, the to and fro from indoors to outdoors, the custom of putting clothes on and taking them off with too little precaution, and all the cares which our excessive sensuality has turned into necessary habits and which then neglecting them or being deprived of them costs us our life or health. If you take into account the fires and earthquakes which consume or topple entire cities, causing their inhabitants to perish by the thousands. In a word, if you combine the dangers which all of these causes constantly gather over our heads, you will sense how dearly nature makes us pay for the contempt we have shown for its lessons.

I will not repeat here what I have said elsewhere about war,[99] but I wish that informed people would be willing or would be daring enough to give, for once, the public a detailed account of the horrors committed in armies by provisioners of food and of hospital supplies. Their none-too-secret maneuverings,

99. Rousseau's reference is unclear. He may refer to what he writes in the main body of the *Discourse on Inequality* about the state of war that follows the establishment of property or the wars among states that follow the establishment of civil society.

by which the most brilliant armies dissolve into less than nothing, would be seen to cause more soldiers to perish than are cut down by the enemy's sword. Another no less astonishing calculation to make is how many men are swallowed up by the sea each year, whether by starvation, or scurvy, or pirates, or fire, or shipwrecks. It is obvious that one must also attribute to established property and consequently to society the assassinations, poisonings, highway robberies, and even the punishment of those crimes—punishments necessary to prevent greater evils, but which, costing two or more lives for the murder of one man, nonetheless actually double the loss to the human species. How many shameful means are there for preventing the birth of human beings and cheating nature? Either by those brutal and depraved tastes which insult its most charming work, tastes which neither savages nor animals ever knew and which arise in civilized countries only from a corrupt imagination; or by those secret abortions, worthy fruits of debauchery and vicious honor; or by the exposure or murder of a large number of children, victims of their parents' misery or of their mothers' shameful barbarity; or, finally, by the mutilation of those unfortunates, a portion of whose existence and their entire posterity are sacrificed to mere songs or, worse yet, to the brutal jealousy of a few men—a mutilation which, in this latter case, doubly outrages nature, both by the treatment inflicted on those who suffer it and by the use to which they are destined.

But are there not a thousand even more frequent and more dangerous cases where paternal rights openly offend humanity? How many talents are buried and inclinations overridden by the imprudent constraint of fathers! How many men who would have distinguished themselves in a suitable profession die miserable and dishonored in another profession for which they had no taste! How many happy but unequal marriages have been broken or disturbed, and how many chaste wives dishonored by that order of social conditions always in contradiction with the order of nature! How many other bizarre unions formed by interest and disavowed by love and reason! Even how many honest and virtuous spouses torment one another for having been ill-matched! How many young and unhappy victims of their parents' greed plunge into vice or spend their sad days in tears, and groan in indissoluble bonds which the heart rejects and which gold alone has forged! Sometimes the fortunate ones are those women whose courage and very virtue tear them from life before some barbaric violence forces them to spend it in crime or in despair. Forgive me, father and mother forever deplorable: I embitter your suffering reluctantly, but may it serve as an eternal and terrifying example to anyone who dares, in the name of nature itself, to violate the most sacred of its rights!

If I have spoken only of those ill-formed unions which are the product of our civilization, are those unions in which love and sympathy have presided themselves thought to be exempt from inconveniences? What would happen if I undertook to show the human species attacked at its very source, and even in the holiest of all bonds, in which one no longer dares heed nature until after having consulted fortune, and in which, with civil disorder mixing up virtues and vices, continence becomes a criminal precaution and the refusal to give life to another fellow human an act of humanity? But without tearing away the veil that covers so many horrors, let us remain content with pointing out the evil for which others must provide the remedy.

Let one add to all this the many unhealthy trades which shorten lives or wreck one's health, such as labor in mines, the various preparations of metals and minerals, especially of lead, copper, mercury, cobalt, arsenic, realgar; those other perilous trades which daily cost the lives of numerous workers, some of them roofers, others carpenters, others masons, others working in quarries. Let all these things be brought together, I say, and one will be able to see in the establishment and perfection of societies the reasons for the reduction in number of the species observed by more than one philosopher.

Luxury, impossible to prevent among men greedy for their own comforts and for the esteem of others, soon completes the evil societies began, and, under the pretext of supporting the poor, who ought not to have been made such in the first place, it impoverishes everyone else and sooner or later depopulates the state.

Luxury is a remedy much worse than the evil it claims to cure. Or, rather, it is itself the worst of all evils in any state whatsoever, whether large or small, and, in order to feed the crowds of lackeys and miserable people it has created, it crushes and ruins both the farmer and the citizen—like those scorching southern winds which, covering the grass and foliage with voracious insects, deprive useful animals of their subsistence and carry famine and death wherever their effects are felt.

From society and the luxury it engenders arise the liberal and mechanical arts, commerce, letters, and all those useless things which make industry flourish, which enrich and ruin states. The reason for this decline is very simple. It is easy to see that by its nature agriculture must be the least lucrative of all the arts, because, since its product is of the most indispensible use to all men, its price must be proportioned to the capacities of the poorest. From the same principle this rule can be derived: that in general the arts are lucrative in inverse ratio to their usefulness, and that those that are most necessary must ultimately become the most neglected. From this it is clear what must be thought of the true advantages of industry and of the actual effect that results from its progress.

Such are the perceptible causes of all the miseries into which opulence ultimately propels the most admired nations. In proportion as industry and the arts spread and flourish, the scorned farmer, burdened with taxes needed for maintaining luxury, and condemned to spend his life alternating between labor and hunger, abandons his fields to go seek in the cities the bread he should be carrying there. The more capital cities strike the stupid eyes of the people as admirable, the more one must groan at seeing the countryside abandoned, fields lying fallow, and the main roads flooded with unfortunate citizens turned beggars or thieves and destined to end their misery one day on the rack or in a dung-heap. This is how the state, while growing rich on the one hand, is weakened and depopulated on the other, and how the most powerful monarchies, after a great deal of work to make themselves opulent and deserted, end up becoming the prey of the poor nations that succumb to the fatal temptation to invade them and that grow rich and weaken themselves in their turn, until they are themselves invaded and destroyed by others.

Let someone deign to explain to us for once what could have produced those hoards of barbarians which have inundated Europe, Asia, and Africa over the course of so many centuries? Was it to the ingenuity of their arts, the wisdom of their laws, the excellence of their civil order that they owed that prodigious population? Let our learned men kindly tell us why, instead of multiplying to such an extent, those ferocious and brutal men—without enlightenment, without restraint, without education—were not slitting one another's throats at every moment while fighting over their food or game? Let them explain to us how these miserable men even had the audacity to look such clever men as we were in the face, we who had such fine military discipline, such fine legal codes, and such wise laws? Finally, why it is that, ever since society was perfected in the countries of the north, and since they went to such trouble to teach men their mutual duties and the art of living together pleasantly and peacefully, they are no longer seen to produce anything like those large numbers of men they used to produce? I rather fear that someone will eventually think of responding to me that all these great things—namely, the arts, sciences, and laws—were very wisely invented by men as a salutary plague to prevent the excessive increase of the species for fear that this world, which is destined for us, might eventually become too small for its inhabitants.

What, then? Must we destroy societies, annihilate thine and mine, and return to live in the forests with bears? A conclusion in the manner of my adversaries which I much rather prefer to anticipate than to leave them the shame of drawing it. O you, to whom the celestial voice has not made itself heard and who recognize no other destiny for your species than to end this short life in peace, you, who are able leave behind in the midst of cities your fatal acquisitions, your anxious minds, your corrupted hearts, and your unbridled desires: reclaim, since it is within your power to do so, your ancient and first innocence; go into the woods to lose sight and memory of the crimes of your contemporaries, and do not fear that you are debasing your species by renouncing its enlightenment in order to renounce its vices. As for men like me, whose passions have forever destroyed their original simplicity, who can no longer feed on grass and acorns nor do without laws and leaders; those who were honored in their first father with supernatural lessons, those who may see in the intention of giving human actions from the outset a morality they would not have acquired for a long time the reason for a precept indifferent in itself and inexplicable in any other system;[100] those, in a word, who are convinced that the divine voice called the entire human species to the enlightenment and happiness of the celestial intelligences: they will all endeavor, by practicing the virtues they obligate themselves to perform as they learn them, to deserve the eternal reward they must expect for doing so; they will respect the sacred bonds of the societies of which they are members; they will love their fellow humans and serve them with all their power; they will scrupulously obey the laws and the men who are their authors and ministers; they will honor above all the good and wise princes who know how to prevent, cure, or palliate that throng of abuses and evils that are always ready to crush us; they will animate the zeal of these worthy leaders by showing them, without fear and without flattery, the greatness of their task and the rigor of their duty. But, for all this, they will have no less scorn for a constitution that can be maintained only with the assistance of so many respectable people—which is desired more often than obtained—and from which, in spite of all their efforts, more real calamities than apparent advantages always arise.

---

100. In this complex and perhaps intentionally evasive sentence, by the "precept indifferent in itself and inexplicable in any other system," Rousseau appears to allude to the divine commandment not to eat the fruit of the knowledge of good and evil (Genesis 2:16–17).

Note X (p. 73). Among the men we know—whether for our own part, or from historians, or from travelers—some are black, others white, others red; some wear their hair long, others have nothing but curly wool for hair; some are almost entirely covered with hair, others do not even have a beard. There have existed, and perhaps there still exist, nations of men of gigantic height; and putting aside the fable about the Pygmies, which may well be merely an exaggeration, Laplanders and especially Greenlanders are known to be well below man's average height. It is even claimed that there are entire peoples that have tails like quadrupeds. And without lending blind faith to the accounts of Herodotus and Ctesias,[101] one can at least draw from them this very likely conclusion: that if good observations had been possible in those ancient times when different peoples followed ways of life more different from one another than they do today, much more striking variations in the shape and bearing of their bodies would also have been noted among them. All these facts, for which it is easy to provide incontestable proofs, can surprise only those who are accustomed to look solely at the objects that surround them, and who are ignorant of the powerful effects of the variety of climates, air, foods, way of living, habits in general, and above all the astonishing force of the same causes when they act continuously over long sequences of generations. Nowadays, when commerce, voyages, and conquests bring different peoples closer together, and when their ways of life constantly grow more alike through frequent communication, certain national differences have perceptibly diminished, and, for example, everyone can see that the French of today are no longer those tall, fair-skinned, and blond-haired bodies described by Latin historians, even though time, together with the admixture of the Franks and Normans, who are themselves fair-skinned and blond, should have restored what contact with the Romans might have taken away from the climate's influence with regard to the natural constitution and complexion of the inhabitants. All these observations regarding the variations that a thousand causes can produce and in fact have produced in the human species make me wonder whether various animal species similar to human beings, which have been taken by travelers without much examination for beasts, either because of certain differences they noted in their exterior structure or simply because these animals did not speak, might not in fact be genuine savage men whose race, dispersed in the woods long ago, did not have the opportunity to develop any of its potential faculties, had not

---

101. Herodotus (5th century BC) relates stories about various exotic peoples in his *Histories*. Ctesias (5th century BC) wrote works about Persia and India.

acquired any degree of perfection, and was still in the primitive state of nature. Let us give an example of what I mean.

"In the Kingdom of the Congo," states the translator of the *Hist[oire] des Voyages*, "are found many of those large animals called Orang-Outangs in the East Indies, which occupy something like a middle position between the human species and baboons. Battel relates that in the forests of Mayomba, in the Kingdom of Loango, two sorts of monsters are seen, the larger of which are called *Pongos* and the others *Enjokos*. The former bear an exact resemblance to a human being, but are much heavier and very tall. Along with a human face, they have very deep-set eyes. Their hands, their cheeks, and their ears are hairless, except for their eyebrows, which are quite long. Although the rest of their body is rather hairy, the hair is not very thick and its color is brown. Finally, the sole feature that distinguishes them from human beings is their leg, which has no calf. They walk upright, holding one another by the hair of the neck; they take shelter in the woods; they sleep in trees, and there make themselves a type of roof which shelters them from the rain. Their foods are fruits or wild nuts. They never eat flesh. The practice of the Negroes who travel through the forest is to light fires at night. They notice that after they have left in the morning, the Pongos take their place around the fire and do not leave until it goes out—for, with all their cleverness, they do not have enough sense to keep it going by bringing wood to it.

"They sometimes walk in groups and kill the Negroes who travel through the forests. They even attack elephants which come to graze in the places where they live and so annoy them by striking them with their fists or with sticks that they force them to run away bellowing. Pongos are never taken alive, because they are so robust that ten men would not be enough to stop them. But the Negroes do take a number of their young after having killed the mother, to whose body they cling tightly. When one of these animals dies, the others cover its body with a pile of branches or greenery. Purchas adds that in the conversations he had with Battel he learned from him that a Pongo kidnapped a little Negro from him who spent an entire month in the society of these animals, for they do no harm to the human beings who surprise them, at least when these humans do not stare at them, as the little Negro had observed. Battel did not describe the second type of monster.

"Dapper confirms that the Kingdom of Congo is full of those animals that in the Indies bear the name of Orang-Outang—that is, inhabitants of the woods—and which the Africans call Quojas-Morros. This beast, he says, is so similar to a man that it occurred to some travelers that it may have been the offspring of a woman and a monkey—a chimera which the Negroes themselves reject. One of these animals was transported from the Congo to Holland and presented to the Prince of Orange, Frederic Henri. It was the height of a child of three and of moderate girth but square and well-proportioned, very agile and very lively, its legs fleshy and robust, the entire front of its body bare, but its back covered with black hair. At first sight its face resembled that of a man, but it had a flat and curved nose; its ears were also those of the human species; its breast—for it was a female—was plump, its navel deep, its shoulders well articulated, its hands divided into fingers and thumbs, its calves and heels fat and fleshy. It often walked upright on its legs, it was capable of lifting and carrying rather heavy loads. When it wanted to drink, it took the cover of a pot in one hand and held the base with the other. Afterwards it gracefully wiped its lips. It lay down to sleep, its head on a pillow, covering itself so skillfully that it might have been taken for a human being in bed. The Negroes tell strange tales about this animal. They insist not only that it violates women and girls, but that it dares to attack armed men. In a word, it is quite likely that it is the Satyr of the Ancients. Merolla perhaps speaks of just this animal when he relates that the Negroes sometimes catch savage men and women in their hunts."[102]

These species of anthropomorphic animals are also spoken of in the third volume of the same *Histoire des voyages*[103] under the name of *Beggos* and *Mandrills*. But restricting ourselves to the preceding accounts, striking conformities with the human species and smaller differences are found in the description of these supposed monsters than those which might be assigned between one man and another. It is not clear from these passages what reasoning the authors rely on in refusing to give the animals in question the name of savage men, but it is easy to conjecture that it is due to their stupidity, and also because they did not speak—weak reasons for those who know that although the organ of speech is natural to man, speech itself is nonetheless not natural to him, and who are aware of the extent to which his perfectibility could have raised civil man above his original state. The small number of lines contain-

---

102. *Histoire des voyages*, 5:87–89. The original source being translated in this collection of travel accounts is Samuel Purchas, whose compilation of travel accounts were published between 1613 and 1625. Purchas recounts the travels of the English merchant Andrew Battel, who traveled through Brazil and Angola from 1589 to 1610, and the Dutch physician and geographer Olfert Dapper's book on Africa (1668), which was itself based on other accounts since Dapper never traveled outside of Holland, and the account of the Congo (1682) by the Franciscan missionary Jerome Merolla.

103. The accounts to which Rousseau refers are actually in the fourth volume of the *Histoire des voyages*.

ing these descriptions enables us to judge how poorly these animals have been observed and with what prejudices they have been seen. For example, they are characterized as monsters and yet it is acknowledged that they reproduce.[104] In one place Battel states that Pongos kill the Negroes who travel through the forest, in another Purchas adds that they do them no harm, even when they surprise them, at least when the Negroes do not stare at them. Pongos gather around fires lit by Negroes when they leave, and they in turn leave when it has gone out. That is the fact, and now here is the observer's commentary: *for, with all their cleverness, they do not have enough sense to keep it going by bringing wood to it*. I would like to guess how Battel or Purchas, his compiler, could have known that the departure of the Pongos was the result of their stupidity rather than of their will. In a climate such as that of Loango, fire is not a very necessary thing for animals, and if the Negroes light them, they do so less against the cold than to frighten ferocious beasts. It is therefore perfectly plain that after having enjoyed the blaze for a time or having thoroughly warmed themselves, the Pongos grow bored of continuing to remain in the same place and go off to forage, which requires more time than if they ate flesh. Besides, the majority of animals, without excepting man, are known to be naturally lazy and to shy away from every kind of task which is not absolutely necessary. Finally, it appears quite strange that the Pongos whose dexterity and strength is praised, the Pongos who know how to inter their dead and make themselves roofs out of branches, do not know how to push kindling into a fire. I recall having seen a monkey perform this very same operation which they want to deny to the Pongos. It is true that, since my ideas were not at that time turned in this direction, I myself made the same mistake for which I reproach our travelers, I neglected to examine whether the monkey's intention was in fact to keep the fire going or whether, as I believe, it was simply to imitate the action of a human being. However that may be, it is well demonstrated that the monkey is not a variety of man, not only because it is deprived of the faculty of speech, but above all because it is certain that its species does not have the faculty of perfecting itself,[105] which is the specific characteristic of the human species — experiments that do not appear to have been made on the Pongo and the Orang-Outang with enough care to be able to draw the same conclusion. There would however be one means by which, if the Orang-Outang or others were of the human species, the crudest observers would be able to satisfy

---

104. In the terminology of Rousseau's time, "monsters" often refers to an animal or plant that cannot reproduce.

105. "The faculty of perfecting itself" translates *la faculté de se perfectionner*. See n. 41 to p. 72.

themselves on this score through a demonstration. But, aside from the fact that a single generation would not suffice for this experiment, it must be regarded as impracticable because what is only a supposition would have to have been demonstrated as true before the test that should verify the fact could be tried innocently.

Judgments which are hasty, and not the fruit of an enlightened reason, are liable to be excessive. Our travelers without further ado take for beasts under the names of *Pongos, Mandrills, Orang-Outangs* the same beings that the ancients took for divinities under the names of *Satyrs, Fauns, Sylvans*. Perhaps after more precise research it will be found that they are neither beasts nor gods, but men. In the meantime, it appears to me that it is just as reasonable to rely in this matter on Merolla — an educated cleric, an eyewitness, and a man who, for all his naïveté, was still an intelligent man — as on the merchant Battel, Dapper, Purchas, and the other compilers.

What judgment would such observers have made regarding the child found in 1694, about whom I spoke above,[106] who gave no sign of reason, walked on his hands and feet, had no language and formed sounds that did not at all resemble those of a man? It was a long time, continues the same philosopher who provides me with this fact,[107] before he could utter a few words, and then he did so in a barbarous manner. As soon as he could speak, he was questioned about his first state, but he remembered no more about it than we remember about what happened to us in the cradle. If, unfortunately for him, this child had fallen into our travelers' hands, there can be no doubt that after having noted his silence and his stupidity, they would have decided to send him back into the woods or to lock him up in a menagerie, after which they would have spoken learnedly about him in fine reports as a very curious beast that very much resembled a man.

For the past three or four centuries the inhabitants of Europe have been inundating the other parts of the world and constantly publishing new collections of voyages and accounts, and yet I am persuaded that we know no other men than Europeans. Still, it appears that, judging by the ridiculous prejudices which have not died out even among men of letters, very nearly everything done by anyone under the pompous denomination of "the study of man" is to study the men of his country. Individuals may well come and go, but it seems that philosophy does not travel, and the philosophy of one people is

106. See note III, p. 121 above.
107. See Condillac, *Essay on the Origin of Human Knowledge* (1746), 1.4.2.23, p. 88.

little suited to another. The reason for this is obvious, at least with regard to distant countries. There are scarcely more than four sorts of men who make extended voyages: sailors, merchants, soldiers, and missionaries. Now, the first three classes should hardly be expected to provide good observers, and as for those of the fourth, even if they were not subject to the prejudices of their station, as are all the others, it has to be believed that being occupied by the sublime vocation that calls them, they would not voluntarily devote themselves to research that appears to be a matter of pure curiosity and that would distract them from the more important labors to which they have dedicated themselves. Furthermore, to preach the gospel with utility only zeal is needed and God grants the rest; but to study men talents are needed which God does not promise to grant to anyone and which are not always the lot of saints. One cannot open a book of voyages without finding descriptions of characters and morals. But it is altogether surprising to see that these people who have described so many things have said only what everyone already knew, that they could perceive at the other end of the world only what they could easily have noticed without leaving their street, and those genuine features which distinguish nations, and which strike those eyes made to see, have almost always escaped theirs. Hence that fine adage of morality, so bandied about by the philosophic rabble, that men are everywhere the same, that since they everywhere have the same passions and the same vices, it is quite useless to try to characterize different peoples—which is about as well reasoned as if one were to say that Peter and James cannot be distinguished because they both have a nose, a mouth, and eyes.

Shall we never see reborn those happy times when peoples did not get mixed up with philosophy, but when the likes of a Plato, a Thales, and a Pythagoras, smitten with an ardent desire to know, undertook the greatest voyages solely to inform themselves and went far away to shake off the yoke of national prejudices, to learn to know men by their conformities and differences, and to acquire that universal knowledge which is not exclusively that of one age or of one country, but which—since it is that of all times and of all places—is, so to speak, the common science of the wise?[108]

The largesse of certain curious people who have, at great expense, made or sponsored voyages to the Orient with learned men and painters to sketch ruins and to decipher or copy inscriptions there is admired. But I have difficulty

---

108. Plato (c. 428–c. 348 BC) traveled to Italy and Sicily and perhaps Egypt. Thales (c. 624–c. 546 BC) is generally regarded as the founder of natural philosophy, was said to have been instructed by Egyptian priests. Pythagoras (c. 570–495 BC) traveled widely through Italy, Greece, and Egypt.

conceiving how, in an age that prides itself on its fine knowledge, it is that one cannot find two like-minded men, both rich—the one in money and the other in genius—both loving glory and aspiring to immortality, for the sake of which the one sacrifices twenty thousand crowns of his fortune and the other ten years of his life for a notable voyage around the world, in order to study, not always rocks and plants, but men and morals for once, and who, after so many centuries spent measuring and examining the house, finally made up their minds that they wanted to know its inhabitants.

The academicians who have traveled through the northern parts of Europe and the southern parts of America had as their objective more to visit them as geometers than as philosophers. However, as they were simultaneously both, the lands seen and described by La Condamine and Maupertuis cannot be regarded as altogether unknown.[109] The jeweler Chardin, who traveled like Plato, has left nothing more to be said about Persia.[110] China appears to have been well observed by the Jesuits. Kaempfer gives a tolerable idea of the little he saw in Japan.[111] With the exception of these accounts, we do not at all know the peoples of the East Indies, who have been visited solely by Europeans more interested in filling their purses than their heads. The entirety of Africa and its numerous inhabitants, as remarkable in terms of their character as in terms of their color, are yet to be examined. The entire earth is covered with nations of which we know only the names, and yet we get mixed up in judging the human race! Let us suppose a Montesquieu, a Buffon, a Diderot, a Duclos, a d'Alembert, a Condillac,[112] or men of that stamp traveling in order to inform

109. Charles Marie de La Condamine (1701–74), French explorer, geographer, and mathematician, published an account of his expedition sent by the French Academy of Sciences to make measurements of the earth at the equator and of his subsequent travels in the Amazon and through South America in 1745. Pierre-Louis Moreau de Maupertuis (1698–1759), French mathematician and philosopher, made a parallel expedition sent by the Academy to Lapland in northern Finland to make measurements of the earth in the high latitudes and delivered his report to the Academy upon his return in 1737.

110. Jean Chardin (1643–1713) was a French jeweler who made several voyages through Persia and the Near East and published a series of works recounting his voyages, culminating in a collection published in 1711.

111. Engelbert Kaempfer (1651–1716) was a German naturalist whose wide travels included an extended time in Japan. His manuscript study of Japanese history and culture was published a decade after his death.

112. Charles-Louis de Secondat, baron de Montesquieu (1689–1755), whose most important work of philosophy was *The Spirit of the Laws* (1748). Georges-Louis Le Clerc, comte de Buffon (1707–88), the great naturalist whose *Histoire naturelle générale et particulère* is an important source for Rousseau. Denis Diderot (1713–84), philosopher and co-editor of the *Encyclopédie*. Charles Pinot Duclos (1704–72), historian and secretary of the Académie Française. Jean le Rond d'Alembert (1717–83), mathematician and co-editor of the *Encyclopédie*. Étienne Bonnot de Condillac (1715–80), philosopher and author of the *Essay on the Origin of Human Knowledge* (1746), to which Rousseau repeatedly refers in the *Discourse on Inequality*. Duclos, d'Alembert, Condillac, and especially Diderot were close friends and associates of Rousseau during the period when he wrote the *Discourse on Inequality*.

their compatriots, observing and describing—as they so well know how to do—Turkey, Egypt, Barbary, the Empire of Morocco, Guinea, the lands of the Bantus, the interior of Africa and its eastern coasts, the Malabars, Mongolia, the banks of the Ganges, the Kingdoms of Siam, Pegu, and Ava, China, Tartary, and above all Japan; then, in the other hemisphere, Mexico, Peru, Chile, the lands by the Straits of Magellan—without overlooking the Patagonias, true or false, Tucumán, Paraguay if possible, Brazil, finally the Caribbean islands, Florida, and all the savage lands—the most important voyage of all and the one that must be undertaken with the greatest care. Let us suppose that these new Hercules, upon returning from their memorable travels, then wrote at their leisure the natural history—moral and political—of what they had seen: we ourselves would see a new world issue from their pens, and we would thereby learn to know our own. I say that when such observers affirm of a given animal that it is a man and of another that it is a beast, they will have to be believed. But it would be very simpleminded to rely in this matter on crude travelers about whom one might sometimes be tempted to ask the same question which they get mixed up in resolving concerning other animals.

Note XI (p. 73). That appears perfectly evident to me, and I cannot conceive from where our philosophers would have arise all the passions they attribute to natural man. With the sole exception of the physically necessary, which nature itself requires, all our other needs are such only by habit, before which they were not needs, or by our desires, and one does not desire what one is not capable of knowing. It follows from this that, since savage man desires only the things he knows and knows only those things whose possession is in his power or are easily acquired, nothing should be so tranquil as his soul and nothing so limited as his mind.

Note XII (p. 76). I find in Locke's *On Civil Government* an objection that appears to me to be too plausible on its face for me to be allowed to conceal it. "The end of society between male and female," states this philosopher, "being not barely procreation, but the continuation of the species, this society between the male and the female ought to last, even after procreation, as long as is necessary to the nourishment and support of the young ones, that is, till they are able to shift and provide for themselves. This rule, which the infinite wise maker hath set to the works of his hands, we find the inferior creatures steadily and exactly obey. In those animals which feed on grass, the society between male and female lasts no longer than the very act of copulation; because the teat of the dam being sufficient to nourish the young, till it be able to feed on grass, the male only begets, but concerns not himself for the female or young, to whose sustenance he can contribute nothing. But in beasts of prey the society lasts longer, because the dam not being able well to subsist herself, and nourish her numerous off-spring by her own prey alone, a more laborious, as well as more dangerous way of living than by feeding on grass, the assistance of the male is entirely necessary to the maintenance of their common family, which cannot subsist till they are able to prey for themselves, but by the joint care of male and female. The same is to be observed in all birds—except some domestic ones, where plenty of food excuses the cock from feeding, and taking care of the young brood—whose young needing food in the nest, the cock and hen continue mates, till the young are able to use their wing and provide for themselves.

"And herein, I think, lies the leading, if not the only, reason why the male and female in mankind are obligated to a longer society than other creatures. This reason is that the female is capable of conceiving, and is commonly with child again, and brings forth a new birth, long before the former is out of a dependency for support on his parent's help and able to shift for himself. Whereby the father, who is bound to take care for those he hath begot, and to undertake that care for a long time, is under an obligation to continue in conjugal society with the same woman by whom he had them, and to remain in that society much longer than the other creatures, whose young being able to subsist of themselves, before the time of procreation returns again, the bond between male and female dissolves of itself, and they are at complete liberty, till that season which customarily beckons the animals to come together obliges them to choose new mates. Wherein one cannot but admire the wisdom of the creator, who having given to man the qualities to lay up for the future, as well as to supply the present necessity, hath wanted and made it necessary that society of man should be much more lasting, than of male and female amongst other creatures; that so their industry might be encouraged, and their interest better united, to make provision and lay up goods for their common issue, which uncertain mixture, or easy and frequent solutions of conjugal society would mightily disturb."[113]

The same love of truth that led me to sincerely present this objection

---

113. Locke, *Second Treatise of Government* (1690), 7.79–80. Locke's original English text is used here with certain necessary changes, generally minor, found in the French version from which Rousseau quotes, with some minor variations of his own. This French version was originally published in 1691 under the title of *Of Civil Government* (*Du governement civil*), the title Rousseau uses in referring to it.

prompts me to accompany it with some remarks, if not to resolve it, at least to clarify it.

1. I will first observe that moral proofs do not have a great deal of force with regard to physical matters, and that they serve rather to make sense of existing facts than to ascertain the real existence of those facts. Now, such is the kind of proof Mr. Locke uses in the passage I have just cited, for although it may be advantageous to the human species for the union of man and woman to be permanent, it does not follow that it was so established by nature, otherwise it would be necessary to say that it had also instituted civil society, the arts, commerce, and everything that is claimed to be useful to men.

2. I do not know where Mr. Locke found out that the society between male and female lasts longer among animals of prey than among those that live on grass, and that one parent helps the other to feed the young. For the dog, cat, bear, or wolf are not observed to recognize their female any better than the horse, ram, bull, stag, or all the other quadruped animals recognize theirs. On the contrary, it seems that if the help of the male were necessary for the female to preserve her young, this would be so above all for species that live solely on grass, because the mother needs a long time to graze and because during this entire time she is forced to neglect her brood, whereas the prey of the female bear or wolf is devoured in an instant and she has more time to nurse her young without suffering hunger. This reasoning is confirmed by an observation regarding the relative number of teats and young that distinguishes the carnivorous from the frugivorous species, and about which I spoke in note VIII. If that observation is correct and general, since the woman has only two teats and rarely gives birth to more than one child at a time, here we have one more strong reason for doubting that the human species is naturally carnivorous, so that it seems that in order to draw Locke's conclusion, his argument would have to be turned completely upside down. This same distinction is no more solid when applied to birds. For who could persuade himself that the union of male and female is more lasting among vultures and ravens than among turtledoves? We have two species of domesticated birds, the duck and the pigeon, which provide us with examples directly contrary to this author's system. The pigeon, which lives solely on grain, remains united with its female and they feed their young in common. The duck, whose voracity is well known, recognizes neither its female nor its young and does nothing to help with their subsistence. And among chickens, a species hardly less carnivorous, the rooster is not observed to trouble himself in the least about the brood. If

the male shares the care of feeding the young with the female in other species, it is because birds, which cannot fly at first and which the mother cannot nurse, are much less capable of doing without the father's assistance than quadrupeds, for whom the mother's teat suffices, at least for a time.

3. There is much uncertainty regarding the principal fact that serves as the basis of Mr. Locke's entire argument. For in order to know whether, as he claims, in the pure state of nature the woman is ordinarily pregnant again and has another child long before the previous one could provide for its needs by itself, experiments would be needed that Locke surely has not made and that no one is in a position to make. The continual cohabitation of husband and wife provides such an ever-present opportunity for exposing them to a new pregnancy that it is rather difficult to believe that chance encounters or the impulse of temperament alone produced such frequent consequences in the pure state of nature as in that of conjugal society—a delay which would perhaps contribute toward making children more robust, and which could more-over be compensated for by extending the capacity of conceiving to a more advanced age for women who have abused it less during their youth. With regard to children, there are many reasons for believing that their strength and their organs develop later among us than they did in the primitive state of which I am speaking. The original weakness they derive from their parents' constitution, the care taken to swaddle and restrain all their limbs, the softness in which they are raised, perhaps the use of milk from someone besides their mother—everything opposes and retards the first progress of nature in them. The concentration they are obliged to give to a thousand things on which their attention is continually fixed while their bodily strength is given no exercise can further considerably hamper their growth. So that if, instead of first over-burdening and exhausting their minds in a thousand ways, their bodies were allowed to be exercised by the continual movements nature seems to ask of them, it is likely that they would be capable of walking, acting, and providing for their needs themselves much earlier.

4. Finally, Mr. Locke proves at most that the man might very well have a motive for remaining attached to the woman when she has a child, but he does not at all prove that he must have been attached to her before the delivery and during the nine months of pregnancy. If a given woman is of no interest to the man during these nine months, if she even becomes unknown to him, why will he assist her after the delivery? Why will he help her raise a child he not only does not know belongs to him, but whose birth he neither planned nor fore-saw? Mr. Locke obviously assumes what is in question: for it is not a matter of

knowing why the man remains attached to the woman after the delivery, but why he becomes attached to her after conception. Once the appetite is satisfied, the man no longer needs a given woman nor the woman a given man. He hasn't the least concern for—nor perhaps the least idea of—the consequence of his action. One goes off in this direction, the other in that, and there is no likelihood that at the end of nine months they have any memory of having known one another. For this type of memory, by which one individual shows a preference for an individual for the act of procreation, requires, as I prove in the text, more progress or corruption of the human understanding than it can be assumed to have in the state of animality in question here. Another woman can therefore satisfy the man's new desires as readily as the one he has already known, and another man can likewise satisfy the woman, assuming she is impelled by the same appetite during pregnancy, which can be reasonably doubted. If, in the state of nature, the woman no longer experiences the passion of love after the child's conception, the obstacle to her society with the man becomes much greater still, because then she no longer needs either the man who has impregnated her or any other. There is therefore no reason for the man to seek out the same woman or any reason for the woman to seek out the same man. Locke's argument therefore falls apart, and all of that philosopher's dialectic has not saved him from the error that Hobbes and the others have committed. They had to explain a fact about the state of nature— that is, about a state in which men lived isolated and in which a given man had no motive to stay by the side of a given man, nor perhaps for men to stay by one another's sides, which is far worse; and they did not think of carrying themselves back beyond the centuries of society—that is, beyond those times when men always have a reason to stay close by one another and when a given man often has a reason to stay by the side of a given man or a given woman.

Note XIII (p. 77). I will refrain from launching into the philosophic reflections that might be made regarding the advantages and inconveniences of this institution of languages. It is not for me to attack vulgar errors, and educated people respect their prejudices too much to tolerate my supposed paradoxes with patience. Let us therefore allow those people to speak for whom it has not been made a crime to dare sometimes to take the side of reason against the opinion of the multitude. *Nor would the happiness of the human race be diminished in any way if, after the ruin and confusion of so many languages has been expelled, [all] mortals practiced [this] one art and if everything were allowed to be explained by signs, movements, and gestures. But now it has been so established that the condition of animals, which are popularly believed to be brutes, is far better than ours in this respect, for they can indicate their feelings and thoughts without an interpreter more promptly and perhaps more felicitously than any mortals, especially when they speak a foreign language.* Is. Vossius de Poëmat, Cant. et Viribus Rhythmi, p. 66.[114]

Note XIV (p. 80). Plato, showing how necessary ideas of discrete quantity and its relations are in the least of arts, rightly mocks the authors of his time who claimed that Palamedes had invented numbers at the siege of Troy, as if, states this philosopher, Agamemnon could not have known until then how many legs he had.[115] Indeed, one senses how impossible it is for society and the arts to have reached the point they had already attained by the time of the siege of Troy without men having used numbers and calculation, but the need to know numbers before acquiring other knowledge does not make their invention any easier to imagine. Once the names of numbers are known, it is easy to explain their meaning and to evoke the ideas that these names represent, but in order to invent them, and before these very ideas were conceived, it was necessary, so to speak, to be familiar with philosophical meditation, to have practiced considering beings in terms of their essence alone and independently of any other perception—a very difficult, very metaphysical, not very natural abstraction without which, however, these ideas never could have been carried from one species or one genera to another nor could numbers have become universal. A savage might separately consider his right leg and his left leg, or look at them together in terms of the indivisible idea of a pair, without ever thinking that he had two of them; for the representative idea that depicts an object to us is one thing, and the numerical idea that determines it another. Still less could he count to five, and although by placing his hands one on top the other he might have noticed that his fingers matched exactly, he was very far from considering their numerical equality. He no more knew the number of his fingers than of his hairs, and if, after having made him understand what numbers are, someone had told him that he had as many toes as fingers, he might perhaps be quite surprised, on comparing them, to discover this was true.

---

114. Isaac Vossius, *De Poematum Cantu et Viribus Rythmi* (1673), quoted by Rousseau in Latin: *Nec quidquam felicitati humani generis decederet, si, pulsâ tot linguarum peste et confusione, unam [hanc] artem [omnes] callerent mortales, et signis, motibus, gesibusque licitum foret quidvis explicare. Nunc vero ita comparatum est, ut animalium quae vulgo bruta creduntur, melior longe quam nostra hac in parte videatur conditio, ut pote quae promptius et forsan felicius, sensus et cogitationes suas sine interprete significent, quam ulli queant mortales, praesertim si peregrino utantur sermone.* Rousseau omits the words in brackets.

115. See Plato, *Republic* 7.522d.

Note XV (p. 83). Pride and self-love—two passions very different in their nature and their effects—must not be confused.[116] Self-love is a natural feeling that inclines every animal to look after its own self-preservation and that, directed in man by reason and modified by pity, produces humanity and virtue. Pride is only a relative feeling, fabricated and born in society, that inclines every individual to attach more importance to himself than to anyone else, that inspires in men all the harm they do to one another, and that is the true source of honor.

This being well understood, I say that in our primitive state, in the genuine state of nature, pride does not exist. For since every individual man regards himself as the sole spectator to observe him, as the sole being in the universe to take an interest in him, as the sole judge of his own merit, it is not possible that a sentiment that derives its source from comparisons he is not capable of making could spring up in his soul. For the same reason, this man could have neither hatred nor a desire for vengeance, passions that can arise only from the opinion that some offense has been received, and as it is contempt or the intention to harm and not the harm itself that constitutes the offense, men who do not know either how to evaluate themselves or how to compare themselves can do one another a great deal of violence, when they derive some advantage from doing so, without ever offending one another. In a word, since each man scarcely views his fellow humans any differently than he would view animals of another species, he can rob the weaker of his prey or give up his own to the stronger without considering these acts of plunder as anything but natural events, without the slightest emotion of insolence or spite, and with no other passion than the sadness or joy of a good or a bad outcome.

Note XVI (p. 97). It is extremely remarkable that for all the years Europeans have been tormenting themselves to bring the savages of various regions of the world around to their way of living, they still haven't been able to win over a single one of them, not even with the assistance of Christianity, for our missionaries sometimes make Christians of them, but never civilized men. Nothing can overcome the invincible repugnance they have for adopting our morals and living in our way. If these poor savages are as miserable as is claimed, by what

116. "Pride" here and in the rest of this note translates *amour-propre* and "self-love" translates *amour de soi-même*. As noted previously, like the English term "pride," *amour-propre* often has the pejorative sense of a corrupted form of self-love as in vanity, a negative sense that Rousseau often emphasizes in his discussions of *amour-propre*, but it also has a potentially positive sense as in "taking pride in one's work." As this note emphasizes, Rousseau's primary point is that there are two different forms of self-love: one natural to humans and other animals and the other developed in society and artificial, at least in the sense of not being original by nature.

inconceivable depravity of judgment do they constantly refuse to become civilized by imitating us or to learn to live happily among us, whereas one reads in a thousand places that Frenchmen and other Europeans have voluntarily taken refuge among these nations, have spent their entire lives there without being able to leave such a foreign way of life, and whereas even sensible missionaries are seen regretting with tender feelings the calm and innocent days they spent among those much despised peoples? If it is replied that they do not possess sufficient enlightenment to judge soundly between their condition and ours, I will reply that the assessment of happiness is less a matter of reason than of feeling. Furthermore, this reply can be turned against us with even greater force, for there is a greater distance between our ideas and the frame of mind required to conceive of the taste savages find for their way of life than there is between the savages' ideas and those that might enable them to conceive of our own way of life. Indeed, after a few observations it is easy for them to see that all our labors are directed toward two objects alone: namely, the comforts of life for oneself and being esteemed by others. But what means do we have for imagining the sort of pleasure a savage takes in spending his life alone in the midst of the forests, or fishing, or blowing into a poorly made flute without ever managing to draw a single note from it and without troubling himself to learn to do so?

On several occasions savages have been brought to Paris, London, and other cities. People have hastened to make a show for them of our luxury, our wealth, and all our most useful and most curious arts. All this has never aroused in them anything but a stupid wonderment, without the slightest movement of covetousness. I recall among others the story of a chief of some North Americans who was brought to the English court thirty years ago. A thousand things were placed before his eyes in order to try to give him some present that might please him without them finding anything that he seemed to care for. Our weapons seemed to him heavy and inconvenient, our shoes hurt his feet, our clothes he found uncomfortable, he refused everything. Finally, it was perceived that, having taken up a wool blanket, he seemed to take pleasure in wrapping it around his shoulders. You will at least admit, someone promptly said to him, the usefulness of this article? Yes, he replied, this appears to me almost as good as an animal skin. Still, he would not have said even that if he had worn them both in the rain.

Perhaps it will be said to me that it is habit which, by attaching each person to his way of life, prevents savages from sensing what is good in ours. And on that score it must, to say the least, appear quite extraordinary that habit should be stronger in preserving the savages' taste for their misery than Europeans' enjoyment of their felicity. But to give an answer to this last objection that leaves not a single word to reply—without citing all the young savages whom people have tried in vain to civilize, without speaking of the Greenlanders and inhabitants of Iceland whom they have tried to raise and feed in Denmark, all of whom sadness and despair have caused to perish, whether from yearning or in the sea, in which they tried to swim back to their country—I will limit myself to citing a single well-attested example and which I offer to be examined by the admirers of European civilization.

"All the efforts of the Dutch missionaries at the Cape of Good Hope have never been capable of converting a single Hottentot. Van der Stel, Governor of the Cape, taking one of them from infancy, had him raised in the principles of the Christian religion and in the observance of European customs. He was richly dressed, he was taught several languages, and his progress answered very well to the care taken for his education. The Governor, expecting much from his mind, sent him to the Indies with a Commissioner General who employed him usefully in the company's business. He returned to the Cape after the death of the Commissioner. A few days after his return, during a visit he made to some Hottentot relatives of his, he made the decision to get rid of his European finery and to dress himself in a sheepskin. He returned to the fort in this new garb, carrying a package which contained his former clothes, and, presenting them to the Governor, he delivered this discourse to him.* *Be so kind, Sir, as to take note that I forever renounce this apparel. I also renounce the Christian religion for the rest of my life; my resolution is to live and die in the religion, the ways, and the customs of my ancestors. The sole favor I ask of you is to let me keep the necklace and cutlass I am wearing. I will keep them for love of you.* Immediately, without waiting for Van der Stel's response, he ran off and was never seen again at the Cape." *Histoire des Voyages*, Volume 5, p. 175.[117]

Note XVII (p. 101). It might be objected to me that amid such a disorder, men, instead of obstinately slitting one another's throats, would have dispersed if there had been no limits to their dispersion. But, first, these limits would at least have been those of the world, and if one thinks of the excessive population that results from the state of nature, it has to be concluded that, in this state, it would not

---

* See the frontispiece.

---

117. The original source reprinted in the *Histoire des voyages* is Peter Kolben, *Description au Cap de Bonne-Espérance* (1719), part 1, chap. 12, §11.

have been long before the earth was covered with men, thereby forced to remain assembled. Furthermore, they would have dispersed if the evil had come swiftly and had this change occurred overnight. But they were born under the yoke; they were in the habit of bearing it by the time they felt its weight, and they limited themselves to awaiting the opportunity to shake it off. Finally, already accustomed to a thousand comforts that forced them to remain assembled, dispersion was no longer so easy as in the first times when, with no one needing anyone but himself, each made his decision without waiting for anyone else's consent.

Note XVIII (p. 103). Marshal de V*** related that in one of his campaigns, when the excessive knavery of a provisioner having made the army suffer and complain, he berated him severely and threatened to have him hanged. This threat does not bother me, the knave boldly answered him, and I have the pleasure to tell you that a man who has a hundred thousand crowns at his disposal does not get hanged. I do not know how it happened, the Marshal naively added, but in fact he was not hanged, even though he deserved it a hundred times over.[118]

Note XIX (p. 113). Distributive justice would even be opposed to that rigorous equality of the state of nature, even if were it practicable in civil society, and as all the members of the state owe it services proportionate to their talents and their resources, the citizens in turn ought to be distinguished and favored in proportion to their services. It is in this sense that a passage in Isocrates must be understood in which he praises the first Athenians for knowing how to discern correctly which was the more advantageous of the two sorts of equality, the first of which consists in apportioning all the same advantages among all the citizens indifferently and the other in distributing them according to each one's merit. These skillful politicians, adds the orator, banishing that unjust equality which establishes no distinction between evil and good men, inviolably adhered to that sort of equality that rewards and punishes each according to his merit.[119] But, first, no society has ever existed, regardless of the degree of corruption it may have attained, in which no distinction was made between evil and good men; and in matters of morals—where the law cannot establish a sufficiently precise standard to serve as a rule for the magistrate—the law, in order not to leave the fate or rank of the citizens at the magistrate's discretion, very wisely forbids him to pass judgment on persons, allowing him only to pass judgment on actions. Only morals as pure as those of

---

118. Claude Louis Hector, Duke of Villars and Marshal General of France (1653–1734), was one of Louis XIV's greatest generals. His memoirs were first published in 1734.

119. Isocrates (436–338 BC) *Areopagitica* 21–22.

the ancient Romans could tolerate censors, and such tribunals would soon have turned everything upside down among us. It is up to public esteem to establish the distinction between evil and good men. The magistrate is judge only of rigorous right, but the people is the genuine judge of morals—an upright and even enlightened judge on this point, sometimes deceived but never corrupted. The ranks of citizens ought therefore to be regulated not according to their personal merit, which would be to let the magistrate have the means to apply the laws almost arbitrarily, but according to the real services they render to the state, which are liable to a more precise assessment.

ON THE

SOCIAL CONTRACT;

OR, PRINCIPLES OF

POLITICAL RIGHT

BY J.-J. ROUSSEAU
CITIZEN OF GENEVA[1]

By an equitable pact
We will make laws.
—*Aeneid* 11[2]

AMSTERDAM
CHEZ MARC MICHEL REY, MDCCLXII

---

1. Rousseau was a citizen of Geneva at the time he published the *Social Contract* in 1762. He had lost his citizenship when he left the city at sixteen years of age and converted to Catholicism, but then regained it in 1754.

2. Virgil *Aeneid* 11.321–22, quoted by Rousseau in Latin: —*foederis aequas / Dicamus leges*. The passage comes from a speech by the king of Latium immediately following the defeat of his army by the Trojans under Aeneas. After lamenting their defeat and commenting that it is unfortunate that they have to deliberate among themselves with the Trojan army at their walls, the king recommends uniting with the victorious Trojans.

NOTICE

THIS SHORT TREATISE is extracted from a more extensive work, undertaken years ago without having consulted my strength and long since abandoned. Of the various portions that could be taken from what had been completed, this is the most considerable and appeared to me to be the least unworthy of being offered to the public. The rest no longer exists.[3]

---

3. Rousseau discusses his project for a more ambitious political work, the *Political Institutions*, in his *Confessions, Collected Writings*, 5:339–42, 432.

TABLE OF THE BOOKS
AND THE CHAPTERS[4]

·◁══════▷·

BOOK I
Investigating how man passes from the state of nature to the
civil state and what the essential conditions of the compact are.

BOOK II
Discussing legislation.

---

4. This table of contents was included in the first edition of the *Social Contract*. For Rousseau's discussion of the table of contents, see his letter to Marc-Michel Rey of February 28, 1762 (*Correspondence complète*, 10:122).

BOOK III

Discussing political laws, that is,
the form of the government.

BOOK IV

*While continuing the discussion of political laws, the means for
strengthening the constitution of the state are explained.*

ON THE

SOCIAL CONTRACT;

OR, PRINCIPLES OF

POLITICAL RIGHT

BOOK I

·⊂━━━━━━━⊃·

I WANT TO INQUIRE whether there can be any legitimate and reliable rule of administration in the civil order, taking men as they are and laws as they can be. In this inquiry I will always try to join what right permits with what interest prescribes, so that justice and utility are not always at odds.

I begin my discussion without proving the importance of my subject. I will be asked whether I am a prince or lawgiver given that I am writing about politics. I reply that I am not, and that it is for this very reason that I write about politics. If I were a prince or a lawgiver, I would not waste my time saying what needs to be done; I would do it, or I would remain silent.

Born a citizen of a free state, and a member of the sovereign, the right to vote there is enough to impose on me the duty to learn about public affairs, regardless of how weak the influence of my voice on them may be. How happy I am, every time I meditate about governments, always to find in my research new reasons to love that of my country!

CHAPTER I
Subject of this First Book

Man is born free, and everywhere he is in chains.[5] He who believes himself the master of others fails not to be a greater slave than they. How did this change

---

5. Two points regarding translation should be noted. First, "man" translates *homme*, which can mean either "man" (that is, a human being of the male sex) or "human being" (applying to both sexes). While it is tempting to translate *homme* as "human being," it is arguable that Rousseau's usage of the word is often not gender-neutral and so the word will be consistently translated as "man" (or "men" in the plural) throughout.

Second, the phrase "Man is born free . . . " (*L'homme est né libre . . .*) could also be translated in the past tense: "Man was born free. . . . " The grammatical structure in French is ambiguous, and Rousseau is perhaps intentionally ambiguous here. On the one hand, if he is using the past tense here, he may be pointing to his account in the *Discourse on Inequality* of the historical emergence of humans from the state of nature into society

come about? I do not know. What can make it legitimate? I do believe I can resolve that issue.

If I were to consider only force and the effect that derives from it, I would say: as long as a people is compelled to obey and does obey, it does well; as soon as it can shake off the yoke and does shake it off, it does even better. For in recovering its freedom by the same right used to rob it of its freedom, either the people is justified in taking it back, or those who took it away from it were not justified in doing so. But the social order is a sacred right that serves as the basis for all the others. Yet this right does not come from nature; it is therefore founded on conventions.⁶ It is a question of knowing what these conventions are. Before coming to that, I should establish what I have just put forward.

CHAPTER 2
On the First Societies

The most ancient of all societies and the only natural one is that of the family. Still, children remain bound to the father only as long as they need him to preserve themselves. As soon as this need ceases, the natural bond dissolves. The children, exempt from the obedience they owed the father, and the father, exempt from the care he owed the children, all equally return to independence. If they continue to remain united, it is no longer so naturally but rather voluntarily, and the family itself is maintained only by convention.

This common freedom is a consequence of man's nature. His first law is to attend to his own preservation, his first cares are those he owes himself, and since, as soon as he has attained the age of reason, he alone is the sole judge of the means proper for preserving himself, he thereby becomes his own master.

The family is therefore, if you will, the first model of political societies. The leader⁷ is the image of the father, the people is the image of the children, and since all are born equal and free, they alienate their freedom only for the sake

---

and eventually into political associations. On the other hand, if he is using the present tense, perhaps thereby setting aside any historical account of this transformation, he is making a claim about the natural freedom of human beings in a moral or legal sense. In this light, compare John Locke, *Second Treatise of Government* (1690), 1.2.4: "To understand political power right, and derive it from its original, we must consider what state all men *are* naturally in, and that is, a state of perfect freedom . . . " (emphasis supplied).

6. "Conventions" here and elsewhere in this work refers to formal agreements such as the social contract itself. Such agreements are also "conventional" in the sense of being non-natural.

7. "Leader" translates *chef*, which might also be translated "chief." The French term *chef* has a number of applications and can be used with regard to the "chief" or "head" of a political or business organization (hence the head of a restaurant kitchen is a "chef"). Although the English term "leader" has a somewhat more democratic connotation than the French term *chef*, especially in Rousseau's time, the term has been translated as "leader" when used with regard to politics.

of their utility. The entire difference is that in the family the father's love for his children rewards him for the care he provides them, whereas in the state the pleasure of commanding takes the place of this love, which the leader does not have for his peoples.

Grotius denies that all human power is established for the benefit of those who are governed. He cites slavery as an example.[8] His most persistent mode of reasoning is always to establish right by fact.* A more consistent method could be used, but not one more favorable to tyrants.

It is therefore doubtful, according to Grotius, whether the human race belongs to a hundred men, or whether those hundred men belong to the human race, and throughout his book he appears to incline to the former view. This is also Hobbes' opinion.[10] So behold the human race divided into herds of cattle, each of which has its leader who tends it in order to devour it.

As a shepherd is of a superior nature to that of his herd, so shepherds of men— who are their leaders—are also of a nature superior to that of their peoples. So reasoned the Emperor Caligula, according to Philo's account, concluding rightly enough from this analogy that kings were gods or that peoples were beasts.[11]

---

* "Learned research into public right is often merely the history of ancient abuses, and those who have taken the trouble to study it too closely have done so with a wrongheaded obstinence." *Treatise on the Interests of France with its Neighbors, by M. le Marquis d'Argenson* (printed by Rey in Amsterdam). This is precisely what Grotius has done.[9]

---

8. See Grotius, *The Rights of War and Peace* (1625), 1.3.8, vol. 1:260–61: "And here we must first reject their opinion, who will have the supreme power to be always, and without exception, in the people; so that they may restrain or punish their kings, as often as they abuse their power. What mischiefs this opinion has occasioned, and may yet occasion, if once the minds of people are fully possessed with it, every wise man sees. I shall refute it with these arguments. It is lawful for any man to engage himself as a slave to whom he pleases. . . . Why should not it not therefore be as lawful for a people that are at their own disposal, to deliver themselves up to any one or more persons, and transfer the right of governing them upon him or them, without reserving any share of that right themselves?"

9. René-Louis de Voyer de Paulmy, marquis d'Argenson, *Considérations sur le gouvernement ancien et présent de la France* (Amsterdam, 1764). At the time of the original publication of the *Social Contract* in 1762, d'Argenson's work existed only in manuscript under the title Rousseau cites in the text. In the first edition of the *Social Contract* Rousseau indicated d'Argenson's name only by the initials "M. L. M. d'A." D'Argenson's *Considérations* was published in 1764 by Marc-Michel Rey, with the passage Rousseau quotes on p. 13.

10. See Hobbes, *Leviathan* (1651), chap. 17, pp. 109–10: "The attaining to this sovereign power is by two ways. One, by natural force, as when a man maketh his children to submit themselves and their children to his government, as being able to destroy them if they refuse, or by war subdueth his enemies to his will, giving them their lives on that condition. The other is when men agree amongst themselves to submit to some man, or assembly of men, voluntarily. . . ."

11. See Philo of Alexandria *On the Embassy to Caius* (or *Gaius*) 11.76: "for as the curators of the herds of other animals, namely cowherds, and goatherds, and shepherds, are neither oxen nor goats, nor sheep, but men who have received a more excellent portion, and a more admirable formation of mind and body; so in the same manner, said he, is it fitting that I who am the leader of the most excellent of all herds, namely, the race of mankind, should be considered as a being of a superior nature, and not merely human, but as one who has received a greater and more holy portion" (trans. Charles Duke Yonge [London: Bohm, 1854–90]).

Caligula's reasoning amounts to that of Hobbes and Grotius. Before any of them, Aristotle had also said that men are not naturally equal, but that some are born for slavery and others for domination.[12]

Aristotle was right, but he mistook the effect for the cause. Every man born in slavery is born for slavery—nothing is more certain. Slaves lose everything in their chains, even the desire to leave them. They love their servitude just as Ulysses' companions loved their brutishness.* If there are slaves by nature, then, it is because there have been slaves contrary to nature. Force made the first slaves, their cowardice perpetuated them.

I have said nothing about King Adam, nor about Emperor Noah, father of the three great monarchs who divided up the universe amongst themselves, as did Saturn's children, with whom they have been identified.[14] I hope that this moderation of mine will be appreciated, for since I am directly descended from one of these princes, and perhaps from the eldest branch, how am I to know whether, upon the verification of titles, I might not find out that I am the legitimate king of the human race? Be that as it may, it cannot be denied that Adam was sovereign of the world just like Robinson was of his island, as long as he was its sole inhabitant.[15] And what made this empire convenient was that the monarch, secure on his throne, had neither rebellions, nor wars, nor conspirators to fear.

CHAPTER 3
On the Right of the Stronger

The stronger is never strong enough to be forever the master unless he transforms his force into right and obedience into duty. Hence the right of the stronger—a right seemingly understood ironically, and in actuality established as a principle. But will this word ever be explained to us? Force is a

---

* See a short treatise by Plutarch entitled *That Animals Use Reason*.[13]

---

12. See Aristotle *Politics* 1.3–6.

13. This work is a brief dialogue between Ulysses and Circe, who had turned Ulysses' men into pigs (see Homer *Odyssey* 10), and then between Ulysses and Gryllus, in which they discuss whether animals use reason.

14. Rousseau alludes to the patriarchal theory most prominently associated with Sir Robert Filmer, who argued in his *Patriarcha* (composed in the 1630s or 1640s and published in 1680) that political authority is inherited through descent from Adam. John Locke wrote his *Two Treatises of Government* (1690), and especially the *First Treatise*, against Filmer's theory, as did Algernon Sidney in his *Discourses Concerning Government* (1698).

15. Rousseau refers to Robinson Crusoe from Daniel Defoe's *Robinson Crusoe* (1719).

physical power. I do not see what morality can result from its effects. To yield to force is an act of necessity, not of will; it is at most an act of prudence. In what sense could it be a duty?

Let us assume this alleged right for a moment. I say that only inexplicable gibberish results. For once force makes right, the effect changes along with the cause. Any force that overcomes the first one succeeds to its right. Once one can disobey with impunity, one can do so legitimately, and because the stronger is always right, it is merely a matter of making it so that one is the stronger. Yet what is a right that perishes when force ceases? If one must obey due to force, there is no need to obey due to duty, and if one is no longer forced to obey, one is no longer obligated to do so. It is clear, therefore, that this word "right" adds nothing to force. It means nothing at all here.

Obey the powers that be.[16] If this is supposed to mean, "yield to force," the precept is good, but superfluous. I say that it will never be violated. All power comes from God, I admit it; but all illness[17] comes from him as well. Does this mean it is forbidden to call the doctor? A brigand takes me by surprise at the edge of a wood: must I not only give him my purse through force, but, even if I could withhold it, am I obligated in conscience to give it? For, after all, the pistol he is holding is also a power.

Let us agree, therefore, that force does not make right, and that one is obligated to obey only legitimate powers. Thus my original question still stands.

CHAPTER 4
On Slavery

Because no man has any natural authority over his fellow human,[18] and because force produces no right, conventions remain as the only basis of all legitimate authority among men.

If a private individual, states Grotius, can alienate his freedom and enslave himself to a master, why can't a people alienate its freedom and subject itself to a king?[19] There are quite a few equivocal words here that need explaining, but let us limit ourselves to the word *alienate*. To alienate is to give or to sell. Now, a man who makes himself a slave to another does not give himself,

---

16. See Romans 13:1.

17. "Illness" translates *mal*, which could also be translated "ill" or "evil."

18. "Fellow human" translates *semblable*. Although the term generally refers to one's fellow humans, it has the root sense of "like" or "similar" and so can also have the more extended sense of beings who are recognized as similar to oneself. See n. 21 (p. 54) of the *Discourse on Inequality*.

19. Grotius, *The Rights of War and Peace* (1625), 1.3.8. See n. 8 (p. 165) above.

he sells himself, at the very least for his subsistence. But a people: why does it sell itself? Far from a king furnishing his subjects with their subsistence, he derives his own from them alone, and according to Rabelais a king does not live cheaply.[20] Do the subjects therefore give their persons on the condition that their goods will be taken as well? I do not see what they have left to preserve.

The despot, it will be said, ensures civil tranquility for his subjects. Perhaps. But what do they gain from it if the wars his ambition brings on them, if his insatiable greed, if harassment by his administration cause them more distress than their own dissensions would have? What do they gain from it if this very tranquility is one of their woes? Life is tranquil in dungeons as well; is that enough to find them good? The Greeks closed up in the Cyclops's cave lived there tranquilly while awaiting their turn to be devoured.

To say a man gives himself gratuitously is to say something absurd and inconceivable. Such an act is illegitimate and null, if only because whoever does so is not in his right mind. To say the same thing of a whole people is to assume a people of madmen. Madness does not make right.

Even if each person could alienate himself, he could not alienate his children. They are born men and free. Their freedom belongs to them, and no one but they themselves has a right to dispose of it. Before they have attained the age of reason, the father can in their name stipulate the conditions for their preservation, for their well-being, but he cannot give them irrevocably and unconditionally, for such a gift is contrary to the ends of nature and exceeds the rights of paternity. For an arbitrary government to be legitimate, therefore, the people at each generation would have to be the master of accepting or rejecting it. But then this government would no longer be arbitrary.

To renounce one's freedom is to renounce one's quality as a man, the rights of humanity, even its duties. There is no possible compensation for someone who renounces everything. Such a renunciation is incompatible with man's nature, and to deprive his will of all freedom is to deprive his actions of all morality. Finally, a convention that stipulates absolute authority for one party and unlimited obedience for the other is vain and contradictory. Isn't it clear that one is in no way bound to someone from whom one has a right to demand everything, and that this condition alone—without any equivalence, without any reciprocity—entails the nullification of the act? For what right would my slave

---

20. François Rabelais's work *Gargantua and Pantagruel* (published c. 1532–64) tells the extravagant stories of two giant kings, lampooning various religious and political institutions of his time.

have against me, because everything he has belongs to me and because, since his right is mine, this right of me against myself is a meaningless expression?

Grotius and the others derive another origin of the alleged right of slavery from war. Since the victor, according to them, has the right to kill the vanquished, the vanquished can buy back his life at the cost of his freedom—a convention all the more legitimate as it works to the profit of both.[21]

But it is clear that this alleged right to kill the vanquished in no way results from the state of war. Men are not naturally enemies if only because when they live in their primitive independence they do not have a stable enough relationship among themselves to constitute either a state of peace or a state of war. It is the relationship between things and not between men that constitutes war, and since the state of war cannot arise from simple personal relations but only from property relations, private war, or war between one man and another, can exist neither in the state of nature, where there is no stable property, nor in the social state, where everything is under the authority of the laws.

Individual combats, duels, occasional conflicts are acts that do not constitute a state; and as for private wars, authorized by the ordinances of Louis IX, King of France and suspended by the Peace of God,[22] these are abuses of feudal government, an absurd system if there ever was one, contrary to the principles of natural right and to all good policy.

War is therefore not a relation between one man and another, but a relation between one state and another, in which private individuals are enemies only by accident—not as men, nor even as citizens,* but as soldiers; not as members of the fatherland,[23] but as its defenders. Finally, each state can have

---

* The Romans, who understood and respected the right of war better than any nation in the world, were so very scrupulous in this regard that a citizen was not allowed to serve as a volunteer without his having expressly enlisted against the enemy, and against that particular enemy by name. When a legion in which the younger Cato was serving for the first time under Popilius had been reorganized, Cato the Elder wrote to Popilius that if he wanted his son to continue serving under him, he would have to have him take a new military

---

21. Grotius, *The Rights of War and Peace* (1625), 1.3.8.

22. Louis IX of France eliminated various legal prohibitions against dueling in 1258. The "Peace of God," or *Pax Dei*, was a proclamation by the Church that granted immunity from violence to various classes of noncombatants.

23. "Fatherland" translates *patrie*. *Patrie* might also be translated "country," in the sense of the phrase "love of country," hence "patriotism." However, aside from the fact that "country" also translates *pays*, which does not have the strong political sense of *patrie*, Rousseau argues that modern peoples can have a "country" (*pays*) without having a true "fatherland" (*patrie*). Although the term "fatherland" in contemporary English often has a pejorative sense stemming from the nationalist movements and wars of the twentieth century, *patrie* will be translated as "fatherland" throughout.

as enemies only other states and not men, inasmuch as no true relationship can be established between things of different natures.

This principle even conforms to the established maxims of all ages and to the constant practice of all civilized peoples. Declarations of war are less warnings to those in power than to their subjects. A foreigner—whether king, or individual, or people—who robs, kills, or detains subjects without declaring war on their prince is not an enemy, he is a brigand. Even in the midst of war, a just prince may well take possession of everything in enemy territory that belongs to the public, but he respects the person and goods of private individuals. He respects the rights on which his own are founded. Since the aim of war is the destruction of the enemy state, one has a right to kill its defenders as long as they bear arms. But as soon as they lay down their arms and surrender, since they thereby cease to be enemies or the enemy's instruments, they once again become simply men and one no longer has a right over their lives. Sometimes a state can be killed without killing a single one of its members. Yet war gives no right that is not necessary to its aim. These principles are not those of Grotius; they are not founded on the authority of poets; rather, they derive from the nature of things, and are founded on reason.

With regard to the right of conquest, it has no other foundation than the law of the stronger. If war does not give the victor the right to massacre the vanquished peoples, this right he does not have cannot be the foundation of that of enslaving them. One has the right to kill the enemy only when one cannot make him a slave. The right to make him a slave therefore does not come from the right to kill him. It is therefore an iniquitous exchange to make him buy his life, over which he does not have any right, at the cost of his freedom. In establishing the right of life and death on the right of slavery, and the right of slavery on the right of life and death, isn't it clear that one falls into a vicious circle?

Even assuming this terrible right to kill everyone, I say that a slave made

---

oath because, the first one being annulled, he could no longer bear arms against the enemy. And the same Cato wrote to his son to be careful not to appear in battle without having taken this new oath.[24] I know that the siege of Clusium and other specific facts could be raised in objection to me, but, as for me, I cite laws, practices. The Romans are the people who least often transgressed their laws, and they are the only one who had such fine ones.

---

24. The story is taken from Cicero *On Duties* 1.11.36. The "younger Cato" in question here is not the better-known "Cato the Younger," the Roman statesman who lived during the period of the fall of the Roman Republic, but rather the son of Marcus Porcius Cato or "Cato the Elder" (234–149 BC), the famously upright Roman statesman and censor.

such through war, or a conquered people, is in no way committed to his master, except to obey him insofar as he is forced to do so. In taking the equivalent of his life, the victor has not spared it. Instead of killing him uselessly, he has killed him usefully. Far from having acquired over him any authority joined to force, therefore, the state of war persists between them as it did beforehand, their relation itself is its effect, and the customs of the right of war presuppose that there has not been any peace treaty. They have made a convention. Perhaps. But this convention, far from destroying the state of war, presupposes its continuation.

Thus, from whatever vantage point one looks at things, the right of slavery is null and void, not only because it is illegitimate, but because it is absurd and meaningless. These words *slavery* and *right* are contradictory; they are mutually exclusive. Whether it is said with reference to one man and another, or one man and a people, the following speech will always be equally absurd: *I am making an agreement[25] with you entirely at your expense and entirely to my benefit, which I will observe so long as I please and which you will observe so long as I please.*

CHAPTER 5
That It Is Always Necessary to Go Back to a First Convention

Even if I were to grant everything I have refuted so far, the champions of despotism would be no better off for it. There will always be a great difference between subjecting a multitude and leading a society. If scattered men, regardless of how many of them there may be, were successively enslaved to a single person, I see there nothing but a master and slaves; I do not see a people and its leader. It is, if you will, an aggregation, but not an association; there is neither public good nor body politic. That man, even if he had enslaved half the world, is still merely a private individual. His interest, being separate from that of the others, is still merely a private interest. If this same man happens to die, his empire is left behind scattered and without a bond, like an oak tree that dissolves and collapses into a heap of ashes after fire has consumed it.

A people, states Grotius, can give itself to a king.[26] According to Grotius, then, a people is a people before giving itself to a king. This very gift is a civil act; it presupposes a public deliberation. Before examining the act by which a people elects a king, therefore, it would be good to examine the act by which a

---

25. "Agreement" here translates *convention*, which is elsewhere translated "convention."
26. Grotius, The Rights of War and Peace (1625), 1.3.8.

people is a people. For this act, being necessarily prior to the other, is the true foundation of society.

Indeed, if there were no prior convention, unless the election were unanimous, wherein lies the obligation for the minority to submit itself to the choice of the majority, and where do one hundred people who want a master get the right to vote on behalf of ten who do not want one? The law of majority rule is itself established by convention and presupposes unanimity at least once.

CHAPTER 6
On the Social Compact

I assume that men have reached that point where the obstacles that interfere with their self-preservation in the state of nature prevail by their resistance over the forces each individual can use to maintain himself in that state. Then that primitive state can no longer persist, and the human race would perish if it did not change its manner of being.

Now, as men cannot engender new forces, but merely unite and direct those that exist, they have no other means for preserving themselves than to form, by aggregation, a sum of forces that might prevail over the resistance, to set them in motion by a single impetus, and to make them act in concert.

This sum of forces can arise only from the cooperation of many. But since each man's force and freedom are the primary instruments of his self-preservation, how can he commit them without harming himself and without neglecting the care he owes himself? This difficulty, as it pertains to my subject, can be expressed in the following terms:

"How to find a form of association that defends and protects the person and goods of each associate with all the common force, and by means of which each, uniting with all, nonetheless obeys only himself and remains as free as before?" Such is the fundamental problem to which the social contract provides the solution.

The clauses of this contract are so completely determined by the nature of the act that the slightest modification would render them null and void. As a result, although they may never have been formally enunciated, they are everywhere the same, everywhere tacitly acknowledged and recognized; they are such until that point when, the social compact having been violated, each person recovers his first rights and regains his natural freedom while losing the conventional freedom for which he renounced it.

These clauses, properly understood, all come down to a single one, namely the total alienation of each associate with all his rights to the whole community. For, in the first place, since each gives himself entirely, the condition is equal for all, and since the condition is equal for all, no one has an interest in making it burdensome for the others.

Moreover, since the alienation is made without reservation, the union is as complete as it can be and no associate has anything further to claim. For if any rights were left to private individuals, as there would be no common superior that could judge between them and the public, each person, being his own judge concerning some issue, would soon claim to be so concerning all of them: the state of nature would persist and the association would necessarily become tyrannical or vain.

Finally, since each gives himself to all, he gives himself to no one, and as there is no associate over whom he does not acquire the same right that he grants him over himself, he gains the equivalent of everything he loses and more force to preserve what he has.

If, then, everything that is not of the essence of the social compact is set aside, it will be found that it comes down to the following terms. *Each of us puts his person and all his power in common under the supreme direction of the general will; and as a body we receive each member as an indivisible part of the whole.*

Instantly, in place of the particular person of each contracting party, this act of association produces a moral and collective body made up of as many members as there are voices in the assembly, which receives from this same act its unity, its common *self*, its life, and its will. This public person thus formed by the union of all the others formerly took the name *city*,* and now takes that

---

* The true meaning of this word has almost entirely vanished among the moderns. Most of them mistake a town for a city and a bourgeois for a citizen.[27] They do not know that houses make the town but that citizens make the city. This same error once cost the Carthaginians dearly. I have not read anywhere that the subjects of a prince have ever been given the title *cives*, not even the Macedonians in ancient times nor, in our days, the English, even though they are closer to freedom than all the others. The French alone colloquially use this name *citizens* because they have no genuine idea of its meaning, as can be seen from their dictionaries. Otherwise, they would be committing the crime of high treason in usurping it: for them, this name expresses a virtue and not a right. When Bodin wanted to speak of our citizens and bourgeois, he made a gross blunder by mistaking the one for the other.[28] M. d'Alembert did not make such a mistake, and in his article *Geneva* he has correctly distinguished the four orders of men (even five, counting simple foreigners) in our town, and only two of which make up the republic.[29] No other French author that I know of has understood the true meaning of the word *citizen*.

---

27. "Town" translates *ville*, which could also be translated "city," and "city" translates *cité*. Rousseau's point here about the true meaning of a city and a citizen would be lost if *ville* were translated "city," and so *ville* has therefore been translated as "town" in this context.

28. See Jean Bodin, *Six Books of the Commonwealth* (1576), 1.6.

29. See Jean le Rond d'Alembert's article "Genève" in the *Encyclopédie* (1757), vol. 7.

of *republic* or of *body politic*, which is called *state* by its members when it is passive, *sovereign* when it is active, *power* when comparing it to similar bodies. With regard to the associates, they collectively take the name *people*, and individually they are called *citizens* as participants in the sovereign authority, and *subjects* as subject to the laws of the state. But these terms are often confused and are mistaken for one another. It is enough to know how to distinguish them when they are used with complete precision.

CHAPTER 7
On the Sovereign

This formulation shows that the act of association encompasses a reciprocal commitment of the public with private individuals, and that each individual, in contracting with himself finds himself, so to speak, engaged in a double relation: namely, as a member of the sovereign toward private individuals, and as a member of the state toward the sovereign. But the maxim of civil right that no one is bound to commitments toward himself cannot be applied in this case, for there is a great difference between being obligated toward oneself and toward a whole of which one is a part.

It must be noted as well that public deliberation, which can obligate all the subjects toward the sovereign—due to the two different relations in terms of which each of the subjects is considered—cannot, for the opposite reason, obligate the sovereign toward itself, and that, consequently, it is contrary to the nature of the body politic for the sovereign to impose a law on itself it cannot break. Since the sovereign can consider itself only under one and the same relation, it is then in the situation of a private individual contracting with himself. It is clear from this that there is not—nor can there be—any type of fundamental law that is obligatory for the body of the people, not even the social contract. This does not mean that this body could not perfectly well enter into a commitment with others regarding anything that does not go against this contract. For with regard to a foreigner, it becomes a simple being, an individual.

But since the body politic or the sovereign derives its being solely from the sanctity of the contract, it can never obligate itself, even toward another, with regard to anything that goes against that original act, such as alienating any part of itself or subjecting itself to another sovereign. To violate the act by which it exists would be to annihilate itself, and whatever is nothing produces nothing.

As soon as this multitude is thus united in one body, none of its members can be harmed without attacking the body, and still less can the body be harmed without its members feeling the effects. Thus duty and interest alike obligate the two contracting parties to help one another, and these same men should endeavor to combine in this double relation all the advantages which depend on it.

Now, since the sovereign is formed solely of the private individuals who make it up, it does not have—and cannot have—any interest contrary to theirs. Consequently, the sovereign power has no need of a guarantor toward the subjects, because it is impossible for the body to want to harm all its members, and we will see below that it cannot harm any of them individually. The sovereign, by the very fact of what it is, is always all that it ought to be.

But this is not so for the subjects in relation to the sovereign: despite their common interest, nothing would vouch for the subjects' commitments unless the sovereign found some means to be assured of their fidelity.

Indeed, each individual can, as a man, have a particular will contrary to or differing from the general will he has as a citizen. His particular interest can speak to him entirely differently than the common interest. His absolute and naturally independent existence can lead him to view what he owes to the common cause as a gratuitous contribution, the loss of which will be less harmful to others than its payment is burdensome to him. And considering the moral person that constitutes the state merely as a being produced by reason because it is not a man, he would enjoy the rights of a citizen without being willing to fulfill the duties of a subject—an injustice whose spread would cause the ruin of the body politic.

Therefore, in order for the social compact not to be an empty formality, it tacitly encompasses the following commitment, which alone can give force to the rest: that whoever does refuse to obey the general will be constrained to do so by the whole body, which means nothing else but that he be forced to be free. For such is the condition that, by giving each citizen to the fatherland, guarantees him against all personal dependence—a condition that makes for the ingenuity and the functioning of the political machine and that alone makes legitimate civil engagements which would otherwise be absurd, tyrannical, and liable to the most enormous abuses.

CHAPTER 8
On the Civil State

This transition from the state of nature to the civil state produces a very remarkable change in man, by substituting justice for instinct in his conduct and by giving his actions the morality they previously lacked. Only then, when the voice of duty replaces physical impulse and right replaces appetite, does man, who until then had considered only himself, see himself forced to act on the basis of other principles and to consult his reason before listening to his inclinations. Although he deprives himself in this state of several advantages he derives from nature, he gains such great advantages from it—his faculties exercised and developed, his ideas enlarged, his feelings ennobled, his entire soul so greatly elevated—that if the abuses of this new condition did not often degrade him beneath the condition he left, he ought to be endlessly thankful for the happy moment that forever tore him away from it, and that, from a stupid and limited animal, made an intelligent being and a man.

Let us reduce the pros and cons to easily comparable terms. What man loses by the social contract is his natural freedom and an unlimited right to everything that tempts him and that he can get. What he gains is civil freedom and property in everything he possesses. In order not to be mistaken about these compensations, one must carefully distinguish between natural freedom, which has as its bounds only the individual's force, and civil freedom, which is limited by the general will, and between possession, which is merely the effect of force or the right of the first occupant, and property, which can be founded only on a positive title.

To the foregoing acquisitions of the civil state might be added moral freedom, which alone makes man truly the master of himself. For the impulsion of appetite alone is slavery, and obedience to the law one has prescribed to oneself is freedom. But I have already said too much about this topic, and the philosophical meaning of the word *freedom* is not my subject here.

CHAPTER 9
On Real Property

Each member of the community gives himself to it at the moment it is formed, such as he then is—himself and all his force, of which the goods he possesses make up a part. It is not the case that by this act possession, by changing hands, changes nature and becomes property in the sovereign's hands. Rather, just as the city's force is incomparably greater than a private individual's, so public possession by this fact also has greater force and is more irrevocable, without being any more legitimate, at least as far as foreigners are concerned. For with regard to its members the state is master of all their goods by the social contract, which within the state serves as the basis of all their rights. But with regard to other powers, it is master only through the right of the first occupant, which it derives from private individuals.

The right of the first occupant, although a more genuine right than the right of the stronger, becomes a true right only after the right of property has been established. Every man naturally has a right to everything he needs, but the positive act that makes him the proprietor of a certain good excludes him from all the rest. Once his portion has been determined, he should limit himself to it, and he no longer has any right to the community of goods. That is why the right of the first occupant, so weak in the state of nature, is respected by everyone in civil society. In this right one respects less what is another's than what is not one's own.

In general, the following conditions are necessary to authorize the right of the first occupant to any piece of land whatsoever. First, that this land not yet be inhabited by anyone. Second, that one occupy only as much of it as one needs to subsist. In the third place, that one take possession of it not by an empty ceremony, but by labor and cultivation — the sole sign of property that should be respected by others in the absence of legal titles.

Indeed, doesn't attributing the right of the first occupant to need and labor extend it as far as it can go? Can't limits be given to this right? Will it be enough to put one's foot on a piece of commonly held land to claim to be its master from then on? Will having the force to drive other men off of it for a moment be enough to deprive them of their right ever to return? How can a man or a people seize an immense territory and deprive the entire human race of it otherwise than by a punishable usurpation, since it deprives the rest of a place to live and foods that nature gave to them in common? When Núñez Balboa, standing upon the shore, took possession of the South Sea and all of South America in the name of the crown of Castile, was that enough to dispossess all its inhabitants and to exclude all the princes of the world? If such is the case, then these ceremonies were multiplied quite needlessly, and all the Catholic king had to do was to take possession of the entire universe all at once from his study — except then afterwards subtracting from his empire what was already possessed by other princes.

It can be conceived how the united and contiguous parcels of land of private individuals become the public territory, and how the right of sovereignty, extending from subjects to the land they occupy, becomes at the same time real and personal, putting those who possess it in a situation of greater dependence and turning their very force into the guarantor of their fidelity. This advantage does not appear to have been fully appreciated by ancient monarchs who, only calling themselves kings of the Persians, of the Scythians, of the Macedonians, seem to have regarded themselves as leaders of men rather than as masters of the country. Those of today more shrewdly call themselves kings of France, of Spain, of England, etc. By thus holding the land, they are quite certain of holding its inhabitants.

What is extraordinary about this alienation is that the community, far from despoiling private individuals of their goods by accepting them, merely assures them of their legitimate possession and transforms usurpation into a genuine right and use into property. Then the possessors, since they are considered as trustees of the public good, with their rights being respected by all the members of the state and secured by all of its force against foreigners, have, through a transfer advantageous to the public and even more so to themselves, so to speak acquired everything they have given—a paradox readily explained by the distinction between the rights which the sovereign and the proprietor have to the same resource, as will be seen below.

It can also happen that men begin to unite before possessing anything and that, subsequently taking possession of a piece of land sufficient for all, they use it in common or divide it up among themselves, either equally or according to proportions determined by the sovereign. Regardless of how this acquisition is made, the right each private individual has to his own resources is always subordinate to the right the community has over everyone, without which there would be neither solidity in the social bond nor actual force in the exercise of sovereignty.

I will end this chapter and this book with a comment that should serve as the basis for the entire social system. It is that rather than destroying natural equality, the fundamental pact on the contrary substitutes a moral and legitimate equality for whatever physical inequality nature may have placed between men, and that while they may be unequal in force or genius, they all become equal through convention and by right.*

END OF THE FIRST BOOK

---

* Under bad governments this equality is only apparent and illusory. It serves only to keep the poor man in his misery and the rich man in his usurpation. In fact, laws are always useful to those who have possessions and harmful to those who have nothing. It follows from this that the social state is advantageous for men only insofar as they all have something and as none of them has too much.

BOOK II

CHAPTER I
That Sovereignty Is Inalienable

The first and the most important consequence of the principles established above is that the general will alone can direct the forces of the state according to the end of its institution, which is the common good. For if the opposition of particular interests has made the establishment of societies necessary, it is the agreement of these same interests that has made it possible. It is what these different interests have in common that forms the social bond, and if there were not some point on which all these interests are in agreement, no society could exist. Hence it is solely on the basis of this common interest that society should be governed.

I say, therefore, that sovereignty—since it is nothing but the exercise of the general will—can never be alienated, and that the sovereign—which is nothing but a collective being—can be represented only by itself. Power may well be transferred, but not will.

Indeed, while it is not impossible for a particular will to be in agreement with the general will on some point, it is at any rate impossible for this agreement to be lasting and continual. For the particular will tends by its nature toward partiality, and the general will toward equality. It is even more impossible to have a guarantee of this agreement, even were it to endure forever: this would not be the result of art, but of chance. The sovereign may very well say, "I currently will what a given man wills, or at least what he says he wills."[30]

---

30. "Will" in this sentence translates various forms of the verb *vouloir*, which could also be translated "want." Depending upon the context, forms of the verb *vouloir* have been translated by the appropriate forms of "to will" and "to want," but the possible alternative translation should be kept in mind.

But it cannot say, "What that man is going to will tomorrow, I too shall will it," because it is absurd for the will to enchain itself with regard to the future, and because it is not up to any will whatsoever to consent to anything contrary to the good of the being that wills. If, then, the people promises simply to obey, it dissolves itself by this act, it loses its status as a people. The moment there is a master, there is no longer a sovereign, and from that point onward the body politic is destroyed.

This is not to say that the commands of leaders cannot be taken for general wills, as long as the sovereign, being free to oppose them, does not do so. In such a case, the people's consent should be presumed from universal silence. This will be explained at greater length.

CHAPTER 2
That Sovereignty Is Indivisible

For the same reason that sovereignty is inalienable, it is indivisible. For the general will is either general* or it is not; it is either the will of the body of the people or only of a part. In the first case, this will when declared is an act of sovereignty and constitutes law. In the second case, it is merely a particular will, or an act of magistracy; it is at most a decree.

But our political thinkers,[31] unable to divide the principle of sovereignty, divide its object. They divide it into force and will, into legislative power and executive power, into rights of taxation, justice, and war, into domestic administration and a power to conduct foreign affairs. Sometimes they mix all these parts together and sometimes they separate them. They turn the sovereign into a fantastical being made up of a motley assortment of pieces. It is as though they constructed a man out of several bodies—one of which had eyes, another arms, another feet—and nothing else. Japanese conjurers are said to carve up a child before the spectators' eyes, then, throwing all of his limbs into the air one after another, they make the child come back down alive and all in one piece. That is more or less like what the juggling acts of our political thinkers are like. After having dismembered the social body by a magic trick worthy of a carnival, they put the pieces back together who knows how.

---

* For a will to be general, it is not always necessary for it to be unanimous, but it is necessary that all the votes be counted. Any formal exclusion destroys the generality.

---

31. "Political thinkers" here and later in this paragraph translates *politiques*, which can refer to political actors of various kinds, including political leaders or political thinkers.

This error comes from not having established precise notions of sovereign authority, and from having mistaken for parts of this authority what are only its manifestations. Thus, for example, the act of declaring war and that of making peace have been regarded as acts of sovereignty, which they are not, because neither of these acts is a law but merely an application of the law, a particular act which decides the case at issue, as will clearly be seen once the idea attached to the word *law* is established.

By examining the other divisions in the same way, one would discover that whenever one believes one sees sovereignty divided, one is mistaken, that the rights which one takes for parts of this sovereignty are all subordinate to it and always presuppose supreme wills which these rights merely implement.

It would be hard to overestimate how much this lack of precision has obscured the judgments of writers on the subject of political rights when they have sought to adjudicate the respective rights of kings and peoples by the principles they have established. Anyone can see in chapters 3 and 4 of the first book of Grotius how that learned man and his translator Barbeyrac have gotten themselves tangled up, caught up in their sophisms, for fear of either saying too much or of not saying enough in accordance with their views, and of offending the interests they had to reconcile. Grotius—taking refuge in France, discontented with his fatherland, and wanting to pay court to Louis XIII, to whom his book is dedicated—spares nothing to strip the people of all their rights and to invest kings with them as artfully as possible. This would certainly also have been to the taste of Barbeyrac, who dedicated his translation to King George I of England. But unfortunately the expulsion of James II, which he calls an abdication, forced him to be on his guard, to be evasive, to equivocate so as not to make a usurper of William.[32] If these two writers had adopted true principles, all their difficulties would have been avoided and they would always have been consistent. But they would have told the truth with regret and would have paid court only to the people. For truth does not lead to fortune, and the people does not confer either embassies, or professorships, or pensions.

---

32. In his *The Rights of War and Peace* (1625), 1.3–4, Grotius discusses the nature of the "supreme power" or sovereignty, where he denies the principle of popular sovereignty, and then the right of subjects to make war on their superiors, which he severely restricts. Hugo Grotius (1583–1645), or Huig de Groot in Dutch, was arrested and imprisoned in 1618 and then, having escaped, fled his native Holland for France in 1621. Grotius published *The Rights of War and Peace* in Paris and dedicated it to King Louis XIII of France. Jean Barbeyrac (1674–1744) translated Grotius' work into French and provided a substantial commentary of his own, publishing the work in 1724 and dedicating it to King George I of England. Barbeyrac characterizes the expulsion of King James II of England in the Glorious Revolution of 1688 that brought William and Mary to the throne as an "abdication" in a note to Grotius' *Rights of War and Peace*, 1.4.9.

CHAPTER 3
Whether the General Will Can Err

From the preceding it follows that the general will is always right[33] and always tends toward the public utility. But it does not follow that the people's deliberations always have the same rectitude. One always wants[34] what is good for oneself, but one does not always see it. Never is the people corrupted, but it is often deceived, and only then does it appear to want what is bad.

There is often a considerable difference between the will of all and the general will.[35] The latter considers only the common interest, while the former considers private interest and is merely a sum of particular wills. But take away from these same wills the pluses and minuses, which mutually cancel each other out,* and the remaining sum of the differences is the general will.

If, when the people deliberates and is adequately informed, the citizens were to have no private communication[37] among themselves, the general will would always result from the large number of small differences and the deliberation would always be good. But when factions—partial associations at the expense of the larger one—are formed, the will of each of these associations becomes general in relation to its members and particular in relation to the state. There can then no longer be said to be as many voters as there are men, but only as

---

* Each interest, states the Marquis d'Argenson, has different principles. The agreement between two individual interests is formed by opposition to that of a third.[36] He might have added that the agreement of all interests is formed in opposition to that of each. If there were no different interests, the common interest, never encountering any obstacle, would scarcely be felt: everything would run by itself and politics would cease to be an art.

---

33. "Right" translates *droit*. The sense of *droit* in this usage is that the general will is "upright" or "rightly directed."

34. Or: "wills," here and elsewhere in this chapter. See n. 30 (p. 179) above.

35. The distinction Rousseau makes between the "will of all" (*volonté de tous*) and the "general will" (*volonté générale*) requires explanation. The word "all" (*tous*) in the "will of all" in this context should be understood not as "all" in the sense of the body of citizens as a whole acting in their collective capacity as sovereign, but as the sum of the wills of "all of them" separately. In other words, the "will of all" is the sum of the wills of all persons acting as private individuals and not the result of the "general will" they all have in their capacity as citizens.

36. D'Argenson, *Considérations sur le gouvernement ancien et présent de la France* (1764), 26–27. Similarly to his citation of d'Argenson above, in the first edition of the *Social Contract* of 1762 Rousseau indicated d'Argenson's name only by the initials "M. d'A." See I.2 and n. 9 above.

37. "Private communication" translates *communication*. Rousseau's point here is not that there should be no communication among the citizens—that is, discussion and debate—but that there should not be any non-public communication among individuals.

many as there are associations. The differences become less numerous and produce a less general result. Finally, when one of these associations is so large that it prevails over all the others, you no longer have for a result a sum of small differences, but rather one single difference. Then there is no longer a general will, and the opinion that prevails is merely a private opinion.

In order for the general will to be expressed well, it is therefore important that there be no partial society in the state and that each citizen give only his own opinion.* Such was the unique and sublime institution of the great Lycurgus. That if there are partial societies, their number must be multiplied and inequality among them must be prevented, as was done by Solon, Numa, Servius.³⁸ These are the only good precautions to ensure that the general will is always enlightened and that the people is not deceived.

CHAPTER 4
On the Limits of the Sovereign Power

If the state or the city is merely a moral person whose life consists in the union of its members, and if its most important concern is that of its own self-preservation, it has to have a universal and compulsory force to move and arrange each part in the manner best suited to the whole. Just as nature gives each man absolute power over all his members, the social compact gives the body politic absolute power over all its members, and it is this same power which, directed by the general will, bears, as I have said, the name "sovereignty."

But aside from the public person, we have to consider the private persons who make it up and whose life and freedom are naturally independent of it. It is a question, therefore, of clearly distinguishing between the respective rights

---

* *It is true*, states Machiavelli, *that some divisions are harmful to republics and some are helpful. Those are harmful that are accompanied by sects and partisans; those are helpful that are maintained without sects and partisans. Thus, since a founder of a republic cannot provide that there be no enmities in it, he has to provide at least that there not be sects.* Florentine Histories, book 7.³⁹

---

38. Solon (c. 638–558 BC) was an Athenian statesman and lawmaker who made democratic reforms. Numa Pompilius was the legendary second king of Rome, and was traditionally held to have ruled from 715 to 673 BC. Servius Tullius was the legendary sixth king of Rome, and was said to have ruled from 578 to 535 BC. For Rousseau's discussion of these institutions by Servius in particular, see IV.4 below.

39. Niccolò Machiavelli, Florentine Histories (1532), 7.1, p. 276, quoted by Rousseau in Italian: *Vera cosa è*, states Machiavelli, *che alcune divisioni nuocono alle republiche, e alcune giovano: quelle nuocono che sono dalle sette e da partigiani accompagnate: gelle giovano che senza sette, senza partigiani si mantengono. Non potendo adunque provedere un fondatore d'una republic ache non siano nimicizie in quella, hà da proveder almeno che non vi siano sette.*

of the citizens and of the sovereign* and between the duties the former have to fulfill in their capacity as subjects and the natural right they should enjoy in their capacity as men.

It is acknowledged that through the social compact each person alienates only that portion of the entirety of his power, his goods, and his freedom the use of which matters to the community, but it must also be acknowledged that the sovereign alone is judge of what matters.

A citizen owes all the services he can render to the state as soon as the sovereign requests them. But the sovereign, for its part, cannot burden the subjects with any chains useless to the community. It cannot even will to do so, for nothing is done without a cause under the law of reason, any more than under the law of nature.

The commitments that bind us to the social body are obligatory only because they are mutual, and their nature is such that in fulfilling them one cannot work for someone else without also working for oneself. Why is the general will always right, and why do all constantly will the happiness of each one of them, if not because there is no one who does not appropriate the word *each* to himself, and who does not consider himself when voting for all? This proves that the equality of right and the notion of justice it produces derives from the preference that each person has for himself and consequently from the nature of man, that the general will—to be truly general—should be so in its object as well as in its essence, that it should come from all in order to be applied to all, and that it loses its natural rectitude when it is directed toward some individual and determinate object, because then, in judging what is foreign to us, we have no true principle of equity to guide us.

Indeed, as soon as it is a question of a particular fact or right, regarding an issue which has not been regulated by a general and prior convention, the matter is in dispute. It is a lawsuit in which the interested private individuals are one of the parties and the public is the other, but in which I see neither what law must be followed nor what judge should decide. It would be ridiculous in this case to try to turn to an express decision of the general will, a decision which can be only the determination of one of the parties and which is, consequently, merely a foreign and particular will as far as the other party is concerned, and which is apt in this situation to be unjust and subject to error. Thus, just as a particular will cannot represent the general will, so the general will in turn

---

* Attentive readers: please do not rush to accuse me of inconsistency here. Given the poverty of the language, I have not been able to avoid some inconsistency in my terminology. But wait.

changes nature when it has a particular object, and, inasmuch as it is general, it cannot decide concerning either a particular man or fact. When the people of Athens, for example, appointed or discharged its leaders, awarded honors to some person, imposed penalties on another, and indiscriminately performed all the acts of government by a multitude of particular decrees, the people then no longer had a general will properly speaking. It no longer acted as a sovereign but as a magistrate. This will appear to be contrary to commonly held ideas, but I must be allowed the time to present my own.

It should be understood from this that what generalizes the will is less the number of voices than the common interest that unites them. For in this institution each necessarily submits to the conditions which he imposes on the others—an admirable agreement of interest and justice which gives the common deliberations an equitable character that is seen to vanish when discussing any particular affair for want of a common interest which unites and identifies the rule of the judge with that of the party.

From whatever direction the principle is approached, the same conclusion is always reached: namely, that the social compact establishes among the citizens an equality such that they all commit themselves under the same conditions and should all enjoy the same rights. Thus, by the nature of the compact every act of sovereignty—that is, every authentic act of the general will—either obligates or favors all of the citizens equally, in such a way that the sovereign recognizes only the body of the nation and does not single out any of those who make it up. What, then, precisely is an act of sovereignty? It is not an agreement[40] between a superior and an inferior, but rather an agreement between the body and each of its members—an agreement which is legitimate because it has the social contract as its basis, equitable because it is common to all, useful because it has no object other than the general welfare, and solid because it has the public force and the supreme power as its guarantor. As long as subjects are subjected only to such agreements, they do not obey anyone, but obey only their own will. And to ask how far the respective rights of the sovereign and the citizens extend is to ask how far they can commit themselves to one another—each toward all and all toward each of them.

It is clear from this that the sovereign power—entirely absolute, entirely sacred, entirely inviolable as it is—does not exceed and cannot exceed the limits of general agreements, and that every man may fully dispose of the por-

---

40. "Agreement" here and in the rest of this chapter translates *convention*, which is elsewhere translated "convention."

tion of his goods and his freedom left to him by these agreements. As a result, it is never right for the sovereign to burden one subject more than another, because in that case, since the matter becomes particular, its power is no longer competent.

Once these distinctions are acknowledged, it is so manifestly false that the social contract involves any genuine renunciation on the part of the private individuals, that, as a result of this contract, their situation actually proves to be preferable to what it had been beforehand, and that, instead of an alienation, they have only made an advantageous exchange of an uncertain and precarious mode of existence for a better and more secure one, of natural independence for freedom, of the power to harm others for their own security, and of their force, which others could overcome, for a right which the social union renders invincible. Their very life, which they have dedicated to the state, is continually protected by it, and when they risk it for its defense what are they then doing except giving back to it what they have received from it? What are they doing that they did not do more frequently and with greater danger in the state of nature, when, waging inevitable battles, they defended the means for preserving their life at the risk of losing it? All have to fight for the fatherland as needed, it is true, but then again no one ever has to fight for himself. Do we not still gain by running only a portion of the risks for the sake of what provides our security as we would have to run for our own sake as soon as we are deprived of it?

CHAPTER 5
On the Right of Life and Death

It is asked how private individuals who have no right to dispose of their own lives can transfer to the sovereign this same right that they do not have. This question appears difficult to resolve only because it is badly posed. Every man has a right to risk his own life in order to preserve it. Has anyone ever said that someone who jumps out of a window to escape a fire is guilty of suicide? Has this crime ever even been imputed to someone who perishes in a storm, even though he was not unaware of its danger when he set out?

The social treaty has as its end the preservation of the contracting parties. Whoever wills the end also wills the means, and these means are inseparable from certain risks, even from certain losses. Whoever wants to preserve his life at the expense of others should also give it up for them when he has to. Hence the citizen is no longer judge of the danger to which the law wills that he be exposed, and when the prince has said to him, "It is expedient to the state that you should die," he ought to die, because it is only on this condition that he has lived in safety until then, and because his life is no longer solely a blessing of nature, but is a conditional gift of the state.

The death penalty imposed on criminals can be considered more or less from the same point of view. It is in order not to become the victim of an assassin that one consents to die if one becomes an assassin oneself. Under this treaty, far from disposing of one's own life, one thinks only of guaranteeing it, and it cannot be presumed that any of the contracting parties is at that time planning to have himself hanged.

Furthermore, in attacking the social right every wrongdoer becomes a rebel and a traitor to his fatherland through his crimes—he ceases to be a member of it in violating its laws and he even wages war against it. Then the preservation of the state is incompatible with his own, so that one of the two must perish, and when the guilty person is put to death, it is less as a citizen than as an enemy. The proceedings, the decision, are the proofs and the declaration that he has broken the social treaty, and consequently that he is no longer a member of the state. Hence as he acknowledges himself to be such, at the very least by his residence, he should be cut off from it by exile as a violator of the compact or by death as a public enemy. For such an enemy is not a moral person, he is a man, and in that case killing the vanquished is the right of war.

But, it will be said, the condemnation of a criminal is a particular act. Agreed. And this condemnation does not belong to the sovereign; it is a right the sovereign can confer without itself having the power to exercise. My ideas all fit together, but I cannot very well present them all at once.

Moreover, the frequency of corporal punishments is always a sign of weakness or idleness in the government. There is not a single wicked person who could not be made good for something. One has only the right to put to death, even as an example, someone who cannot be preserved without danger.

With regard to the right to pardon, or to exempt a guilty person from the penalty prescribed by the law and pronounced by the judge, it belongs only to the one who is above the judge and the law—that is, to the sovereign. Still, its right in this matter is not altogether clear, and the occasions for exercising it are quite rare. In a well-governed state there are few punishments, not because many pardons are granted, but because there are few criminals. The high number of crimes ensures their impunity when the state is declining. Under the Roman Republic never were the senate or the consuls tempted to grant pardons; nor did the people itself do so, although it sometimes revoked its own verdict. Frequent pardons proclaim that crimes will soon no longer need them, and anyone can see where that leads. But I feel my heart murmur and hold back my pen. Let us leave these questions to be discussed by the just man who has never lapsed and who has never himself been in need of pardon.

CHAPTER 6
On Law

Through the social compact we have given existence and life to the body politic. It is now a question of giving it movement and will through legislation. For the original act through which this body is formed and united does not determine anything further about what it should do to preserve itself.

What is good and in accordance with order is so by the nature of things and independently of human conventions. All justice comes from God; he alone is its source. But if we knew how to receive it from on high, we would need neither government nor laws. Without doubt, there is a universal justice emanating from reason alone. But in order to be acknowledged among us, this justice must be reciprocal. Considering things from a human standpoint, the laws of justice are ineffectual among men for want of a natural sanction. They merely benefit the wicked and harm the just when the latter observes them toward everyone while no one observes them toward him. Conventions and laws are therefore necessary to unite rights with duties and to bring justice back to its object. In the state of nature, where everything is common, I owe nothing to those to whom I have promised nothing, I recognize as belonging to someone else only what is useless to me. This is not so in the civil state, where all rights are settled by the law.

But what in the end, then, is a law? As long as people are satisfied with attaching only metaphysical ideas to this word, they will continue reasoning without understanding one another, and when they have stated what a law of nature is, they will not thereby have any better idea of what a law of the state is.

I have already said that there is no general will regarding a particular object. Indeed, this particular object is either within the state or outside of the state. If it is outside of the state, a will that is foreign to it is not general in relation to it. And if this object is within the state, it is part of it. Then a relation is formed between the whole and its part that makes of them two separate beings, of which the part is one and the whole minus that part is the other. But the whole minus a part is not the whole, and as long as this relation persists there is no longer a whole but only two unequal parts, from which it follows that the will of one of them is no longer general in relation to the other.

But when the whole people enacts statutes regarding the whole people, it considers only itself, and if a relation is then formed, it is between the entire object from one point of view toward the entire object from another point of view, without any division of the whole. Then the subject matter of the statute is general like the will that enacts. It is this act that I call a law.

When I say that the object of the laws is always general, I mean that the law considers the subjects as a body and their actions in the abstract, never any man as an individual or any particular act. Thus, the law can very well enact that there will be privileges, but it cannot confer them on anyone by name. The law can create several classes of citizens, even specify the qualifications for having a right to membership in these classes, but it cannot name this or that person for admission to them. It can establish a royal government and a hereditary succession, but it cannot elect a king or name a royal family. In a word, any function that relates to an individual object does not belong to the legislative power.

With this idea in mind, it is immediately clear that it is no longer necessary to ask to whom it belongs to make laws, because they are acts of the general will; nor whether the prince is above the laws, because he is a member of the state; nor whether the law can be unjust, because no one is unjust toward himself; nor how one is both free and yet subject to the laws, because they merely register our wills.

It is also clear that, since the law combines the universality of the will and that of the object, what any man—regardless of who he may be—orders on his own authority is not a law. What even the sovereign orders concerning a particular object is not a law either, but is instead a decree, nor is it an act of sovereignty, but instead one of magistracy.

I therefore call a republic any state ruled by laws, whatever the form of administration may be: for then alone does the public interest govern and does the commonwealth truly exist. Every legitimate government is republican.* I will explain later what government is.

The laws are, strictly speaking, nothing but the conditions of the civil association. The people subject to the laws should be their author. It belongs only to those who are forming an association to regulate the conditions of the society. But how will they regulate them? Will it be by a common accord, through a sudden inspiration? Does the body politic have an organ to enunciate its wills? Who will give it the foresight necessary to formulate its acts and publish them in advance, or how will they be declared in time of need? How will a blind multitude, which often does not know what it wants because it

---

* By this word I do not mean only an aristocracy or a democracy, but in general any government guided by the general will, which is the law. In order to be legitimate, not only must the government not be confounded with the sovereign, but it must be its minister. In this case, monarchy itself is a republic. This will become clearer in the following book.

rarely knows what is good for it, carry out by itself an undertaking as vast, as difficult as a system of legislation? By itself the people always wants the good, but by itself it does not always see it. The general will is always right, but the judgment that guides it is not always enlightened. It must be made to see objects as they are, sometimes as they should appear to it to be, be shown the good path it seeks, be safeguarded against seduction by particular wills, be brought to regard considerations of time and place, to weigh the appeal of present and perceptible advantages against the dangers of remote and hidden evils. Private individuals see the good they reject; the public wants the good it does not see. All are equally in need of guides. The first must be obliged to make their wills conform to their reason; the latter must be taught to know what it wants. Then the union of understanding and will in the social body results from public enlightenment, and from this union results the smooth working of the parts, and, finally, the greatest force of the whole. From this arises the need for a lawgiver.

CHAPTER 7
On the Lawgiver

To discover the best rules of society suited to each nation would require a superior intelligence who saw all of men's passions and experienced none of them, who had no relation to our nature and who knew it profoundly, whose happiness was independent of ours and who was yet quite happy to attend to ours; finally, one who, preparing distant glory for himself in the fullness of time, could work in one age and enjoy the reward in another.* Gods would be needed to give laws to men.

The same reasoning that Caligula used with respect to fact was used by Plato with respect to right in order to define the civil or royal man he seeks in his book on ruling.[41] But if it is true that a great prince is a rare man, what

---

* A people becomes famous only once its legislation begins to decline. No one knows for how many centuries the institutions established by Lycurgus produced the Spartans' happiness before the rest of Greece took note of them.

---

41. For Caligula's remark, see the passage from Philo of Alexandria *On the Embassy to Caius* (or *Gaius*) (*De Legatione ad Caium*) cited in n. 11 to p. 165. For Plato, see *Statesman* 261c-d: "To supervise the soulless things, as if it were a master-builder's job, is never the characteristic of the royal science, but it is nobler and grander, always in possession of its power in the case of animals and about these very things. . . . But we won't find the statesman at least to be a nurse-in-private, like the oxdriver or horse-groom, but with more of a resemblance to a horse-feeder or cattle-feeder" (trans. Seth Bernardete [Chicago: University of Chicago Press, 1984]).

about a great lawgiver? The first need merely follow the model which the second must propose. The latter is the mechanic who invents the machine, the former is merely the workman who puts it together and makes it work. At the birth of societies, states Montesquieu, it is the leaders of republics who create the institutions, and afterward it is the institutions that form the leaders of republics.[42]

He who dares to undertake to establish a people's institutions must feel that he is capable of changing, so to speak, human nature; of transforming each individual, who by himself is a complete and solitary whole, into a part of a greater whole from which that individual receives as it were his life and his being; of weakening man's constitution in order to reinforce it; of substituting a partial and moral existence for the physical and independent existence we have all received from nature. In a word, it is necessary for him to take away man's own forces in order to give him forces which are foreign to him and of which he cannot make use without the help of others. The more these natural forces are dead and annihilated, the more powerful and lasting are the ones he has acquired, and the more solid and complete is the institution as well. As a result, when each citizen is nothing, can do nothing, except with all the others, and when the force acquired by the whole is equal or superior to the sum of the natural forces of all the individuals, the legislation can be said to be at the highest point of perfection it might attain.

The lawgiver is in every respect an extraordinary man in the state. If he must be so by his genius, he is no less so by his office. It is not magistracy; it is not sovereignty. This office, which constitutes the republic, is not part of its constitution. It is a particular and superior function which has nothing in common with the human realm. For if he who has command over men should not have command over the laws, so neither should he who has command over the laws have command over men. Otherwise, his laws— ministers of his passions—would often serve merely to perpetuate his injustices, and he could never avoid having particular views debase the sanctity of his work.

When Lycurgus gave his fatherland laws, he began by abdicating the kingship. It was the custom of most Greek cities to entrust the establishment of their laws to foreigners. The modern republics of Italy often imitated this practice.

---

42. Montesquieu, *Considerations on the Causes of the Greatness of the Romans and Their Decline* (1734), chap. 1, p. 25. This passage first appeared in the 1748 edition of the *Considerations*.

The republic of Geneva did likewise, and to good effect.* Rome in its finest period beheld all the crimes of tyranny reborn in its midst, and found itself on the verge of perishing as a result of having united the lawgiving authority and the sovereign power in the same hands.

Yet even the Decemvirs themselves never arrogated to themselves the right to have any law passed on their authority alone. *Nothing we propose to you,* they would say to the people, *can become law without your consent. Romans, be yourselves the authors of the laws that should create your happiness.*[44]

He who drafts the laws, therefore, does not have and should not have any legislative right. And the people itself cannot—even if it wanted to—divest itself of this nontransferable right, because according to the fundamental compact it is only the general will that obligates private individuals, and because there can be no assurance that a particular will is consonant with the general will until it has been submitted to the free suffrage of the people. I have already said this, but it is not useless to repeat it.

Thus one finds at one and the same time two seemingly incompatible things in the work of the legislator: an undertaking beyond human strength and, to execute it, an authority that amounts to nothing.

A further difficulty warrants attention. The wise who want to speak in their own language to the vulgar rather than in the language of the vulgar cannot be understood by them. For there are a thousand kinds of ideas which are impossible to translate into the language of the people. Overly general views and overly remote objectives are equally beyond its grasp. Each individual, appreciating no other plan of government than that which bears on his particular interest, has difficulty perceiving the advantages he is to derive from the constant privations imposed by good laws. In order for a nascent people to be able to appreciate sound maxims of politics and to follow the fundamental rules of statecraft, the effect would have to become the cause: the social spirit that is to be

---

* Those who consider Calvin merely as a theologian fail to understand the extent of his genius. The drawing up of our wise edicts, in which he played a large part, does him as much honor as his *Institutes*. Whatever revolution time may bring about in our rites, as long as love of the fatherland and of freedom is not extinguished among us, never will the memory of that great man cease to be blessed.[43]

---

43. Jean Calvin (1509–64) was a French theologian whose *Institutes of the Christian Religion* (1536) was one of the most influential works of the Protestant Reformation. In the same year as he published this work, he was invited to Geneva to reform church government and religious rites.

44. The Decimvirs was a commission of ten men appointed for one year by the Romans in 452 BC to draw up a code of laws. After their year in office, the commissioners were reappointed for a second year, after which they refused to leave office, causing an uprising by the Roman people that forced them to resign.

the work of the institution would have to preside over the institution itself, and men would have to be prior to the laws what they are to become through the laws. Hence, therefore, since the lawgiver can use neither force nor reasoning, he must of necessity have recourse to an authority of a different order which might be able to motivate without violence and persuade without convincing.

This is what has at all times forced the fathers of nations to resort to the intervention of heaven and to honor the gods with their own wisdom, so that peoples—subject to the laws of state as to those of nature, and recognizing the same power in the formation of man as in that of the city—obey with freedom and bear the yoke of public felicity with docility.

This sublime reason, which exceeds the grasp of vulgar men, is the reason whose decisions the legislator puts into the mouth of the immortals, in order to motivate by divine authority those who could not be swayed by human prudence.* But it does not belong to just any man to make the gods speak, or to make himself believed when he proclaims himself their interpreter. The great soul of the lawgiver is the true miracle that must prove his mission. Any man can engrave stone tablets, or bribe an oracle, or feign secret dealings with some divinity, or train a bird to speak in his ear, or find other crude ways to impress the people. Someone who can do only this much might even by chance assemble a mob of madmen, but he will never found an empire, and his extravagant work will soon perish along with him. Trifling tricks may form a fleeting bond; only wisdom makes it lasting. The Jewish law, which still endures, that of Ishmael's child, which has ruled half of the world for ten centuries, even today still proclaim the great men who dictated them. And whereas proud philosophy or the blind spirit of partisanship sees in them merely lucky imposters, the true politician admires in their institutions that great and powerful genius that presides over enduring establishments.[45]

One need not conclude from all this with Warburton that among us politics

---

* *And truly,* states Machiavelli, *there was never any orderer of extraordinary laws for a people who did not have recourse to God, because otherwise they would not have been accepted. For a prudent individual knows many goods that do not have in themselves evident reasons with which one can persuade others.* Discourses on Titus Livy, book 1, chapter 11.[46]

---

45. "Politician" here translates *politiques.* See n. 31 to p. 180. Rousseau appears to allude here to Voltaire, whose play *Fanaticism, or Mohammed* (1741) presents Mohammed as a charlatan. See Rousseau, *Letter to d'Alembert, Collected Writings,* 10:271–73, 360.

46. Machiavelli, *Discourses on Livy* (1531), 1.11, p. 35, quoted by Rousseau in Italian: *E veramente,* states Machiavelli, *mai non fù alcuno ordinatore di leggi staordinarie in un popolo, che non ricorresse a Dio, perche altrimenti non sarebbero accettate; perche sono molti beni conosciuti da uno prudente, i quali non hanno in se raggioni evidenti da potergli persuadere ad altrui.*

and religion have a common goal, but that at the origin of nations the one serves as an instrument of the other.[47]

CHAPTER 8
On the People

Just as an architect, before putting up a large building, examines and tests the soil to see whether it can support the weight, so the wise founder does not begin by drawing up laws which are good in themselves, but first examines whether the people for whom he intends them is fit to bear them. It is for this reason that Plato refused to give laws to the Arcadians and the Cyrenians, since he knew those two peoples were wealthy and could not tolerate equality.[48] It is for this reason that there were good laws and wicked men in Crete, as Minos had merely disciplined a people teeming with vices.

A thousand nations on earth have shined which could never have tolerated good laws, and even those that could have tolerated them could do so only a very short time in their entire lifetimes. Most peoples, like most men, are docile only in their youth; they become incorrigible as they grow old. Once customs are established and prejudices rooted, it is a dangerous and futile undertaking to seek to reform them. The people cannot even bear having what ails it touched so as to destroy it, like those stupid and cowardly patients who tremble at the sight of the doctor.

This is not to say that, just as certain illnesses unhinge men's minds and deprive them of their memory of the past, there are not sometimes violent periods during the lifetimes of states when revolutions have the same effect on peoples as certain crises have on individuals, when the horror of the past serves as a kind of forgetting, and when the state, set ablaze by civil wars, is so to speak reborn from its ashes and recovers the vigor of youth as it escapes death's clutches. Such was Sparta at the time of Lycurgus, such was Rome after the Tarquins, and such with us were Holland and Switzerland after the expulsion of the tyrants.

But these events are rare. They are exceptions the reason for which is always found in the particular constitution of the state so excepted. They cannot even occur twice with the same people, for it can free itself as long as it is merely barbarous, but it can no longer do so when the civil mainspring is worn

---

47. See William Warburton, *The Divine Legation of Moses Demonstrated on the Principles of a Religious Deist*, 2 vols., (1737–41), bk. 2, sect. 5.

48. See Plutarch *Life of Lucullus* 2.

out. Then disturbances may destroy it without revolutions being able to re-store it, and as soon as its chains are broken, it falls apart and no longer exists. From then on it needs a master and not a liberator. Free peoples, remember this maxim: freedom can be acquired, but is never recovered.

Youth is not childhood. For nations as for men there is a time of youth—or of maturity, if you wish—that must be awaited before subjecting them to laws. But the maturity of a people is not always easy to recognize, and if one acts too soon the work is ruined. One people is capable of being subjected to discipline at birth, another is not capable of it after ten centuries. The Russians will never be truly civilized because they were civilized too soon. Peter had the genius of imitation.[49] He did not have true genius—that which creates and makes everything from nothing. Some of the things he did were good, but most were ill-advised. He saw that his people was barbarous, but he did not see that it was not ripe for political ordering. He sought to give it culture when he needed only to make it warlike. He first sought to make Germans or English-men when he needed to begin by making Russians. He prevented his subjects from ever becoming what they could be by persuading them that they were something they are not. It is like when a French tutor forms his pupil to shine for a moment during his childhood and then never to amount to anything. The Russian empire will seek to subjugate Europe and will itself be subjugated. The Tartars, its subjects, or its neighbors will become its masters and ours. This revolution appears inevitable to me. All the kings of Europe are working in concert to hasten it.

CHAPTER 9
Continued

Just as nature has set limits to the stature of a well-formed man, beyond which it no longer produces anything but giants or dwarfs, likewise there are bounds, with regard to the best constitution of a state, to the size it can have for it to be neither too large to be able to be well governed nor too small to be able to be self-sustaining. In every political body there is a maximum of force which it cannot exceed, and from which it often deviates by dint of growing larger. The more the social bond extends, the looser it grows, and in general a small state is proportionately stronger than a large one.

---

49. Czar Peter I "The Great" of Russia (1672–1725) traveled incognito to Western Europe to observe its politics and economics and then enacted sweeping reforms aimed at modernizing Russia.

A thousand reasons prove this maxim. First, administration becomes more difficult over great distances, just as a weight becomes heavier at the end of a longer lever. It also becomes more burdensome in proportion as the number of levels multiplies. For, to begin with, each city has its own administration for which the people pays, each district has its own which is also paid for by the people, then each province, then the large-scale governments, the satrapies, the viceroyalties which always have to be paid more the higher one climbs, and always at the expense of the wretched people; last comes the supreme administration, which crushes everything. Such excessive taxation continually exhausts the subjects. Far from being better governed by these various orders, they are less well governed than if there were just one over them. Yet hardly any resources are left for extraordinary situations, and when recourse to them is necessary, the state is always on the brink of ruin.

That is not all. Not only does the government have less vigor and speed to enforce the laws, prevent vexations, correct abuses, forestall seditious enterprises which may be occurring in faraway places, but the people have less affection for their leaders, whom they never see, for a fatherland that is like the world in their eyes, and for their fellow citizens, who for the most part are strangers to them. The same laws cannot suit such a variety of provinces, which have different morals, live in varying climates, and cannot tolerate the same form of government. Different laws give rise to nothing but trouble and confusion among peoples who—living under the same leaders and in constant communication with one another—move back and forth or intermarry with one another, and who, since they are subject to different customs, never know whether their patrimony is really theirs. Talents are buried, virtues unrecognized, vices unpunished in this multitude of men who do not know one another and whom the seat of the supreme administration has brought together in the same place. The leaders, overwhelmed with work, see nothing by themselves. Functionaries govern the state. In the end, the measures which have to be taken in order to maintain the general authority—which so many distant officials want either to shirk or abuse—absorb all public attention, nothing is left for the people's happiness, and there is barely anything left for its defense in case of need, and this is how a body too large for its constitution collapses and perishes, crushed beneath its own weight.

On the other hand, the state should provide itself with a sure footing so as to have solidity, so as to withstand the shocks it is bound to experience and the efforts it will be compelled to make in order to sustain itself. For all peoples have a kind of centrifugal force by which they continually act against one another and tend to grow at their neighbors' expense, like Descartes' vortices.[50] Thus the weak risk being quickly swallowed up, and scarcely can any people preserve itself except by establishing a kind of equilibrium with all the others, which makes the pressure everywhere more or less equal.

It is clear from this that there are reasons to expand and reasons to contract, and that it is not the least of the politician's talents to find the proportion between these two sets of reasons which is most advantageous for the state's preservation. In general, it can be said that the former reasons, since they are merely external and relative, should be subordinated to the latter, which are internal and absolute. A healthy and strong constitution is the first thing that must be sought, and one should rely more on the vigor arising from a good government than on the resources a large territory provides.

Moreover, there have been states that were so constituted that the necessity for conquests entered into their very constitution and that were forced to grow continually larger in order to maintain themselves. Perhaps they heartily congratulated themselves on this happy necessity, which however revealed to them, along with the limit to their size, the inevitable moment of their downfall.

CHAPTER 10

Continued

A body politic can be measured in two ways. Namely, by the extent of the territory and by the number of the people, and there is a proper ratio between these two measures that determines the state's genuine size. It is men who make up the state and it is the land that feeds the men. This ratio therefore consists in there being enough land to support its inhabitants, and as many inhabitants as the land can feed. It is in this proportion that the maximum of force of a given number of people consists, for if there is too much land, its defense is burdensome, its cultivation insufficient, its yield superfluous. This is the proximate cause of defensive wars. If there is not enough land, the state finds itself at the discretion of its neighbors for what more is needed. This is the proximate cause of offensive wars. Any people which, owing to its location, has no other alternative than commerce or war is inherently weak. It is dependent on its

---

50. René Descartes (1596–1650) postulated a theory of planetary motion in which the planets and other celestial bodies adopted fixed orbits when the outward or centrifugal or force of their motions in relation to one another was balanced by an inward or centripetal force.

neighbors; it is dependent on events. It never has anything but an uncertain and brief existence. Either it subjugates and changes its situation, or it is subjugated and is nothing. It can preserve its freedom only by dint of being either very small or very large.

It is therefore impossible to calculate a fixed ratio between the extent of the land and the number of men by which they are mutually sufficient—as much due to the differences in the properties of the soil, its degree of fertility, the nature of its products, the influence of climate, as to the differences observed in the temperament of the men who inhabit it, some of whom consume little in a fertile country, others who consume a great deal on an unforgiving soil. One must also take into account the greater or lesser fertility of women, what the country can offer in terms of what is more or less favorable to growth in population, to the number of people the lawgiver can hope to contribute to this population growth through the institutions he establishes. Hence, he should not base his judgment on what he sees but on what he foresees, nor focus as much on the present state of the population as on the condition it should naturally attain. Finally, there are a thousand occasions when the accidental features of a place require or permit more land to be included than appears necessary. Thus, it can be extended a great deal in a mountainous country, where the natural products—namely, woods, pastures—require less work, where experience teaches that women are more fertile than in the plains, and where large stretches of sloping terrain leave only a small amount of level area, which can alone be considered for planting vegetation. By contrast, it can be restricted by the seashore, even among nearly barren rocks and sand, because there fishing can in large measure make up for the products of the earth, because men have to assemble more closely to repulse pirates, and moreover because it is easier to relieve the country of its surplus inhabitants by means of colonies.

To these conditions for instituting a people, it is necessary to add one that cannot substitute for any other, but without which all the rest are useless: the enjoyment of prosperity and peace. For the time when a state is being organized, like that when a battalion is being drawn up in formation, is the moment when the body is least capable of resistance and easiest to destroy. Better resistance would be offered in the midst of absolute disorder than in a moment of fermentation when each person is preoccupied with his rank and not with the danger. Should a war, a famine, an uprising occur in such a time of crisis, the state will inevitably be overthrown.

Not that many governments haven't been established during such storms; but then it is those governments themselves that destroy the state. Usurpers always provoke or choose these times of trouble, taking advantage of the public's panic, to get destructive laws passed which the people would never adopt when cool-headed. The choice of the moment of institution is one of the most reliable features that can be used to distinguish the work of a legislator and that of a tyrant.

What people, then, is suited for legislation? One that, while finding itself already bound by some union of origin, interest, or convention, has not yet borne the true yoke of laws. One that has neither deeply rooted customs nor superstitions. One that does not fear being overrun by a sudden invasion, which, without taking part in its neighbors' quarrels, can resist any of them alone or enlist the aid of one to repulse the other. One in which each member can be known to all, and where one is not forced to burden any one man with a greater load than a man can bear. One that does not have to depend on other peoples and on which no other people has to depend.* One that is neither rich nor poor and can be self-sufficient. Finally, one that combines the stability of an ancient people with the docility of a new people. What makes the work of legislation difficult is less what must be established than what must be destroyed. And what makes success so rare is the impossibility of finding the simplicity of nature joined with the needs of society. These conditions, it is true, are difficult to bring together. So, one sees few well-constituted states.

In Europe there is still a country capable of receiving legislation: it is the island of Corsica. The valor and constancy with which that brave people has been able to recover and defend its freedom would amply deserve having some wise man teach it how to preserve it. I rather suspect that one day this small island will astonish Europe.

---

* If one of the two neighboring peoples could not do without the other, this situation would be very hard for the one and very dangerous for the other. In such a case, any wise nation will very promptly endeavor to relieve the other of this dependence. The republic of Tlaxcala, an enclave in the Mexican Empire, preferred doing without salt to buying it from the Mexicans, and even to accepting it free of charge. The wise Tlaxcalans saw the trap hidden beneath this generosity. They preserved their freedom, and this small state, enclosed within that great empire, was in the end the instrument of its ruin.[51]

---

51. As Rousseau remarks, the Tlaxcalans held an independent enclave within the Aztec Empire. They allied themselves with the Spanish and took part in the war that eventually led to the fall of the Aztec Empire in 1521.

CHAPTER II
On the Various Systems of Legislation

If one investigates in what precisely consists the greatest good of all—which should be the end of every system of legislation—one will find that it comes down to the following two principal objects: *freedom* and *equality*. Freedom, because any particular dependence is that much force taken away from the body of the state. Equality, because freedom cannot endure without it.

I have already said what civil freedom is. With regard to equality, this word must not be understood to mean that the degrees of power and wealth should be absolutely the same, but rather that, with regard to power, it should be incapable of any violence and never be exercised except by virtue of rank and the laws, and that, with regard to wealth, no citizen should be so extremely rich that he can buy another and none so poor that he is constrained to sell himself. This presupposes moderation in goods and influence on the part of the great, and moderation in avarice and covetousness on the part of the lowly.*

This equality, they say, is a chimera of speculation that cannot exist in practice. But if the abuse is inevitable, does it follow that it ought not to at least be regulated? It is precisely because the force of things always tends to destroy equality that the force of legislation should always tend toward maintaining it.

But these general objects of every good institution should be modified in each country according to the relations that arise as much from local conditions as from the character of the inhabitants, and it is on the basis of these relations that each people has to be assigned a particular system of institution which is best, not perhaps in itself, but for the state for which it is intended. For example, is the soil unforgiving and barren, or the country too limited in size for the inhabitants? Turn toward industry and the arts, the products of which you can exchange for the foodstuffs you lack. On the contrary, do you occupy rich plains and fertile hillsides? Do you have a good soil yet lack inhabitants? Devote all your efforts to agriculture, which multiplies men, and chase away the arts, which would only result in depopulating the country by concentrating the few inhabitants it has in a few places across the

---

* Do you, then, want to give the state stability? Bring the extremes as close together as possible. Tolerate neither extremely rich people nor beggars. These two conditions—naturally inseparable—are equally fatal to the common good. From one come the fomenters of tyranny and from the other tyrants. It is always between these two that trafficking in public freedom occurs: one buys it and the other sells it.

territory.* Do you occupy extensive and convenient shores? Cover the sea with ships, cultivate commerce and navigation: you will have a brilliant and brief existence. Does the sea bathe nothing but nearly inaccessible rocks along your shores? Remain barbarous and fish-eaters: you will live there more tranquilly, perhaps better, and certainly more happily. In a word, aside from the maxims common to all peoples, each people contains in itself some cause that orders these maxims in a particular manner and makes its legislation appropriate for it alone. This is how the Hebrews long ago and the Arabs recently have had religion for their principal object, the Athenians letters, Carthage and Tyre commerce, Rhodes seafaring, Sparta war, and Rome virtue. The author of *The Spirit of the Laws* has shown through swarms of examples the art by which the lawgiver directs the institution toward each of these objects.[52]

What makes a state's constitution genuinely solid and durable is when matters of suitability are so well observed that natural relationships and the laws always turn out to agree on the same points and that the latter serve, so to speak, merely to secure, accompany, and rectify the former. But if the lawgiver, being mistaken in his object, adopts a principle different from that which arises from the nature of things—such that one principle tends toward servitude and the other toward freedom, one toward wealth and the other toward population, one toward peace and the other toward conquests—the laws will be found to grow imperceptibly weaker, the constitution to deteriorate,[54] and the state

---

* Any branch of foreign commerce, states the M. d'Argenson, diffuses almost nothing but a deceptive benefit in a kingdom generally. It may enrich a few private individuals, even a few cities, but the nation as a whole gains nothing from it, and the people is no better off for it.[53]

---

52. See Montesquieu, *Spirit of the Laws* (1748), esp. 11.5, p. 156: "Although all states have the same purpose in general, which is to maintain themselves, yet each state has a purpose that is peculiar to it. Expansion was the purpose of Rome; war, that of Lacedaemonia; religion, that of the Jewish laws; commerce, that of Marseilles; public tranquility, that of the laws of China; navigation, that of the laws of the Rhodians; natural liberty was the purpose of the police of the savages. . . . " For Montesquieu's discussion of the role of the lawgiver, see *Spirit of the Laws*, bk. 29.

53. D'Argenson, *Considérations sur le gouvernement ancien et présent de la France* (1764), p. 20: "A branch of commerce acquired at the expense of money obtains merely a deceptive benefit for a kingdom generally and enriches a few cities or a few private individuals that are already prosperous." Similarly to his citation of d'Argenson above, in the first edition of the *Social Contract* of 1762 Rousseau indicated d'Argenson's name here only by the initials "M. d'A." See I.2 and n. 9 above.

54. "Deteriorate" translates *s'altérer*. As noted in n. 17 to p. 51 of the *Discourse on Inequality*, although *altérer* in its various grammatical forms as a verb, noun, or adjective can mean simply "alter" or "change," it generally has a negative connotation of distortion, degeneration, corruption, or adulteration. In the *Social Contract* Rousseau uses this word almost exclusively in its negative sense, and so it has been translated by "deteriorate," or "vitiate," or occasionally "disrupt" throughout this work.

will not cease being disturbed until it is either destroyed or changed, and until invincible nature has regained its empire.

CHAPTER 12
Classification of Laws

To order the whole, or to give the commonwealth the best possible form, various relations have to be considered. First, the action of the entire body acting on itself—that is, the relation of the whole to the whole, or of the sovereign to the state, and this relation is comprised of the relations between the intermediary terms, as we will see below.

The laws that regulate this relation bear the name "political laws," and are also called "fundamental laws"—not without some reason if these laws are wise. For if there is but a single good way of ordering any given state, the people that has found it should hold on to it. But if the established order is bad, why should those laws that prevent it from being good be considered as fundamental? Furthermore, a people is in any case always master of changing its laws—even the best ones. For if it likes harming itself, who has the right to prevent it from doing so?

The second relation is that of the members with one another or with the entire body, and this relation should be as small as possible with respect to the first and as large as possible with respect to the second. As a result, each citizen is in a position of perfect independence with respect to all the others and in a position of excessive dependence with respect to the city. This is always achieved by the same means, for it is only the state's force that creates its members' freedom. It is from this second relation that civil laws arise.

It is possible to consider a third sort of relation between a man and the law, namely that of disobedience in relation to penalty, and this relation gives rise to the establishment of criminal laws, which at bottom are less a particular type of law than the sanction for all the others.

To these three sorts of laws may be added a fourth—the most important of all. One which is not engraved on marble or bronze, but in the hearts of the citizens; which is the genuine constitution of the state; which daily acquires new force; which, when the other laws grow old or die out, revives them or replaces them, preserves the people in the spirit of its institution and imperceptibly substitutes the force of habit for that of authority. I speak of morals, customs, and especially opinion—a part of the laws unknown to our politicians, but upon which the success of all the others depends, a part to which the great lawgiver attends in secret while he appears to restrict himself to particular regulations which are merely the sides of the arch of which morals—slower to arise—ultimately form the unshakeable keystone.

Among these various classes, political laws, which constitute the form of the government, are the only ones relevant to my subject.

END OF THE SECOND BOOK

BOOK III

BEFORE DISCUSSING the various forms of government, let us try to determine the precise meaning of this word, which has not yet been especially well explained.

CHAPTER I
On Government in General

I warn the reader that this chapter should be read with due care, and that I do not know the art of being clear for those who are not willing to be attentive.

Every free action has two causes which concur to produce it: one moral, namely the will which determines the act, the other physical, namely the power which executes it. When I walk toward an object, it is necessary first of all for me to will to go to it, and, in the second place, that my feet carry me to it. Let a paralyzed man will to run, let an agile man will not to do so: both will stay where they are. The body politic has the same motive forces; force and will are likewise distinguishable in it: the latter under the name *legislative power*, the former under the name *executive power*. Nothing is done in it—or nothing should be done in it—without their cooperation.

We have seen that the legislative power belongs to the people, and can belong only to it. On the contrary, it is easy to see, by the principles established above, that the executive power cannot belong to the general public in its legislative or sovereign capacity, because this power consists solely in particular acts which are not within the province of the law nor, consequently, within that of the sovereign, all of whose acts can be nothing but laws.

The public force must therefore have its own agent, which unites it with and puts it into action in accordance with the directives of the general will, which serves as a means of communication between the state and the sovereign, which does in a sense in the public person what the union of soul and body does in man. This is the reason why there is government in the state — government which is improperly confused with the sovereign, of which it is merely the minister.

What, then, is the government? An intermediary body established between the subjects and the sovereign for their mutual communication, and charged with the execution of the laws and the maintenance of freedom, civil as well as political.

The members of this body are called "magistrates" or *kings*, that is, *governors*, and the body as a whole bears the name *prince*.*[55] Thus those who claim that the act by which a people subjects itself to leaders is not a contract are perfectly correct. It is absolutely nothing but a commission, an office in which, as mere officers of the sovereign, they exercise in its name the power it has vested in them and which it can limit, modify, and take back whenever it so pleases, since the alienation of such a right is incompatible with the nature of the social body and contrary to the goal of the association.

I therefore call *government* or "supreme administration" the legitimate exercise of the executive power, and "prince" or "magistrate" the man or the body charged with this administration.

It is in the government that one finds the intermediate forces whose relations[56] make up that of the whole to the whole or of the sovereign to the state. This latter relation can be expressed as the relationship between the extreme terms of a continuous proportion whose proportional mean is the government. The government receives from the sovereign the commands which it then gives to the people, and in order for the state to be in proper equilibrium it is necessary, taking everything else into account, for the product or power of the government taken by itself to be equal to the product or power of the citizens, who are sovereigns from one perspective and subjects from another.[57]

---

* So in Venice the college of senators is given the name *Most Serene Prince*, even when the Doge is not in attendance.

---

55. Rousseau's highly unusual — and pointedly anti-monarchical — usage of the term "prince" should be kept in mind throughout.

56. "Relations" translates *rapports*, which could also be translated as "ratios" in the mathematical sense of the term. Rousseau's ensuing discussion of the "relations" or "relationships" between different parts of the state and the proportions or "ratios" between them plays on the ambiguity of this French term.

57. An example of a "continuous" or geometric proportion would be A : B :: B : C, etc., or, for example, $4 : 6 :: 6 : 9$. The "extreme terms" in these examples would be A and C, or 4 and 9 in the numerical example. The "mean proportional" would be $A \times C = B \times B = B^2$, or, $4 \times 9 = 6 \times 6 = 6^2$ in the numerical example. Rousseau applies this reasoning to the relations among the sovereign, the government, and the citizens considered as subjects to the laws they make as sovereign, with the sovereign and the citizens being

Moreover, none of these three terms can be changed without immediately destroying the proportion. If the sovereign tries to govern, or if the magistrate tries to give laws, or if the subjects refuse to obey, disorder replaces rule, force and will no longer act in concert, and the state, being dissolved, thereby falls into despotism or into anarchy. Finally, as there is only one proportional mean for each ratio, there is also only one good government possible in a given state. But as a thousand events can change these relations within a people, not only can different governments be good for various peoples, but they can be good for the same people at different times.

In order to try to give some idea of the various relations which might obtain between these two extreme terms, I will take as an example the number of the people, as this relation is easier to express.

Let us assume that the state is made up of ten thousand citizens. The sovereign can be considered only collectively and as a body. But each private individual in his capacity as a subject is considered as a single individual. Thus, the sovereign is to the subject as ten thousand to one. That is, each member of the state has for his share only one ten-thousandth a part of the sovereign authority, even though he is entirely subjected to it. If the people is made up of one hundred thousand men, the condition of the subjects does not change, and each one bears the full dominion of the laws equally, whereas his vote, being reduced to one hundred-thousandth, has ten times less influence on the drafting of the laws. In that case, since the subject always remains one, the ratio of the sovereign to the subject increases in proportion to the number of citizens.[58] From which it follows that the more the state grows, the more freedom diminishes.

When I say that the ratio increases, I mean that it moves further away from equality. Thus the greater the ratio in the geometers' sense of the term, the smaller the relation is in the ordinary sense. In the first sense, the ratio—considered in terms of quantity—is measured by the quotient, and in the latter sense—considered in terms of likeness—is assessed by similarity.[59]

---

the "extreme terms" and the government being the "mean proportional." So, if *Sovereign* = A, *Government* = B, and *Citizens* = C, then *Sovereign* : *Government* :: *Government* : *Citizens*. Or, alternatively, *Sovereign* × *Citizens* = *Government²*.

58. The subject always remains "one" because the laws must apply to each individual subject equally. When translated into the mathematical language Rousseau uses in this context (A : B :: B : C, where *Sovereign* = A, *Government* = B, and *Citizens* considered as subjects to the law = C), then C is always equal to 1.

59. See n. 56 above on the ambiguity of the French term *rapport*, which is translated in this paragraph by both "ratio" and "relation." Rousseau's point is that a ratio which is "greater" in the geometric sense, as measured by the size of the quotient—as 1/100,000 is "greater" than 1/10,000—produces a relation between

Now, the smaller the ratio between particular wills and the general will—that is, between morals and the laws—the more repressive force should increase. Then, for the government to be good, it should be relatively stronger in proportion as the people is more numerous.

On the other hand, since the expansion of the state offers the trustees of the public authority more temptations and more means for abusing their power, as the government should have more force to restrain the people, the sovereign, in its turn, should have more force to restrain the government. I am not speaking here about absolute force, but about the relative forces of the various parts of the state.

It follows from this double ratio that the continuous proportion between the sovereign, the prince, and the people is not an arbitrary idea, but a necessary consequence of the nature of the body politic. It further follows that since one of the extreme terms—namely, the people considered as subject—is fixed and represented by unity, whenever the double ratio increases or decreases, the single ratio similarly increases or decreases, and that the middle term is correspondingly changed as a consequence.[60] This makes it clear that there is no unique and absolute constitution of government, but that there can be as many governments differing in nature as there are states differing in size.

If, ridiculing this system, someone were to say that, according to me, to find this proportional mean and to form the body of the government, one need only take the square root of the number of the people, I would reply that I am here only taking this number as an example; that the ratios about which I am speaking are not measured only by the number of men, but more generally by the amount of activity, which is the result of a great many causes; that, moreover, if I momentarily borrow the terminology of geometry to express myself in fewer words, I am however not unaware that geometrical precision does not obtain in moral quantities.

---

the two terms ($1 : 10,000$ vs. $1 : 100,000$) which grows "smaller" as the ratio between them increases, or, as Rousseau states, the two terms grow less "like" or "similar."

60. Once again taking Rousseau's mathematical description of the relations among the sovereign, the government, and the citizens considered as subject to the law ($A : B :: B : C$, where $Sovereign = A$, $Government$ or $Prince = B$, and $Citizens = C$), then $Sovereign : Government :: Government : Citizens$, or, alternatively, $Sovereign \times Citizens :: Government^2$. Following his argument above that the citizens considered as subject to the laws should always be considered as a "unity," which he rephrases here as "the people" (or the body of the citizens) is always "fixed and represented as unity," then $C = 1$ in the equation. As a consequence, $Sovereign = Government^2$. In Rousseau's terminology $Government^2$ is a "double ratio" and it is the "middle term" (B) in the above equation. His point is that the size and power of the government will vary with the size of the people, and that an increase in the size of the people results in a proportional geometric increase in the power of the government.

The government is on a small scale what the body politic that contains it is on a large scale. It is a moral person endowed with certain faculties, active like the sovereign, passive like the state, and which can be broken down into other similar ratios from which a new proportion consequently arises, and then within this yet another proportion according to the way in which judicial tribunals are organized, until one reaches an indivisible middle term—that is, a single leader or supreme magistrate—which might be represented as the unity in the middle of this progression between the series of fractions and that of whole numbers.

Without getting caught up in this proliferation of terms, let us be satisfied with considering the government as a new body in the state, distinct from both the people and the sovereign, and intermediate between them.

There is this essential difference between these two bodies: that the state exists by itself, and that the government exists only by virtue of the sovereign. Thus, the prince's dominant will is not—or should not be—anything but the general will or the law. Its force is nothing but the public force concentrated in it, and as soon as it tries to originate some absolute and independent act by itself, the bond tying together the whole begins to grow slack. If it eventually came to pass that the prince had a particular will more active than the sovereign's and that, in obeying this particular will, it used the public force in its hands so that that there were, so to speak, two sovereigns—one by right and the other in fact—the social union would instantly vanish and the body politic would be dissolved.

Yet in order for the body of the government to have existence, a real life which distinguishes it from the body of the state, in order for all of its members to be able to act in concert and to heed the end for which it was instituted, it must have a particular *self*, a sensibility common to its members, a force, a will of its own that tends toward its self-preservation. This particular existence presupposes assemblies, councils, a power to deliberate, to resolve, rights, titles, privileges which belong exclusively to the prince and which make the position of the magistrate more honorable to the degree that it is more demanding. The difficulties lie in ordering this subordinate whole within the whole in such a way that it does not vitiate the general constitution by consolidating its own, that it always distinguishes between its particular force, which is intended for its own self-preservation, and the public force, which is intended for the state's preservation, and that, in a word, it is always ready to sacrifice the government to the people and not the people to the government.

Furthermore, although the artificial body of the government is the product of another artificial body, and although it has, as it were, merely a borrowed and subordinate life, this does not prevent it from being able to act more or less vigorously or promptly, or from enjoying, so to speak, more or less robust health. Finally, without directly departing from the goal of its institution, it may deviate from that goal to a greater or lesser extent depending on how it is constituted.

It is from all these differences that the various relations which the government should have with the body of the state arise, according to the accidental and particular relations by which this same state is modified. For often the government that is best in itself will become the most vicious unless its relations are modified according to the defects of the body politic to which it belongs.

CHAPTER 2
On the Principle That Constitutes the Different Forms of Government

In order to present the general cause of these differences, it is necessary to distinguish here between the prince and the government, just as I have distinguished above between the state and the sovereign.

The body of the magistracy can be made up of a greater or lesser number of members. We have said that the ratio of the sovereign to the subjects was greater to the degree that the people was more numerous, and by an obvious analogy we can say the same about the government with regard to the magistrates.

Now, since the total force of the government is always that of the state, it does not vary. From which it follows that the more it uses this force on its own members, the less it has left to act on the whole people.

Therefore, the more numerous the magistrates, the weaker the government. As this maxim is fundamental, let us endeavor to clarify it more fully.

We can distinguish three essentially different wills in the person of the magistrate. First, the individual's own will, which tends solely to his particular advantage. Second, the common will of the magistrates, which is concerned exclusively with the advantage of the prince, and which may be called the corporate will, which is general in relation to the government and particular in relation to the state of which the government is a part. In the third place, the will of the people or the sovereign will, which is general, as much in relation to the state considered as the whole as in relation to the government considered as part of the whole.

In perfect legislation, the particular or individual will should be null, the government's corporate will very subordinate, and consequently the general or sovereign will always dominant and the sole rule for all the others.

According to the natural order, on the contrary, these different wills become more active in proportion as they are concentrated. Thus the general will is always the weakest, the corporate will has the second place, and the particular will is the first of all. As a result, each member within the government is first of all himself, and then a magistrate, and then a citizen—a gradation directly opposed to that required by the social order.

Given this, let the whole government be in the hands of a single man. Then the particular will and the corporate will are perfectly united, and consequently the corporate will attains the highest degree of intensity it can have. Now, as the use of force depends on the degree of will and as the government's absolute force does not vary, it follows that the most active of governments is that of a single man.

On the contrary, let us combine the government with the legislative authority; let us make a prince out of the sovereign, and all the citizens into so many magistrates. Then the corporate will, merged with the general will, will not have more activity than it, and will leave the particular will with its full force. Thus the government, always having the same absolute force, will be at its minimum relative force or activity.

These relations are incontestable, and are further confirmed by other considerations. It is clear, for example, that each magistrate is more active within his corporate body than each citizen in his, and that, consequently, the particular will will have far more influence in the actions of the government than in those of the sovereign. For each magistrate is almost always charged with some function of government, whereas each citizen by himself exercises no function of sovereignty. Furthermore, the more the state expands, the more its real force increases, although it does not increase in proportion to its size. Rather, since the state remains the same, the magistrates may well multiply but the government does not thereby acquire greater real force because this force is the force of the state, whose extent is still the same. Thus the relative force or activity of the government diminishes without its absolute or real force being able to increase.

It is also certain that business gets done less expeditiously in proportion as more people are responsible for it; that by overestimating prudence, not enough attention is given to chance; that opportunity is lost; and that the fruits of deliberation are often lost by dint of deliberating.

I have just proved that government grows slack in proportion as magistrates multiply, and I have proved above that the more numerous the people, the more repressive force should increase. From which it follows that the ratio of the magistrates to the government should be the inverse of the ratio of the subjects to the sovereign. That is, the more the state grows, the more the government should contract, such that the number of leaders diminishes in proportion to the increase of the people.

Still, I am speaking here only about the government's relative force, and not about its rectitude. For, on the contrary, the more numerous the body of the magistracy, the more closely the corporate will approaches the general will, whereas under a single magistrate this same corporate will is, as I have said, merely a particular will. Thus one loses on the one hand what might be gained on the other, and the lawgiver's art consists in knowing how to determine the point at which the government's force and will, which are always inversely proportional, are to be combined in the ratio most advantageous to the state.

CHAPTER 3
Classification of Governments

We have seen in the previous chapter why the different types or forms of government are distinguished according to the number of members that make it up. It remains to be seen in this chapter how this classification is made.

The sovereign can, in the first place, entrust the government to the whole people or to the majority of the people, so that there are more citizens who are magistrates than citizens who are simple private individuals. This form of government is given the name *democracy*.

Or else it can restrict the government to the hands of a small number, so that there are more ordinary citizens than magistrates, and this form bears the name *aristocracy*.

Finally, it can concentrate the entire government in the hands of a single magistrate from whom all the others derive their power. This third form is the most common, and is called *monarchy* or royal government.

It should be noted that all these forms—or at least the first two—are liable to a greater or lesser degree, and even have a rather wide range. For democracy can include the whole people or be restricted to as few as half. Aristocracy, in turn, can be restricted anywhere from half of the people to the smallest number. Even royalty can be shared to a certain extent. Sparta consistently had two kings by its constitution, and the Roman Empire was known to have up to eight emperors at once without its being possible to say that the empire was divided. Thus there is a point at which each form of government blends with the next one, and it is clear that, under these three names alone, government can in actuality take as many different forms as the state has citizens.

What is more, since this same government can in certain respects be subdivided into further parts, with one administered in one way and another in different way, a multitude of mixed forms can result from the combination of these three forms, each of which can be multiplied by all the simple forms.

There has always been a great deal of dispute regarding the best form of government without considering that each of them is the best in certain cases and the worst in others.

If the number of supreme magistrates in different states should be inversely proportional to the number of citizens, it follows that in general democratic government suits small states, aristocratic governments medium-sized ones, and monarchical large ones. This rule is derived directly from the principle. But how to count the multitude of circumstances which might furnish exceptions?

CHAPTER 4

On Democracy

He who makes the law knows better than anyone how it should be executed and interpreted. It therefore seems that there could be no better constitution than that in which the executive power is combined with the legislative. But this is precisely what makes this government inadequate in certain respects, because things that should be kept distinct are not, and because, since the prince and the sovereign are nothing but the same person, they form, so to speak, nothing but a government without a government.

It is not good for he who makes the laws to execute them, nor for the body of the people to turn its attention away from general considerations to particular objects. Nothing is more dangerous than the influence of private interests in public affairs, and the abuse of the laws by the government is a lesser evil than the corruption of the legislative body[61]—the infallible consequence of particular considerations. In that case, since the state is vitiated in its very substance, all reform becomes impossible. A people that would never abuse government would not abuse independence either. A people that would always govern well would not need to be governed.

In the strict sense of the term, a genuine democracy never has existed, and

61. "Legislative body" translates *législateur*, which is otherwise translated as "lawgiver." In this instance, however, Rousseau uses the term to refer to the legislative body, that is, the people in its capacity as sovereign.

never will exist. It is against the natural order for the larger number to govern and for the smaller number to be governed. It is unimaginable that the people could remain constantly assembled to attend to public affairs, and it is readily apparent that it could not establish commissions to do so without the form of administration changing.

Indeed, I do believe I can state as a principle that when the government's functions are divided among several tribunals, the least numerous will sooner or later acquire the greatest authority, if only due to the ease of expediting affairs, which naturally leads to their acquiring it.

Furthermore, think of how many things this form of government presupposes which are difficult to combine. First, a very small state where the people is easily assembled and where each citizen can easily know all the others. Second, great simplicity of morals, which forestalls all manner of business and thorny discussions. Next, great equality of ranks and fortunes, without which equality of rights and authority could not long endure. Finally, little or no luxury, for luxury either is the result of wealth or it makes it necessary. It simultaneously corrupts rich and poor, the former by its possession, the latter by its covetousness. It sells out the fatherland to softness, to vanity. It deprives the state of all its citizens in order to enslave some of them to others, and all of them to opinion.

This is why a famous author has named virtue as the principle of a republic, for all these conditions could not endure without virtue.[62] But for want of making the necessary distinctions, this noble genius has often lacked precision, sometimes clarity, and he failed to see that since the sovereign authority is everywhere the same, the same principle should apply in every well-constituted state—to a greater or lesser degree, it is true, according to the form of government.

Let us add that there is no government as subject to civil wars and intestine turmoil as democratic or popular government, because there is none which tends so strongly and so constantly to change form or which requires greater vigilance and courage to maintain in its own form. It is in this constitution above all that the citizen ought to arm himself with force and steadfastness,

---

62. The "famous author" is Charles-Louis de Secondat, baron de Montesquieu (1689–1755), who argues in his *Spirit of the Laws* (1748) that each form of government has a "principle" that makes it act and states: "There need not be much integrity for a monarchical or despotic government to maintain or sustain itself. The force of the laws in the one and the prince's ever-raised arm in the other can rule or contain the whole. But in a popular state there must be an additional spring, which is VIRTUE" (3.3, p. 22).

and every day of his life to say from the bottom of his heart what a virtuous Palatine* said in the Diet of Poland: *I prefer dangerous freedom to quiet servitude.*[63]

If there were a people of gods, it would govern itself democratically. So perfect a government is not suited to men.

CHAPTER 5
On Aristocracy

We have here two very distinct moral persons—namely the government and the sovereign—and consequently two general wills, one in relation to all the citizens and the other solely to the members of the administration. Thus, even though the government may regulate its internal administration as it pleases, it can never speak to the people except in the name of the sovereign, that is, in the name of the people itself. This must never be forgotten.

The first societies governed themselves aristocratically. The heads of families deliberated among themselves about public affairs. Young people deferred without any difficulty to the authority of experience. Hence the names *priests*, *elders*, *senate*, *gerontes*. The North American savages still govern themselves in this way in our times, and they are very well governed.

But in proportion as institutional inequality came to prevail over natural inequality, wealth or power† was given preference over age, and aristocracy became elective. Eventually power was transmitted from father to children along with goods, families became patrician, government was made hereditary, and there were twenty-year-old senators.

There are, therefore, three kinds of aristocracy: natural, elective, hereditary. The first is suited only to simple peoples. The third is the worst of all governments. The second is the best: it is aristocracy properly so-called.

Aside from the advantage of distinguishing between the two powers, this government has that of choosing its members; for in popular government all citizens are born magistrates, but this type limits them to a small number and

---

* The Palatine of Poznan, father of the King of Poland, Duke of Lorraine.

† It is clear that among the ancients the word *optimates* did not mean the best, but the most powerful.

---

63. Quoted by Rousseau in Latin: *Malo periculosam libertatem quam quietum servitium.* This remark is attributed by Stanisław Leszczyński, King of Poland and Duke of Lorraine (1677–1766), to his father, Rafał Leszczyński, Palatine of Poznan. The statement is a version of the Roman adage, *Malim inquietam libertatem quam quietam servitium*: "I would prefer unquiet freedom to quiet servitude."

they become such only through election*—a means by which probity, enlightenment, experience, and all the other reasons for public preference and esteem are so many new guarantees that they will be wisely governed.

Moreover, assemblies are more conveniently held, business is discussed better and dispatched in a more orderly and diligent manner, the state's prestige is better upheld abroad by venerable senators than by an unknown or despised multitude.

In a word, the best and most natural order is for the wisest to govern the multitude, as long as it is certain that they will govern it for its advantage and not for their own. Mechanisms must not be multiplied needlessly, nor must twenty thousand men do what one hundred well-chosen men could do even better. But it must be noted that the corporate interest begins here to direct the public force less in accordance with the rule of the general will, and that another inevitable decline takes from the laws a portion of the executive power.

With regard to particular circumstances of suitability, a state must not be so small nor a people so simple and so upright that the execution of the laws follows immediately from the public will, as happens in a good democracy. Nor either must a nation be so large that the leaders, dispersed in order to govern it, can make decisions on behalf of the sovereign each in their own department, and begin by making themselves independent so as ultimately to become the masters.

But if aristocracy requires somewhat fewer virtues than popular government, it also requires others that belong to it, such as moderation among the rich and contentment among the poor. For it seems that rigorous equality would be out of place there. It was not even adhered to in Sparta.

Besides, while this form of government includes a certain inequality of fortune, it is rather so that in general the administration of public affairs may be confided to those who can best devote all their time to them, but not, as Aristotle claims, so that the wealthy may always be preferred.[64] On the contrary, it

---

* It is very important to regulate the formalities of electing magistrates by laws. For if it is left to the will of the prince, it is impossible to avoid falling into hereditary aristocracy, as has happened in the republics of *Venice* and of *Bern*. And so the first has long been a dissolute state, but the second has maintained itself through the extreme wisdom of its senate. This is a most honorable and a most dangerous exception.

---

64. Aristotle nowhere claims that the wealthy should be preferred in an aristocracy. Whether intentionally or not, Rousseau ignores the important distinction Aristotle makes between an aristocracy, which is a proper form of regime in which the virtuous rule for the common benefit, and an oligarchy, an improper form of regime in which the wealthy rule and do so for their own benefit (see esp. *Politics* 3.7). However, Aristotle does concede that the tendency in aristocratic regimes is for wealth to accumulate in a few hands (see *Politics* 5.7).

is important that an opposite choice occasionally teach the people that men's merit offers more important reasons for preference than wealth.

CHAPTER 6

On Monarchy

So far we have considered the prince as a moral and collective person, united by the force of laws, and the trustee of the executive power in the state. We now have to consider this power united in the hands of a natural person, an actual man, who alone has the right to employ it in accordance with the laws. This is what is called a monarch or a king.

In total contrast to the other forms of administration, in which a collective being represents an individual, in this one an individual represents a collective being. As a result, the moral unity which constitutes the prince is at the same time a physical unity in which all the faculties that the law unites in the other forms of administration with so much difficulty are naturally united.

Thus the people's will, and the prince's will, and the public force of the state, and the particular force of the government all respond to the same motive force, all the springs of the machine are in the same hands, everything moves toward the same goal, there are no opposing motions which cancel out one another, and no constitution of any kind whatsoever can be imagined in which less effort produces greater action. Archimedes quietly sitting on the shore and effortlessly lifting a large vessel out of the water is my image of a skillful monarch governing his vast states from his study and making everything move while himself appearing immobile.[65]

But while there is no government that is more vigorous, there is none in which the particular will has greater sway and more easily dominates the others. Everything moves toward the same goal, it is true, but that goal is not public felicity, and the very force of the administration constantly works to the detriment of the state.

Kings want to be absolute, and from afar there are those who cry out to them that the best means for being so is to make themselves loved by their peoples. This maxim is very fine, and even very true in certain respects. Unfortunately, it will always be ridiculed at court. The power that comes from peoples' love is doubtless the greatest. But it is precarious and conditional: never will princes be satisfied with it. The best kings want to be able to be

---

65. The Greek mathematician and scientist Archimedes (c. 287–c. 212 BC) invented a number of military machines, including one that was said to be able to lift attacking ships out of the water.

wicked if they so please without ceasing to be masters. A political sermonizer may well tell them that since the force of the people is their own, their greatest interest is for the people to be prosperous, numerous, formidable. They know perfectly well that this is not true. Their personal interest is first of all for the people to be weak, wretched, and never able to resist them. I admit that, assuming the subjects to be always perfectly submissive, the prince's interest would in that case be for the people to be powerful so that this power, being his, would make him formidable to his neighbors. But as this interest is merely secondary and subordinate, and since the two assumptions are incompatible, it is natural for princes always to prefer the maxim more immediately useful to them. This is what Samuel so forcefully impressed upon the Hebrews.[66] This is what Machiavelli has so clearly proved. While pretending to teach lessons to kings, he taught great ones to peoples. Machiavelli's *Prince* is the book of republicans.*

We have found on the basis of general relations that monarchy is suited only to large states, and we again find this to be the case upon examining monarchy in itself. The more numerous the public administration, the more the ratio of the prince to the subjects decreases and approaches equality, so that this ratio is one to one, or equality itself, in democracy. This same ratio increases in proportion as the government contracts, and it is at its maximum when the government is in the hands of one alone. Then the distance between the prince and the people is too great, and the state lacks cohesion. In order to create this cohesion, intermediate orders are therefore needed: princes, grandees, nobility are needed to fill them. Now, none of this is suited to a small state, which all these different levels ruin.

---

* Machiavelli was an honest man and a good citizen. But being attached to the house of the Medici, he was forced during the oppression of his fatherland to disguise his love of freedom. The choice of his execrable hero alone is enough to manifest his secret intention, and the conflict between the maxims of his book *The Prince* and those of his *Discourses on Titus Livy* and his *Florentine Histories* demonstrates that this profound political thinker has so far had only superficial or corrupt readers. The Court of Rome has severely prohibited his book. I should think so. It is this court that he most clearly depicts.[67]

---

66. See 1 Samuel 8, where the Jewish people ask Samuel to appoint a king over them and Samuel foretells the misfortunes that will come to the people from having a king.

67. Niccolò Machiavelli (1469–1527) was a high-level Florentine political administrator who fell from power in 1512 when the Medici family returned to Florence and overthrew the republic he served. After falling from power, Machiavelli turned to writing works of political theory, most importantly *The Prince* and *Discourses on Livy*, and history, notably the *Florentine Histories*. The "execrable hero" of *The Prince* is Cesare Borgia, son of Pope Alexander VI, whose ruthless actions to acquire rule in northern Italy in the late 1490s and early 1500s Machiavelli himself observed and later wrote about in *The Prince*. First published in 1532, *The Prince* was placed on the Catholic Church's ("the Court of Rome's") Index of Prohibited Books in 1559.

But if it is difficult for a large state to be well governed, it is much more difficult for it to be well governed by a single man, and everyone knows what happens when the king appoints agents.

An essential and inevitable defect which will always make monarchical government inferior to republican is that in the latter the public voice almost never elevates to the highest places any but enlightened and capable men who fill them with honor, whereas those who succeed in monarchies are most often only petty bunglers, petty knaves, petty schemers whose petty talents, which allow them to attain high positions at court, serve only to reveal their ineptitude to the public as soon as they have attained them. The people is much less frequently mistaken in this choice than the prince, and a man of true merit is almost as rare in a royal ministry as a fool is at the head of a republican government. As such, when by some happy accident one of those men who are born to govern takes the helm of public affairs in a monarchy which has been almost ruined by a pack of fancy administrators, everyone is utterly amazed at the resources he discovers, and this marks an epoch in a country's history.

For a monarchical state to be able to be well governed, its size or extent would have to be commensurate with the faculties of he who governs. It is easier to conquer than to rule. Given an adequate lever, a single finger can move the world, but it takes the shoulders of Hercules to hold it up. If the state is the least bit large, the prince is almost always too small. When, on the contrary, the state happens to be too small for its leader, which is very rarely the case, it is still badly governed because the leader, always pursuing his grandiose views, forgets the people's interest and makes them no less unhappy by abusing his excessive talents than would a leader who is limited by his lack of talents. The kingdom would, so to speak, have to expand or contract with each reign according to the capacity of the prince, whereas, since the talents of a senate have more fixed bounds, in that case the state can have stable boundaries and the administration run no less well.

The most perceptible inconvenience of the government of one alone is the lack of that continuous succession which forms an unbroken bond in the two other forms of government. When one king dies, another one is needed. Elections leave dangerous intervals, they are stormy, and unless the citizens have a disinterestedness, an integrity which scarcely belongs to this government, intrigue and corruption enter in. It is difficult for he to whom the state has sold itself not to sell it in turn, and to compensate himself at the expense of the weak for the money the powerful have extorted from him. Sooner or later everything becomes venal under such an administration, and the peace which is then enjoyed under kings is worse than the disorder of interregna.

What has been done to prevent these evils? Crowns have been made hereditary within certain families and an order of succession has been established which prevents any dispute upon the death of kings. That is, by substituting the drawback of regencies for that of elections, apparent tranquility has been chosen over wise administration, and the risk of having children, monsters, and imbeciles for leaders has been preferred to having to argue over the choice of good kings. They failed to consider that by thus taking a chance on the alternative, they stack the odds almost entirely against themselves. It was a very sensible reply that Dionysius the Younger made when his father, reproaching him for a shameful action, said, "Did I set such an example for you?" "Ah," replied his son, "your father was not a king!"[68]

Everything conspires to deprive a man brought up to command others of justice and reason. Great pains are taken, they say, to teach young princes the art of ruling. It does not appear that this education does them any good. It would be better to begin by teaching them the art of obeying. The greatest kings celebrated by history were not brought up to rule. It is a science that is never known less well than after it has been learned too well, and it is acquired better by obeying than by commanding. *The most practical and shortest means of distinguishing between what is good and what is bad, is to think what you yourself would or would not have wished for under another prince.**[69]

One consequence of this lack of coherence is the instability of royal government which, sometimes guided by one plan and sometimes by another depending on the character of the prince who rules or of the people who rule for him, cannot have a fixed objective or a consistent mode of conduct for long—a variability which causes the state forever to vacillate from maxim to maxim, from project to project, and does not occur in the other forms of government in which the prince is always the same. As such, it is clear in general

---

* Tacitus, *Histories*, bk. 1.

---

68. Plutarch *Sayings of Kings* 175e. In the original, Dionysius the Younger calls his father a "tyrant" and not a "king." Dionysius the Elder (c. 432–367 BC) was tyrant of Syracuse in Sicily and was succeeded by his son, Dionysius the Younger (c. 397–343 BC).

69. Tacitus *Histories* 1.16, quoted by Rousseau in Latin: *Nam utilissimus idem ac brevissimus bonarum malarumque rerum delectus, cogitare quid aut nolueris sub alio Principe aut volueris.* The passage comes from a speech in AD 69 by the Emperor Galba in which he adopted Piso as his successor in the midst of the dispute over the empire, reminding the Romans that his own tumultuous reign was preferable to that of his predecessor, Nero. Galba was assassinated two weeks after giving this speech.

that while there is more cunning at court, there is more wisdom in a senate, and that republics pursue their ends by means of plans which are more consistent and better followed, whereas every revolution in the royal ministry produces one in the state, seeing that the maxim common to all ministers, and almost all kings, is to do the opposite in all things as their predecessor.

This very incoherence also provides the solution to a sophism very familiar to royalist politicians: which is, not only to compare civil government to domestic government and the prince to the father of a family, an error already refuted, but also to liberally endow this magistrate with all the virtues he would need and always to assume the prince is what he should be—an assumption with whose help royal government is obviously preferable to any other because it is incontestably the strongest, and because all it lacks in order to be the best as well is a corporate will more consistent with the general will.

But if, according to Plato,* a king by nature is such a rare person, how often will nature and fortune cooperate to crown him, and if a royal education necessarily corrupts those who receive it, what is to be expected from a succession of men brought up to rule? It is therefore surely deliberate self-deception to confuse royal government with that of a good king. In order to see what this government is in itself, it must be considered under limited or wicked princes. For either they are like this when they come to the throne, or the throne will make them such.

These difficulties have not escaped the notice of our authors, but they have not been hindered by them. The remedy, they say, is to obey without a murmur. God in his wrath gives us bad kings, and they must be endured as punishments from Heaven. This discourse is edifying, no doubt. But I wonder whether it would be better suited to the pulpit than to a book on politics. What would one say about a doctor who promised miracles and whose entire art consisted of exhorting the sick to be patient? Everyone knows perfectly well that when there is a bad government it must be endured. The question would be to find a good one.

CHAPTER 7
On Mixed Governments

Properly speaking, there is no simple government. A single leader has to have subordinate magistrates. A popular government has to have a leader. Thus in

* *The Statesman.*[70]

70. Plato *Statesman*, esp. 297b-c.

the distribution of executive power there is always a gradation from the larger to the smaller number, with the difference that sometimes the larger number depends on the smaller, and sometimes the smaller on the larger.

Sometimes there is an equal distribution, either when the constitutive parts are mutually dependent, as in the government of England, or when the authority of each part is independent but incomplete, as in Poland. This latter form is bad, because there is no unity in the government and because the state lacks cohesion.

Which is better, a simple government or a mixed government? A question much debated among political thinkers, and to which the same response should be given which I gave above about every form of government.

Simple government is the best in itself, for the very reason that it is simple. But when the executive power is not sufficiently dependent on the legislative—that is, when the ratio between the prince and the sovereign is greater than that between the people and the prince—this lack of proportion must be remedied by dividing the government. For then all of its parts have no less authority over the subjects, and their division makes all of them combined weaker as against the sovereign.

The same inconvenience can also be prevented by establishing intermediary magistrates which, leaving the government whole, serve merely to balance the two powers and to maintain their respective rights. Then the government is not mixed, it is tempered.

The opposite inconvenience can be remedied by similar means, and when the government is too slack, tribunals can be established to concentrate it. This has been the practice in all democracies. In the first case, the government is divided in order to weaken it, and in the second in order to reinforce it. For the maximum of both strength and weakness are likewise found in simple governments, whereas mixed forms produce a moderate force.

CHAPTER 8

That Every Form of Government Is Not Suited to Every Country

Freedom, since it is not a fruit of every climate, is not within the reach of every people. The more one meditates on this principle established by Montesquieu,[71] the more one senses its truth. The more one challenges it, the more opportunities one provides to establish it by new proofs.

---

71. See esp. Montesquieu, *Spirit of the Laws* (1748), 17.1: "Political servitude depends no less on the nature of the climate than do civil and domestic servitude."

In all the governments of the world the public person consumes and yet produces nothing. Where, then, does the substance it consumes come from? From its members' labor. It is the excess production of private individuals which produces what is necessary for the public. From this it follows that the civil state can subsist only as long as the product of men's labor exceeds their needs.

Now, this surplus is not the same in all the countries of the world. In some it is considerable, in others very moderate, in others nil, in others negative. This relation depends on the fertility of the climate, the kind of labor the soil requires, the nature of its products, the force of its inhabitants, the greater or lesser amount they need to consume, and several other similar relations of which it is composed.

On the other hand, all governments are not of the same nature. Some are more or less voracious, and the differences among them are based on the additional principle that the farther public contributions are from their source, the more burdensome they are. This burden ought to be measured not by the amount of taxes but by the distance they have to travel to return to the hands from which they came. When this circulation is prompt and well established, it does not matter whether one pays a little or a lot: the people is always rich and finances are always in good shape. By contrast, regardless of how little the people gives, when this small amount does not come back to them, it is soon exhausted by constantly giving: the state is never rich, and the people is always destitute.

It follows from this that the more the distance between the people and the government increases, the more burdensome taxes become. Thus, in democracy the people is least burdened, in aristocracy more so, in monarchy it bears the greatest weight. Monarchy is therefore only suited to opulent nations, aristocracy to states of moderate wealth as well as size, democracy to small and poor states.

Indeed, the more one reflects on this, the greater the difference one finds in this respect between free states and monarchies. In the former everything is used for the common utility; in the latter, public and private forces are reciprocal, and one increases through the weakening of the other. Finally, instead of governing the subjects in order to make them happy, despotism makes them miserable in order to govern them.

Here, then, are some natural causes in every climate on the basis of which one can assign the form of government toward which the force of the climate directs it, and even say what type of inhabitants it should have. Unforgiving and barren places where the product is not worth the labor should be left un-cultivated and uninhabited, or peopled only by savages. Places where men's labor yields precisely what is barely necessary should be inhabited by barba-rous peoples—any polity would be impossible there. Places where the excess of produce over labor is moderate suit free peoples. Those where abundant and fertile soil yields a great deal of product with little labor demand to be governed monarchically, so that the prince's luxury might consume the sur-plus of the excessive production of the subjects, for it is better to have this surplus absorbed by the government than frittered away by private individu-als. There are exceptions, I know, but these very exceptions confirm the rule in that sooner or later they produce revolutions which bring things back to the order of nature.

Let us always distinguish between general laws and the particular causes which can modify their effect. Even were the entire south covered with repub-lics and the entire north with despotic states, it would be no less true that due to the effect of climate despotism suits warm countries, barbarism cold cli-mates, and good polity the intermediate regions. I also see that, while granting the principle, there might be some dispute concerning its application. It might be said that there are some very fertile cold countries and some very unforgiv-ing southern ones. But this is a difficulty only for those who do not examine the matter with an eye to all its relations. It is necessary, as I have already said, to take into account the relations of labor, force, consumption, etc.

Let us assume that given two equal pieces of land, one yields five and the other ten. If the inhabitants of the former consume four and those of the latter nine, the surplus of the first product will be $1/5$ and that of the second $1/10$. Since the ratio of these two surpluses is therefore the inverse of the ratio of the products, the piece of land that produces only five will yield a surplus double that of the piece of land that produces ten.

But getting double the yield is out of the question, and I do not believe that anyone dares claim that in general the fertility of cold countries is even equal to that of warm countries. Nonetheless, let us assume this equality. Let us, if you wish, equate England with Sicily and Poland with Egypt. Farther south we will have Africa and the Indies, farther north we will have nothing more. To achieve this equality in the yield, what difference is required in cultivation? In Sicily one need only scratch the soil, while in England what effort it takes to work it! Now, where more hands are needed to produce the same yield, the excess production must necessarily be less.

Consider, on top of this, that the same number of men consume much less in warm countries. The climate there requires them to be temperate to stay healthy. Europeans who try to live there as they do at home all perish of dysentery and stomach ailments. *We are*, states Chardin, *carnivorous beasts, wolves, by comparison to Asians. Some attribute the Persians' temperance to the fact that their country is less cultivated, and, as for me, I believe, on the contrary, that their country is less abundant in foodstuffs because the inhabitants need less of them. If their frugality,* he continues, *were an effect of scarcity in the country, it would only be the poor who ate little, whereas in general everyone does so, and they would eat more or less in each province in accordance with the fertility of the country, whereas the same temperance is found throughout the kingdom. They highly congratulate themselves on their manner of living, saying that one need only look at their complexion to see how much more excellent their manner of living is than that of the Christians. Indeed, the Persians' complexion is clear. They have fair, delicate, and smooth skin, whereas the complexion of the Armenians, their subjects, who live in the European manner, is coarse, blotchy, and their bodies are fat and heavy.*[72]

The closer one gets to the equator, the less people live on. They eat almost no meat. Rice, maize, couscous, millet, cassava are their usual foods. In the Indies there are millions of men whose diet costs no more than a penny per day. In Europe itself we see perceptible differences of appetite between the peoples of the north and those of the south. A Spaniard will live for a week on a German's dinner. In countries where men are more voracious, objects of consumption also become luxury items. In England they exhibit it by a table laden with meats. In Italy you are regaled with sugar and flowers.

Luxury in clothing also exhibits similar differences. In climates where the changes of season are abrupt and violent, they have better and simpler clothes, while in those climates where they dress merely for display, they strive more for ostentation than utility, and clothes themselves are a luxury there. In Naples you will daily see men strolling along the Posilippo in gold-embroidered jackets and no stockings. The same is true for buildings. Everything is devoted to magnificence when no damage is to be feared from the weather. In Paris, in London, they want to be housed warmly and comfortably. In Madrid they have superb drawing rooms, but no windows that close, and they sleep in rat-holes.

Foods are much more substantial and succulent in warm countries. This is a third difference which cannot fail to influence the second. Why do they eat so many vegetables in Italy? Because there they are good, nourishing, extremely

72. Jean Chardin, *Voyages du Chevalier Chardin en Perse* (1711), 3.76, 83–84.

tasty. In France, where they are grown only with water, they are not at all nutritious, and count for almost nothing at meals. Yet they take up no less land and require at least as much effort to cultivate. It is a matter of experience that the wheats of Barbary, although otherwise inferior to those of France, yield much more flour, and that those of France in turn yield more than the wheats of the north. It can be inferred from this that a similar gradation generally obtains when moving in the same direction from the equator to the north pole. Now isn't it a clear disadvantage to get a smaller amount of nourishment from an equal amount of food?

To all these various considerations I can add another one which follows from them and reinforces them. It is that warm countries need fewer inhabitants than cold countries, yet could feed more of them. This produces a double excess of production which is always to despotism's advantage. The larger the area inhabited by a given number of inhabitants, the more difficult revolts become: because they cannot act in concert promptly or secretly, and because it is always easy for the government to get wind of the plans and cut off communication. But the closer together a numerous people draws, the less the government is able to usurp the sovereign. The leaders deliberate as securely in their chambers as the prince does in his council, and the crowd assembles as quickly in public squares as the troops do in their barracks. The advantage of a tyrannical government in this regard is therefore that of acting over great distances. With the help of fulcrums it sets up, its force increases with distance, like that of levers.* The force of the people, by contrast, acts only when concentrated, since in spreading it evaporates and vanishes, like the effect of gunpowder scattered on the ground and which ignites only one grain at a time. The least populous countries are thus those most appropriate for tyranny. Wild beasts reign only in wildernesses.

CHAPTER 9
On the Signs of a Good Government

Therefore, when it is asked which form of government is absolutely the best, this is to pose a question that is insoluble since it is indeterminate. Or, if you

---

* This does not contradict what I said above—book II, chapter 9—regarding the inconveniences of large states. For there it was a question of the government's authority over its members, and here it is a question of its force against its subjects. Its scattered members serve it as fulcrums for acting on the people at a distance, but it has no fulcrums to act directly on these members themselves. Thus, in the one case the length of the lever creates its weakness and in the other case its strength.

wish, it has as many good solutions as there are possible combinations of the absolute and relative situations of peoples.

But if one were to ask by which sign one might know whether a given people is well or badly governed, this would be another thing altogether, and the question of fact could be resolved.

Yet it is not resolved, because everyone wants to resolve it in his own way. Subjects praise public tranquility, citizens the freedom of private individuals; one prefers security of possessions, and the other that of persons; one would have it that the best government is the most severe, the other maintains that it is the mildest; this one wants crimes to be punished, and that one for them to be prevented; one thinks it a fine thing to be feared by one's neighbors, the other prefers to be ignored by them; one is satisfied when money circulates, the other demands that the people have bread. Even if they were to agree on these and other similar points, would we have gotten any farther? Since moral quantities lack a precise measure, even if there were agreement regarding the sign, how can there be so regarding the way to estimate it?

As for me, I am always astonished that people overlook such a simple sign or that they have the bad faith not to agree upon it. What is the end of the political association? It is the preservation and prosperity of its members. And what is the surest sign that they are preserving themselves and prospering? It is their number and their population. Look no further, then, for this much disputed sign. All other things being equal, the government under which the citizens—without external aid, without naturalizations, without colonies—populate and multiply most is infallibly the best. That under which a people grows smaller and wastes away is the worst. Calculators, it is now up to you: count, measure, compare.*

---

* The same principle should be used to judge which epochs deserve preference in terms of the prosperity of the human race. People have too much admired those in which the letters and arts have been seen to flourish, without having fathomed the secret object of their cultivation, without considering their fatal effect—*and this in their ignorance they called humanity when it was but part of their servitude.*[73] Will we never see in the maxims of books the crass interest which moves the authors to speak? No. Regardless of what they may say, when for all of its brilliance a country is depopulated, it is not true that all goes well, and it is not enough for one poet to have an income of a hundred thousand pounds for his age to be the best of all. Less consideration should be given to apparent repose and to the tranquility of leaders than to the well-being of entire nations and especially to the most numerous social stations. Hail may desolate a few cantons, but it rarely causes famine. Riots, civil

---

73. Tacitus *Agricola* 21, quoted by Rousseau in Latin: *idque apud imperitos humanitas vocabatur, cum pars servitutis esset.* The passage from which this quotation is taken describes the Britons' growing acceptance of the Roman customs spread by the Roman provincial governor Agricola.

CHAPTER 10
On the Abuse of Government and Its Tendency to Degenerate

Just as the particular will continually acts against the general will, so the government makes a constant effort against sovereignty. The greater this effort grows, the more the constitution is vitiated, and as there is here no other corporate will that balances the will of the prince by resisting it, sooner or later it must come to pass that the prince will eventually oppress the sovereign and break the social treaty. This is the inherent and inevitable vice which, from the birth of the body politic, relentlessly tends to destroy it just as old age and death destroys man's body.

There are two general paths by which a government degenerates: namely, when it contracts or when the state dissolves.

The government contracts when it goes from a larger number to a smaller one, that is, from democracy to aristocracy, and from aristocracy to royalty. This is its natural tendency.* If it were to retrogress from a smaller number to a larger one, it might be said that it slackens, but this reverse movement is impossible.

---

wars greatly alarm leaders, but they do not cause the true woes of peoples, which may even have some respite while there is dispute over who will tyrannize over them. It is their permanent condition which gives rise to their real prosperities and calamities. When everything is crushed beneath the yoke, it is then that everything perishes; it is then that leaders destroy them at their leisure, *and where they produce desolation, they call it peace.*[74] When the quibbling of the great caused turmoil in the kingdom of France, and when the coadjutor of Paris carried a dagger in his pocket when he went to the Parlement, this did not prevent the French people from living happily and in large numbers in honest and free affluence.[75] Long ago Greece flourished in the midst of the cruelest wars. Blood flowed like water, and the entire country was covered with men. It seemed, states Machiavelli, that in the midst of murders, proscriptions, civil wars our republic became more powerful. The virtue of its citizens, their morals, their independence did more to reinforce it than all its dissentions had done to weaken it. A little agitation gives vitality to souls, and what truly causes the species to prosper is not so much peace as freedom.[76]

* The slow formation and the development of the Republic of Venice amidst its lagoons offers a notable example of this sequence, and it is rather astonishing that after more than twelve hundred years the Venetians still seem to be only at the second stage, which began with the *Serrar di Consiglio* in 1198. As for the ancient

---

74. Tacitus *Agricola* 30, quoted by Rousseau in Latin: *ubi solidtudinem faciunt, pacem appellant.* The passage from which this quotation is taken comes from a speech by a Briton to rally his people against the Romans, at whom this remark is directed.

75. Rousseau refers to Jean François Paul de Gondi, cardinal de Retz (1613–79), who was made coadjutor to the archbishop of Paris (an official designated to assist the diocesan bishop in his duties) and who was a leading figure during the mid-seventeenth-century conflicts in France over the powers of the crown and the parlements. Retz relates the story in his memoirs.

76. See Machiavelli, *Florentine Histories* (1532), Preface.

Indeed, never does the government change form except when its worn-out mainspring leaves it too weak to be able to preserve its form. Now, if it were to slacken by expanding, its force would become completely nil, and it would be even less able to subsist. It is therefore necessary to rewind and tighten the mainspring in proportion as it gives way, otherwise the state which it supports would fall into ruin.

The situation in which dissolution of the state can come about occurs in two ways.

Doges on whose account they are reproached, regardless of what the *squitinio della libertà veneta* may say about them, it has been proved that they were not their sovereigns.[77]

The Roman Republic will not fail to be raised in objection to me, whose development, they will say, followed a completely opposite course, moving from monarchy to aristocracy, and from aristocracy to democracy. I am very far from thinking of it in this way.

Romulus' initial establishment was a mixed government which promptly degenerated into despotism. The state perished prematurely owing to certain particular causes, just as a newborn dies before having reached manhood. The expulsion of the Tarquins was the genuine period of the Republic's birth. But it did not at first take a consistent form, because in not abolishing the patriciate only half of the work was accomplished. For in this way since the hereditary aristocracy—which is the worst of legitimate administrations—remained in conflict with the democracy, the form of the government—forever uncertain and fluctuating—was not settled, as Machiavelli has proved, until the establishment of the tribunes.[78] Only then was there a true government and a genuine democracy. Indeed, the people was then not only sovereign but also magistrate and judge, the senate was merely a subordinate tribunal to temper and concentrate the government, and the consuls themselves—although patricians, although the first magistrates, although absolute generals in wartime—were, in Rome, merely the presiding officers of the people.

From that time on, the government was also seen to follow its natural inclination and to tend strongly to aristocracy. With the patriciate having abolished itself as if of its own accord, the aristocracy no longer consisted in the body of patricians, as it does in Venice and Genoa, but in the body of the senate, which was composed of both patricians and plebeians, and even in the body of the tribunes once they began to usurp active power. For words do not make things, and when the people has leaders who govern on its behalf, regardless of the name the leaders may bear, it is still an aristocracy.

From the abuse of the aristocracy the civil wars and the Triumvirate arose. Sulla, Julius Caesar, Augustus became veritable monarchs in fact, and ultimately under Tiberius' despotism the state was dissolved.[79] Roman history therefore does not disprove my principle. It confirms it.

---

77. The *Serrar* (or *Serrata*) *di Consiglio* (Closing of the Council) refers to the limitation of members of the Great Council to families that had provided members in the past, thus creating a hereditary aristocracy, which was passed in Venice in 1297 (not 1198, as Rousseau claims). The *squitinio della libertà veneta* (*Scrutiny of Venetian Liberty*) was an anonymous writing published in 1612 that sought to establish the Holy Roman Emperors' claim of sovereignty over Venice.

78. See Machiavelli, *Discourses on Livy* (1531), 1.2.

79. The First Triumvirate was a private arrangement among the generals and politicians Pompey the Great (106–48 BC), Gaius Julius Caesar (100–44 BC), and Marcus Licinius (c. 115–53 BC) formed in the aftermath of the first civil wars in Rome in opposition to the aristocratic party in Rome. The breakdown of the First Triumvirate led to renewed civil war and the ultimate victory of Caesar. Lucius Cornelius Sulla (c. 138–78 BC) was the leader of the more aristocratic or senatorial faction during first civil wars in Rome and used his position as dictator to make constitutional reforms. Augustus (63 BC–AD 14) was the first Roman emperor. Tiberius (42 BC–AD 37) was Augustus' heir as emperor.

First, when the prince no longer administers the state in accordance with the laws and usurps the sovereign power. Then a remarkable change occurs: namely, it is not the government but the state that contracts. I mean that the large state dissolves and another one is formed within it, composed solely of the members of the government, and which is no longer anything for the rest of the people minus its master and its tyrant. As a result, the moment the government usurps sovereignty, the social compact is broken and all ordinary citizens, returned by right to their natural freedom, are forced—but not obligated—to obey.

The same situation also comes about when the members of the government separately usurp the power they should exercise only as a body. This is a no less serious an infraction of the laws, and it produces even greater disorder. Then there are, so to speak, as many princes as magistrates, and the state, no less divided than the government, perishes or changes form.

When the state dissolves, any abuse of government whatsoever takes the general name *anarchy*. To distinguish, democracy degenerates into *ochlocracy*, aristocracy into *oligarchy*. I would add that royalty degenerates into *tyranny*, but this latter word is equivocal and calls for explanation.

In the vulgar sense of the term, a tyrant is a king who governs with violence and without regard for justice and the laws. In the precise sense of the term, a tyrant is a private individual who arrogates the royal authority to himself without having a right to it. It is in this manner that the Greeks understood the word "tyrant." They applied it indiscriminately to good and to bad princes whose authority was not legitimate.* Thus, *tyrant* and *usurper* are two perfectly synonymous words.

In order to give different names to different things, I call a *tyrant* the usurper of royal authority and a *despot* the usurper of sovereign power. The tyrant is he who imposes himself against the laws in order to govern in accordance with

---

* For all those are both considered and called tyrants who exercise perpetual power in a city that is accustomed to freedom. Cornelius Nepos, Life of Miltiades.[80] It is true that Aristotle—*Nicomachean Ethics*, bk. 8, chap. 10—distinguishes between a tyrant and a king, in that the first governs for his own utility and the second solely for his subjects' utility. But, aside from the fact that generally all Greek authors have used the word "tyrant" in a different sense, as is apparent above all in Xenophon's *Hiero*, it would follow from Aristotle's distinction that there had never existed a single king since the beginning of the world.[81]

---

80. Cornelius Nepos (c. 100–c. 24 BC), Lives of Eminent Commanders, "Life of Miltiades" 8, quoted by Rousseau in Latin: *Omnes enim et habentur et dicuntur Tyranni qui potestate utuntur perpetua, in ea Civitate quae libertate usa est.*

81. See Aristotle *Nicomachean Ethics* 8.10 (1060b). *Hiero* by Xenophon (c. 430–354 BC) is a dialogue on the life of the tyrant.

the laws. The despot is he who puts himself above the laws themselves. Thus, the tyrant cannot be a despot, but the despot is always a tyrant.

CHAPTER II
On the Death of the Body Politic

Such is the natural and inevitable tendency of the best-constituted governments. If Sparta and Rome perished, what state can hope to last forever? If we want to form a lasting establishment, let us therefore not dream of making it eternal. To succeed, one must not attempt the impossible, nor flatter oneself with giving the work of men a solidity that human things do not allow.

The body politic—just like the body of man—begins to die right from the moment of its birth and carries within itself the causes of its destruction. But both of them can have a constitution that is more or less robust and suited to preserve it for a longer or shorter period of time. The constitution of man is the work of nature, that of the state is the work of art. It does not belong to men to prolong their lives; it does belong to them to prolong that of the state as far as possible by giving it the best constitution it might have. The best constitution will come to an end, but later than another, if no unforeseen accident brings about its downfall before its time.

The principle of political life lies in the sovereign authority. The legislative power is the heart of the state, the executive power is its brain, which gives movement to all the parts. The brain can become paralyzed and the individual still live. A man can remain an imbecile and yet live. But as soon as the heart has stopped functioning, the animal is dead.

It is not through the laws that the state subsists; it is through the legislative power. Yesterday's law does not obligate today, but tacit consent is presumed from silence, and the sovereign is assumed to be constantly confirming the laws it does not repeal while being able to do so. Everything that it has once declared it wills, it still wills unless it revokes it.

Why, then, is so much respect accorded to ancient laws? Because of their very antiquity. It is to be believed that nothing but the excellence of these ancient wills could have preserved them for so long. If the sovereign had not continually recognized them as salutary, it would have revoked them a thousand times over. This is why the laws, far from weakening, constantly acquire new force in every well-constituted state. The prejudice in favor of antiquity makes them daily more venerable, whereas wherever the laws grow weaker as they grow older, it is proof that there is no longer any legislative power and that the state is no longer alive.

CHAPTER 12

How Sovereign Authority Is Maintained

Since the sovereign has no force other than the legislative power, it acts only through the laws, and since the laws are simply the authentic acts of the general will, the sovereign can act only when the people is assembled. "The people assembled!" it will be said, "What a chimera!" This is a chimera today, but it was not so two thousand years ago. Have men changed their nature?

The limits of the possible in moral matters are less narrow than we think. It is our weaknesses, our vices, our prejudices that contract them. Base souls do not believe in great men; vile slaves smile mockingly at the word "freedom."

Let us consider what can be done by what has been done. I will not speak of the ancient republics of Greece, but the Roman Republic was, it seems to me, a large state and the city of Rome a large city. The last census accorded Rome four hundred thousand citizens bearing arms, and the last enumeration of the Empire more than four million citizens, not counting subjects, foreigners, women, children, slaves.

What difficulty is there that might not be imagined about frequently assembling the immense populace of that capital and its environs? Yet few weeks went by without the Roman people being assembled, and even several times. Not only did it exercise the rights of sovereignty, but a portion of those of government as well. It dealt with some business, it judged some cases, and at the public square this entire people was magistrate nearly as often as citizen.

By going back to the earliest times of nations, one would find that most ancient governments, even monarchical ones such as those of the Macedonians and Franks, had similar councils. Be that as it may, this single indisputable fact answers all the difficulties: the inference from what exists to what is possible appears sound to me.

CHAPTER 13

Continued

It is not enough for the assembled people to have once and for all settled the state's constitution by giving sanction to a body of laws. It is not enough for it to have established a perpetual government or to have provided, once and for all, for the election of magistrates. Aside from extraordinary assemblies which unforeseen circumstances might demand, there must be regular and periodic ones that nothing can abolish or prorogue, so that on the designated day the people is legitimately convened by the law without needing any further formal convocation.

But except for these assemblies, lawful by their date alone, any assembly of the people that has not been convened by the magistrates appointed for that purpose and in accordance with the prescribed forms ought to be held to be illegitimate and everything done there as null and void because the order to assemble itself ought to emanate from the law.

As for the frequency of the meeting of legitimate assemblies, this depends on so many considerations that precise rules cannot be given on that point. It can only be said that in general the more force the government has, the more frequently ought the sovereign assert itself.

This, I will be told, may be good for a single town,[82] but what is to be done when the state includes several of them? Is the sovereign authority to be shared, or should it rather be concentrated in a single town and all the rest subjected to it?

I reply that neither should be done. First, the sovereign authority is simple and single, and it cannot be divided without destroying it. In the second place, a town no more than a nation can be legitimately subjected to another, because the essence of the body politic consists in the agreement between obedience and freedom, and because the words *subject* and *sovereign* are identical correlatives whose concept is combined in the single word "citizen."

I further reply that it is always an evil to unite several towns into a single city, and that anyone wanting to create this union should not flatter himself with having avoided the natural drawbacks. The abuses of large states must not be urged as an objection against someone who wants only small ones. But how are small states to be given enough force to resist large ones? Just like the Greek towns in times past resisted the Great King, and more recently just like Holland and Switzerland resisted the House of Austria.[83]

Nonetheless, if the state cannot be limited to proper bounds, one resource still remains. It is to not allow a capital, to have the seat of government alter-

---

82. "Town" translates *ville*, which could also be translated "city." In this context, however, Rousseau will also use the term *cité*, which has been translated "city." See I.6 and n. 27 to p. 173.

83. I.e., through confederation. The Greek city-states allied under the leadership of Athens and Sparta and successfully resisted the Persians ("the Great King") during the fifth century BC. The Dutch provinces under the leadership of Holland successfully revolted against Habsburg rule ("the House of Austria") during the latter part of the sixteenth and beginning of the seventeenth centuries. The Swiss Confederation expanded and consolidated its power through victories over the Habsburgs during the fifteenth century.

nately located in each town, and also to convene the country's estates in each of them by turn.

Populate the territory evenly, extend the same rights throughout, spread abundance and life throughout it—this is how the state will become simultaneously the strongest and the best governed as possible. Remember that the walls of towns are only built with the wreckage of farmhouses. In every palace I see rise in the capital, I believe I see an entire countryside reduced to hovels.

CHAPTER 14
Continued

The moment the people is legitimately assembled as a sovereign body, the entire jurisdiction of the government ceases, the executive power is suspended, and the person of the humblest citizen is as sacred and inviolable as that of the first magistrate, because where the represented is present, there is no longer a representative. Most of the tumults which arose in Rome in the comitia came from having been ignorant of that rule or having neglected it. Then the consuls were only the presiding officers of the people, the tribunes mere speakers,* the senate was nothing at all.

These intervals of suspension, during which the prince recognizes or should recognize the presence of a superior, have always been threatening to it, and these assemblies of the people, which are the aegis of the body politic and the curb on government, have in all times been an object of dread for leaders. As such, they never spare efforts, or objections, or difficulties, or promises to deter the citizens from having them. When the latter are greedy, cowardly, pusillanimous, more enamored with tranquility than freedom, they do not hold out for long against the redoubled efforts of the government. This is how, with the force of resistance constantly increasing, the sovereign authority ultimately vanishes, and how most cities fall and perish before their time.

But an intermediate power is sometimes introduced between sovereign authority and government which has to be discussed.

CHAPTER 15
On Deputies or Representatives

As soon as public service ceases to be the principal business of citizens, and as soon as they prefer to serve with their pocketbooks rather than with their per-

---

* Approximately in the sense given to this term in the English Parliament. The similarity between these functions would have led to conflict between the consuls and the tribunes, even had all jurisdiction been suspended.

sons, the state is already close to its ruin. Must they march into battle? They pay troops and stay home. Must they attend the council? They name deputies and stay home. By dint of laziness and money they eventually have soldiers to enslave the fatherland and representatives to sell it.

It is the hustle and bustle of commerce and the arts, it is the avid interest in gain, it is the softness and love of comforts, that transform personal services into money. One gives up a portion of one's profit to increase it at one's leisure. Give money, and soon you will have chains. This word *finance* is a slave's word; it is unknown in the city. In a truly free state the citizens do everything with their hands and nothing with money. Far from paying to exempt themselves from their duties, they would pay to fulfill them themselves. I am quite far from commonly held notions. I believe that corvées are less contrary to freedom than taxes.

The better constituted the state, the more public affairs prevail over private ones in the citizens' minds. There are even far fewer private affairs, because, since the sum of the common happiness contributes a more considerable share of the happiness to each individual, he needs to seek less of it through his own pursuits. In a well-run city each person flies to the assemblies. Under a bad government no one likes to take a step to go to them, because no one takes an interest in what is done there, because they foresee that the general will won't predominate there, and, finally, because domestic concerns are all-consuming. Good laws lead to making better ones, bad laws bring about worse ones. As soon as someone says, *What do I care?* about the affairs of state, the state should be regarded as lost.

The cooling of the love of the fatherland, the activity of private interest, the immensity of states, conquests, the abuse of the government have led people to devise the measure of using deputies or representatives of the people in the nation's assemblies. This is what people in certain countries dare to call the Third Estate. Thus, the particular interest of two orders is assigned first and second place, and the public interest only the third.

Sovereignty cannot be represented for the same reason that it cannot be alienated. It consists of its essence in the general will, and the will cannot be represented. Either it is the same or it is different—there is no middle ground. The people's deputies therefore are not, nor can they be, its representatives. They are merely its agents. They cannot conclude anything definitively. Any law the people has not ratified in person is null and void. It is not a law. The English people thinks it is free; it is greatly mistaken. It is so only during the election of members of Parliament; as soon as they are elected, it is a slave, it is nothing. Given the use it makes of its freedom in the brief moments it has it, it certainly deserves losing it.

The idea of representatives is modern. It comes to us from feudal government—from that iniquitous and absurd government in which the human species is degraded and in which the name of man is dishonored. Among the ancient republics and even among monarchies, never did the people have representatives. That very word was unknown. It is quite striking that in Rome, where the tribunes were so sacred, no one even imagined that they might usurp the functions of the people, and that, amidst such a great multitude, they never attempted to pass a single plebiscite on their authority alone. Yet the trouble the crowd sometimes caused may be judged by what happened at the time of the Gracchi, when a portion of the citizens voted from the rooftops.[84]

Where right and freedom are everything, inconveniences are nothing. Among this wise people everything was given its proper due. It allowed its lictors to do what its tribunes would not have dared to do. It did not fear that its lictors would want to represent it.

In order to explain how the tribunes sometimes did represent it, however, it is enough to understand how the government represents the sovereign. Since law is nothing but the declaration of the general will, it is clear that the people cannot be represented in its legislative power, but it can and must be represented in its executive power, which is nothing but force applied to law. This makes it clear that, on proper examination, very few nations would be found to have laws. Be that as it may, it is certain that the tribunes, since they did not possess any portion of the executive power, could never represent the Roman people by the rights of their office, but only by usurping those of the senate.

Among the Greeks, everything the people had to do it did by itself. It was constantly assembled in the public square. It inhabited a mild climate, it was not greedy, slaves did its work, its chief business was its freedom. No longer having the same advantages, how are the same rights to be preserved? Your harsher climates give you more needs,* six months of the year the public place is unbearable, your muted languages cannot be heard in the open, you give more thought to your gain than to your freedom, and you fear slavery much less than poverty.

---

* In cold countries, to adopt the luxury and softness of the peoples of the Orient is to want to give oneself their chains. It is to submit to them even more necessarily than they do.

---

84. The two Gracchi brothers, Tiberius and Gaius, were tribunes of the second century BC who attempted to pass legislation that would have redistributed land from the patricians to the plebeians.

What! Freedom can be maintained only with the help of servitude? Perhaps. The two extremes meet. Everything that is not in nature has its inconveniences, and civil society more than all the rest. There are certain unfortunate situations in which one cannot preserve one's freedom except at the expense of someone else's and in which the citizen can be perfectly free only if the slave is utterly enslaved. Such was the situation of Sparta. As for you, modern peoples, you do not have slaves, but you yourselves are slaves. You pay for their freedom with your own. Boast as you may of this choice; I find in it more cowardice than humanity.

I do not mean by all this that it is necessary to have slaves or that the right of slavery is legitimate, since I have proved the contrary. I simply state the reasons why modern peoples who believe themselves to be free have representatives, and why ancient peoples did not have them. Be that as it may, the moment a people gives itself representatives, it is no longer free. It no longer exists.

All things considered, I do not see that it is henceforward possible among us for the sovereign to preserve the exercise of its rights unless the city is very small. But if it is very small, won't it be subjugated? No. I will show below* how the external power of a great people can be combined with ease of administration and the proper ordering of a small state.

CHAPTER 16
That the Institution of the Government Is Not a Contract

Once the legislative power is well established, it is a matter of likewise establishing the executive power. For this latter power, which operates only through particular acts, since it is not of the essence of the former, is naturally separate from it. If it were possible for the sovereign, considered as such, to have the executive power, right and fact would be so confounded that it would no longer be possible to tell what is and what is not the law, and the body politic, thereby denatured, would soon fall prey to the violence against which it was instituted.

Since the citizens are all equal through the social contract, what all ought to do may be prescribed by all, whereas no one has the right to require another to do something that he does not himself do. Now, it is precisely this right, indispensible for making the body politic live and move, that the sovereign gives to the prince by instituting the government.

---

* This is what I had proposed to do in the sequel to this work, when, in dealing with foreign relations, I would have come to federations. This subject is entirely new and its principles have yet to be established.

Some have claimed that the act of this establishment was a contract between the people and the leaders it gives to itself—a contract by which the conditions between the two parties were stipulated under which the one obligated itself to command and the other to obey. Everyone will agree, I am sure, that this is indeed a strange way of contracting! But let us see whether this opinion is tenable.

First, the supreme authority can no more be modified than it can be alienated: to limit it is to destroy it. It is absurd and contradictory for the sovereign to give itself a superior. To obligate oneself to obey a master is to return to one's full freedom.

Moreover, it is evident that this contract between the people and certain specific persons would be a particular act. From this it follows that this contract could not be either a law or an act of sovereignty, and that consequently it would be illegitimate.

It is also clear that, with respect to one another, the contracting parties would be under the law of nature alone and without any guarantor of their reciprocal engagements, which is in every way incompatible with the civil state. Since whoever controls the force is always the master of the outcome, one might as well give the name "contract" to the act of one man who said to another, "I give you all of my goods, on the condition that you will give back to me as much as you please."

There is only one contract in the state, which is that of the association, and that contract alone excludes any other. It is impossible to imagine any other public contract that would not be a violation of the first one.

CHAPTER 17
On the Institution of the Government

How, then, ought the act by which the government is instituted be understood? I will begin by noting that this act is complex or composed of two others, namely the establishment of the law and the execution of the law.

By the first, the sovereign enacts that there will be a governmental body established under some specific form, and it is clear that this act is a law.

By the second, the people appoints the leaders who will be given responsibility for the government that has been established. Now, since this appointment is a particular act, it is not a second law, but merely a consequence of the first and a function of government.

The difficulty is to understand how there can be an act of government before the government exists, and how the people, which is only either sovereign or subject, can become prince or magistrate in certain circumstances.

Here, again, is revealed one of those astonishing properties of bodies politic by which apparently contradictory operations are reconciled. For this reconciliation is accomplished through a sudden conversion of sovereignty into democracy, in such a way that, without any perceptible change and solely through a new relationship of all to all, the citizens, having become magistrates, proceed from general acts to particular acts and from the law to its execution.

This change of relationship is not some speculative subtlety without any example in practice. It takes place daily in the British Parliament, where the lower house on certain occasions turns itself into a committee of the whole in order to better discuss business, and thereby becomes a simple commission in the place of the sovereign court it had been the moment before. In this way it then reports to itself in its capacity as the House of Commons on what it has just settled in its capacity as a committee of the whole, and deliberates anew under one title what it has already resolved under another.

Such is the peculiar advantage of democratic government that it can be established in effect through a simple act of the general will. After this, this provisional government either remains in office if such is the form adopted, or it establishes in the name of the sovereign the government prescribed by the law, and everything is thus in order. It is not possible to institute the government in any other legitimate way, and without renouncing the principles established above.

CHAPTER 18
A Means for Preventing the Usurpations of the Government

From these clarifications it follows—in confirmation of chapter 16—that the act that institutes the government is not a contract but a law, that the trustees of the executive power are not the people's masters but its officers, that the people can establish them and dismiss them whenever it so pleases, that it is not a question of them contracting but of obeying, and that in assuming the functions the state imposes on them, they are merely fulfilling their duty as citizens without in any way having the right to debate the conditions.

When, therefore, it happens that the people institutes a hereditary government, whether it is monarchical within one family or aristocratic within one order of citizens, this is not an engagement it takes on. It is a provisional form it gives to the administration until such time as it so pleases to order it otherwise.

It is true that these changes are always dangerous, and that an established government must never be touched until it becomes incompatible with the public good. But this circumspection is a maxim of politics and not a rule of right, and the state is no more bound to leave the civil authority to its leaders than the military authority to its generals.

It is true as well that one cannot be too careful in such a case about observing all the requisite formalities for distinguishing a regular and legitimate act from a seditious tumult and the will of an entire people from the clamors of a faction. It is especially in such cases that no more must be conceded to the temporary suspension of rights[85] than what cannot be denied to it in the full rigor of the law, and that it is also from this obligation that the prince derives a great advantage for preserving its power in spite of the people, without it being possible to say that it has usurped it. For while appearing to use only its rights, it is very easy for it to extend them and, on the pretext of public tranquility, to prevent assemblies intended to reestablish good order. As a result, the prince takes advantage either of a silence which it prevents from being broken or of irregularities it itself has caused to be committed so as to presume that the attitudes of those whom fear has silenced are in its favor and to punish those who dare to speak. This is how the Decimvirs, after having at first been elected for one year, then continuing for another year, tried to hold on to their power in perpetuity by no longer allowing the comitia to assemble.[86] And it is by this simple means that all the governments of the world, once they are invested with the public force, sooner or later usurp the sovereign authority.

The periodic assemblies of which I have spoken above are suitable for preventing or postponing this misfortune, especially if they do not need formal convocation. For then the prince cannot prevent them without openly declaring itself to be a violator of the laws and an enemy of the state.

Those assemblies which have as their object solely the maintenance of the social treaty ought always to be opened with two motions which may never be omitted and which are to be voted on separately:

---

85. Such temporary suspensions of rights by the government when it deemed their exercise to be dangerous to the state was known in France by the old legal term *cas odieux*, which is the term Rousseau uses here. A somewhat parallel example would be the suspension of the writ of habeas corpus possible under the US Constitution or British law, although in the French context such suspensions did not occur in accordance with any regularized or constitutional procedures.

86. For the Decimvirs, see n. 44 to p. 192.

The first: Whether it so pleases the sovereign to retain the present form of government?

The second: Whether it so pleases the people to leave its administration in the hands of those who are currently charged with it?

I assume here what I do believe I have demonstrated, namely that there is no fundamental law in the state that cannot be revoked, not even the social compact. For if all the citizens were to assemble in order to break this compact by common agreement, there can be no doubt that it was very legitimately broken. Grotius even thinks that each person can renounce the state of which he is a member, and regain his natural freedom and his goods on leaving the country.*[87] Now, it would be absurd for all the citizens combined not to be able to do what each of them can do separately.

END OF THE THIRD BOOK

---

* It being well understood that the person does not leave in order to evade his duty and avoid serving the fatherland when it needs us. Fleeing would then be criminal and punishable; it would no longer be withdrawal, but desertion.

---

87. See Grotius, *The Rights of War and Peace* (1625), 2.5.24, vol. 2:553–55.

BOOK IV

CHAPTER I
That the General Will Is Indestructible

As long as several men united together regard themselves as a single body, they have only a single will which relates to their common preservation and to the general welfare. Then all the mainsprings of the state are vigorous and simple, its maxims are clear and luminous, there are no tangled, contradictory interests, the common good is everywhere clearly evident and requires only good sense to be perceived. Peace, union, equality are enemies of political subtleties. Upright and simple men are difficult to deceive due to their simplicity: traps, sophisticated pretexts do not deceive them. They are not even sharp enough to be duped. When, among the happiest people in the world, one sees bands of peasants settling affairs of state beneath an oak and always acting wisely, how can one help but scorn the sophistication of other nations which make themselves illustrious and miserable with so much art and mystery?

A state so governed needs very few laws, and in proportion as it becomes necessary to promulgate new ones, this necessity is universally seen. The first person who proposes them merely states what everyone has already sensed, and there is no question of intrigues or eloquence to pass into law what each has already resolved to do as soon as he is certain that the others will do likewise.

What misleads reasoners is that since they see only states that have been badly constituted from their origin, they are struck by the impossibility of maintaining similar political order in them. They laugh when they imagine all the foolishness of which a smooth talker could persuade the people of Paris or London. They do not know that Cromwell would have been sentenced to hard labor by the people of Bern, and the duc de Beaufort to the reformatory by the Genevans.[88]

But when the social knot begins to grow slack and the state to grow weak, when particular interests begin to make themselves felt and small societies to influence the large one, the common interest is vitiated and meets opposition, unanimity no longer prevails in voting, the general will is no longer the will of everyone,[89] contradictions and disagreements arise, and the best advice is not accepted without disputes.

Finally, when the state, close to its ruin, continues to subsist only in an illusory and empty form, when the social bond is broken in all hearts, when the basest interest brazenly assumes the sacred name of the public good: then the general will becomes mute, everyone, guided by secret motives, no longer offer their opinions as citizens—no more so than if the state had never existed—and iniquitous decrees which have as their goal merely particular interest are falsely passed under the name of laws.

Does it follow from this that the general will is annihilated or corrupted? No, it is always constant, unalterable, and pure. But it is subordinated to others which prevail over it. Each person, detaching his interest from the common interest, sees clearly that he cannot completely separate them, but his share of the evil that then befalls the public appears as nothing to him compared to the exclusive good he intends to get for himself. Except for this particular good, he wills the general good for his own interest just as strongly as anyone else. Even in selling his vote for money, he does not extinguish the general will within himself; he evades it. The mistake he makes is to change the status of the question and to reply to something different from what he is asked. As a result, instead of saying with his vote, *it is advantageous to the state*, he says, *it is advantageous to a given man or a given party for such and such an opinion to pass*. Thus the law of public order in assemblies consists not so much in maintaining the general will as in seeing to it that it is always questioned and that it always replies.

I could offer quite a few reflections here regarding the simple right to vote in every act of sovereignty—a right that nothing can take away from the cit-

---

88. Oliver Cromwell (1599–1658), English military and political leader who led the overthrow of the monarchy and establishment of the Commonwealth, then acquiring dictatorial powers as "Lord Protector." The duc de Beaufort is François de Vendôme (1616–69), who was a leader of the armed struggle by a number of French nobility against an increasingly absolute monarchy.

89. "Will of everyone" translates *volonté de tous*. This term is translated "will of all" in II.3, where Rousseau distinguishes between the "general will" (*volonté générale*) and the "will of all," that is, the sum of the wills of all persons acting as private individuals (see n. 35 to p. 182). However, in this context it is clear that he is not referring to the "will of all" in that sense.

izens—and regarding the right to voice an opinion, to make propositions, to divide the question, to debate, which the government always takes great care to allow only to its members. But this important matter would require a separate treatise, and I cannot say everything in this one.

CHAPTER 2
On Voting

It is clear from the previous chapter that the way in which general affairs are handled can provide a fairly reliable indication of the current state of morals and the health of the body politic. The more concord reigns in assemblies— that is, the closer opinions approach unanimity—the more the general will is dominant as well. But long debates, dissensions, tumult herald the ascendancy of particular interests and the decline of the state.

This appears less evident when two or more orders are included in its constitution, as in Rome with the patricians and the plebeians, whose quarrels often disturbed the comitia even in the finest period of the Republic. But this exception is more apparent than real. For in that case by the inherent vice of the body politic there are, so to speak, two states in one. What is not true of the two together is true of each separately. And, indeed, even in the very stormiest times, the plebiscites of the people always proceeded calmly and by a large majority when the senate did not interfere in them. Since the citizens had but one interest, the people had but one will.

At the other extreme of the circle, unanimity returns. That is when the citizens, having fallen into servitude, no longer have either freedom or will. Then fear and flattery turn voting into acclamations; they no longer deliberate, they worship or they curse. Such was the abject manner of expressing opinions in the senate under the emperors. Sometimes this was done with ridiculous precautions. Tacitus notes that under Otho the senators, while heaping execration on Vitellius, sought to make a terrific noise at the same time so that, if by chance he were to become master, he could not tell what any one of them had said.[90]

From these various considerations arise the maxims that should regulate the manner in which votes are counted and opinions compared, according to whether the general will is more or less easy to know and the state more or less in decline.

There is only a single law that by its nature requires unanimous consent.

---

90. Tacitus *Histories* 1.85.

This is the social compact. For the civil association is the most voluntary act in the world; since every man is born free and master of himself, no one may, on any pretext whatsoever, subjugate him without his consent. To decide that the son of a slave is born a slave is to decide that he is not born a man.

If, then, at the time of the social compact there are some who are opposed to it, their opposition does not invalidate the contract; it merely keeps them from being included in it: they are foreigners among the citizens. Once the state is instituted, consent consists in residence; to inhabit the territory is to submit oneself to sovereignty.*

Except for this primitive contract, the vote of the greatest number always obligates all the rest. This is a consequence of the contract itself. But it is asked how a man can be free and yet be forced to conform to wills that are not his own. How are those who are opposed both free and subject to laws to which they have not consented?

I reply that the question is badly put. The citizen consents to all the laws—even to those passed despite him, and even to those that punish him when he dares to violate one of them. The constant will of all the members of the state is the general will; it is through it that they are citizens and free.† When a law is proposed in the assembly of the people, what they are being asked is not precisely whether they approve the proposal or whether they reject it, but whether or not it is conformable to the general will that is theirs. Each expresses his opinion on this by voting, and the declaration of the general will is taken from the counting of the votes. When, therefore, the opinion contrary to my own prevails, this proves nothing except that I was mistaken, and that what I deemed to be the general will was not. If my particular opinion had prevailed, I would have done something other than what I had willed, and it is then that I would not have been free.

This presupposes, it is true, that all the characteristic features of the general will are still in the majority. Once they cease to be so, there is no longer any freedom regardless of which side one takes.

---

* This should always be understood to refer to a free state. For elsewhere family, goods, lack of place of refuge, necessity, violence may keep an inhabitant in the country despite himself, and then his merely living there no longer implies his consent to the contract or violation of the contract.

† In Genoa the word *Libertas* can be read on the front of the prisons and on the chains of galley slaves. This application of the motto is fine and just. Indeed, it is only the malefactors of all social stations who keep the citizens from being free. In a country where all such people were in the galleys, the most perfect freedom would be enjoyed.

When showing above how particular wills took the place of the general will in public deliberations, I indicated clearly enough the means practicable for preventing this abuse. I will say more about this below. With regard to the proportion of votes required to declare this will, I have also provided the principles by which it can be ascertained. The difference of a single vote breaks a tie, a single opposing vote destroys unanimity. But between unanimity and a tie there are many unequal vote shares, the requisite number for each of which can be ascertained according to the condition and the needs of the body politic.

Two general maxims can serve to regulate these ratios. The first, that the more important and serious the deliberations are, the more the opinion that prevails should approach unanimity. The second, that the greater dispatch the business at hand requires, the smaller the prescribed difference in the division of opinions should be. In deliberations that must be finished on the spot, a majority of a single vote should suffice. The first of these maxims appears better suited to the laws, and the second to public affairs. Be that as it may, it is on the basis of a combination of the two that the best ratios for the deciding majority are to be established.

CHAPTER 3
On Elections

With regard to elections of the prince and the magistrates, which are, as I have said, complex acts, there are two ways to go about them: namely, by choice and by drawing lots. Both of them have been used in various republics, and a very complicated mixture of the two is still seen today in the election of the Doge of Venice.

Voting by drawing lots, states Montesquieu, is of the nature of democracy.[91] I agree, but why is this so? Drawing lots, he continues, is a manner of electing that distresses no one; it leaves each citizen a reasonable hope of serving the fatherland. These are not reasons.

If one keeps in mind that the election of leaders is a function of government and not of sovereignty, it will be clear why election by drawing lots is more in keeping with the nature of democracy, where administration is better to the extent that its acts are fewer in number.

---

91. Montesquieu, *Spirit of the Laws* (1748), 2.2, p. 13.

In every genuine democracy the magistracy is not an advantage but is an onerous responsibility which cannot be fairly imposed on one individual rather than another. The law alone can impose this responsibility on the person to whom it falls by lot. For then, since the condition is equal for everyone and since the choice does not depend on any human will, there is no particular application that vitiates the universality of the law.

In aristocracy the prince chooses the prince, the government preserves itself of its own accord, and it is there that voting is appropriate.

Far from destroying this distinction, the example of the election of the Doge of Venice confirms it. This mixed form is suited to a mixed government. For it is an error to take the government of Venice for a genuine aristocracy. While the people have no part in the government, the nobility there is itself the people. A multitude of poor Barnabites never came close to attaining any magistracy, and has to show for its nobility merely the empty title of "Excellence" and the right to attend the Grand Council. Since this Grand Council is as numerous as our General Council in Geneva, its illustrious members have no more privileges than our ordinary citizens do. It is certain that, putting aside the extreme disparity between the two republics, the Genevan bourgeoisie is exactly analogous to the Venetian patriciate, our natives and inhabitants are analogous to the townsmen and people of Venice, our peasants are analogous to the subjects on the mainland. Finally, apart from its size, in whatever way this republic is considered, its government is not any more aristocratic than our own. The entire difference is that since we have no leader for life, we do not have the same need to draw lots.

Elections by drawing lots would have few drawbacks in a genuine democracy, where—since everyone is equal by their morals and talents as well as by their maxims and fortunes—the choice would become almost indifferent. But I have already said that there is no genuine democracy.

When choice and drawing lots are combined, the former should fill the positions that require appropriate talents, such as military offices. The latter is suited to those where good sense, justice, integrity are enough, such as judicial responsibilities, because in a well-constituted state these qualities are common to all the citizens.

Neither drawing lots nor voting has any place in monarchical government. Since the monarch is by right the only prince and sole magistrate, the choice of his lieutenants belongs to him alone. When the abbé de St. Pierre suggested multiplying the councils of the king of France and electing their members by ballot, he did not see that he was proposing to change the form of the government.[92]

It would remain for me to speak of the manner in which votes are cast and collected in the assembly of the people, but perhaps the history of the Roman administration regarding these matters will explain more tangibly all the maxims I might establish. It is not unworthy of a judicious reader to see in some detail how public and private affairs were conducted in a council of two hundred thousand men.

CHAPTER 4
On the Roman Comitia

We have no really reliable records of the earliest times in Rome. It is even quite likely that most of what is retailed about it are fables,* and in general the most instructive part of the annals of peoples, which is the history of their establishment, is the part we most lack. Experience daily teaches us about the causes that give rise to the revolutions of empires. But as no new peoples are being formed any longer, we have hardly anything but conjectures to explain how they were formed.

The practices that one finds established at minimum attest that these practices had an origin. Among those traditions that go back to those origins, those which the greatest authorities support and which the strongest reasons confirm must pass for the most certain. These are the maxims I have tried to follow in investigating how the freest and the most powerful people on earth exercised its supreme power.

After the founding of Rome, the emerging republic—that is, the army of the founder, made up of Albans, Sabines, and foreigners—was divided into three classes which took from this division the name *tribes*. Each of these tribes was subdivided into ten curiae, and each curia into decuriae, at the head of which were placed leaders called *curions* and *decurions*.

Aside from this, a body of one hundred horsemen or knights, called a "century," was drawn from each tribe, from which it is clear that these divisions,

---

* The name *Rome*, which supposedly comes from *Romulus*, is Greek and means *force*. The name *Numa* is also Greek, and means *law*. How likely is it that the first two kings of that city would have borne names that anticipated in such a highly relevant way what they did?

---

92. Charles-Irénée Castel, abbé de Saint-Pierre, *Discours sur la Polysynodie* (1719). For Rousseau's summary of the work and commentary on it, see his *Polysynody*, in *Collected Writings*, vol. 11.

scarcely needed in a market town, were at first solely military in character. But it seems that an instinct for greatness led the little city of Rome to give itself in advance an administration suited to the capital of the world.

From this first apportionment a drawback soon resulted. It was that since the tribe of the Albans* and that of the Sabines† remained ever in the same condition while the tribe of foreigners‡ continually grew due to the perpetual influx of their kind, it was not long before this last tribe surpassed the other two. The remedy Servius[93] found for these dangerous abuses was to change the division, and to substitute for the division based on race, which he abolished, another one derived from the districts of the city occupied by each tribe. Instead of three tribes, he created four. Each of them occupied one of the hills of Rome and bore its name. Thus at the same time as he remedied the existing inequality, he also prevented it from occurring in the future. And in order that this division not be merely one of districts but of men, he forbade the inhabitants of one quarter from moving to another, which prevented the races from mixing together.

He also doubled the three previously formed centuries of knights and added twelve more to them, but still under the previous names—a simple and judicious means by which he succeeded in distinguishing the body of knights from that of the people, without causing the latter to grumble.

To these four urban tribes Servius added fifteen more, called rural tribes because they were formed of the inhabitants of the countryside, apportioned into the same number of cantons. Later, the same number of new ones was created, and the Roman people eventually found itself divided into thirty-five tribes, the number at which they remained fixed until the end of the Republic.

From this distinction between urban tribes and country tribes an effect resulted that is worthy of note because there is no other example of it, and because Rome owed to it both the preservation of its morals and the growth of its empire. The urban tribes might have been expected to have soon arrogated power and honors to themselves and to lose no time in degrading the rural tribes. Yet the very opposite occurred. The taste of the earliest Romans for country life is well known. They owed this taste to the wise founder who

---

* *Ramnenses.*
† *Tatienses.*
‡ *Luceres.*

---

93. **Servius** Tullius was the legendary sixth king of Rome, and was said to have ruled from 578–535 BC.

joined rustic and military labors to freedom, and so to speak relegated arts, crafts, intrigue, riches, and slavery to the town.

Thus, since all those who were most illustrious in Rome lived in the countryside and cultivated the land, they became accustomed to look only there for the mainstays of the Republic. Since this condition was that of the worthiest patricians, it was held in honor by everyone: the simple and hard-working life of villagers was preferred to the idle and cowardly life of city-dwellers in Rome, and someone who would have been merely a miserable proletarian in the city became a respected citizen as a farmer in the countryside. It is not without reason, stated Varro, that our magnanimous ancestors established villages as the nursery of those robust and valiant men which defended them in time of war and fed them in time of peace.[94] Pliny states with assurance that the tribes of the countryside were honored due to the men who made them up, whereas cowards whom they wanted to degrade were transferred to those of the city as a disgrace.[95] When the Sabine Appius Claudius came to settle in Rome, he was loaded with honors and inscribed in a rural tribe which afterwards took the name of his family.[96] Finally, freedmen all entered the urban tribes, never the rural ones, and there was not a single instance during the entire period of the Republic of any of these freedmen attaining any magistracy even though he had become a citizen.

This maxim was excellent, but it was pushed so far that ultimately there resulted from it a change and certainly an abuse in the administration.

First, the censors, after having long arrogated to themselves the right of arbitrarily transferring citizens from one tribe to another, allowed most of them to inscribe themselves in whichever one they pleased—a permission which was surely not good for anything, and which deprived the censorship of one of its greatest mainsprings. Moreover, since the great and the powerful all had themselves inscribed in the country tribes, and since freedmen who had become citizens remained in the urban ones along with the populace, the tribes in general no longer had either a district or a territory, but rather all of them were so intermingled that the members of each could no longer be identified except by consulting the registers, with the result that the word *tribe* thereby shifted from propertied residence to persons or, rather, it became almost a chimera.

It further came about that the urban tribes, being closer at hand, were often

---

94. Varro *De Re rustica* 3.1.

95. Pliny the Elder *Naturalis Historiae* 18.3.

96. Appius Claudius was a semi-legendary Sabine who was said to come to Rome in 504 BC after the Sabines were defeated by the Romans.

the strongest in the comitia and sold the state to those who deigned to buy the votes of the rabble who composed them.

With regard to the curiae, since their founder had created ten of them in each tribe, the entire Roman people then enclosed within the city walls was composed of thirty curiae, each of which had its temples, its gods, its officers, its priests, and its festivals called *compitalia*, similar to the *paganalia* later held by the rural tribes.

At the time of Servius' new apportionment, since this number thirty could not be split up equally among his four tribes, he did not want to change them, and the curiae independent of the tribes became a separate division of Rome's inhabitants. But there was no question of curiae either among the rural tribes or among the people who composed them because, since the tribes had become a purely civil establishment and a different administration had been introduced for raising troops, Romulus' military divisions proved superfluous. Thus, although every citizen was inscribed in a tribe, nowhere near everyone was inscribed in a curia.

Servius made yet a third division which bore no relation to the first two and which by its effects became the most important of all. He distributed the entire Roman people into six classes, which he distinguished neither by district nor by persons, but by goods, so that the first classes were filled with the rich, the last ones with the poor, and the middle ones with those who enjoyed a moderate fortune. These six classes were subdivided into one hundred ninety-three further bodies called "centuries," and these bodies were so distributed that the first class alone included more than half of them and the last one was formed of only a single one. It was thereby the case that the class with the smallest number of men had the largest number of centuries, and the entire last class was counted as only one subdivision, even though it alone contained more than half of Rome's inhabitants.

So that the people would not see through the consequences of this last form, Servius pretended to give it a military cast. He inserted two centuries of armor makers into the second class and two centuries of weapons makers into the fourth. In each class, except the last, he distinguished the young from the old, that is, those who were obliged to bear arms from those whose age exempted them by law from doing so—a distinction which, even more than that of goods, made it necessary to frequently do a new census or enumeration. Finally, he wanted the assembly held at the Campus Martius and for all those who were of an age to serve to come there with their arms.

The reason why he did not follow the same division into young and old in the last class is that the populace of which it was composed was not accorded the honor of bearing arms for the fatherland. It was necessary to have hearths to obtain the right to defend them, and among those countless crowds of beggars who today make the armies of kings shine, there was not a single one of them, perhaps, who would not have been contemptuously expelled from a Roman cohort in the days when soldiers were the defenders of freedom.

In the last class, however, they further distinguished between the *proletarians* and those called *capite censi*. The first, not completely reduced to nothing, at least gave citizens to the state, sometimes even soldiers when there was a pressing need. As for those who had nothing at all and who could be enumerated only by head, they were regarded as completely nil, and Marius was the first who deigned to enroll them.[97]

Without deciding here whether this third enumeration was good or bad in itself, I do believe I can assert that it was only the simple morals of the earliest Romans, their disinterestedness, their taste for agriculture, their contempt for commerce and for the ardor for gain that could have made it practicable. Where is the modern people whose devouring greed, uneasiness of mind, intrigue, continual moving about, perpetual revolutions of fortune would allow such an establishment to last twenty years without overturning the whole state? It must even be carefully noted that morals and censorship—stronger than this institution—corrected its vice in Rome, and that a rich man could see himself relegated to the class of the poor for having made an excessive display of his wealth.

From all this, it is easy to understand why mention is almost never made of more than five classes, even though there were really six. The sixth, since it provided neither soldiers to the army nor voters at the Campus Martius* and was of almost no use in the Republic, was rarely taken into account.

Such were the various divisions of the Roman people. Let us now see what effect they produced in the assemblies. These assemblies when legitimately convened were called *comitia*. They were usually held in the Roman forum or the Campus Martius, and were distinguished into comitia by curiae, comitia by centuries, and comitia by tribes, according to which of these three forms they were organized. The comitia by curiae were instituted by Romulus, those

---

* I say at the *campus martius* because it was there that the comitia assembled by centuries. In the two other forms, the people assembled in the *forum* or elsewhere, and then the *capite censi* had as much influence and authority as the first citizens.

---

97. Gaius Marius (157–86 BC) was a Roman general and statesman who first authorized recruiting landless citizens into the army.

by centuries by Servius, those by tribes by the tribunes of the people. No law was sanctioned, no magistrate was elected except in the comitia, and as there was not a single citizen who was not inscribed in a curia, a century, or a tribe, it follows that no citizen was excluded from the right to vote and that the Roman people was genuinely sovereign both by right and in fact.

For the comitia to be legitimately assembled and for what was done by them to have the force of law, three conditions had to be met. First, that the body or the magistrate that convened it was invested with the necessary authority to do so. Second, that the assembly was held on one of the days permitted by law. Third, that the auguries were favorable.

The reason for the first regulation does not need to be explained. The second is a matter of administration, so the comitia were not allowed to be held on holidays and market days, when the people of the countryside, coming to Rome to do their business, did not have the time to spend their day in the public square. By means of the third the senate held in check a proud and restless people and, when necessary, tempered the ardor of seditious tribunes, but the latter found more than one means of getting around this constraint.

The laws and the election of the leaders were not the only issues submitted to the judgment of the comitia. Since the Roman people had usurped the most important functions of the government, the fate of Europe may be said to have been decided in its assemblies. This variety of objects gave rise to the various forms these assemblies took according to the matters they had to decide.

In order to judge these various forms, it is enough to compare them. In instituting those of the curiae, Romulus had in mind restraining the senate by the people and the people by the senate while dominating both alike. By means of this form, therefore, he gave the people the authority of numbers to balance the authority of power and wealth he left to the patricians. But in accordance with the spirit of monarchy, he nevertheless gave a greater advantage to the patricians through the influence of their clients in the majority of votes. This admirable institution of patrons and clients was a masterpiece of politics and humanity, without which the patriciate, so contrary to the spirit of the Republic, could not have survived. Rome alone had the honor of giving to the world this fine example, which never led to any abuse and yet has never been followed.

Since this same form of curiae continued under the kings until Servius, and since the reign of the last Tarquin was not held to be legitimate, the royal laws were generally identified by the name of *leges curiatae*.

Under the Republic, the curiae, still limited to the four urban tribes and no longer containing anyone but the populace of Rome, were no longer suited either to the senate, which was at the head of the patricians, or to the tribunes, who, while plebeians, were at the head of the well-off citizens. They therefore fell into discredit, and their degradation was such that their thirty lictors assembled did what the comitia by curiae should have been doing.

The division by centuries was so favorable to aristocracy that it is at first not clear why the senate did not always prevail in the comitia that bore that name and by which the consuls, censors, and other curule magistrates were elected.[98] Indeed, of the one hundred ninety-three centuries which formed the six classes of the entire Roman people, since the first class was made up of ninety-eight of them and the votes were counted solely by centuries, this first class alone prevailed over all the others by the number of votes. When all of its centuries were in agreement, they did not even continue to collect the ballots. What the smallest number had decided was taken for a decision of the multitude, and it might be said that in the comitia by centuries affairs were settled by the majority of money much more so than by that of votes.

But this extreme authority was tempered by two means. First, since usually the tribunes—and always a large number of plebeians—were among the class of the rich, they balanced the influence of the patricians in this first class.

The second means consisted in this: that instead of first having the centuries vote in order, in which case they would have always begun with the first one, they drew one by lot, and that one* alone proceeded to hold an election, after which, all the centuries being summoned on another day in the order of their rank, they repeated the same election and usually confirmed it. In this way the authority of example was taken away from rank in order to give it to lot in accordance with the principle of democracy.

Another further advantage resulted from this practice: that the citizens of the countryside had time between the two elections to inform themselves about the merit of the candidate provisionally nominated, so that they might give their votes knowledgeably. But under the pretext of a need for dispatch, they succeeded in abolishing this practice and the two elections took place on the same day.

The comitia by tribes were properly speaking the council of the Roman people. They were convened only by the tribunes. The tribunes were elected

---

* That century thus drawn by lot was called *prae rogativa* due to the fact that it was the first to be asked for its vote, and this is where the word *prerogative* comes from.

---

98. The "curule seat" was a chair upon which certain high-level magistrates were entitled to sit.

in them and their plebiscites were passed in them. Not only did the senate not have any standing in them, it did not even have the right to attend them, and forced to obey laws on which they could not vote, the senators in this regard were less free than the humblest citizens. This injustice was completely mistaken and was alone enough to invalidate the decrees of a body to which not all of its members were admitted. Even had all the patricians attended these comitia according to their right as citizens, since in that case they became ordinary private individuals, they would have had hardly any influence on a form of voting based on counting heads, and in which the lowliest proletarian counted for as much as the prince of the senate.

It is therefore clear that aside from the fact that these various divisions for collecting votes from such a large people were not indifferent in themselves, each of them had effects relative to those considerations that led it to be preferred.

Without going into greater detail on the above subject, it follows from the preceding clarifications that the comitia by tribes were the most favorable to popular government and the comitia by centuries to aristocracy. With regard to the comitia by curiae, in which the populace of Rome alone formed the majority, as they were good only for promoting tyranny and evil designs, they had to fall into disrepute, with the seditious parties themselves abstaining from using a means that all too clearly exposed their schemes. It is certain that the entire majesty of the Roman people was found only in the comitia by centuries, which were alone complete, seeing that the comitia by curiae lacked the rural tribes and the comitia by tribes lacked the senate and the patricians.

As for the manner of collecting votes, among the earliest Romans it was as simple as their morals, although still less simple than in Sparta. Each person called out his vote aloud, a clerk wrote them down as they were given. In each tribe a majority of votes determined the vote of the tribe, a majority of votes among the tribes determined the vote of the people, and likewise for the curiae and centuries. This practice was good as long as honesty reigned among the citizens and as long as each person was ashamed to vote publicly for an unjust opinion or an unworthy candidate. But when the people grew corrupt and votes were bought, it was agreed that they would vote in secret in order to restrain buyers through mistrust and to provide scoundrels with a means not to be traitors.

I know that Cicero condemns this change and attributes the ruin of the Republic in part to it.[99] But although I am sensible of the weight that Cicero's

99. See Cicero *Laws* 3.15.

authority should have here, I cannot share his opinion. I think, on the contrary, that the loss of the state was hastened for not having made enough similar changes. Just as the regimen for healthy people is not fit for the sick, so one must not try to govern a corrupt people by the same laws that suit a good people. Nothing proves this maxim better than the duration of the Republic of Venice, of which the simulacrum still exists solely because its laws are suited only to wicked men.

Tablets were therefore distributed to the citizens so that each could vote without anyone knowing his opinion. New formalities were also established for collecting tablets, counting votes, comparing numbers, etc. This did not prevent the fidelity of the officers charged with these functions* from often being suspected. Eventually, to prevent intrigue and trafficking in votes, they passed edicts whose number demonstrates their uselessness.

Toward the end, they were often compelled to resort to extraordinary expedients in order to make up for the inadequacy of the laws. Sometimes miracles were alleged; but this means, which might fool the people, did not fool those who governed it. Sometimes an assembly was suddenly convened before the candidates had had the time to engage in their intrigues. Sometimes an entire session was consumed by talk when it was seen that the people had been won over and was ready to make a bad choice. But ultimately ambition eluded everything, and what is incredible is that in the midst of so many abuses, this immense people, thanks to its ancient regulations, did not cease to elect its magistrates, pass laws, judge cases, expedite private and public affairs with almost as much ease as the senate itself might have done.

CHAPTER 5

On the Tribunate

When an exact proportion cannot be established between the constitutive parts of the state, or when indestructible causes constantly disrupt the ratios between them, then a special magistracy is instituted which is not incorporated with the others, which restores each term to its true ratio, and which creates a link or middle term either between the prince and the people, or between the prince and the sovereign, or on both sides at the same time if necessary.

This body, which I will call the *tribunate*, is the preserver of the laws and of the legislative power. It serves sometimes to protect the sovereign against the

---

* Custodes, Diribitores, Rogatores suffragiorum.

government, as the tribunes of the people did in Rome, sometimes to sustain the government against the people, as the Council of the Ten does now in Venice, and sometimes to maintain the balance between one part and another, as the ephors did in Sparta.

The tribunate is not a constitutive part of the city, and should not have any share in the legislative or executive power, but it is for this very reason that its power is greater. For while it can do nothing, it can prevent everything. It is more sacred and more revered as the defender of the laws than the prince which executes them and the sovereign which makes them. This was seen quite clearly in Rome when those proud patricians, who always despised the entire people, were forced to bow down before a simple officer of the people who had neither patronage nor jurisdiction.

A wisely tempered tribunate is the firmest support of a good constitution. But if it has even a little too much force, it overturns everything. With regard to weakness, it is not in its nature, and provided that it counts for something, it is never less than it has to be.

It degenerates into tyranny when it usurps the executive power of which it is merely the moderator, and when it tries to issue the laws it should merely protect. The enormous power of the ephors, which posed no danger as long as Sparta preserved its morals, accelerated its corruption once it began. The blood of Agis, murdered by those tyrants, was avenged by his successor. The crime and punishment of the ephors both equally hastened the downfall of the republic, and after Cleomenes Sparta no longer counted for anything.[100] Rome also perished in the same way, and the excessive power gradually usurped by the tribunes ultimately served, along with the help of laws that had been made for freedom, as a safeguard for the emperors who destroyed it. As for the Council of Ten in Venice, it is a bloody tribunal, equally abhorrent to the patricians and the people and which, far from loftily protecting the laws, after their degradation no longer serves any purpose other than to strike blows in the shadows of which no one dares take notice.

The tribunate, like the government, is weakened by the multiplication of its members. When the tribunes of the Roman people, at first two in number, then five, wanted to double this number, the senate let them do so, quite certain that it could check some by means of the others, which did not fail to happen.

---

100. Agis, king of Sparta from 245–241 BC, tried to revive Lycurgus' institutions and was assassinated by the ephors, who opposed him. Cleomenes became king of Sparta in 235 BC and, after having removed the ephors, instituted many of Agis' reforms.

The best means for preventing usurpations by such a formidable body—a means which has so far not occurred to any government—would be not to make this body permanent, but rather to stipulate intervals during which it would be suspended. These intervals, which should not be long enough to allow abuses the time to become consolidated, can be fixed by law in such a way that it is easy to shorten them when needed by extraordinary commissions.

This means appears to me to be without any inconvenience because, as I have said, the tribunate, since it does not make up part of the constitution, can be removed without the constitution suffering for it; and it appears to me to be efficacious because a newly established magistrate does not start with the power his predecessor had, but with that which the law grants him.

CHAPTER 6
On the Dictatorship

The inflexibility of laws, which prevents them from being adapted to events, can in certain cases make them pernicious, and they themselves can cause the downfall of the state during a crisis. The orderliness and slowness of legal formalities requires a period of time that circumstances sometimes do not allow. A thousand cases can arise which the lawgiver had not foreseen, and it is a very necessary foresight to sense that not everything can be foreseen.

One must therefore not try to consolidate political institutions to the point of depriving oneself of the power to suspend their effect. Sparta itself allowed its laws to sleep.

But only the greatest dangers can outweigh the danger of disrupting the public order, and the sacred power of the laws should not be suspended except when the salvation of the fatherland is at stake. In these rare and manifest cases, a special act provides for public safety, giving the responsibility to the most worthy. This commission can be granted in two ways according to the type of danger.

If increasing the activity of the government is enough to remedy the danger, it is concentrated in one or two of its members. Thus, it is not the authority of the laws that is disrupted but merely the form of their administration. Yet if the peril is such that the apparatus of the laws is itself an obstacle to defending them, then a supreme leader is named who silences all the laws and temporarily suspends the sovereign authority. In such a case, the general will is not in doubt, and it is evident that the foremost intention of the people is that the state not perish. In this way, the suspension of the legislative authority does not abolish it. The magistrate who silences it cannot make it speak; he dominates it without being able to represent it; he can do everything, except make laws.

The first means was used by the Roman senate when it charged the consuls by means of a consecrated formula with providing for the salvation of the Republic. The second occurred when one of the two consuls named a dictator,* a practice for which Alba had set the precedent for Rome.

In the beginnings of the Republic, they very frequently had recourse to the dictatorship because the state still did not have a firm enough basis to be able to sustain itself by the force of its constitution. Since morals then rendered superfluous many of the precautions which would have been necessary in other times, there was no fear that either a dictator would abuse his authority, or that he would attempt to keep it beyond his term. It seemed, on the contrary, that so great a power was a burden to the person who had been invested with it, so quickly did he hasten to get rid of it, as though taking the place of the laws were too painful and too dangerous an assignment!

As such, it is not the danger of abuse but rather the danger of degradation which leads me to blame the indiscriminate use of this supreme magistracy in the earliest times. For while it was being lavished on elections, dedications, pure formalities, there was reason to fear that it would become less formidable when needed and that people would become accustomed to consider it as an empty title used only in empty ceremonies.

Toward the end of the Republic, the Romans, having become more circumspect, used the dictatorship sparingly with as little reason as they had formerly used it prodigally. It was easy to see that their fear was ill-founded, that by then the weakness of the capital guaranteed its safety against the magistrates who were in its midst, that a dictator could in certain cases defend public freedom without ever being able to violate it, and that Rome's chains would not be forged in Rome itself, but in its armies. The feeble resistance Marius offered Sulla, and Pompey offered Caesar, showed clearly enough what could be expected from internal authority in opposing external force.[101]

---

* This nomination was done at night and in secret, as if they were ashamed to place a man above the laws.

---

101. The Roman generals and statesmen Gaius Marius (157–86 BC) and Lucius Cornelius Sulla (c. 138–78 BC) were the two principal opponents in the first civil wars in Rome. The generals and statesmen Gnaeus Pompeius Magnus, or Pompey the Great (106–48 BC), and Gaius Julius Caesar (100–44 BC) were initially allies and then enemies in the later civil wars that ultimately led to the downfall of the Roman Republic.

This error caused them to make great mistakes. As, for example, that of failing to name a dictator in the Catiline affair, for as the issue was such that it concerned only the interior of the city, and at most some province in Italy, a dictator, with the unlimited authority the laws gave him, would have easily suppressed the conspiracy, which was suppressed only by a concurrence of happy accidents which human prudence could never have anticipated.[102]

Instead, the senate contented itself with handing over all of its power to the consuls. From this it came about that, in order to act effectively, Cicero was constrained to exceed this power on a crucial point, and that while the first outbursts of joy voiced approval of his conduct, he was later justly called to account for the blood of the citizens shed in violation of the laws — a reproach that could not have been made against a dictator. But the consul's eloquence prevailed over everything, and since he himself, although a Roman, loved his glory more than his fatherland, he did not seek the most legitimate and most certain means for saving the state so much as the means that brought him all the honor from this affair.* As such, he was justly honored as Rome's liberator and justly punished as a breaker of the laws. However brilliant his recall, it is certain that it was a pardon.[103]

Furthermore, in whatever manner this important commission may be conferred, it is important for its duration to be fixed to a very short term which can never be extended. In the crises that lead to its being established, the state is soon destroyed or saved, and, once the pressing need is past, the dictator becomes tyrannical or useless. In Rome, since the dictators had terms of only six months, most of them abdicated before their term was over. If the term had been longer, perhaps they would have been tempted to extend it further, as the Decimvirs did with a term of one year. The dictator had only the time to attend to the need that led to his being elected; he did not have the time to think up other projects.

---

* This is what he could not have been confident of in proposing a dictator, since he did not dare to name himself and he could not be sure that his colleague would name him.

---

102. The Catiline affair refers to the attempt by Lucius Sergius Catilina (108–62 BC) to overthrow the Roman Republic. His principal opponent, who uncovered the plot and then urged the senate to take action, was Marcus Tullius Cicero (106–43 BC), who was consul at the time.

103. Cicero had the conspirators in the Catiline affair killed without a trial, and he was therefore exiled four years after the event when one of his opponents had a law passed against such acts that clearly had Cicero as its target. After about a year of exile, the senate recalled Cicero.

CHAPTER 7
On the Censorship

Just as the declaration of the general will is done through the law, the declaration of the public judgment is done through the censorship. Public opinion is a type of law of which the censor is the minister and which he does no more than apply to particular cases, following the example of the prince.

Far from the censorial tribunal being the arbiter of the people's opinion, therefore, it does no more than declare it, and as soon as it departs from it, its decisions are useless and ineffective.

It is useless to distinguish between the morals of a nation and the objects of its esteem, for all of these things stem from the same principle and are necessarily intermingled. Among all the peoples of the world, it is not nature but opinion that determines the choice of their pleasures. Reform men's opinions and their morals will be purified of themselves. One always likes what is noble or what one finds to be so, but it is about this judgment that one may be mistaken; it is therefore a matter of regulating this judgment. He who judges morals judges honor, and he who judges honor derives his law from opinion.

The opinions of a people arise from its constitution. Although law does not regulate morals, it is legislation that causes them to arise. When legislation grows weak, morals degenerate, but by then the censors' judgment will not be able to do what the force of the laws has not done.

It follows from this that the censorship can be useful for preserving morals, never for restoring them. Establish censors while the laws have all their vigor. Once they have lost it, all is hopeless. Nothing legitimate has force any longer when the laws no longer have any.

The censorship maintains morals by preventing opinions from becoming corrupt, by preserving their uprightness through wise applications, sometimes even by determining them when they are still indeterminate. The use of seconds in duels, which became a mania in the kingdom of France, was abolished there by the following words alone in an edict of the king: *as for those who are so cowardly as to call upon seconds*. This judgment, by anticipating the public's, immediately determined it. But when the same edict tried to proclaim that it was also an act of cowardice to fight a duel—which is very true, but contrary to common opinion—the public ridiculed this decision, about which its judgment was already settled.

I have said elsewhere* that since public opinion is not subject to constraint, there ought not be any vestige of constraint in the tribunal established to represent it. The artfulness with which this mechanism—entirely forgotten among the moderns—was bought into play among the Romans and even better so among the Lacedaemonians cannot be too admired.

When a man of bad morals offered a good opinion in the council of Sparta, the ephors, without taking notice of him, had the same opinion proposed by a virtuous citizen. What an honor for one, what a disgrace for the other, without either of them being given either praise or blame! Some drunkards from Samos† defiled the ephors' tribunal. The next day the Samians were given permission by a public edict to be filthy. A real punishment would have been less severe than such impunity. When Sparta had declared what was or was not decent, Greece did not appeal its judgments.

CHAPTER 8
On Civil Religion

Men at first had no other kings than the gods, nor any other government than a theocratic one. They reasoned like Caligula, and then they reasoned correctly. A lengthy degeneration of sentiments and ideas is needed before they could bring themselves to accept their fellow human as a master, and to flatter themselves that this would be a good thing.

By the sole fact that god was placed at the head of each political society, it followed that there were as many gods as peoples. Two peoples foreign to one another, and almost always enemies, could not recognize the same master for long. Two armies engaged in battle could not obey the same leader. Thus from national divisions resulted polytheism, and from it theological and civil intolerance, which are naturally the same thing, as will be stated below.

The extravagant notion the Greeks had of rediscovering their gods among barbarian peoples came from the notion they also had of regarding themselves as the natural sovereigns of these peoples. But in our day it is an erudition of

---

* I merely indicate in this chapter what I have discussed at greater length in the *Letter to M. d'Alembert*.[104]
† They came from another island which the delicacy of our language does not allow to be named in this context.[105]

---

104. See Rousseau, *Letter to M. d'Alembert* (1758), *Collected Writings*, 10:300ff.

105. They were from the island of Chios, but Rousseau avoids the term "Chiots" because of the potential play on words with *chiens*, or "dogs."

the most ridiculous sort that centers on the identity of the gods of different nations—as if Moloch, Saturn, and Cronos could be the same god, as if the Phoenicians' Baal, the Greeks' Zeus, and the Latins' Jupiter could be the same, as if chimerical beings bearing different names could have anything in common!

It might be asked: why were there no wars of religion under paganism, where each state had its own form of worship and its gods? I reply that it was precisely because each state had its own form of worship as well as its own government that they did not distinguish between its gods and its laws. Political war was also theological: the dominions of the gods were, so to speak, determined by the boundaries of nations. The god of one people had no right over other peoples. The gods of the pagans were not jealous gods; they divided up the empire of the world among themselves. Even Moses and the Hebrew people sometimes went along with this idea in speaking of the God of Israel. They did, it is true, regard as naught the gods of the Canaanites—proscribed peoples, destined for destruction, and whose stronghold they were to occupy. But see how they spoke about the divinities of neighboring peoples they were forbidden to attack! *The possession of what belongs to Chamos your god*, said Jephthah to the Ammonites, *is it not legitimately your due? We possess by the same token the lands that our victorious god has acquired.** This, it seems to me, was a clearly acknowledged parity between the rights of Chamos and those of the god of Israel.

But when the Jews, subjected to the kings of Babylon and subsequently to the kings of Syria, obstinately sought to recognize no other god than their own, this refusal, regarded as rebellion against the victor, brought down on them the persecutions we read of in their history and of which no other example is seen prior to Christianity.†

Since each religion was therefore tied exclusively to the laws of the state that prescribed it, there was no other way of converting a people than enslaving it nor any other missionaries than conquerors, and since the obligation to

---

* *Nonne ea quae possidet Chamos deus tuus tibi jure debentur?* This is the text of the Vulgate. Father de Carrières has translated it: "Do you not believe you have the right to possess what belongs to Chamos your god?" I do not know the thrust of the Hebrew text, but I see that in the Vulgate Jephthah positively acknowledges the right of the god Chamos, and that the French translator weakens this acknowledgment by an "according to you" that is not in the Latin.[106]

† It is perfectly evident that the war against the Phocians called the "sacred war" was not a war of religion. It had as its object to punish sacrileges and not to subjugate nonbelievers.[107]

---

106. Judges 11:24. Louis de Carrières published his Latin-French translation of the Bible with commentaries between 1709 and 1716.

107. The "sacred war" was fought in 356–346 BC by the Thebans and their allies against the Phocians and their allies in revenge for the Phocians' having plundered the treasury of the temple of Delphi.

change their form of worship was the law for the vanquished, it was necessary to begin by being victorious before discussing such a thing. Far from men fighting for the gods, it was, as in Homer, the gods who fought for men: each people asked his own for victory, and paid for it with new altars. The Romans, before taking a place, called upon its gods to abandon it, and when they let the Tarentians keep their irate gods, it was because in that case they recognized these gods as subject to their own and forced to pay them homage. They left the vanquished their gods just as they left them their laws. A crown for the Capitoline Jupiter was often the sole tribute they imposed.

Eventually, the Romans, having extended their empire, their form of worship, and their gods, and having themselves often adopted the gods of the vanquished by granting them as well as their own gods legal status in the city, the peoples of that vast empire imperceptibly found themselves with multitudes of gods and forms of worship, more or less everywhere the same. And this is how paganism eventually became one and the same religion throughout the known world.

It was under these circumstances that Jesus came to establish a spiritual kingdom on earth, which, by separating the theological system from the political system, made it so that the state ceased to be a unity, and caused the intestine quarrels which have never ceased to convulse Christian peoples. Now, since the pagans could never get this new idea of an otherworldly kingdom through their heads, they always regarded Christians as veritable rebels who, beneath a hypocritical submission, were merely looking for the opportunity to make themselves independent and the masters, and to craftily usurp the authority they pretended to respect due to their weakness. Such was the cause of persecutions.

What the pagans feared came to pass. Then everything took on a different appearance, the humble Christians changed their tune, and soon this supposedly otherworldly kingdom was seen to become under a visible leader the most violent despotism in this world.

Yet as a prince and civil laws still existed, this dual power has resulted in a perpetual conflict over jurisdiction which has made any good polity impossible in Christian states, and no one has ever been able to figure out who — the master or the priest — he was obligated to obey.

Some peoples, however, even in Europe or near it, have tried to preserve or restore the previous system, but without success. The spirit of Christianity has won out over everything. The sacred cult has always remained or again become independent of the sovereign and without any necessary tie to the body of the state. Mohammed had very sound views: he tied his political system together well, and as long as the form of his government endured under his successors the caliphs, this government was strictly unified, and good for that reason. But once the Arabs had become prosperous, lettered, polished, soft, and cowardly they were subjugated by barbarians. Then the division between the two powers began anew. Although this division is less apparent among Muslims than among Christians, it is still there, especially in the sect of Ali, and there are states, such as Persia, in which it never ceases to make itself felt.

Among us, the kings of England have established themselves as heads of the church, and the czars have done the same. But through this title they have made themselves not so much its masters as its ministers. They have acquired less the right to change it than the power to maintain it; they are not its lawgivers, they are merely its princes. Wherever the clergy constitutes a body,* it is the master and the lawgiver in its dominion. There are therefore two powers, two sovereigns, in England and in Russia, just as everywhere else.

Of all Christian authors, the philosopher Hobbes is the only who clearly saw the disease and the remedy, who dared to propose reuniting the two heads of the eagle and the complete return to political unity, without which neither state nor government will ever be well constituted. But he should have seen that the domineering spirit of Christianity was incompatible with his system and that the interest of the priest would always be stronger than that of the state. It is not so much what is horrible and false in his politics as what is correct and true that has made it odious.†[108]

---

* It must especially be noted that it is not so much formal assemblies, like those in France, which bind the clergy into a body as it is the communion of churches. Communion and excommunication are the clergy's social compact, a compact by which they will always be the master of peoples and kings. All priests who are in communion with one another are fellow-citizens, even though they may come from the opposite ends of the earth. This invention is a masterpiece of politics. There was nothing like it among the pagan priests. As such, never did they make up a body of clergy.

† See, among other things, in a letter by Grotius to his brother of April 11, 1643, what this learned man approves and disapproves of in the book *De Cive*. It is true that, being inclined to be indulgent, he appeared to pardon the author for his good points for the sake of the bad ones. But not everyone is so lenient.[109]

---

108. Thomas Hobbes (1588–1679) proposed placing religious authority in the hands of the sovereign, including in his *On the Citizen* (1642) and *Leviathan* (1651). His works were widely criticized, in large part because of his argument for absolute sovereignty.

109. In this letter, Grotius wrote: "I have seen *De Cive*, and am pleased by what it says on behalf of kings. But I cannot approve of the foundations upon which these arguments rest. It says that by nature there is a war between all men and has some other ideas which do not match mine. Thus it says that it is the duty of the private citizen to follow the religion established in his country, if not in his conscience then at least in outward worship. There are some other things I cannot approve of" (cited by Richard Tuck, *Philosophy and Government 1572–1651* [Cambridge: Cambridge University Press, 1993], 200).

I believe that by elaborating on the historical facts from this point of view, it would be easy to refute the opposing sentiments of Bayle and Warburton, the first of whom claims that no religion is useful to the body politic, and the latter of whom maintains to the contrary that Christianity is its firmest support.[110] One would prove to the first that no state has ever been founded except with religion as its base, and to the second that the Christian law is at bottom more harmful than useful to the strong constitution of the state. To make myself fully understood, it is only necessary to give a little more precision to the overly vague ideas about religion relative to my subject.

Religion considered in relation to society, which is either general or particular, can also be divided into two types: namely, the religion of man and that of the citizen. The first—without temples, without altars, without rites, limited to the purely internal form of worship of the supreme God and to the eternal duties of morality—is the pure and simple religion of the Gospel, true theism, and what may be called divine natural right. The latter, inscribed in a single country, gives it its gods, its own tutelary patrons: it has its dogmas, its rites, its exterior form of worship prescribed by the laws. Outside the single nation that follows it, everything for it is infidel, alien, barbarous. It does not extend the duties and the rights of man any farther than its altars. Such were all the religions of the earliest peoples, to which the name of civil or positive divine right may be given.

There is a third, more bizarre sort of religion which, by giving men two bodies of legislation, two leaders, two fatherlands, subjects them to contradictory duties and prevents them from being able to be simultaneously devout men and citizens. Such is the religion of the Lamas, such is that of the Japanese, such is Roman Catholicism. This sort can be called the religion of the priest. It results in a sort of mixed and unsociable right which has no name.

Considering these three sorts of religion in terms of politics, they all have their defects. The third is so manifestly bad that it is a waste of time to amuse oneself with demonstrating it. Everything that destroys social unity is worthless. All institutions that put man in contradiction with himself are worthless.

The second is good in that it combines divine worship and the love of the

---

110. Pierre Bayle (1647–1706) notoriously argued in his *Various Thoughts on the Occasion of a Comet* (1682) that a society of atheists was possible and also preferable to a superstitious society, an argument many readers took to mean that a society of atheists was preferable to a society with any religion. For William Warburton, see *The Divine Legation of Moses Demonstrated on the Principles of a Religious Deist* (1737–41).

laws, and since it makes the fatherland the object of the citizens' worship, it teaches them that to serve the state is to serve its tutelary god. It is a type of theocracy in which there should be no pontiff other than the prince, nor other priests than the magistrates. In that case, to die for one's country is to be martyred, to violate the laws is to be impious, and to subject a guilty person to public execration is to deliver him to the wrath of the gods: *sacer estod*.[111]

But it is bad in that, being founded on error and falsehood, it deceives men, makes them credulous, superstitious, and drowns the true worship of the divinity in empty ceremony. It is also bad when, becoming exclusive and tyrannical, it makes a people bloodthirsty and intolerant, so that it breaths only murder and massacre, and believes it is performing a sacred deed by killing whoever does not accept its gods. This puts such a people into a natural state of war with all others, which is very harmful to its own security.

There therefore remains the religion of man or Christianity, not that of today but that of the Gospel, which is altogether different. Through this saintly, sublime, genuine religion, men — children of the same god — all recognize one another as brothers and the society that unites them does not dissolve even at death.

But this religion, since it has no particular relation to the body politic, leaves the laws with only the force they derive from themselves without adding any other force to them, and, due to this, one of the great bonds of any particular society remains ineffectual. What is more, far from attaching the citizens' hearts to the state, it detaches them from it as it does from all earthly things. I know of nothing more contrary to the social spirit.

We are told that a people of true Christians would form the most perfect society that could be imagined. I see only one major difficulty with this supposition, which is that a society of true Christians would no longer be a society of men.

I even say that, for all its perfection, this supposed society would be neither the strongest nor the most durable. By dint of being perfect, it would lack cohesion: its fatal vice would lie in its very perfection.

Each person would fulfill his duty; the people would be subject to the laws, the leaders would be just and moderate, the magistrates honest, incorruptible,

111. Or *sacer esto*: "Let him be accursed." The formula is found in the Twelve Tables of Roman law, among other places.

the soldiers would despise death, there would be neither vanity nor luxury. All that is very well, but let us look further.

Christianity is a wholly spiritual religion, exclusively concerned with the things of Heaven: the Christian's fatherland is not of this world. He does his duty, it is true, but he does it with a profound indifference with regard to the success or failure of his efforts. Provided he has nothing to reproach himself for, it does not much matter to him whether everything goes well or badly down here on earth. If the state prospers, he hardly dares to enjoy the public felicity, he fears taking pride in his country's glory. If the state declines, he blesses the hand of God that weighs down on his people.

For society to be peaceful and for harmony to be maintained, it would be necessary for all the citizens without exception to be equally good Christians. But if unfortunately there is a single ambitious person, a single hypocrite—a Catiline, for example, a Cromwell—that man will most certainly get the better of his pious compatriots.[112] Christian charity does not easily allow one to think ill of one's neighbor. Once he has discovered the art of tricking them through some ruse and of seizing a portion of the public authority, behold a man vested with dignity; God wills that he be respected. Soon behold a power; God wills that he be obeyed. Does the repository of this power abuse it? This is the scourge with which God punishes his children. To drive out the usurper would be to trouble one's conscience; one would have to disturb public tranquility, resort to violence, shed blood. All of this is not at all in keeping with the mildness of the Christian. And, after all, what does it matter whether one is a freeman or a serf in this vale of tears? The essential thing is to go to paradise, and resignation is merely one more means for doing so.

Does a foreign war break out? The citizens march into battle without difficulty; none of them thinks of fleeing. They do their duty, but without being passionate for victory; they know how to die rather than to win. What does it matter if they are the victors or the vanquished? Doesn't providence know better than they what must be for them? Imagine how a proud, impetuous, passionate enemy can take advantage of their stoicism! Pit them against those generous peoples who were consumed by the ardent love of glory and of the fatherland, suppose your Christian republic confronted with Sparta or Rome: the pious Christians will be beaten, crushed, destroyed before having the time to realize what is happening, or they will owe their salvation solely to the con-

---

112. For Catiline, see n. 102 to p. 261. For Cromwell, see n. 88 to p. 244.

tempt their enemy will conceive for them. To my mind it was a fine oath that Fabius' soldiers took: they did not swear to die or to win, they swore to return the victors, and they kept their oath.[113] Never would Christians have taken such an oath; they would have believed they were tempting God.

But I am mistaken in speaking of a Christian republic: each of these two words excludes the other. Christianity preaches nothing but servitude and dependence. Its spirit is too favorable to tyranny for tyranny not always to profit from it. True Christians are made to be slaves. They know it and are scarcely moved by it; this brief life has too little value in their eyes.

Christian troops are excellent, we are told. I deny it. Will someone show me some? As for me, I do not know of any Christian troops. Someone will cite the Crusades to me. Without arguing about the valor of the crusaders, I will point out that far from being Christians, they were the soldiers of the priest, they were citizens of the Church; they were fighting for their spiritual country, which the Church had made temporal, no one knows how. Strictly speaking, this should be included under paganism. Since the Gospel does not establish a national religion, a holy war is impossible among Christians.

Under the pagan emperors, Christian soldiers were brave. All Christian authors attest this, and I believe it: there was a spirit of emulation for honor against pagan troops. As soon as the emperors were Christians, this spirit of emulation no longer survived, and when the cross had driven out the eagle, all Roman valor disappeared.

But leaving aside political considerations, let us return to right and determine what principles obtain concerning this important point. The right the social compact gives to the sovereign over the subjects does not, as I have said, exceed the bounds of public utility.* The subjects therefore do not owe the sovereign an account of their opinions except insofar as those opinions matter

---

* *In a republic*, states the marquis d'Argenson, *each person is perfectly free with respect to what does not harm others*. This is the unvarying limit. It cannot be stated more precisely. I have not been able to deny myself the pleasure of sometimes citing this manuscript, even though it is unknown to the public, in order to honor the memory of an illustrious and respectable man who, even in the office of a royal ministry, preserved the heart of a true citizen and upright and healthy views regarding the government of his country.[114]

---

113. Quintus Fabius Maximus (c. 280–203 BC) was a politician and general who led Rome during the Second Punic War.

114. René-Louis de Voyer de Paulmy, marquis d'Argenson (1694–1757) was a government minister, ultimately serving as foreign minister under Louis XV until he was compelled to resign in 1747, after which he devoted himself to literary pursuits. See n. 9 to p. 165.

to the community. Now, it is certainly important to the state that each citizen have a religion which makes him love his duties, but the dogmas of that religion are of no interest either to the state or its members except insofar as those dogmas relate to morality and to the duties which anyone who professes it is bound to fulfill toward others. Beyond these, each person can have whatever opinions he pleases, without it belonging to the state to know them. For as it is has no competence in the other world, whatever the fate of the subjects may be in the life to come is none of its business provided they are good citizens in this one.

There is, therefore, a purely civil profession of faith whose articles it belongs to the sovereign to determine, not precisely as dogmas of religion but as sentiments of sociability, without which it is impossible to be a good citizen or a loyal subject.* Without being able to obligate anyone to believe them, it may banish from the state anyone who does not believe them. It may banish him, not as impious but as unsociable, as incapable of sincerely loving the laws, justice, and if need be of sacrificing his life to his duty. If anyone, after having publicly acknowledged these same dogmas, behaves as though he does not believe them, let him be punished with death. He has committed the greatest of crimes: he has lied before the laws.

The dogmas of the civil religion should be simple, few in number, stated with precision, without explanations or commentaries. The existence of a powerful, intelligent, beneficent, foresighted, and provident divinity, the life to come, the happiness of the just, the punishment of the wicked, the sanctity of the social contract and the laws: these are the positive dogmas. As for the negative dogmas, I limit them to a single one: that is, intolerance. It belongs with the forms of worship we have excluded.

Those who distinguish between civil intolerance and theological intolerance are mistaken, in my view. These two intolerances are inseparable. It is impossible to live in peace with people one believes are damned; to love them would be to hate God who punishes them; they absolutely must be brought back into the fold or tormented. Wherever theological intolerance is allowed,

* In pleading for Catiline, Caesar tried to establish the dogma of the mortality of the soul. Cato and Cicero, in order to refute it, did not waste their time philosophizing; they contented themselves with showing that Caesar was speaking like a bad citizen and was advancing a doctrine pernicious to the state. Indeed, this was what the Roman senate had to pass judgment on, and not on a question of theology.[115]

115. See Sallust *Conspiracy of Catiline* 52.

it is impossible for it not to have some civil effect.* And as soon as it does, the sovereign is no longer sovereign, even in the temporal realm. From then on, the priests are the true masters; kings are merely their officers.

Now that there is no longer and can no longer be an exclusive national religion, all those which tolerate the others should be tolerated insofar as their dogmas contain nothing contrary to the duties of the citizen. But whoever dares say, *no salvation outside of the church*, should be driven out of the state, unless the state is the church and the prince is the pontiff. Such a dogma is good only in a theocratic government; in any other it is pernicious. The reason for which Henri IV is said to have embraced the Roman religion should make any honest man—and especially every prince who knows how to reason— leave it.[116]

CHAPTER 9
Conclusion

After having set forth the true principles of political right and having tried to found the state on that basis, it would remain to buttress it through its external relations, which includes the law of nations, commerce, the right of war and of conquests, public law, alliances, negotiations, treaties, etc. But all this forms a new object, too vast for my short sight. I should have always set my sights closer to myself.

END

---

* Marriage, for example, since it is a civil contract, has civil effects without which it is even impossible for society to endure. Let us suppose, then, that a clergy succeeds in obtaining for itself alone the right of performing this act—a right that it must inevitably usurp in any intolerant religion. Then isn't it clear that by exercising the authority of the church in this matter, it will render vain that of the prince, who will have no other subjects than those the clergy is so pleased to give it? As master of marrying or of not marrying people according to whether they will or will not have one doctrine or another, according to whether they will accept or reject one religious formula or another, according to whether they will be more or less devoted to it, isn't it clear that by behaving prudently and remaining firm the clergy alone will dispose of inheritances, offices, the citizens, the state itself—which cannot endure once it consists of nothing but bastards? But, it will be said, these abuses will be appealed, summonses issued, warrants served, temporal holdings seized. What a pity! The clergy, for as little—I do not say courage—but good sense they may have, will allow this to happen and will go on its way. It will calmly allow appeals, summonses, warrants, seizures, and will end up being the master. It is not, it seems to me, a great sacrifice to give up a part when one is certain of prevailing over the whole.

---

116. Henri IV of France (1553–1610) was said to have said "Paris is worth a mass" when he converted from Protestantism to Catholicism when he became king in 1594.

BIBLIOGRAPHY OF
ROUSSEAU'S SOURCES

·⊂══════⊃·

Included here are only those works to which specific page citations to English editions have been given in the editorial notes.

Burlamaqui, J. J. *The Principles of Natural and Politic Law* (1748). Translated by Thomas Nugent. Indianapolis: Liberty Fund Press, 2006.

Condillac, Etienne Bonnot, abbé de. *Essay on the Origin of Human Knowledge* (1746). Translated by Hans Aarsleff. New York: Cambridge University Press, 2001.

Cumberland, Richard. *A Treatise of the Laws of Nature* (1672). Edited by Jon Parkin. Translated by John Maxwell. Indianapolis: Liberty Fund Press, 2005.

Grotius, Hugo. *The Rights of War and Peace* (1625). Edited by Richard Tuck. Indianapolis: Liberty Fund Press, 2005.

Hobbes, Thomas. *On the Citizen* (1642). Edited by Richard Tuck and Michael Silverthorne. New York: Cambridge University Press, 1998.

Hobbes, Thomas. *Leviathan* (1651). Edited by Edwin Curley. Indianapolis: Hackett Publishing Company, 1994.

Locke, John. *An Essay Concerning Human Understanding* (1690). Edited by Peter H. Nidditch. Oxford: Oxford University Press, 1979.

Locke, John. *Two Treatises of Government* (1690). Edited by Peter Laslett. 3d ed. New York: Cambridge University Press, 1988.

Machiavelli, Niccolò. *Discourses on Livy* (1531). Translated by Harvey C. Mansfield and Nathan Tarcov. Chicago: University of Chicago Press, 1998.

Machiavelli, Niccolò. *Florentine Histories* (1532). Translated by Laura F. Banfield and Harvey C. Mansfield. Princeton: Princeton University Press, 1988.

Mandeville, Bernard. *Fable of the Bees* (1732). Edited by F. B. Kaye. Indianapolis: Liberty Fund Press, 1988.

Montaigne, Michel de. *Essays* (1580–92). Translated and edited by Donald M. Frame. Stanford: Stanford University Press, 1958.

Montesquieu, Charles-Louis de Secondat, baron de. *Considerations on the Causes of the Greatness of the Romans and Their Decline* (1734). Translated and edited by David Lowenthal. Indianapolis: Hackett Publishing, 1999.

Montesquieu, Charles-Louis de Secondat, baron de. *The Spirit of the Laws* (1748). Translated by Anne M. Cohler, Basia Carolyn Miller, and Harold Samuel Stone. Cambridge: Cambridge University Press, 1989.

Pufendorf, Samuel. *The Whole Duty of Man, According to the Law of Nature* (1673). Edited by Ian Hunter and David Saunders. Indianapolis: Liberty Fund Press, 2002.

Sidney, Algernon. *Discourses Concerning Government* (1698). Edited by Thomas G. West. Indianapolis: Liberty Fund Press, 1996.

INDEX

This index covers all of the writings by Rousseau contained in this volume but not the editor's introduction, editorial notes, etc. References to items in Rousseau's own footnotes are indicated by the page number and note symbol (* or †).